Fundamentals of Experimental Psychology

PRENTICE-HALL, INC., Englewood Cliffs, New Jersey 07632

Paul W. Robinson

Brigham Young University

SECOND EDITION

Fundamentals of Experimental Psychology

Library of Congress Cataloging in Publication Data

ROBINSON, PAUL W
    Fundamentals of experimental psychology.

    Bibliography: p.
    Includes index.
    1. Psychology, Experimental. I.–Title.
[DNLM: 1.–Psychology, Experimental. BR181
R663f]
BF181.R62–1981   150'.724   80-23454
ISBN   0-13-339135-3

Editorial/production supervision and interior design: Alison D. Gnerre
Cover design: Infield/D'Astolfo Associates
Manufacturing buyer: Edmund W. Leone

Printed in the United States of America

10 9 8 7 6 5 4 3 2 1

PRENTICE-HALL INTERNATIONAL, INC., *London*
PRENTICE-HALL OF AUSTRALIA PTY. LIMITED, *Sydney*
PRENTICE-HALL OF CANADA, LTD., *Toronto*
PRENTICE-HALL OF INDIA PRIVATE LIMITED, *New Delhi*
PRENTICE-HALL OF JAPAN, INC., *Tokyo*
PRENTICE-HALL OF SOUTHEAST ASIA PTE. LTD., *Singapore*
WHITEHALL BOOKS LIMITED, WELLINGTON, *New Zealand*

Dedicated to

BILL ROBINSON, who put up with so much for so long

Contents

PREFACE TO THE FIRST EDITION   xi

PREFACE TO THE SECOND EDITION   xv

1   AN OVERVIEW   1

Psychology in Perspective   2
Primary Work Activities of Psychologists   5
Role of an Undergraduate Experimental Psychology Course   8
Skills Required of a Psychologist   11
Overview of the Text   13
Steps in Conducting an Experimental Investigation   17
Summary   27

**2   HISTORY OF EXPERIMENTAL PSYCHOLOGY
AND THE SCIENTIFIC METHOD   29**

Assumptions Underlying the Scientific Method   32
Psychology—A Scientific Approach   37
Scientific Paradigms in Psychology   45
Proper Subject Matter: The Problem   53
Summary   61

3   TYPES OF INVESTIGATIONS   63

Controlled Laboratory Experiments   67
Field Experiments   76
Ex Post Facto Field Studies   80
Ex Post Facto Laboratory Studies   83
Summary   86

4   VARIANCE   88

What Is Variance?   90
Methods of Controlling Secondary Variance   100
Sources of Secondary Variation   108
Summary   115

5   NONDESIGN EXPERIMENTAL PROCEDURES   117

Selection of Subjects   119
Ethical Issues in Research   126
Selection of the Dependent Variable   132
Selection of the Independent Variable   139
Elimination and Constancy as Nondesign Control Techniques   140
Experimenter Bias   141
Pilot Studies   142
Instrumentation   143
Summary   143

6   METHODS OF DATA COLLECTION   145

Threshold Measurement   147
Scaling Techniques   156
Interviews   165
Psychological Tests   167
Application of Data-Collection Methods   176
Summary   178

7   NONEXPERIMENTAL DESIGNS   179

Quasi-Experimental Designs   181
Correlational Designs   183

Contrast Designs   195
Case Study Designs   197
Advantages and Disadvantages of Nonexperimental Designs   201
Summary   202

8   EXPERIMENTAL DESIGNS   204

What are Experimental Designs?   205
Types of Experimental Designs   212
One-Group Designs   217
Summary   222

9   TWO-GROUP DESIGNS   224

Logical Analysis of Two-Group Designs   225
Types of Two-Group Designs   228
Advantages and Disadvantages of Two-Group Designs   249
Summary   251

10   MULTIGROUP DESIGNS WITH ONE INDEPENDENT VARIABLE   252

Logical Analysis of One-Way Anovar Designs Using an f Test   255
Types of Anovar Designs   264
Advantages and Disadvantages of One-Way Anovar Designs   278
Summary   280

11   FACTORIAL DESIGNS   282

Logical Analysis of Factorial Designs   288
Randomized Factorial Designs   294
Randomized Blocked Factorial Designs   298
Statistical Control with Factorial Designs   301
Advantages and Disadvantages of Factorial Designs   305
Summary   305

12   SMALL-*N* DESIGNS

Origin of Small-N Designs   308
Logical Analysis of Small-N Designs   311
ABA Small-N Designs   314
Other Types of Small-N Designs   320
Comparison of Small-N and Large-N Designs   324
Small-N Designs in the Applied Setting   330
Advantages and Disadvantages of Small-N Designs   333
Summary   334

13   DATA ANALYSIS—STATISTICAL TECHNIQUES   336

Statistical Terms and Concepts   338
Chi-Square Nominal Statistical Test   348
Mann-Whitney U Test: An Ordinal Significance Test   354
Summary   356

14   COMMUNICATION IN PSYCHOLOGY   357

Role of the Report   358
Objectives of the Report   360
Organization of the Report   362
Dry Facts and Some Requirements of Style   375
Peer Communication   377
Summary   388

APPENDICES   391

REFERENCES   403

INDEX   407

Preface
to the First Edition

As the manuscript draws toward completion, I begin to reflect in a serious vein on whether these long hours of writing have produced what others will consider a unique addition to the field. In looking over the final product, I think there are several aspects of the text that make it a functional contribution.

First is the approach. Experimental psychology texts can be grossly divided into three types. First, there are content oriented texts, which concentrate on theoretical and empirical concepts in specific areas of psychology, such as perception, learning, motivation, and cognitive processes. Second, there are methodologically oriented texts dealing mostly with the role of experimental designs in research and important statistical concepts. The third type of experimental text is also methodologically oriented, but it emphasizes procedural, rather than statistical dimensions of psychological investigations. This text falls into the third category. It emphasizes procedural aspects of psychological investigations such as selection of independent and dependent variables, means of controlling secondary variables, criteria for selecting subjects, and so on.

This text is distinguished from other texts on several other points also. It is geared for a contemporary experimental psychology course in which a large portion of the students are headed for applied psychology careers. All types of psychological investigations are covered, from clinical case studies in the field to the use of factorial designs in controlled laboratory experiments. Similarities and differences between analytical approaches, such as two-group designs, baseline designs, case studies, and quasi-experimental designs, are presented in an easy-to-understand manner. Experimental dimensions are organized into simplified categories (for example, four primary types of psychological investigations, six basic steps in conducting an experiment, five main ways of measuring a dependent variable) to help the student master the fundamentals involved. To avoid a long explanation of statistical theory (usually required to ready the student for correctly analyzing experimental data), I have provided with every type of experimental design covered complete step-by-step examples of how to statistically analyze data. (Unfortunately, these examples make the book look highly statistical to anyone just thumbing through.)

Although experimental investigations involving one or two subjects have been employed in psychology since its inception (Wundt's experiments on introspection, Pavlov's on classical conditioning, to name just two), only in the last twenty years with the growing use of behavior modification has the valid use of a small-N analytical approach begun to grow widely. One of the chapters in the text shows not only what the basic parts of a small-N approach include, but also what the similarities and differences are between large-N and small-N designs. This type of comparative coverage is not available in any other experimental psychology text.

Most experimental psychology courses require students to perform an experiment and write a report on their findings. Instructors must either prepare handouts on how to write a report or require their students to purchase a separate manual. This text, in Chapter Fourteen, gives detailed instructions for writing a report in the APA style and provides many examples. A section on how to look up articles in *Psychological Abstracts* is also included.

Every instructor has his own research interest and special area of expertise, be it learning, perception, psychophysical scaling, sensory processes, or some other area. This text does not include special-interest content material, so that each instructor can flavor the content in the course according to his own interest by combining this text with other readings. No attempt is made to slant the text toward animal-versus-human or behavioral-versus-cognitive research. The procedures presented are general and can be employed in almost any subfield of psychology. My overall purpose is to present general analytical approaches rather than specialized research techniques.

The publication of any book is the product of many people's work. I would like to express appreciation to some of those who played a role in this one. As the major sources of my undergraduate and graduate intellectual stimulation, Peter C. Wolff and David R. Stone deserve first mention. Being one of possibly many who left their tutorship without letting them know how much their association meant, I am grateful for the opportunity to express my debt and gratitude to them. I am indebted also to the Prentice-Hall staff for effectively completing this project, including Neale Sweet (subject editor), Margery Carazzone (production editor), and Dwight Osborn, who prompted the writing of the text. Thoughtful advice and suggestions regarding the manuscript from Geoffrey Keppel (University of California, Berkeley), Jay M. Finkelman (City University of New York), Frank B. McMahon (Southern Illinois University, Edwardsville), T. S. Krawiec (Skidmore College), Ron Norton (University of Winnipeg), and James J. Jenkins (University of Minnesota) are appreciated. A special thank you goes to Charles Vance for his illustrations; and Dennis Clayson, Richard Storm, Stephanie Price, Steve Rowley, and Carolyn Bridges for their assistance with the manuscript. Less obvious, but equally important, is the patience and forbearance shown by my wife, Carol.

P. W. Robinson

Preface
to the Second Edition

As I completed the first edition, I began to wonder, like most authors, whether my peers would see experimental psychology as I do and accept the book as a valuable addition to the field. The overwhelming adoption of the book across the country in both large and small universities was quite gratifying. I received a large number of comments from professors in the field about the book. Almost without exception they reported students had a relatively easy time with the writing style of the book. There were a few suggestions for changes which were consistent among commentors. Suggestions included adding material on helping students with the problem of selecting a topic, discuss ethical issues in experimenting, historically and logically tie in small-N and large-N analytical approaches, discuss in a rather nonstatistical way statistical terms like parametric-nonparametric tests, and omit Chapter Thirteen, which was an overview of some of the more classical experiments in various areas of psychology.

I greatly appreciate those who took the time to write, many of whom I have been unable to reply to. Bill Buskist, Tim Newby, Martin Brown (Keene State College), Dr. M. M. Gittis (Youngstown State University), John Monahan (Central Michigan University), Dewey Rundus (The University of South Florida), and Peter Senkowski (Northern Illinois University) provided valuable feedback as the manuscript was made ready for production. Leigh Anne Best did a superb job converting my penmanship into a typed manuscript.

P. W. Robinson

I. **Psychology in Perspective**
II. **Primary Work Activities of Psychologists**
III. **Role of an Undergraduate Experimental Psychology Course**
IV. **Skills Required of a Psychologist**
    A. *Analytical Prowess*
    B. *Knowledge of Psychological Principles*
    C. *Skill in Communicating Ideas to Professional Peers*
    D. *Skill in Communicating Ideas to Laymen*
    E. *Ability to Evaluate Research*
V. **Overview of the Text**
VI. **Steps in Conducting an Experimental Investigation**
    A. *Defining the Problem*
    B. *Classifying Variables*
    C. *Selecting the Type of Investigation*
    D. *Planning and Carrying out the Method*
    E. *Analyzing Results*
    F. *Drawing Conclusions*
VII. **Summary**

An Overview

1

Often a student of psychology goes through an undergraduate program without gaining an overall perspective of what psychological training entails, what the field of psychology includes, and what should be known when he or she complets training. The purpose of the first four sections of this chapter is to help the student gain an idea of what the field of psychology involves, what skills the psychologist needs, and what role an experimental psychology course can play in developing those skills, The fifth section provides a brief résumé of each chapter so that the reader can visualize how a particular chapter fits into the overall scheme of the text. The sixth section lists the steps involved in conducting an experimental investigation. This is possibly the most important part of the chapter—and the book, for that matter—for that is what the text is all about—how to design and carry out an appropriate psychological investigation.

PSYCHOLOGY IN PERSPECTIVE

Psychology is most commonly referred to as "the study of behavior and its correlated processes." Its goal is generally expressed to be the "identification, explanation, and prediction of the behavioral principles and processes by which people operate." Although correct, these statements are somewhat misleading, for they imply that psychologists spend most of their time on basic research geared toward isolating new behavioral principles. The definition does a satisfactory job in representing psychology as a scholarly and scientific discipline, but the field is more than an academic area of investigation. It is also a profession concerned with offering guidance on and assistance with everyday problems. In fact, only about 18 percent of the profession's time is spent in basic research; the rest is given over to providing services for intrapersonal problems.

Defining psychology as an area of scientific investigation was more appropriate in its formative stages. Since 1879 the proportion of psychol-

2

ogists involved in laboratory research has declined. This has not been due to lack of interest in research, however, for research is a prime area of concern for all psychologists. There are three interrelated reasons for this decrease in the percentage of experimental psychologists. The first is the development of psychology into an applied science. In the late 1800s the field of psychology was in its infancy. Like all other applied sciences in this stage of development, the emphasis had to be on basic research. One of the objectives of psychology was to become a functional part of everyday life situations. To adequately develop an applied psychology, however, the proper groundwork had to be laid in terms of devising appropriate analytical techniques and empirically based theoretical structures. As the years passed, more behavioral principles and analytical procedures became available, and with increased confidence and new techniques came programs for training applied psychologists.

This development generated the second major reason for the decrease in the percentage of experimentalists. The demand for applied psychologists went beyond all expectations. With society taking over a greater responsibility for ensuring the health and physical welfare of its members, individuals began concentrating more on inter- and intrapersonal problems. People became more concerned with juvenile delinquency, peer conflicts, mental retardation, learning difficulties, phobias, compulsions, and other such problems. As a result, psychology was inundated with requests for professionals knowledgeable in the dynamics of behavioral relationships. The demand significantly stimulated the increased production of applied psychologists.

The third reason for the decreased proportion of psychologists labeling themselves as strictly experimentalists is the increased experimental training in all subfields of psychology. There has been an increased concern over the years for psychologists in all subfields of psychology to strengthen their experimental skills. Society has increased its demands for psychologists to scientifically demonstrate the effectiveness of what they do. Because of society's concern with mental health, well over 70 percent of the monies received by psychologists comes directly or indirectly through governmental funding. State mental hospitals, university training and research programs, county social services, community mental health centers, and governmental research centers are maintained through governmental funds. And governmental agencies are increasing their requirements for psychologists involved in the mental health programs to demonstrate their effectiveness. As a consequence, clinical psychologists, counselors, child psychologists, social psychologists, and school psychologists have had to increase their skills in scientific methodology for determining causal relationships. With the increased experimental emphasis throughout psychology, the distinction between an experimental psychologist and other psychologists becomes less clear. With improved methodological technology, the psychologist with analytical skills may easily pass through boundaries of the laboratory to the outside world and perform a scientific investigation with almost the same amount of internal validity as can be obtained in the laboratory. Many prospective experimental psychologists have found that their scientific appetite and curiosity can now be satisfied in nonlaboratory settings by delving into everyday, practical problems (often called outcome research).

With these points in mind, we can more appropriately classify psychologists as a group interested in contributions to knowledge about human and animal behavior, the communication of such information, and its applications. Figure 1–1 presents psychology in terms of its various subfields. The percentages represent the proportion of psychologists in that area. It is apparent that psychology has proliferated along many dimensions. Psychologists specializing in a particular subfield, such as social, developmental, educational, and physiological psychology, have become welcome additions to the profession.

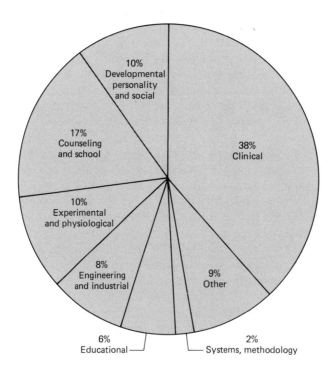

FIGURE 1–1   Subfields of psychology, 1978
(Adapted from *Careers in Psychology*, 1978, p. 17. Copyright 1978 by the American Psychological Association. Reprinted by permission.)

PRIMARY WORK ACTIVITIES
OF PSYCHOLOGISTS

With psychology's diversity of interests has come an increasing range of work activities. A psychologist may be found doing almost anything, from analyzing the mating behavior of the ground squirrel to arbitrating a labor dispute. Figure 1–2 shows who employs psychologists. The types of activities required of psychologists by these employers may include the following.

Clinical and Counseling.   As mentioned previously, the largest proportion of psychologists are concerned with the use and application of psychological techniques and principles in face-to-face, individual situations. Psychologists in these categories are frequently concerned with intrapersonal problems involving anxiety, adjustment, motivation, communication, and vocational or educational attainment.

Management and Administration.   Every year more psychologists are being drawn into industrial administrative posts and other organizations. Psychologists in these executive positions find themselves planning, developing, organizing, and executing various programs. Schools, hospitals,

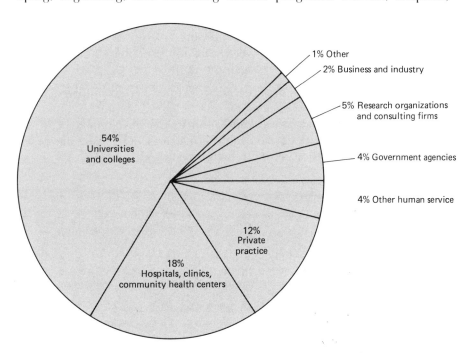

FIGURE 1–2   Employers of psychologists, 1978
(Adapted from *Careers in Psychology*, 1978, p. 17. Copyright 1978 by the American Psychological Association. Reprinted by permission.)

5

clinics, private businesses, corporations, and research laboratories are a few of their employers. Administration is considered to. be one of the most open and lucrative fields for the future.

Testing. One of the most widely known areas of psychology to the layman deals with the assessment and evaluation of psychological tests. Psychologists in this area may be involved with the development, administration, or interpretation of tests designed to measure intelligence, achievement, aptitude, interests, vocational suitability, and personality disorders.

Research. Psychology, like all other sciences, is actively involved in research. Research carried out to advance our understanding of behavior is accomplished by investigations centered around both theoretical and practical problems. One investigator may be involved with determining the internal processes involved in personality development, while another may be attempting to develop a new technique for eliminating phobias. Psychologists carrying out research can be found in hospitals, universities, and industrial and governmental laboratories throughout the country. They are also found outside the laboratory—in supermarkets studying buying trends, in forests studying animal behavior, and in schools analyzing the behavioral patterns of children.

Teaching. The main function of one third of all psychologists is teaching. Psychologists work as professors at institutions of higher learning. They are also hired to develop and implement training programs in industry and governmental organizations.

Consulting. There are many requests from industry, business, and governmental agencies for psychological expertise on a part-time basis. Psychologists are called to aid in the development of instructional programs, help develop educational toys, and assist in applying laboratory findings to everyday situations.

Insight
Changes in Careers in Psychology

By comparing the 1978 census information shown in Figures 1–1 and 1–2 to information published by the American Psychological Association in 1963 (Figures 1–3 and 1–4), some insights into trends in psychological careers may be seen. A close look at Figures 1–1 and 1–3 shows little change in the percentages of the differing subfields in psychology. For example, over the 15-year period, clinicians still compose just under 40 percent of all psychologists. While the 1978 figures show only 6 percent educational psychologists, the 13 percent figure presented for 1963 included school psychologists. Notice that the combined percentage of educational, school, and counseling psychologists is 23 percent in 1978 compared to 24 percent in 1963. While

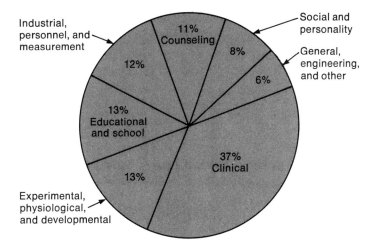

FIGURE 1-3 Subfields of psychology, 1963
(Adapted from Ross and Lockman, 1963, p. 8, Copyright 1963 by the American Psychological Association. Reprinted by permission.)

the proportion of experimental psychologists dramatically declined from 1879 to the 1960s, little change has occurred during the past 15 years.

While the proportion of the subfields has changed little over the past 15 years, the employment setting percentages have changed substantially in several categories. Employment of psychologists in university settings has risen from 35 to 54 percent from 1963 to 1978. The proportion of psychologists in private practice has nearly doubled. The proportion of psychologists hired by government has declined from

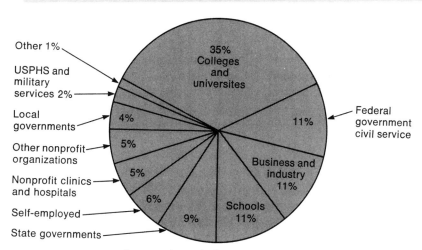

FIGURE 1-4 Employers of psychologists, 1963
(Adapted from Ross and Lockman, 1963, p. 12. Copyright 1963 by the American Psychological Association. Reprinted by permission.)

7

24 to 4 percent. Psychologists hired by business and industry has declined from 11 to 2 percent. Psychologists employed by hospitals and mental health clinics has risen from 5 to 18 percent.

What are the career opportunities in psychology? How much do psychologists make? What type of activities are psychologists involved in? What training and educational requirements are there for the different subfields of psychology? Where is psychology headed? Information concerning these questions may be obtained by writing for a free booklet entitled *Careers in Psychology* to Publication Sales Department, American Psychological Association, 1200 17th Street, N.W., Washington, D.C. 20036.

ROLE OF AN UNDERGRADUATE EXPERIMENTAL PSYCHOLOGY COURSE

With such diversity in contemporary psychology and a smaller proportion of psychologists spending their time in laboratory research, we could question the importance of an experimental psychology course for all undergraduates majoring in psychology. Most psychology majors intend to become applied psychologists. They are interested in training to become clinical, industrial, or educational psychologists, or counselors. They therefore see little value in taking experimental psychology. But psychology is an analytical field, and one of the prime duties of any psychologist is evaluation. He or she should be able to apply psychological principles and evaluate the effects of these principles in specific situations. To do this effectively requires two kinds of training. First, from content courses such as learning, developmental, personality, and abnormal psychology, principles of behavior and what events influence them are learned. The content courses provide the psychology student with the facts as they are currently understood. The student learns such things as the stages a child goes through in development toward adulthood, the perceptual processes people use in dealing with the world, the anatomical divisions of the nervous system and their correlated behavioral functions, the different types of behavioral disorders, the factors involved in personality, and the processes involved in learning.

Second are courses in analysis. Here the student learns how to identify problems, how to apply the behavioral principles learned in content courses, and how to evaluate whether or not the principles are effective in the situation of the moment. A student in psychology requires two types of analytical courses. First are analytical courses that deal with the basic formats used in scientific investigations. These teach the prospective psychologist the alternative types of investigatory procedures that are accepted by professional psychologists and that will be employed as a professional. They deal with what types of investigations a psychologist can carry out, what steps are necessary, and how to implement the various experimental designs. The formats are very general in nature; they are basic investigation types used in all areas of psychology irrespective of the specific area of emphasis. An educational psychologist or a social psychologist, for example, may employ a manipulatory investigation involving two randomized groups. This type of investigation is a common approach used to analyze cause-and-effect relationships, even in disciplines other than psychology.

The second type of analytical course is more related to specific subfields in psychology and is much more restricted in applicability. Psychotherapeutic procedures, for example, are based on general experimental methods that have been modified to deal with specialized case situations encountered by the clinical psychologist. These procedures may not be functional for educational psychologists. A child psychologist may be interested in exploring the ability of children to distinguish between different colors, so the subjects are asked to identify verbally the colors they see. A comparative psychologist interested in animal behavior may want to study the ability of nonhuman organisms to identify colors. Perceptual studies such as this can be done with monkeys, rats, or pigeons although these creatures cannot talk. Though both the child and the comparative psychologist may use the same basic experimental design, their graduate courses in analysis will have taught them what special modifications are necessary in the experimental procedures to deal with their respective situations.

An undergraduate course in experimental psychology is intended to give the student an understanding of the general types of investigatory methods available to all psychologists. Generally speaking, it is the only course in analysis the undergraduate student will have before entering graduate school, for the emphasis of other undergraduate courses is on content rather than procedure. This course should provide an opportunity to develop general analytical skills and sharpen the ability to diagnose which type of scientific investigation should be used in any given situation.

Unfortunately, many students have difficulty in visualizing the importance of experimental psychology if they plan to be applied psychologists. They cannot see any practical application for experimental design problems in human situations, especially when the instructor consistently uses examples with rats running through mazes and pigeons pecking little plastic keys. I recall an example given in my first experimental psychology course. With a gleam in his eye, the professor began explaining the steps involved in a scientific investigation. He used as his example an investigation concerning rats turning right or left in a maze. Although that gleam over the rats' behavior was initially interpreted as an indication of senility, I later came to appreciate it as an honest effort by an intelligent and sensitive scholar to arouse the students' interest in experimental psychology. The wise student should actively attempt to relate the material in this course to the chosen area of interest.[1] Many graduate students have spent long hours learning principles of scientific analysis they failed to pick up in their undergraduate experimental psychology courses because they saw no relevance to them at the time.

There is also growing pressure for graduate psychology programs to increase students' training in experimental procedures. More and more, society is requiring that psychologists demonstrate the effectiveness of their programs. Boards of education now expect educational psychologists to document their views on such issues as whether teaching machines are more effective than teachers, whether students do better when graded or not graded, and whether low student-teacher ratios result in better student performance than high ratios. The clinical psychologist in charge of the county mental health program may be required to carry out investigations to show that an innovative group therapy program (which is expensive) is more effective than some less costly program, or that the drug crisis program is worth the money needed to continue it.

It is also important that psychologists stay well versed in experimental procedures so that they may be able to apply various techniques accurately, as indicated in the following story. A psychiatrist was employed by a state to deal with special behavioral problems that arise in grade school children. One of his cases involved a second-grade girl who had a skill at profanity that would put a sailor to shame. After reading an article on the use of pennies to operantly condition normal talking behavior in certain mute children, the psychiatrist decided to try the same thing on this girl. The following week the girl was brought into his office and seated across the desk from him. His plan was to give her a penny each time she spoke without using profanity, in the hope that he could eventually bring her language under control by paying her to speak nicely.

He sat quietly on his chair with pennies lined up in front of him on the desk and waited for her to speak, just as the psychologist had done in the article he read. "What's wrong?" she asked. Smiling, he slid a penny across the desk to her. She looked down at the penny, back up at him, and back down at the penny. "What's this for?" she asked. A second penny was pushed toward her. "Is this a game?" she asked, while looking at the two pennies in front of her. Again without comment he sent another coin her way. "What the hell's the matter with you? Cat got your tongue?"—no penny. After fifteen minutes of this (and increasing emotion being displayed by the child in response to the "mute" psychiatrist), he told her, "Well, that's all today. I'll see you tomorrow." Quickly the girl got up and started walking toward the door. "Aren't you going to take your pennies?" he asked. In reply she told him exactly where he could stick those pennies.

---

[1] In an effort to help the student see the relevance, I have attempted to use examples from all subfields in psychology, not just animal experiments in the laboratory.

Later, after recounting the incident at a meeting, the psychiatrist adamantly maintained that his situation demonstrated that techniques currently being used by many psychologists in behavior modification programs were ineffective and potentially damaging due to the frustration and anxiety they may develop in children. There are a number of things wrong with his situation. He should not have drawn that conclusion from such an uncontrolled situation. There are several potential explanations for the results he obtained, other than the one he presented. He used an experimental procedure with which he was unfamiliar, besides not understanding the principles involved. A better background in carrying out scientific investigations would have saved him from making such unfounded claims and from the verbal chastisement he received from his audience.

SKILLS REQUIRED OF A PSYCHOLOGIST

There is a common misconception held by many students interested in psychology that the only thing a psychologist needs to know is principles. Psychological training is envisioned by these students as a program in which the prospective psychologist is fed facts and figures about behavioral relationships until all there is to know about psychological principles is known. These principles include such things as the different stages an infant goes through in becoming an adult, how people react in crowds, and what makes the mind work. Actually, psychological training involves much more than learning facts and figures. A potential psychologist must learn more than one skill to become a professional. There are five skills which all psychologists need to develop in becoming a professional, no matter what subfield of psychology they select:

1. Analytical prowess.
2. Knowledge of psychological principles.
3. Skill in communicating ideas to professional peers.
4. Skill in communicating ideas to laymen.
5. Ability to evaluate research.

Analytical Prowess

More than anything else, the psychologist is trained to be an analyst. Society presents behavioral problems to be solved: Why are there so many divorces? Why are people violent? How do mistakes help a person learn? As would be expected, there is more than one way of answering these questions. Laboratory experiments could be performed, surveys could be conducted, observations could be made, case histories could be reviewed.

A large portion of psychological training involves teaching the apprentice psychologist how to answer these questions. The student learns what types of investigatory procedures are available, the advantages, and disadvantages of each type of procedure, and in what situations each may be used.

The psychologist's role is similar to that of an aeronautical engineer. An engineer may be called in to investigate why a particular plane crashed or to come up with a better landing device. A main reason for hiring the engineer is that he or she has been trained to analyze such situations. The engineer knows how to design scientific investigations that can answer these questions. The psychologist is also an expert on how to design a scientific investigation, but in behavioral rather than aeronautical situations.

Knowledge of Psychological Principles

The medical doctor is our society's authority on physical health, to whom people turn for solving medical and surgical problems. He or she either knows the appropriate medicine to give in a particular situation or where to find out. The same is true of psychologists in regard to the mental health of society. The psychologist spends many course hours learning what is known about the psychological composition of people in terms of their actions and thought processes. At first, the training consists of a general foundation in all content areas of psychology, including learning, thinking, physiological mechanisms, motivation, perception, growth and development, personality, social, and abnormal psychology. Later this training becomes confined to a special area of interest such as child psychology, experimental analysis, psychological testing, physiological mechanisms, or learning. As in medicine, so much is currently known in subfields of psychology that it is impossible for one person to know all areas well. The psychologist selects a certain area of psychology to specialize in and becomes intimately familiar with what is known in that area.

Skill in Communicating Ideas to Professional Peers

The psychologist needs to be able to communicate with other professionals in his or her field. Every academic area has its own jargon and style of writing. Special terminology and ways of presenting information have been devised in psychology so that new findings can be presented to other psychologists. Certain formats are considered acceptable for presenting new results, ideas, hypotheses, and theories to others in the field by means of professional journals and presentations at psychological conventions.

Learning the proper form and writing style is an important part of psychological training, and it is a skill that should not be taken lightly.

Skill in Communicating Ideas to Laymen

The psychologist must also be able to develop a good rapport with the nonprofessional. Success as a psychologist is highly dependent on the ability to relate to laymen and explain the solutions to psychological problems in their terms. Although this is especially true of clinical and other applied psychologists, it is also true of research and academic psychologists, who must make their program needs known to administrators and funding agencies.

Ability to Evaluate Research

Progress is continually being made in psychology. More becomes known every day. New principles are being discovered, new approaches are being developed, and new needs are arising. To keep abreast, the psychologist must spend at least a few hours each month reading professional journals. He or she needs not only to read but also to be able to evaluate the results of the published research. In many instances more than one conclusion can be drawn from the results of a research project. Psychologists must rely on their training in how to carry out investigations to help in interpreting the strong and weak points of a new innovative technique reported by a peer and to be able to note the strong and weak aspects of articles that show conflicting results.

OVERVIEW OF THE TEXT

The objective of this text is to introduce the reader to the analytical dimensions of psychology. In the thirteen chapters that follow the reader will be exposed to the various tactics and methods psychologists currently use in carrying out psychological investigations. This may sound like a sizable chore for one textbook, and it is, for there are literally hundreds of different strategies used in psychological investigations. If one were to try to learn all the different psychological investigatory designs individually, it would take hundreds of books and more than one lifetime. What this book attempts to do is show that all the hundreds of designs are derived from a few basic elements or building blocks. Just as the thousands of words in our language are derived from the twenty-six letters of the alphabet, so the different psychological strategies are derived from a few basic methodological dimensions.

The essence of all psychological investigations is to identify causal relationships between variables. A psychologist, for example, may be concerned with the effect of LSD on people's attitudes and actions. To anlayze this relationship, he or she may devise a scientific investigation in which one group of subjects receives LSD and a second group receives a placebo. The investigator tries to make sure that the two groups are the same in terms of age, IQ, ethnic background, and so on, so that any behavioral differences that show up can be attributed to the LSD, not to something else. A second psychologist may be in a country that does not allow the use of LSD in experimentation. To answer the question "what effect does LSD have," resort is made to an alternative type of scientific investigation. The researcher may interview people who have taken the drug or may observe people who have been arrested and are still under the influence of the drug. These are only three of hundreds of different approaches psychologists could use to determine the cause-effect relationship between LSD and behavior.

What would all the different types of investigations have in common? All would be trying to show that LSD and not some other variable present caused some effect on behavior. All would want to be able to state with some degree of validity that LSD has such and such an effect on actions. How could all the alternative investigations differ? They could differ on many variables, such as how much LSD was given and what type of behavior was measured. In terms of validity, however, they will all differ according to how well they control for the possibility that some variable (commonly called a secondary variable) other than LSD may have caused the actions being recorded. Control of secondary variables, then, is the crucial aspect of all psychological investigations and is generally the building block dimension for providing alternative types of investigations. As we shall see in Chapter Four, there are five basic ways of controlling secondary variables upon which scores of alternative types of psychological investigations are based.

The main purpose of the book, then, is to tell the reader what are the basic dimensions of psychological investigations that can be mixed or matched to provide the psychologist with the numerous tactical alternatives at his or her disposal. The steps involved in carrying out a psychological investigation are presented along with the basic points that must be taken into consideration to design and carry out any investigation or to analyze a past investigation. A brief synopsis of the text chapters is presented here to give an overview of what is to be covered. This text is designed for interested students who have no more knowledge of psychology than that obtained in a general psychology course, although a background in statistics would be helpful.

Chapter Two attempts to give the reader some idea of how the general analytical approach used by psychologists originally developed. The major schools of thought are presented along with the methodological approaches they advocated.

Chapter Three categorizes psychological investigations along two dimensions: (1) whether they occur in a controlled laboratory setting or in the natural environment and (2) whether a variable is manipulated (experimental research) or not (ex post facto research). The main steps involved in carrying out these different types of investigations are discussed with strong emphasis on their similarities and differences, advantages and disadvantages. Five reasons for carrying out psychological research are also included.

One of the prime objectives of the book is to aid the reader to understand that scientific investigations center around analyzing variations brought about by variable fluctuations. Variation and its causes are initially covered in Chapter Four in the comparison of the terms *variation* and *variance*. Total variation is then divided into *systematic* and *secondary* components to emphasize the fact that an investigator is concerned with different sources of variation. Five methods for controlling unwanted variables in an experimental investigation are presented. These are elimination, constancy, randomization, making the unwanted variable a second independent variable, and statistical control. The advantages of these five techniques are compared. After defining variation and the different ways of controlling it, the general sources from which unwanted variation may arise are covered. Chapter Four is an important chapter, for it presents the rationale behind all psychological investigations that involve the actual manipulation of some factor.

Chapter Five discusses several important facets of scientific investigations that do not have to do with how the investigation is designed. Issues such as selecting appropriate independent and dependent variables, experimenter bias, and instrumentation problems are presented.

As mentioned in Chapter Four, not all scientific investigations involve the manipulation of some variable where one group is given something (e.g., LSD) and a second group is not. Chapters Six and Seven introduce the reader to nonmanipulatory (ex post facto) research designs and alternative methods of data collections. Although manipulatory investigations are preferred over ex post facto analyses, the psychologist is often confronted with a situation that does not lend itself to experimental manipulation. For example, it would be difficult to carry out a manipulatory study to find out why people commit suicide. Several types of ex post facto investigations are presented that are as scientifically sound as experimental investigations, yet are less powerful for identifying cause-effect relationships.

Chapters Eight through Eleven present sixteen of the most commonly used experimental (manipulatory) designs in behavioral research. All sixteen designs involve performing statistical tests such as a *t*-test and an F test to aid the investigator in determining whether the manipulated factor did have an effect. Not all readers will at this stage of their training have had a course in statistics. Although a course in statistics would be beneficial, it is certainly not necessary. The main purpose of these chapters is to show the student how these designs are used, where they are used, and when to use them, rather than emphasize the importance of statistics. A logical analysis of the statistical computations is provided, however, for the students with and without a statistical background who may be interested in the reasoning behind the statistics. Mathematical examples of each design are presented in a step by step fashion so that the reader may in fact carry out the statistical computations needed without knowing statistics. The numerical examples are also included for another reason. The student should keep this book as part of his or her personal reference library. When later a certain type of investigation needs to be carried out and the student has forgotten how the statistical computations are done, he or she can turn to the appropriate example and carry them out in cookbook fashion.

The use of small-*N* experimental designs in basic psychological research and applied behavior modification therapy is generally considered to be one of the most significant innovations in analysis since the implementation of statistical tests in research. Chapter Twelve presents the experimental analysis of behavior based on operant conditioning procedures using a small number of subjects rather than larger numbers of subjects, as is the case with the experimental designs presented in Chapters Eight through Eleven. The rationale behind such investigatons, plus examples, is included. The development of experimental analysis procedures that can be carried out on as few as one or two subjects has provided the practicing psychologist with the opportunity to carry out sound manipulatory investigations unthought of years ago.

Chapter Thirteen presents several of the more common statistical tests (other than analysis of variance) employed by psychologists. Although most universities have a statistics course as a prerequisite for enrolling in experimental psychology, it is not uncommon for students to still be grasping for a basic understanding as to what statistical tests are and how they work. This chapter is designed to provide additional statistical explanations and illustrations for these students.

As previously mentioned, writing skills are important to a psychologist. Students are generally expected to develop their technical writing skills in the undergraduate experimental psychology course. Chapter Fourteen presents the principles required to write in the style approved by the American Psychological Association. The reader is also introduced to the various journals in psychology and their main areas of concentration.

STEPS IN CONDUCTING AN EXPERIMENTAL INVESTIGATION

Students in an experimental psychology course generally find themselves in a contradictory situation. On the one hand, they are told that they need to finish the course to be able to carry out experimental investigations, and on the other hand they are told they must design and conduct an adequate experiment before the course is over. To help the student in this situation, the basic steps involved in a scientific investigation are presented here so that the student may have some idea of how to plan and properly carry out an investigation. If a particular step is unclear after this brief discussion, the reader may turn to one of the later chapters for a more in-depth coverage.

How many steps are there in a scientific investigation? That depends on which experimental psychology text you look at. If you were to ask twenty different experimental psychologists, "How many steps are there in carrying out an investigation?", you would probably get twenty different answers. Although they would all agree basically on what needs to be done, they would not agree on how many steps into which to divide the overall task. The situation is analogous to asking three chefs how many pieces there are in a pie. Though they would agree on what the whole pie is, they might disagree on how to divide it up. The important point here is that there are no universally accepted specified steps for carrying out research. This text will divide an investigation into six steps. Actually, the number of steps varies somewhat depending on what type of investigation is carried out (experimental or ex post facto). The steps presented here are for experimental types of investigations because most courses require students to carry out an experimental rather than an ex post facto investigation, because experimental investigations are superior in determining cause-effect relationships, and students should have the experience of carrying them out. If the student does happen to carry out an ex post facto investigation as a class project, Chapter Three will provide him or her with the steps involved in such studies.

There are six basic steps in planning and carrying out a psychological research project:

1. Selecting a research topic.
2. Classifying variables.
3. Selecting an appropriate design.
4. Planning the method for carrying out the project, and carrying it out.
5. Analyzing the results.
6. Drawing conclusions about the relationships involved.

First, the student decides what to investigate. At the end of this step the student writes down exactly the phenomenon to be analyzed. Second, the variables are identified and divided into three categories: the independent variable, the dependent variable, and the important secondary variables. Third, a research design is chosen. A research design is simply a way of setting up the experimental situation that allows secondary variables to be controlled by applying one or more of the five control procedures that form the basis of all research designs. Fourth, the exact steps in carrying out the investigation (e.g., the subjects are seated in a classroom, shown a film, and fill out a questionnaire) are specified and carried out. Fifth, the results obtained are analyzed. (Normally this involves performing some statistical test.) Sixth, conclusions are drawn about what happened in the experiment and generalized statements are made regarding the value of this project to situations other than the specific experimental situation. Perhaps an example will better illustrate the role of these steps in conducting an investigation. The following is an account of a former student who had to select and conduct an independent research project for course credit.

Sid was a junior when he enrolled in an undergraduate experimental psychology course. Although listed as a psychology major, he was not sure whether he wanted to become a physiological psychologist or go into the medical profession. Like most of the other students in the class, he had no idea what he would do for the independent research project assignment, which was due at the end of the term. After having had no luck thinking of something to do, he asked the instructor for suggestions. The instructor then asked him what his interests were and what professions he was considering. Sid mentioned he was interested in physiological psychology and the problem of drug addiction. He was told to look through *Psychological Abstracts*,[2] especially the sections dealing with the use of drugs. He found from his readings that very little had been done in actually working with people while they were under the influence of a drug. Some articles had even suggested that it was impossible to work with persons under the influence of certain drugs (e.g., LSD, apomorphine) that caused them to act in seemingly uncontrollable ways. After going through the *Abstracts* and having a few more discussions with the instructor, Sid decided on a project.

He proposed injecting rats with apomorphine and trying to get them to work at some task. Why did he select rats for subjects and apomorphine as the drug? Like all research situations, there were restrictions. Drug research on humans by students is not ethically acceptable, and most addicting drugs are not available for experimental use. Drug research on animals under supervision was acceptable; and apomorphine was available. Apomorphine is commonly used in hospitals in large doses to make a

---

[2] *Psychological Abstracts* is a reference journal published monthly that summarizes every psychological research investigation published in any journal that month.

person vomit. In small doses it causes infants to chew compulsively and rats to gnaw. In previous articles rats had been observed to chew wood, sandpaper, and even their own tails under the influence of apomorphine.

Sid wanted to carry out a research project on the effects of apomorphine. Rather than merely observe rats given the drug, he wanted to get a measure of how strong a motivational state apomorphine caused. He took 12 rats and divided them into two 6-rat groups. All the rats were put in individual metal restraining tubes $2\frac{1}{2}$ inches in diameter, which allowed the rat's head to protrude at one end. They were then trained to swing their heads to the right and to gnaw on a block of wood for 15 seconds as reinforcement. When a head turn was made, the block was presented to the subject by means of a retractable bar. Six rats were given an injection of apomorphine during the sessions; the remaining six were not. After ten daily 1 hour sessions, the drugged rats were averaging 114 head turns per hour, while the undrugged rats were only averaging 3. From the results, Sid concluded that apomorphine did have a motivational effect and that subjects under the influence of the drug could be conditioned to respond to what was going on around them.

When doing an experiment, you should fill out a planning form on the proposed experiment. Figures 1–5 and 1–6 show an example of such a form for Sid's project.

Defining the Problem

Selecting a research problem is difficult for most students. Generally, they are unfamiliar with what is currently going on in terms of psychological research. Consequently, they do not know what to try and they do not know what has been done. One solution is for the student to skim through *Psychological Abstracts*. A second source for research topics is the instructor, who is usually full of ideas, especially feasible projects. Frequently, students decide on a project that is too large or complex to be handled by the novice experimenter. The instructor will usually help steer the student away from such situations.

The step of selecting a research project actually has two parts: (1) deciding on what the general intent of the investigation is and (2) defining exactly what is to be analyzed. In Sid's case the general problem was to determine whether subjects could be made to attend to environmental conditions while under the influence of a strong drug. Notice that this is a broad statement and indicates what general area the investigation involves. To carry out an experiment, however, the investigator must specify clearly how it is to be analyzed. This is the reason for the statement of an operationally defined hypothesis. The hypothesis in Sid's situation was "to determine the effect of apomorphine on the head-turning behavior

---

RESEARCH PLANNING FORM

I. Definition of Problem

   A. General reason for the study   *To determine whether an organism under the influence of a strong drug could be made to attend*

   B. Operationally defined hypothesis *To determine the effects of apomorphine on the gnawing behavior of the rat, and to see if the rat could be conditioned to turn his head while under the influence of apomorphine*

II. Classification of Variables

   A. IV *Apomorphine*

   B. DV *Head turning*

   C. Secondary Variables *Concentration of drug, how it is applied, species of rat, weight of subjects*

III. Type of Investigation

   A. General type of investigation *Laboratory experiment*

   B. Specific type of design *Randomized two-group design*

IV. Method *(See reverse side)*

V. Type of Analysis *t-test*

VI. Conclusions

   1. Apomorphine does induce a compulsive gnawing syndrome in rats.

   2. The effects of apomorphine can be empirically quantified.

   3. Subjects under the influence of a powerful drug can be worked with and conditioned to emit behaviors.

FIGURE 1–5   Sid's research planning form, front side

of the rat." Why are two statements made, one general and one specific? The general statement tells what the basic area of concern is. As in the example, however, there is more than one way to study drugs and behavior. The specific statement pinpoints more closely how it is going to be studied.

IV. Method

A. Subjects *Twelve female Long-Evans hooded rats, three months old and weighing 240 to 290 grams*

B. Instrumentation *A steel restraining tube 2¼ inches in diameter, and 7 inches long, was used to hold the rat during experimental sessions. Two bolts, one at each end of the tube, ran through the diameter of the tube to keep the rat in. A photoelectric cell was placed 1 inch in front of the tube and 1½ inches to the right of the center of the tube.*

C. Procedure

1. *Each rat was run for a one-hour daily session for ten consecutive days.*
2. *During each session a rat was placed in the tube with his head protruding at one end.*
3. *Every time the rat turned his head far enough to the right to break a photoelectric beam, a wooden block was presented in front of him to gnaw on for 15 seconds, by means of a retractable bar.*
4. *Six rats were placed in the tube each day without being injected with a drug, while the other six were injected interperitoneally with 2.0 mg/kgm of apomorphine 20 minutes prior to being put in the tube.*
5. *The number of head turns each subject made per hour was recorded.*
6. *A t-test was run on the data using the following formula:*

$$t = \frac{(\bar{X}_A - \bar{X}_B)}{\sqrt{\dfrac{SS_A + SS_B}{(n_A - 1) + (n_B - 1)}\left(\dfrac{1}{n_A} + \dfrac{1}{n_B}\right)}}$$

FIGURE 1–6   Sid's research planning form, reverse side

Classifying Variables

After stating a hypothesis, the investigator takes stock of exactly what variables are involved in the project. First, he or she defines the variable that is going to be investigated. This is called the *independent variable* (IV), which in Sid's situation was apomorphine. Then it is decided which variable will be measured to determine whether the IV had an effect. This is generally called the *dependent variable* (DV), and in Sid's case it was head-turning behavior. Sid was not really so interested in head-turning behavior; he simply chose that as one means of measuring the effect of the drug. All other variables (secondary variables) in the situation that could influence the head-turning behavior were then listed. This is an important step in carrying out research, for the objective of an investigation is to determine the influence some IV has on a DV. To do this, the investigator's main job is to make sure the secondary variables in the situation were controlled so they could not have caused changes in the DV. Chapter Five elaborates on the selection of the IV and DV of an experiment. Chapter Four discusses secondary variables and ways to control them.

Selecting the Type of Investigation

Over the years psychologists, like other scientists, have learned that there is more than one way to analyze a given problem scientifically. Some investigations involve the manipulation of an IV; others do not. Some are carried out in a controlled laboratory situation; others may be carried out under everyday conditions. Psychological investigations can be divided into four types:

1. Controlled laboratory experiments (IV manipulated in controlled setting)
2. Field experiments (IV manipulated in everyday setting)
3. Ex post facto laboratory studies (IV not manipulated in controlled setting)
4. Ex post facto field studies (IV not manipulated in field setting)

Why have psychological investigations been divided into these four categories? There are a number of different ways investigations could be categorized—for example, dividing them according to whether they are carried out on animals or humans, or dividing them according to their content area of investigation (e.g., perceptual, developmental, social). Whether an IV was actively manipulated or not and whether it is carried out in a controlled laboratory situation or in the field were chosen because they are so important in determining what conclusions may be drawn about cause and effect relationships. Scientists feel safer in concluding that cigarette smoking causes cancer after carrying out a manipulatory investigation (e.g., raising some mice in a smoke-filled chamber and raising other mice in a smoke-free chamber) than after carrying out a nonmanipulatory study (e.g., observing more smokers get cancer than nonsmokers). In a nonmanipulatory study there is a greater chance of drawing incorrect conclusions because the cause in question is not actively applied and removed. There is a greater possibility that some secondary variable is responsible for the effect.

Whether an investigation is carried out in the laboratory or in the field is also an important dimension in determining whether a cause and effect relationship may be concluded. In a laboratory situation the investigator has much greater control over the secondary variables, making it less likely that an incorrect conclusion will be drawn about what caused what. Chapter Three divides psychological investigations into the four categories listed and compares them in terms of similarities and differences, advantages and disadvantages. The student should decide which of the four types of investigations to carry out (notice that Sid decided on a laboratory experiment).

After choosing the general type of investigation to be used, the investigator selects a specific design. A design is a way of setting up the investigation, a procedure for arranging the situation to analyze a certain problem. There are two-group designs, factorial designs, randomized one-way ANOVAR designs, and many more. If an investigator wants to determine whether drinking influences driving ability, he or she may randomly select two groups of people: one is given alcoholic beverages before driving and the other group, nothing. This investigator has chosen a randomized two-group design to compare the two groups on how they drive and determine whether alcohol has an effect. If an investigator wished to determine which of three types of teaching machines was most effective in the classroom, she or he might select a three-group one-way ANOVAR design; a two-group design would be inappropriate.

How many different designs are there? There are scores of designs from which a researcher may choose. Chapter Eight lists sixteen basic designs, and the wise student should at least look over this chapter before deciding to use a specific design.

Planning and Carrying Out the Method

After the appropriate design has been selected, the investigator plans the method. Method may sound like an inappropriate word here, but it is the accepted term in professional journals, so we will use it. If you look in any experimental psychology journal, you will find a section labeled "Method." This section lists step by step exactly how the investigation was carried out. The section is usually divided into three parts: subjects, apparatus, and procedure.

Subjects.   In the subjects portion the investigator lists all the pertinent information about the subjects used, such as the species, sex, age, IQ, their number, or anything else that may be relevant.

Apparatus. If any elaborate equipment, such as timers, test chambers, and so forth, is used, the investigator briefly describes it in this portion of the report.

Procedure. In the procedure subsection the investigator lists all the things done in carrying out the experiment. For instance, in Sid's experiment he listed how the rats were divided into groups, what concentration of drug was used, how it was injected, how the head-turning behavior was conditioned, how long the reinforcement was presented, how many sessions were run, and so on.

The method section is important because the investigator must know exactly what needs to be done before starting. The method section is also important after the project is finished, when the investigator writes up a report. If anyone wants to replicate the experiment, the method section reproduces exactly the research investigation. Replication plays a prominent role in research, so the investigator should be sure the method section of the report is complete.

Deciding just how the investigation is to be carried out is also a difficult step. Like someone planning a vacation, the investigator may find that some important points have been forgotten. How can a student guard against this? There is no way to guarantee that the investigator will not miss some important point, but there are things to do to make it less likely. First, *Psychological Abstracts* should be consulted to see how similar investigations were carried out. The authors of such published articles are professionals and have thought out their research carefully. Use their experience to your advantage by reading their articles and noting the procedures they used.

Some students try to design and set up an experiment without first reviewing related published material. The student taking this position is doing the project the hard way. Reviewing literature first can make carrying out a project much faster and easier, besides helping the student select a higher-quality project. Looking over previously published studies can help the student pick an appropriate problem; it will also indicate what design to use, the procedural steps, what to look for, and what statistical test to use. In fact, not reviewing the literature first is the worst mistake the beginning investigator can make.

Analyzing Results

After the results of the investigation have been recorded, they are analyzed. Analysis usually involves performing some sort of statistical computation to determine whether the IV had an effect. Isn't it possible simply to compare the means of the two groups in the investigation and if they differ conclude that the IV had an effect? No, because it is highly unlikely that the means would ever be exactly equal even if the IV had no effect on the group of subjects it was given to. Suppose an investigation was carried out to see what effect displacement prisms[3] would have on a subject's accuracy in throwing darts at a bull's eye on a dartboard. First, a subject throws three darts at a board without the prisms and then throws one dart with the prisms on. Theoretically, the three darts thrown without the prisms should hit the target in the same place. Actually they do not, however, because the conditions are not exactly the same for each throw. Stance may differ, wind conditions may change, or the darts may be held differently each time. The variation in the distance the three darts landed from the bull's eye is termed *error variation*, for it is due to small errorlike fluctuations in the situation that cannot be controlled. If there was a variation in the accuracy of the three throws without the prisms, then we should hardly expect the throws with the prisms on to be exactly the same as those without, even if the prisms did not distort the visual field at all.

At this point the reader may be saying to himself, "Well, if there is always variation in scores between groups, how do you determine whether the IV had an effect?" The answer to this question is simple and is discussed at length in Chapter Four. Briefly, what is done is this: a measure of variation without the IV present is obtained along with a measure of the variation with the IV present. Table 1–1 presents theoretical scores of the dart situation as an example. First, a mean of the three throws without the glasses is calculated:

$$\left(\overline{X} = \frac{4 + 6 + 8}{3} = 6 \right)$$

The average absolute amount each dart "varied" from the mean is calculated:

$$\left(\frac{|4 - 6| + |6 - 6| + |8 - 6|}{3} = \frac{4}{3} = 1.33 \right)^{[4]}$$

Then the distance the dart thrown with the prisms on varies from the mean is calculated ($14 - 6 = 8$). The amount of variation found with the prisms on is then divided by the amount of variation without

$$\left(\frac{8}{1.33} = 6.01 \right)$$

[3] These may be a specially ground pair of glasses that makes an object look 10 degrees farther to the left than it actually is.
[4] The vertical lines in the numerator indicate that absolute values should be used. The mathematical calculations performed here are designed to serve as an illustration and do not represent the exact procedure used in such cases.

TABLE 1–1	*Distance (in inches) from the Bull's eye for Each Dart Throw*
Without Prisms	*With Prisms*
4	14
6	
8	
$\bar{X} = 6$	

to give a rating of how many times larger is the variation from throws with the prisms versus without the prisms in contrast to variation in throws just without. Putting the glasses on causes over six times as much variation as without the glasses. Can we conclude, then, that the prisms did influence accuracy? After the ratio is calculated, the investigator looks up 6.01 on a table which states the probability that a ratio this size could occur by chance. If there is a 5 percent possibility or less that 6.01 could have been obtained by chance, the investigator concludes the IV (prisms) did influence accuracy.

What has just been covered is the basic idea behind a statistical analysis. Because scores will naturally vary due to chance, the investigator carries out statistical computations to obtain a ratio of the amount of variation found when an IV is applied divided by the amount of chance variation found when no IV is present. A table that gives the probability that such a ratio would occur by chance is then consulted. In this text the student will be shown exactly how the statistical computations are carried out for each type of design. Once a student selects a design, the type of statistical analysis it involves should be located and recorded in step five. Then, after the data are collected, turn to the chapter containing the type of design used and follow the example given for how to perform the computations required.

Students seem to dread the statistical analysis of an experimental investigation more than any other part, perhaps because they do not understand how statistics are derived. It is not the objective of the book to teach statistics, but to show the student where statistics are used in scientific investigations, a bit of the rationale for their use, and step by step examples of how they are used.

Drawing Conclusions

Drawing conclusions is the reason for carrying out investigations in the first place. The investigator wants to make some statement about the problem that could not be made without conducting the research. Sid was interested in finding out what effect apomorphine had, and if it was possible to get subjects under the influence of the drug to attend to things around them. From his analysis he now can draw these conclusions: (1) apomorphine does induce a strong gnawing compulsion; and (2) even though the subjects did not seem to be aware of what was going on around them while they were under the influence of the drug, conditions could be set up so that they would attend to external conditions. In Sid's case this meant they would emit some behavior to get the chance to chew on a block of wood.

Injecting rats with a drug and having them turn their heads in order to get a block of wood to chew on may not sound like an investigation that would have any value in solving human drug addiction. It is an important addition to scientific knowledge, however, because it shows that you can get subjects to respond under the influence of a powerful drug. It suggests that it may be possible to interact with humans who are under the influence of strong drugs, and this is an important step in understanding how strongly drugs may control people's behavior. Studies are currently being carried out on alcoholics to determine how much control alcohol has over them by seeing how hard they will work to get alcoholic beverages.

The ability to perceive the value of a seemingly trivial investigation is a skill which the psychologist develops. The more research the psychologist has been involved in, the better he or she usually is at determining how valuable projects are. Having students evaluate the results of investigations is an important part of psychological training.

SUMMARY

Psychology has expanded during its hundred-year history to become both an academic and an applied discipline. The various subfields of psychology include learning, experimental, developmental, clinical, counseling, social, industrial, physiological, educational, personality, abnormal, and perception. The primary work activities of psychology include clinical work, counseling, management and administration, testing, research, teaching, and consulting.

Most undergraduate psychology courses deal mainly with content. In a content course the student learns the facts regarding behavioral relationships as presently understood. In contrast to the content course, the experimental psychology course is designed to teach the student how to analyze psychological situations and devise appropriate procedures for answering the questions with which psychologists are faced.

A professional psychologist needs five skills: (1) the ability to devise means for analyzing psychological problems, (2) expertise on the principles of behavior and why people act as they do, (3) the ability to write in a professional manner and present ideas to professional peers, (4) the ability to communicate with laymen, and (5) the ability to evaluate research.

The last section of this chapter presents the steps involved in planning and carrying out an experimental investigation. These are (1) selecting an appropriate topic, (2) Classifying the variables (IVs, DVs, secondary variables), (3) selecting the design to be used, (4) planning and carrying out the basic steps, (5) analyzing the results, and (6) drawing conclusions about the relationships involved.

I. **Assumptions Underlying the Scientific Method**
II. **Psychology—A Scientific Approach**
    A. The Early Years
    B. Formation of Psychology as a Scientific Discipline
    C. The Era of the Great Schools
III. **Scientific Paradigms in Psychology**
    A. Experiential Control
    B. Development of an Internally Verifiable Large-N Experimental Paradigm
    C. Development of an Internally Verifiable Small-N Experimental Paradigm
IV. **Proper Subject Matter—The Problem**
    A. Reasons for Experimentation
    B. Different Approaches to Problems
    C. Identifying Possible Research Topics
    D. Things to Consider When Selecting a Problem
V. **Summary**

History of
Experimental
Psychology and the
Scientific Method

2

Chapter Two attempts to give the reader some idea of how the general analytical approach used by psychologists originally developed. The scientific method is presented here as the basic format for all psychological investigations. After covering what the scientific method involves, we will take a historical look at the attempt to understand the behavior of people from the earliest times up through the formation of psychology as a separate discipline to study behavior using the scientific method.

One of the most intriguing puzzles that people have tried to solve is the cause of their behavior. Even with all the technological advances that have taken place, such as going to the moon, few topics arouse as much interest as why people act the way they do; can people read others' minds; can a person be controlled by means of mental telepathy? There is a demonstration you can carry out to see how captivated people are with human behavior. When you are with a small group of friends, relatives, or roommates, tell them you want to demonstrate the ability of one person to influence another by means of mental telepathy. Ask each of them to take a piece of paper and a pencil and then be seated. After they are seated and you have their attention, say the following:

All of you should sit comfortably, relax, and close your eyes. I want you to clear your mind of all thoughts and concentrate on my voice. I am not going to hypnotize you, but I am going to try mentally to pass something to you which you are to write down when I tell you. First, to help clear your mind of other thoughts, I am going to give you a few simple mathematical problems to solve in your minds. Do not say the answers to the problems out loud, just say them to yourself.

What is the sum of 5 plus 1? (Wait about three seconds before giving the second math problem.)

What is the sum of 3 plus 3? (Again wait three seconds.)

What is the sum of 2 and 4? (Wait.)

The sum of 0 and 6? (Wait.)

The sum of 1 and 5? (Wait.)

Now, as quick as you can, open your eyes and write down the name of the first vegetable that comes to mind.

About 80 percent of the people will write down the word *carrot*. After you have given them time to write an answer, ask them one by one to tell the others what they wrote down. Then, from your pocket casually remove a card on which you have earlier written the word *carrot*. For the rest of the evening everyone will be asking you how you did it.[1]

There is only one thing people enjoy more than a magical trick, and that is knowing how it is done. The same is true in psychology. As much as the layman respects the psychologist for knowledge of behavioral principles, the psychologist is held in esteem more for seemingly extraordinary powers of analysis. Patients are continually surprised at the ability of the practicing psychologist to identify the source of a problem that may have been bothering them for years. How was the psychologist able to analyze and solve the situation, while the patient was not? Didn't the patient know as much about the condition—even more, possibly—than the psychologist?

College students are frequently impressed by the writings of well-known psychologists such as Hull, Piaget, Skinner, Kohler, and Guthrie, and wonder what it was that enabled these men to find some of the answers to understanding the actions of people. Too often this question is answered by saying, "These men are unique; they have almost supernatural powers of observation and analysis." There is, however, a much more parsimonious explanation. What all of them have done, in fact, is to employ a rather elementary method of analysis that is not unique to the area of psychology at all. Rather, it was borrowed from other disciplines and found quite effective in solving almost any kind of problem. This type of analysis is called the *scientific method*. The reader may be somewhat let down at this point, having expected the answer to be something other than the oft-mentioned scientific method, a sort of objective and empirical approach to looking at things. Doesn't everybody use the scientific method to some extent in solving everyday problems such as what clothes to buy and what would be the best car to buy? Why should psychologists, and especially famous psychologists, be any more effective in finding out why people behave as they do if all they are using is an approach that most people know of and use to some extent?

The answer lies in the fact that psychologists are something like skilled fishermen. Two persons may have access to the same kinds of poles, reels, and bait, yet not catch the same amount of fish. The expert fisherman can take a fishing outfit and catch the limit of trout in a

---

[1] Why people generally respond with *carrot* is unclear. Carrots are certainly not the most common vegetable. The reason has something to do with the number 6, however, for the demonstration works best when 6 is the answer to each of the math problems.

particular lake while the Sunday fisherman may catch one or two small fish, barely large enough to keep. What is the difference between the two? There are two reasons why the expert fisher gets superior results—skill from experience and knowledge of the capabilities of the equipment used. The expert knows what type of rod, reel, and bait to use when going after a particular kind of fish, and what the next best outfit would be if the best is unavailable. Brown trout prefer flies. Not having any, however, the expert knows what type of bait (worms, eggs) is the next best to try. The skill of fishing, like most skills, comes from practice. The expert spent many hours working on the fundamentals of casting, baiting up, and so on. While learning, he or she may have questioned why things are done a certain way when no relevance was apparent at the time. Later, when applying skills and seeing the results, the value of the apparent idiosyncracies became evident.

Just as the fisherman has basic equipment, the psychologist has the scientific method. Just as the fisherman may select different types of poles, reels, and the like, so may the psychologist employ two-group experimental designs, systematic observation, case study analysis, and correlational designs. The psychologist has learned what the scientific method involves, what variations are possible with it, how to apply it, and when to apply it. The psychologist knows the best approach to solve a particular type of problem; and if it cannot be used, the psychologist knows the next best alternative. For example, it is known that experimental designs involving the manipulation of an IV are a more powerful type of analysis for finding cause-effect relationships than ex post facto procedures. However, there are problems (e.g., suicide) that do not lend themselves to an experimental type of analysis.

Why are some psychologists better than others in their ability to analyze? Mainly because they have more effectively developed their analytical skill by experience and spent more time in learning when, where, and how various scientific procedures should be used. It is true that everyone does not have the same intellectual ability and that part of the success of well-known psychologists is due to better than average intellectual ability. Extra time and effort by the psychologist, however, play a major role in success. B. F. Skinner, for example, once mentioned that many of his research data sheets have entries dated December 25.

ASSUMPTIONS UNDERLYING THE SCIENTIFIC METHOD

The term scientific method has been used so frequently and in so many different situations that it might be wise to say just what it stands for here. It is somewhat of an elusive term in that its exact definition has been

scientific method

stated differently by various scientists. Generally, however, it may be said to be a method of analysis based on four assumptions: empiricism, determinism, parsimony, and testability.[2]

Empiricism.   This term has already been introduced, but let us define it further. The empirical assumption simply says, "Let's look and see." Years ago the common belief was that nerves were hollow tubes through which "animal spirits" ran. Then one day someone cut open a corpse and found that this is really not the case. Empiricism dictates that the statement must be proved, that one must look and see. Without it, rampant speculation, superstition, and hearsay have often stood for scientific truth in the past. Even today, scientific authority is sometimes misused to support unverified speculations.

Determinism.   Another basic assumption a scientist holds is that there is a law and order to which all events bow. Indeed, without law and order we could not be sure of even the most common, everyday things. We could not assume that the sun was coming up the next morning. We could not predict that the presence of rain and subfreezing temperatures means snow. Scientists are investigators of the laws of the universe and consequently hold that the universe is an orderly place. How does this belief apply to the psychologist?

   The psychologist assumes that behavior follows this lawful order and can be linked to causal factors, even if at first they are not readily apparent. Therefore, the psychologist observes behavior and every surrounding condition to try to identify these factors. It is assumed that in the course of observation, once the causal factors are identified, they can be manipulated to modify or control the behavior to which the factors are linked. Knowing these factors and the degree to which behavior can be changed, the psychologist then may apply the principles and techniques to abnormal behavior and bring about normal behavior in the subject. The mental patient can be helped to function in normal society, the criminal to learn to control behavior, or the college student to bring up his or her grades.

Parsimony.   When it comes to speculation or hypotheses about the cause of a scientific phenomenon, the scientist is extraordinarily parsimonious. Parsimony is the assumption that the scientist will never hypothesize a complicated or more abstract scientific explanation unless all the simpler explanations have been experimentally ruled out. In the early years of medical research it was supposed to be common knowledge that demons caused schizophrenia and other mental illnesses. Today, more parsimonious causes for mental illness are considered. Extensive investigation into organic disorders is being done, as is investigation into the environmental

[2] Adapted from Whaley and Surratt [1968]. Reprinted by permission.

control of mental illness on the assumption that something more parsimonious than demons causes the illness.

Testability. Last, but certainly not least, of the assumptions of a scientist is testability. For an event to undergo a scientific analysis, there must be procedures available to the scientist by which empirical observations can be manipulated in such a way that conclusions can be drawn. A scientific approach requires the investigator to use an analytical system that takes all the empirical data available into consideration. In the past there have often been situations in which empirical observations were available, but no method of analysis. Empirically, other planets could be seen, but people could only speculate about what it was like on the surface, how much water they had, and so on. Certain aspects of the stars could be scientifically analyzed (e.g., their movements), but many dimensions could not. Whenever we speculate about a situation without using some empirically based analytical procedure, we leave the realm of science.

In some cases the investigator carries out an analytical testing procedure of some sort, but fails to take into consideration all the available empirical data. An investigator may consciously or unconsciously attend only to aspects of those data that support the research, while ignoring contradictory information. Selectively attending to certain empirical observations while discarding others is, in scientific circles, totally unacceptable.

To get a better understanding of exactly what the scientific method involves, let us take a look at a situation in which an analysis that violates the assumptions of science was carried out.

The Two Faces of Jane Green

The first time Jane Green came to my office was late in December of 1959. She pretended to have come to inquire about having her adenoids removed and gave the impression of being upset when I told her I only did that kind of work on weekends. But there was something else about the small wisp of a girl which made me uneasy. Perhaps it was the large skull and crossbones she had tatooed on the back of her right hand or the football cleats she wore on her feet. I could sense that there was something strange and different about Jane. We chatted for a time about this and that, and Jane's husband, who played the piano for a living, but had recently suffered a double hernia when he joined a marching band. After she had gone, I thought about her for some time. There was something weirdly remarkable about Jane Green. I was soon to learn she had a multiple personality.

Most of us have but one personality we can call our own; good or bad, it is ours for life. In some rare instances, however, an individual may develop two or even three distinctly different personalities. In these cases it is almost as if one is dealing with distinct individuals, so great are the changes in behavior, mannerism, and even physical appearance.

There is some discussion concerning the cause of multiple personalities. One theorist contends that these individuals have an unconscious urge to beat the government out of tax money by declaring each of their personalities as dependents. I am certain, however, that the true cause is a web-like growth in the cerebral cortex causing a schism or "split" in the personality.

It was almost six months after her first visit that Jane Two appeared. I greeted her at the door and immediately noticed the familiar skull and cross bones tattoo. It did not take me long to discern that there was something "different" about Jane. She had always been a small girl, barely over four feet tall and weighing no more than 75 pounds. On that day she was at least six feet five and weighed well over 250 pounds. Her hair which had previously been long and blond was now jet black and crew cut. She had a heavy dark beard and a long ugly scar over her left eye. Even the tattoo, which had previously been on the back of her right hand, was now on her left wrist. She spoke in a gruff voice and told me that her name was Ed Molduleski, and she was here to fix the air conditioner. I was both shocked and amused by the drastic change in her personality. I thought it best that I not show or reveal that I had detected a new personality. "How is your husband?" I asked politely. "Is his hernia better?" Jane appeared to become quite upset and struck me swiftly in the mouth with her amazingly large fist. Before I could regain my composure, she had left the office muttering obscenities under her breath.

While I must admit that her rash behavior took me unaware, it is to be expected from individuals suffering from a multiple personality. In such cases there is always one personality whose behavior is entirely unpredictable, unmanageable, and unanalyzable by any scientific methods.

After that incident, I never saw Jane Two again. It was as though that single encounter had obliterated that other half of Jane Green's personality, leaving only the plain, simple girl I had met on that first day in my office. Jane is now doing quite well and has almost fully recovered from her adenoid operation. She, of course, is completely unaware of that other Jane and of the fact that she once suffered from a multiple personality.[3]

The analysis carried out in this somewhat humorous situation was certainly not scientific. Every one of the assumptions of science was violated. The writer of this article violates the attitude of empiricism when he says that he is certain that the true cause of a multiple personality is a weblike growth in the brain causing a split in the person's personality. No empirical observations were mentioned that would support such a conclusion. A scientist must be careful to make sure any conclusive statements made are based on empirical observations.

The writer suggests that the rash behavior of Jane Two took him by surprise, but if he had thought about it, he would have remembered that such individuals always exhibit one particular personality which is unpredictable, unmanageable, and unanalyzable by any scientific method. In doing so he violates determinism. We must always assume that things are

[3] From Whaley and Surratt [1968], © 1967, 1968 by Donald L. Whaley. Reprinted by permission. The book is a composite of many such fictional situations constructed and analyzed to better one's basic understanding of what the philosophy of science involves.

caused and that these causes can be identified through diligent effort, experimentation, and scientific observation. It may possibly happen that we will, at some future date, run into things which we apparently cannot explain in terms of natural causes, but for now determinism is critical to all science.

The writer attributes the vast differences observed on two occasions in his office to the idea of multiple personalities, He assumes that the conversations he had with the individuals he calls Jane One and Jane Two were really with the same person. He states that the differences can be attributed to a multiple personality. It is obvious to most readers, however, that there is a simpler explanation for the great differences in appearance and mannerism observed in these two instances. Therefore, the writer violates parsimony. It is obvious from the statement that he has made two serious errors. He uses very slim evidence to conclude that conversations held on two different occasions were with the same person. He then reasons that since the behavior, mannerisms, and appearance of the individual on these two occasions is so different, the individual must be suffering from a multiple personality. The reader has no difficulty in seeing that a much simpler explanation is possible, that is, the writer was actually dealing with two different people. This error, of course, is not one that most people would make, and great artistic license has been taken in order to stress the point. Psychologists seem to have more problems with parsimony than most other scientists. This is at least partly due to the fact that so much is still unknown about controlling forces; in addition, people have always seemed to enjoy explanations that are more mystical in nature.

The writer makes an error that violates testability when he assumes that two similar tattoos indicate that he is dealing with the same person. The writer observes the tattoo on the individual he labels Jane Green One and observes a similar tattoo on a later occasion. He makes the error of selectively attending to the tattoos and ignoring differences such as height, weight, and hair color. An investigator must be extremely careful when carrying out an analysis so as not to omit potentially relevant empirical data.[4] Because it is so easy to make an honest mistake on this point, it is an accepted procedure that an investigator should report as much of the data as possible when writing a report.[5]

---

[4] Adapted from Whaley and Surratt [1968]. Reprinted by permission.
[5] There are cases when an investigator may omit part of the data, e.g., if he or she is very sure some of the fluctuations in data are due to an irrelevant variable that fluctuated in the situation. Suppose an investigator gave a subject the wrong instructions and did not realize it until after data were recorded on that subject. This subject's scores may then be excluded from the analysis.

PSYCHOLOGY—A SCIENTIFIC APPROACH

The Early Years

Psychology was founded as a unique discipline in the late 1800s. Its prime purpose was the analysis of humanity. This in itself was not new, for people have sought an explanation of existence since the beginning of time. Two aspects of the quest for knowledge that changed over the years stimulated the analysis of humanity using a scientific approach. The first deals with the explanation of why events occurred. Mankind has always believed that life is made up of cause and effect relationships. We considered behavior to be a function of something, though we were not quite sure of what.

Primitive people believed destiny was in the hands of animistic forces that had the ability to dispense pleasure or pain at will. The initial organization of civilization into groups or clans generally centered around a supreme object of worship, now often called a totem. The totem could be an animal, a body of water, a volcano, or any other natural phenomenon people believed had power over them. Animistic beliefs are still found in today's primitive societies and in many children's explanations of the reason certain events occur. Though animism was an incorrect explanation, it implied a rigorous determinism that is considered one of the first steps toward understanding, predicting, and controlling behavior.

Later, the control of people shifted from belief in forces of nature to deities and celestial beings not subject to terrestrial bondage. Though the new explanation of behavior still placed humanity at the mercy of supernatural forces, it was a significant change in terms of the control people felt they had over themselves. With animism, people devised various magical rites in an attempt to influence good or evil forces. It was believed that through the development of imitative dances and certain objects these forces could be influenced. A person could sap the strength of another by the possession of hair, teeth, or a doll replica. Although most believed deities could be influenced to some extent, mythology placed a more pessimistic attitude toward the ability to influence one's destiny and more dependence on fate.

Then astrology entered the picture. The first attempt to explain behavior in some sort of systematic fashion is generally credited to the ancient Egyptians. They observed the movements of heavenly bodies and concluded human behavior could be accounted for by the regularity of the celestial spheres. The sign under which a person was born became important, for it determined the course of his or her life. Although the explanation of behavior in terms of celestial motion was as fallacious as animism and mythology, it was one more step toward a scientific explanation. Both animistic and mythological explanations of behavior are metaphysical, in that they go beyond the physical world by defining human action in terms of nonphysical entities and deities. This is an important point, for the astrological explanation allowed an opportunity for verification by means of physical manipulation. Unlike animism and mythology, astrological relationships between the stars and behavior could be empirically determined and possibly manipulated by investigators in future years. Unfortunately, the importance of explanations in terms of physical dimensions was not accepted at this time. In fact, people seemed to prefer metaphysical explanations and strongly opposed any attempts at a more parsimonious physical explanation.

In ancient Greece and for centuries after, philosophy was considered the main route to understanding. At the present time philosophy proposes that there are different means to obtain knowledge: rationalism, metamorphism, and empiricism. Each of the three is considered a legitimate avenue to understanding, though each is verified in different ways. Rationalism is based on logic. With logical uniformity, something is said to be true if it is logical and false if it is illogical. It would be false, for example, to say, "Two particular objects are exactly the same along every conceivable dimension, yet they are different." Metamorphism considers knowledge to be a function of symbolic and intuitive cognitions based on an intangible or metaphysical foundation. Empiricism is a source of knowledge dependent on the analysis of physical dimensions that can be observed and measured.

The early Greek philosophers had a strong bent toward a metamorphic, rationalistic approach to knowledge. They believed in empiricism, and even spent time carrying out observations directed at physical relationships. Unfortunately, however, philosophers found themselves in a situation in which they believed there was an explanation for everything, yet had little empirical data upon which those explanations might be based. The sudden illness and death of a loved one who shared the same food and housing as healthy relatives was difficult to explain in terms of physical events alone. Not being familiar with viruses and bacteria, an explanation in terms of a nonphysical spirit was found to be more logical. Just as a child might have the superior ability to inflict pleasure and pain on a captive pet, people thought it more rational to explain their actions by taking into consideration the possibility of a supernatural deity. This approach was considered more justifiable than believing in physical events that could not then be observed—bacteria, molecules, electromagnetic forces.

Metaphysical and magical explanations were coined for every situation, including those now considered part of the natural sciences. Wind velocity, like volcanic action, was accepted as being controlled by supernatural forces. The healing ability of certain herbs was credited to their nonphysical characteristics.

As time passed, people explained more events in terms of physical relationships. Physicians, sailors, explorers, and traders found themselves making more progress toward an understanding of life that would allow them to predict and control their environment than the educated monks and philosophers. Functionality, then, was the second reason for the shift to a scientific approach. The simplistic empirical concept of trying something to see if it worked led to mediation and speculation being surpassed by manipulation as the procedure by which knowledge could be obtained and built upon. Philosophers such as Copernicus, Galileo, Descartes, and Newton aided these developments with their stronger dependence on empiricism in their speculative formulations regarding physics and biology.

More scholars turned their talents toward empirical investigations. Better analytical procedures were developed, and empirical information accumulated. The productivity of the empirical approach led people to realize that the prediction and control they sought in most fields of knowledge were possible without relying on metaphysical explanations. This led to the formation of the natural sciences, who divorced themselves from metamorphism and began an exclusive courtship with logical empiricism. One branch of knowledge remained in philosophy's camp. Most people still felt that their actions must be under the influence, at least partially, of events outside the physical dimension. In fact, even as late as the eighteenth century, anyone advocating that behavior was a function of natural laws was met with hostility or violent punishment.

Formation of Psychology as a Scientific Discipline

Psychology's emergence as a science resulted from the fusion of certain philosophical movements and the rapid advance in experimental physiology during the nineteenth century. Table 2–1 presents some of the more important events since the 1600s that led to the formation of psychology as a separate science.

Philosophical Root of Psychology.   It was approximately 1,700 years after Aristotle that a significant trend toward an empirical approach to the mind appeared. In France, the mathematician and philosopher René Descartes proposed a dual mind-body concept similar to Plato's, except that he took a strong mechanistic stand on behavior and urged the use of the empirical method of dissection. This helped stimulate the development of experimental physiology. A push toward an empirical approach to studying the mind was made by Thomas Hobbes, John Locke, David Hartley, and others. They believed, in essence, that people learn through sensation and

---

TABLE 2–1   *Roots of Psychology*

PHILOSOPHICAL ROOT		EXPERIMENTAL, PHYSIOLOGICAL ROOT	
Date	*Event*	*Date*	*Event*
1650	René Descartes proposed a dual concept of mind and body and urged empirical analysis	1811	Charles Bell and François Magendie discovered sensory and motor nerves
1651	Thomas Hobbes presented the idea of associationism	1833	Johannes Muller proposed specific energies of nerves
1690	John Locke extended Hobbes's idea and proposed that an infant mind is like a *tabula rasa* at birth and gains knowledge by experience	1846	Ernst Weber derived the first quantitative law in psychology
		1850	Marshall Hall pioneered in the investigation of reflex behavior
1749	David Hartley combined all the previous ideas of empiricism and association into a school of thought called associationism	1859	Charles Darwin proposed his theory of evolution
		1861	Paul Broca pioneered in the clinical method of determining brain functions
1860	John Mill argued that the mind must be considered as a whole unit	1869	Francis Galton studied individual differences and began regression analysis
		1870	Gustav Fritsch and Eduard Hitzig used electrical stimulation to study the brain

---

that the origin of the "mind" comes through experience. They proposed experiences should be broken up and analyzed empirically if people were to be understood. Not all empirical philosophers proposed a molecular analysis, however. John Mill, for example, suggested a molar type of analysis, much like the gestalt psychologists to come.

Physiological Root of Psychology.   Due to the fact that dissection was not tolerated by society, even with animals, until the 1800s, the main discoveries leading toward a discipline of experimental physiology occurred in the nineteenth century. The 1800s began with Charles Bell and François Magendie discovering that sensory fibers of the spinal nerves enter the dorsal portion of the cord, whereas motor fibers leave the cord in a ventral root. Johannes Muller developed the concept of specific nerve energies, which basically held that each different sense quality (coldness, warmness, sweetness, sourness, color, and so forth) has its own specialized sensory mechanism that informs the brain of the quality's presence. Ernst Weber took the experimental methods of physiology and employed them in psychological investigations on humans. He developed some of the first quantitative psychophysical methods with his investigations on sensory thresholds. Charles Darwin's presentation of his theory of evolution had a strong effect on the development of psychology as a separate discipline because of its implications about human behavior.

These comments have given some perspective on the events that led to the launching of a scientifically based discipline concerned with understanding people and their actions. While philosophers were drawing toward an empirical analysis of mental processes, physiologists were investigating the neurological basis of behavior and developing objective analytical procedures. Both played an important role in the formation of psychology as a scientific discipline.

The Era of the Great Schools

Modern experimental psychology began in 1879 with the establishment of the first psychological laboratory by Wilhelm Wundt at Leipzig, Germany. Most agree that Wundt was the first person to be correctly called a psychologist. Born in 1832, Wundt took his degree in medicine and emphasized physiology in his early graduate work. He became interested in human sensation and perception. His conversion to psychology was complete with the opening of the first psychological laboratory. Wundt was an intellectual who wrote not only about psychology, but also about logic, ethics, and scientific metaphysics. Although slowed down somewhat when he injured his sight while experimenting on himself, he published 54,000 pages of psychological material before his death in 1920.

Psychology as an independent discipline, as undertaken by Wundt, was selectively directed toward the investigation of sensation and perception. Even before the end of the nineteenth century, however, the realm of psychology had expanded. Like most scientific disciplines in their early stages of development, psychology had to address two issues: (1) what is the proper subject matter of psychology, and (2) what are appropriate scientific procedures for investigating that subject matter. These two points seemed almost inseparable at first, so for the first 50 years different schools formed around different views of what psychology should be. Table 2–2 lists the major historical schools of psychology, their major areas of interest, and the types of analytical procedures they advocated.

Structuralism.   The first major school of psychology began with two men, Wilhelm Wundt and Edward Titchner. Titchner, a bright young Englishman, went to Germany to study under Wundt and later went to America, where he was responsible for the propagation of structuralism. Wundt believed that the primary subject matter of psychology should be the analysis of conscious experiences using a method called introspection. Introspection, as employed by Wundt, was a highly specialized form of self-observation in which a trained psychologist analyzed his or her own

TABLE 2–2   *Major Historical Schools of Psychology*

DATE	SCHOOL	INVESTIGATION PROCEDURE	AREA OF INTEREST	IMPORTANT INDIVIDUALS
1879	Structuralism	Introspection	The "structure" of mental processes and their analysis through personal experience	Wilhelm Wundt (1832–1920) Edward Titchner (1867–1927)
1900	Functionalism	Introspection, objective observation	The utilization of mental processes to fulfill needs	William James (1842–1910) John Dewey (1859–1952)
1902	Psychoanalysis	Clinical method— free association and dream analysis	Underlying causes of mental disorders, causal determination of behavior in childhood	Sigmund Freud (1856–1939)
1914	Behaviorism	Experimental method	Analysis of overt behavior	John Watson (1878–1958)
1915	Gestalt psychology	Phenomenology	Organization of perceptual processes	Max Wertheimer (1880–1943) Wolfgang Kohler (1887–) Kurt Kofka (1886–1941)

private experiences while they were occurring, or immediately thereafter. Structuralists felt that all the complex higher processes were derived from three basic elements—images, sensations, and affective states. For them, the main objective of psychology was to analyze experience by means of introspection in an attempt to discover how these three elements combine to produce complex mental processes.

Because structuralism was based on introspection, its scope was considered too narrow and restrictive by many psychologists. Introspection required considerable laboratory training before it was believed to produce valid results. This limited its application, for it could not be used by children, animals, or mentally disturbed individuals; only the normal adult human could serve as a subject. Titchner claimed these dimensions could be analyzed indirectly, however, using introspection by analogy. In these situations the psychologist was to carefully observe the behavior of the subject, and then to take the subject's place and try to interpret what the individual was experiencing. This was considered one of the weakest links in structuralism, and most felt it was the reason interest in the structuralist position waned. Structuralism is generally given credit for bringing the scientific method to psychology and making psychology a science.

Functionalism. Psychologists not content with the limitations of introspective structuralism sought alternatives, one of the most popular of which was called functionalism. Functionalism was a form of psychology promoted by a number of American psychologists whose main concern was a study of the mind as it functions in allowing the organism to adjust to its environment. Rather than restrict its analysis to the way higher mental processes were "organized," functionalism stressed the importance of finding out how these processes were "utilized" by people in coping with their environment. The main emphasis was on how a person used the processes of perception, attention, thinking, and emotion to fulfill needs.

Introspection was accepted as an analytical technique, especially in investigating conscious awareness. The funtionalist went beyond introspection, however, and emphasized the use of objective observation. As time went on, functionalists moved away from introspection and relied more heavily on objective observation. Not being restricted to introspection, functionalism was able to increase its area of concern far beyond that of structuralism. Investigations could be carried out on children, animals, and mentally disturbed individuals. Psychologists could pursue their interests in the unique as well as the average adult; the abnormal as well as the normal; individuals of all ages, from conception to death. The impetus toward a functionalist approach to people played a significant role in developing the applied dimension of psychology.

Psychoanalysis. Technically speaking, psychoanalysis was not actually a school of psychology. It was not the product of any academic circle within psychology, nor was it considered a complete area designed to explain all the dimensions of psychology, such as attention, perception, sensation, and learning. Psychoanalysis initially was the product of an attempt to deal with the causes, development, and treatment of mental disorders. It was considered a practice involving nonexperimental techniques for treating patients suffering from psychologically induced physical disorders. Its effect on the academic dimensions of psychology became significant with its emphasis on unconscious determinants of behavior and the importance of the formative years in psychological adjustment.

Methodologically, most of the analysis of behavior was carried out using observation. In drawing his theoretical conclusions regarding psychological processes, Sigmund Freud depended on observations of patients' behavior and inductive reasoning. He did use certain methods in applied situations, but did little in carrying out investigations to determine their effectiveness. The clinical analysis of psychological disorders was, however, an important contribution to the advancement of psychology as a science.

Psychoanalysis kindled the interest of society in psychological problems as no other development in psychology had before.

Behaviorism.   Although John Watson graduated from the University of Chicago, which was the center of the funtionalist movement after the turn of the century, he did not agree with the strong mentalistic approach upon which both structuralism and functionalism were based. He became interested in animal research during his graduate studies and carried that interest on into later life. Although functionalism as a school of thought came about through the efforts of many psychologists (William James, John Dewey, James Angell, Harvey Carr), behaviorism as a school of thought was conceived and nurtured in its early years mainly by one man—Watson. Watson believed consciousness was an unscientific residue that philosophical psychologists had carried over from the days of mental philosophy. To Watson, concepts such as mind, volition, images, and consciousness were not tangible items open to objective analysis by scientific methods.

Watson felt the real problem with structuralism and functionalism was their methodology. Introspectionists were disagreeing among themselves on basic issues concerning the conscious processes. The results from introspection were not being reliably supported through replication. Although the introspectionist blamed this on faulty training of the investigator, Watson argued introspection was at fault; it was too subjective. A science of psychology had to be based on better analytical techniques than that. From the natural sciences he saw the importance of using controlled analytical situations involving the elimination and holding constant of important factors in the situation that might influence the dimension being investigated. In his animal investigations he controlled the rest, diet, activity, and hereditary strain of his subjects, variables which, if left uncontrolled, could lead to incorrect behavioral relationships. He strongly advocated the use of manipulatory investigations in psychology, rather than the ex post facto type of analysis predominant at the time. His use of experimental procedures in studying emotional behavior in infants was one of the greatest advances in methodological procedures in psychology.

Gestalt Psychology.   While structuralism, functionalism, and behaviorism were busy debating their strengths and weaknesses, a new school was underway in Germany. The new movement argued against the approaches being used by the other three schools. Gestaltists said experience and behavior could not be analyzed into elements of consciousness, as claimed by the structuralists; nor could they be broken down into stimulus-response units, as the behaviorists claimed. Behavior and experience were to be analyzed only in terms of wholeness and could not be broken down into basic elements. The new movement began with Max Wertheimer's interest in perceptual illusions such as the phi phenomenon, an illusion of movement typified by the sequential turning on and off of lights on theater marquees or the turning barber's pole. The gestaltists argued such perceptual phenomena demonstrated the patterning of stimuli much as a painting represented something more than its basic parts (canvas and so much paint). The gestalt method of analysis centered around the use of observation as an evaluative tool. Gestaltists would observe how humans or animals responded in certain situations. They employed phenomenology, which was the analysis of verbal reports given by naive subjects regarding their experiences, in contrast to the trained introspective approach used by structuralists and functionalists. Although the schools differed in terms of what they felt the subject matter of psychology should be and the procedures by which it should be analyzed, they did agree that psychology should be approached in a scientific way.

SCIENTIFIC PARADIGMS IN PSYCHOLOGY

By the time the field of psychology reached its fiftieth birthday (in the late 1920s), the heyday of the school era was on the wane. A reflective look at what those 50 years had accomplished produced mixed emotions. On the one hand, it was apparent that society's curiosity and desire to understand behavior was more than sufficient to support the propagation of this field. The relatively few nuggets of factual information that had been unearthed during that half-century gave strong indication that there was a wealth of scientific information yet to be uncovered. Although there were a substantial number of educated men during psychology's formative years who believed a scientific study of humanity was not possible, the research findings of that time convinced most psychologists that scientific investigations could identify the causes of people's actions.

However, by the 1920s there was a growing dissatisfaction over the relatively few psychological facts identified. Psychology was advancing much slower than expected. The social sciences were not making the progress the physical sciences were, even though both were employing the scientific method. Most agree [e.g., Woodworth, 1938; Gee, 1950] that psychology adopted its scientific approach from the natural sciences where it had been employed for quite some time. This approach focused on the scientific assumptions of empiricism and testability and was called *experimentation*. Basically, the idea of experimentation was to *manipulate* the variables under investigation. Rather than be a passive observer to the unfolding of natural relationships, a scientific experimenter helped nature along by constructing situations and *manipulating* the elements in question. Chemists would mix elements such as sulfur, oxygen, nitrogen, and calcium and note the results. (Engineers presently experiment on model planes in wind tunnels to study stress on the wings.) Beginning in the late 1800s, the schools of psychology popularized experimentation in psychology and "armchair psychologizing" began to decline.

As experimentation flourished during the school era, a major distinction between the natural and social sciences became apparent: psychology had a much greater problem with *controlling background variables.* A chemist interested in experimentally analyzing the effects of mixing sodium hydroxide and hydrocloric acid had very little problem with the intrusion of factors into the experimental situation that might cause incorrect conclusions of results to occur. Assuming the ingredients were relatively free from impurities, the temperature was within reason, and the mixing vials were clean and free from contamination, any observed chemical reaction could easily be ascribed to the elements being mixed. Holding the room temperature relatively *constant,* and *eliminating* impurities in the vials and the to-be-mixed elements were the only two control procedures the chemist needed to carry out. Chemical elements do not think or reason; atoms of sulfur are identical. All changes in chemical compounds result from easily identifiable outside sources. Nature has provided a substantial amount of experimental control for the natural scientist by making the elements studied physically and mentally inert.

For social scientists, the experimental situation was not as stable. Some type of sensing, reasoning, and reacting organism was part of any psychological experiment. The psychologist had to deal with a number of *background variables* (i.e., differences in past experiences, subject attitudes and mental sets, problems of subject attention) that natural scientists did not need to worry about. Social scientists soon came to the realization that the key to effective experimental analysis is the ability to control background variables in the analytical situation. As Dorothy Thomas [1929, p. 1] said, "Scientific method centers around control, i.e., the measurement of the influence of a given variable by excluding all interfering stimuli." It became apparent that the experimental formats of the natural scientist, consisting basically of eliminating or physically holding constant secondary variables, provided insufficient control for the effective experimental analysis of behavior. Thomas [1929] also noted that, while an experimental approach presents relatively few problems in the physical sciences, the almost impossible task of controlling background variables in the social sciences makes proper use of an experimental approach impractical in most situations.

Experiential Control

Realizing that social scientists faced a somewhat different type of experimental situation, psychologists began their experimental assault on behavior by incorporating *experiential control* into the experimental situation, along with the control methods of elimination and constancy. Experiential control entailed using the past experience of the investigator to control for background variables. Suppose, for example, Ann, an experimental psychologist of the 1890s, was interested in determining the effects of some drug on a rat's behavior. Ann would inject the drug into the rat and then take notes on the rat's behavior (it turned around, bit its tail nineteen times, chewed on the walls of the observation chamber, and so on) until the drug wears off. Later she would compare the drugged rat's behavior to the behavior of rats she had previously encountered in her graduate school training and postdoctoral experiences. The effects of the drug, then, were those behaviors of the drugged rat that she could not recall seeing in rats before.

Training programs during psychology's first 50 years were mainly designed to provide the necessary experiences and seasoning for the experimentalist to adequately employ experiential control. With this system of experimentation, the more seasoned the experimenter, the more likely the conclusions concerning behavioral relationships would be valid. While training in structuralism focused strongly on a certain type of experiential training, all schools emphasized the acquiring of experiences and the development of the powers of observation in their students. Psychological experimentation during the school era relied heavily on external verification through experiential control to identify causal relationships.

Development of an Internally Verifiable Large-*N* Experimental Paradigm

By the middle of the 1920s it was apparent that the scientific analysis of people was possible, but that the proper scientific paradigm had not been identified yet. Psychological experimentation did not include the control methods necessary to adequately extract valuable data about behavioral relationships. What was needed was a scientific paradigm that was internally verifiable. Instead of relying on rather subjective past experience, an experimental format was needed that inherently included ways of controlling background variables. Such a paradigm was introduced to psychology by R. A. Fisher with the 1925 publication of his book, *Statistical Methods for Research Workers*. Most psychologists agree that the experimental paradigm put forth by Fisher in his book has been the greatest analytical breakthrough in the history of psychology. The Fisherian experimental movement (begun in the 1920s) developed an experimental paradigm that was internally verifiable. Instead of experimenters having to rely on past experience and training to separate the fluctuations in behavioral measures due to the IV from the fluctuations caused by uncontrolled background variables, a variety of experimental formats was designed that would perform this separation. Fisher accomplished this by introducing three procedures to an experiment. First, *control subjects* were included in the experiment. Instead of comparing subjects experiencing an IV and using subjects encountered in the investigator's past as control subjects, Fisher advocated including more than two or three subjects in an experiment, and using some of those additional subjects as control subjects. Second, Fisher explained how an investigator should select subjects so that (1) background variables could be controlled and (2) the results obtained in the experiment could be generalized to other subjects. This subject selection procedure is called *randomization*. Third, he introduced the idea of *statistical testing* to make the comparison of DV measures for the control subjects and the subjects receiving the IV even more objective.[6]

It would be difficult to overstate the importance of R. A. Fisher's experimental approach to psychology. Within a short time this intergroup experimental approach (also referred to as large-N experimentation) became accepted as *the* scientific paradigm for psychology. It was not long before experimentation relying on *experiential control* was no longer accepted for publication in psychological journals. Figure 2–1 clearly illustrates how the number of subjects employed in psychological experimentation rose after the introduction of large-N experimentation in the 1920s. After 50 years of searching, psychology finally had a scientific experimental paradigm viable for social scientists. The rate of experimental discovery in psychology began to rise. The number of journals publishing behavioral research rose from a handful in the 1910s to over 200 in 1978.

Development of an Internally Verifiable Small-N Experimental Paradigm

Presently, experimental psychology has a second internally verifiable experimental paradigm in use that does not require the psychologist to use a large number of subjects. This new approach is based on the use of sequential *control conditions* rather than *control subjects*. In contrast to the Fisherian large-N approach, a few experimental psychologists felt that an experiment with few subjects (often referred to as a small-N experiment) could provide an effective means of experimentally analyzing behavior. Among those who resisted the rush to large-N experimentation was B. F.

---

[6] Actually, Fisher's book was not the first publication showing the use of these three procedures. There were some published studies using control subjects [e.g., Winch, 1908] and some earlier studies demonstrating the use of statistical tests [e.g., W. S. Gosset, 1908]. Fisher, however, is generally given credit for putting all the pieces of a new innovative experimental approach together and for playing a substantial role in refining the approach over the next four decades.

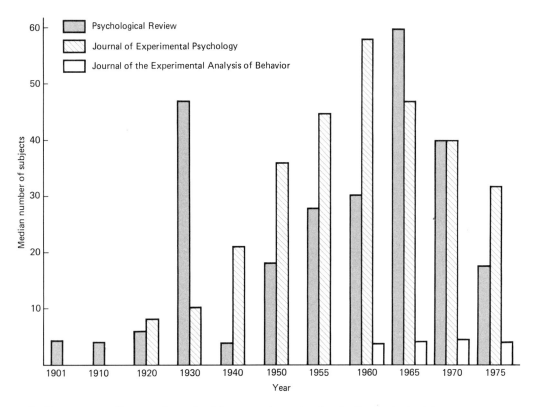

FIGURE 2–1 Median number of subjects per investigation in *Psychological Review, Journal of Experimental Psychology* (begun in 1916), and *Journal of the Experimental Analysis of Behavior* (begun in 1958, and devoted to small-*N* investigation).

Skinner, who felt, as did some other experimenters, that understanding of an organism's behavior was possible by carefully controlling and monitoring the experimental situation. To them, an experimental analysis of behavior did not require a large number of subjects, randomization, or statistical tests. According to Skinner [1956], "The pattern of behavioral research is simple: establish the behavior in which you are interested, submit the organism to a particular treatment, and then look again at the behavior." The small-*N* approach involves basically three phases or conditions. First, establish a baseline of behavior. That is, measure the behavior under investigation over a certain length of time to determine how the organism reacts without the IV in question. Second, apply the IV and continue to record the DV measure, noting any changes. Third, remove the IV and continue to monitor the DV for a specified time. With this approach the subject acts as its own control; thus, no control group is required. The baseline phase of the experiment serves as a control condition, eliminating the need for control subjects. The baseline is also important because it provides a time in which the investigator can control for background variables. The basic idea behind a small-N approach is to take a large number of response measures from one or two subjects rather than one or two response measures from a large number of subjects.

Over the past three decades, the small-N experimental approach has been continually modified and refined; now it is becoming an accepted alternative to large-N experimenitation. Due to the fact that over 85 percent of the students enrolling in experimental psychology courses will become applied psychologists finding themselves dealing with an individual client's problem(s), it is not surprising psychologists are welcoming this new scientific experimental paradigm that can be effectively employed in both applied and basic research circles. Chapter Twelve discusses the small-N experimental approach in more detail.[7]

Insight
Brief History of Experimentation in Psychology

Over psychology's 100-year history, three important analytical trends have occurred: (1) the pre-1920 experimental era, (2) the development of large-N experimental formats, and (3) the development of small-N experimental formats.

Pre-1920 Experimental Psychology

Prior to 1920, causal relationships were investigated using two different analytical approaches, *individual psychology* and *experimental psychology*; the latter had a more restricted definition than it does today. Individual psychology and experimental psychology developed independently of each other [Boring, 1950]. The first attempted to identify behavioral relationships by using statistical manipulation of variables (now known as correlational analysis; then called the "statistical method"); the second sought to identify relationships through direct physical manipulation of conditions in the situation (then called the "experimental method").

---

[7] While the undergraduate experimental psychology course at most universities includes coverage of large-N and small-N experimentation, more undergraduate courses are arising that focus specifically on small-N research methods. P. W. Robinson and D. F. Foster's *Experimental Psychology: A Small-N Approach* published by Harper & Row, Inc., New York, 1979, compares the similarities and differences of the two paradigms in terms of both procedural technology and application. It is designed to be used in conjunction with a basic large-N experimental text or as the basic reader in a small-N experimental psychology course.

Individual psychology was considered a distinct alternative to experimental psychology. According to Gee [1950, p. 273], a main reason for the development and use of the statistical method was that the experimental method was not being used with much effect in the social sciences. Chaddock [1925] contended the experimental method in the social sciences was inadequate because it lacked control. The statistical method, he argued, was the only means for obtaining the required analytical objectivity. When Francis Galton published *Hereditary Genius*, a study of genius along family lines, he initiated the statistical method. He worked out a method of statistical correlation and, with W. F. R. Weldon and K. Pearson, founded the journal *Biometrika* in 1901 for the publication of articles aimed at using correlational rather than experimental methods.

The experimental and statistical methods of the pre-1920 era differed in their stand on the number of subjects required in an investigation. Whereas individual psychology emphasized the use of large number of subjects in order to increase the validity of the relationships sought, experimental psychology advocated the use of few subjects, to increase control. The later development of large-*N* investigations by Fisher and others to study behavior was seen by individual psychology as a means of reducing the number of subjects needed to identify relationships; experimental psychology perceived it as a move toward increasing the number of subjects necessary to study behavior experimentally.

Large-*N* Experimentation

Fisher's book in 1925 launched the era of the large *N* group comparison experiment. The publication of this book was largely the result of two events that occurred in 1908. W. H. Winch [1908] performed a landmark experiment in psychology in which a relatively large number of subjects and a control group were incorporated into the design of the investigation. The experiment, entitled "The Transfer of Improvement of Memory in School Children," was one of the first investigations to use two groups, one experiencing a pretest (the IV) and a posttest, and the other (the control group) experiencing only the posttest. Also in 1908, W. S. Gosset, under the pen name "Student," published a paper, "The Probability Error of a Mean," which introduced the *t*-test as a means of determining the significance of differences between group means.

With the support of W. S. Gosset, E. Somerfield, and W. A. MacKenzie, Fisher wrote *Statistical Methods for Research Workers*, advocating the use of groups to control background variables. It was demonstrated that the ratio of the variance between groups experiencing different levels of some IV could be used to indicate the probability that the difference between group means was the result of chance. Fisher established what is now known as the F table which helps an investigator determine whether the IV in his investigation does have an affect.

With an analysis of variance possible, experimentation shifted from the small-*N* approach employing one or two subjects and no statistical analyses of the data to large-*N* experimentation consisting of the random assignment of a larger sample of subjects to two or more comparison groups and statistical analyses of the results.

With the overwhelming demonstration of the effectiveness of the statistics-based large-*N* approach in identifying cause-effect relationships, statistics courses became part of the required program in the psychologist's academic curriculum. These courses emphasized such points as the following:

1. The way to control for the effects of background variables is to have a control group and to statistically determine the significance of data.

2. Significance levels must be set before the experimenter can determine the effects of an IV.
3. Increasing the number of subjects employed in the experiment increases the investigator's ability to detect the effect of an IV.
4. Large numbers of subjects must be employed if one wants to generalize the results.

Small-*N* Experimentation after 1920

In 1938 Skinner published *The Behavior of Organisms*, a work devoted exclusively to small-*N* research. By 1946 there was sufficient interest in Skinner's work to justify convening the first Conference on the Experimental Analysis of Behavior, a three-day affair held at Indiana University. Further conferences were held during the 1950s in conjunction with the annual meetings of the American Psychological Association. Because the majority of psychological journals refused to accept small-*N* research for publication, the *Journal of the Experimental Analysis of Behavior* was launched in 1958. Since that time, several new journals have arisen that are chiefly devoted to small-*N* behavioral research. These include the *Journal of Applied Behavioral Analysis* (begun in 1967), which features small-*N* studies with an applied orientation. The rapid proliferation of texts and journals devoted to small-*N* research has marked its emergence from the dominant shadows of large-*N* experimentation.

Although the small-*N* approach has been employed in psychology for more than three decades, it has had an almost exclusive courtship with a certain group of psychologists whose research interests have centered mainly in the area of operant conditioning. Only within the last 10 years have psychologists outside the behaviorally oriented group become aware of the utility of a small-*N* approach and realized that adoption of such an approach does not presuppose adoption of the behaviorist viewpoint.

A small-*N* experimental approach has several aspects that distinguish it from a large-*N* experimental approach. First, it requires constant and close monitoring of each subject's behavior with repeated measures (in many experiments, thousands of responses), instead of the large-*N* "one-shot" measure of each subject. Small-*N* experimentation employs intra-subject comparison of IV effects before, during, and after introduction of the IV; large-*N* experimentation employs an intergroup comparison. Small-*N* investigators may actually manipulate the DV by explicitly adjusting secondary variables. This may be done to develop stability in the DV prior to the introduction of the IV. In this way the effects of the IV become more apparent. In contrast, using an automotive analogy, a large-*N* experimentalist would randomly select 100 or so cars, randomly divide them into two groups, and apply a gasoline additive being tested to one group of cars without directly adjusting secondary variables. In such a large-*N* experiment, the effect of the gasoline additive (the IV) will be identified—if the amount of background noise caused by secondary variables (e.g., carburation differences, spark plug firing variation, variation in clogged air filters) does not mask the effect of the additive. (The principle is analogous to identifying the effect of a rock thrown into water having either a smooth or a choppy surface.)

PROPER SUBJECT MATTER: THE PROBLEM

Now that the issue of an appropriate scientific paradigm has been addressed, let us look at psychology's second big concern: the proper subject matter of psychology. This question hits home to the student enrolled in an experimental psychology course when he or she is required to carry out an experiment as a course requirement. Most students feel perplexed when asked to select a good topic for psychological research. And why shouldn't they? Psychology spent a major portion of its efforts during its first 50 years trying to identify the proper subject matter for psychological research, so why wouldn't an undergraduate student feel uncomfortable trying to do the same thing in a few weeks? Often, professors show little patience with students who have a difficult time selecting a worthy topic, when, to the professor, there appears to be a host of topics available. To get a better idea of what is involved in selecting a research problem, we will consider three aspects of problem selection: (1) reasons for experimenting, (2) how a student and professor differ in their approaches to problem selection, and (3) the things a student should consider when selecting a problem.

Reasons for Experimentation

Why do psychologists conduct laboratory experiments? The standard answer to this question has traditionally been, "to test a theory." Theorizing was the main function of psychologists in the past when few principles of behavior were known. It was felt that evaluating a theory was the only acceptable reason for conducting psychological investigations. Over the years that view has changed, however, and now there are several acceptable reasons for conducting experiments. Sidman [1960] lists several reasons besides theory evaluation that the apprentice psychologist should be aware of.

Evaluation of a Theory.   The most common reason by far for carrying out research is to investigate hypotheses and relate them to a particular theory. Experiments that test the adequacy of theories in terms of their ability to provide explanations for relationships between events are important in the scientific community. The basic premise of science, as you may recall, is to identify the relationships between variables. The next logical step up the ladder of experimental sophistication is to identify the relationships between relationships. But before this gets too confusing, let us analyze what has been said so far by means of an example.

If parents are interested in an individual behavior of their child, for example, bedwetting, the parents might hypothesize the fact that the child drinks a full glass of water each night before going to bed as the cause of the bedwetting. If, after making sure the child no longer drinks water before going to bed, the bedwetting stops, the parents accept water drinking as the cause and confirm their hypothesis. Thus, parents deal with particular facts, simple and exact, and from them try to discover some singular relationship between the two.

To discover the relationship between relationships would be our next experimental step. If we were to take the relationship of early childhood bedwetting and that of later success in life, ability to adjust, IQ, or any number of other relationships or laws, and relate these to a particular theory or theories, we would be taking that next step. We would no longer be concerned with only one event involving a particular child, but with the relationship between events in a more global framework. We now hypothesize the relationship between bedwetting and its effect on certain situations that may influence achievement later in life. Thus, we are dealing with determining the relationship between previously noted relationships (water-bedwetting and certain situations-achievement). Theory building involves hypothesizing about the relationship between simple relationships or facts noted.

Satisfaction of Curiosity.   The second most frequent reason for carrying out a scientific experiment or investigation is to satisfy the researcher's curiosity.[8] A person may be little concerned with integrating the results of his or her study into some theory, but still may be interested in finding the answer to a particular question or problem: for example, "Do dogs have ESP?" or "What effect does LSD have on memory?" After finding a problem to be solved, the researcher then sets out to solve it employing the six steps given in the previous chapter.

Those who conduct psychological research seem to follow one of two general routes, the first of which involves developing a theory in one particular area or field and with undeviating vigor exploring *only* that area. Herman Ebbinghaus was an experimenter of this sort. He developed a theory of memory and explored only those areas directly related to it. The second route is taken by those who are not bound by any particular

---

[8] Satisfying one's own curiosity is the most common reason for experiments being carried out in the experimental psychology course, rather than natural causes. A standard requirement of an experimental psychology course is to have the student create and carry out an experiment. This places the student in a situation where the instructor may evaluate her or his ability to carry out the steps involved in scientific research.

theory or area. They are interested in problems and solutions utilizing the scientific method in whatever areas those problems may be. Theories, then, become the product of experimentation and data, not vice versa. B. F. Skinner and many others display varied interests and tend to follow those interests wherever they lead. Theories may develop from their explorations, but they are secondary to solving problems and gathering data.

Demonstration of a New Method or Technique.   A main reason for the development of psychology as a scientific discipline in both the applied and research dimensions has been improvement of laboratory methodology and applied psychological techniques. Prior to the development of the Skinner box, for example, it was difficult to carry out investigations on rats that involved more than one type of response from the subject at a time. Generally, the maze was used as the test apparatus, and the only response measured was how long it took for the rat to traverse the maze or which way it turned in the maze at choice points. With the Skinner box, a subject could be given two or more response bars to push at one time. Now it was possible to analyze what effect changing one task might have on a second task that was not changed. A practical everyday example of this type of research would be answering a question such as, "Will punishing a child for doing something wrong make him withdraw more from other activities also?" In applied psychology, the application of operant conditioning procedures in mental institutions is an example of an improvement in technique. People with certain types of mental problems, such as autism, had not responded very well to therapies based on verbal interaction between the therapist and the patient. Wolf, Risley, and Mees [1964] applied operant conditioning procedures to autistic children and found them to be a welcome addition to other therapeutic procedures.[9]

Demonstrations of a Behavioral Phenomenon.   Another area in which experimentation is used is in demonstrating a new phenomenon. In discovering what is now called state-dependent learning, Girden and Culler in 1937 demonstrated through their experiments that, if a conditioned response was acquired by a dog in a drugged state, that response would thereafter be performed only when the dog was drugged.

The discovery of a new phenomenon is, above all else, a creative activity, though many times accident plays a more important role than most of us would like to admit. The question of how new phenomena are discovered has no set answer. They may be discovered by accident, by

[9] Before a graduate student in psychology receives a master's or doctorate, he or she is generally required to carry out research and write a paper on some topic that will advance the field of psychology. Often this research is in the development of a new procedure or the application of a standard procedure to a different problem area. However, the most important criterion in the resulting data is its quality, not the uniqueness of a technique.

prediction, from theories, from casual observation, from systematic experimentation, or by any number of other ways. Many different areas other than psychology may contribute to the discovery of new psychological phenomena (e.g., sociology, anthropology, and physiology). These other disciplines often provide new insights or suggest new avenues for psychological investigation.

Investigation of Conditions Influencing Behavioral Phenomena. Following the discovery of a new phenomenon, the next step is to integrate the discovery and its data into what is already known and into acceptable theories. The initial phenomenon then becomes integrated by further experimentation, study, and replication. Following Girden and Culler's [1937] discovery and pioneer work with state-dependent learning, many others (Barry, 1968; Bellville, 1964; Heistad and Torres, 1959; Holmgren, 1965; Miller, 1961; and Overton, 1964) tried to analyze the different conditions and effects under which state-dependent learning occurs. They varied the type of drugs, the quantity, and the tasks required, all of which expanded and deepened our understanding of the initial discovery and by doing so aided in its integration.

Different Approaches to Problems

If a psychology professor and an undergraduate psychology student are both asked to come up with a problem to investigate, they will do so from somewhat different vantage points. From a deep well of experience and training and with little hesitancy, the professor may list several potential research topics. The experience and training is typically focused in a particular subfield of psychology—learning, motivation, personality, or the like. The professor has had to become familiar with the theories, the behavioral phenomenon, and the methods employed in the subfield to the extent of knowing what has and has not been done experimentally. The professor would have little difficulty in designing an experiment from any of the five reasons just listed for experimenting. The student, on the other hand, has relatively little experience and training. His or her knowledge of method and technique is limited, so this is not a rich source of ideas. In fact, it is one reason for taking the experimental course in the first place. Most undergraduate content courses (i.e., learning, motivation, social) focus on the basic, well-established principles of a given area and devote little time to the behavioral frontiers research ideas are currently focusing on.[10] Typically, contemporary research coverage is mainly left to

[10] Keep in mind that it take 3 to 5 years on the average for a textbook to be written. This automatically puts the student in the position of reading yesterday's news from the researcher's point of view.

graduate programs. And even when an undergraduate instructor does bring up current issues and topics, there is insufficient time to present the supporting material necessary for the student to conceptualize the area well enough to germinate a research problem. A student project demonstrating a behavioral phenomenon is then also improbable.

Of the five reasons listed for conducting research, the student is most likely suited to draw from two: (1) experimentation for curiosity and (2) experimentation to study conditions influencing behavioral phenomenon. Taking the second reason first, in previous courses the student has heard of several behavioral phenomena, such as the following: Facial expressions, gestures, and other body movements convey emotional meaning. Young persons learn concepts through associations. Certain perceptual capacities are present in organisms at birth. Reinforcement can affect learning. After learning such behavioral principles, the student often wonders such things as: are facial expressions of emotion innate or learned; what is the relationship between language and concept learning; what affects learning more, punishment or reinforcement? These are all potential research problems that may be addressed in one way or another in an experimental psychology course. Often, however, such topics require special equipment, subject facilities, and a sound understanding of surrounding issues. Will the student's university have the necessary equipment and facilities? Most likely it will, if the psychology department has a faculty member who has research interests in that particular area.

With this in mind, if a student decides to carry out an experiment that involves demonstrating the conditions influencing a behavioral phenomenon, he or she should do one of two things. First, find out the interests of the members of the psychology department and see if any of their interests might provide an idea for an interesting and suitable project. Second, select a topic that does not require special facilities or equipment. The first suggestion is generally more profitable to the student than the second. In either case, one should check with the course instructor and see what is available in terms of equipment and the like before selecting a topic.

Satisfying one's curiosity provides, possibly, the most likely area for undergraduate research topics. While a student's scientific curiosity may be dormant, often there are a number of practical, everyday issues that could supply a research topic. Do married college students get better grades than single students? Does one food product actually taste better than another as television advertisements suggest? Will people downtown be more likely to follow someone crossing the street against red lights if a person crossing the street is well dressed or dirty and poorly clothed? There are a multitude of experimental questions such as these that can be answered. Although such questions may have little "scientific" value, they can still provide an appropriate situation for one to develop skills in conducting an experiment. Too often students feel their project should break some scientific barrier and become disenchanted when unable to develop such an idea. Remember, the main objective of experimental projects is to develop experimental skills.

Identifying Possible Research Topics

As a child you were full of curiosity and questions. How does a seed turn into a tree? Why does Daddy have no hair on his head? Why is the inside of people's mouths wet? As years went by, that type of curiosity is forced to give way to what many consider practical thinking. Prompting an individual to come up with an experimental idea is asking him or her to return to asking "why" again. In doing so, the student may come up with questions the same way he or she did when younger—by observation. One of the best ways to come up with a research idea is to look at the people around you for ideas relating to practical problems. Do college students select mates with higher or lower IQs? Do out-of-state students get more traffic tickets than in-state students? Can students study better in the library or their apartment? Do certain brands of margarine taste like butter as TV commercials imply?

Look at textbooks, magazines, and psychological journals. From textbooks you may learn that "behavioral differences between the sexes

TABLE 2–3   *Questions for Potential Research Topics*

 1. Can people distinguish between some brands of margarine and butter?
 2. Do married college students get better grades than single students?
 3. Do college men marry women with lower IQs? College women?
 4. Are different sentences given to drunk drivers, depending on whether they are wealthy or poor?
 5. Can students study as well with music? as without?
 6. Do women get better grades than men during their freshman year?
 7. Can students trace a star while looking through a mirror better with their dominant or nondominant hand? (The results may surprise you).
 8. What are the perceptions of college students concerning the relationship between job type and income?
 9. What is the relationship between marital happiness and length of courtship?
10. What type of social factors influence eating behavior in the obese?
11. Does an animal's perception of important environmental cues enhance learning?
12. Does the meaningfulness of words enhance a person's ability to memorize them?
13. Do males and females of all adult ages have the same sexual attitudes?
14. What is the correlation between a parent's level of permissiveness and the child's willingness to model after his or her parents?
15. Will Siamese fighting fish (*Betta splendens*) attack only other *Betta splendens* or other fish that may look similiar to *Betta splendens*?

may be due to genetic and cultural factors." You may then try to identify certain behavioral differences in men and women; then set about designing an experiment that attempts to culturally manipulate some of these behaviors.

Table 2–3 lists fifteen questions resulting from observation that a student could address for getting experience in the use of the experimental method.

Insight
Student Experimental Fears

In a book entitled *Doing Psychology Experiments*, David Martin discusses the problem of students coming up with experimental ideas from a somewhat different angle. In a delightful, light-hearted and thoroughly enjoyable style he lists nine fears students may have that could inhibit their ability to come up with a research idea:

Geniephobia: an unfounded student fear that they do not have the genius required to come up with a proper scientific problem.

Imitatophobia: the fear of proposing an idea that is not absolutely original— an idea that was thought of long ago.

Paraphernaliophobia: a student fear of the sophisticated equipment necessary to conduct an experiment.

Manuphobia: a feeling of inadequacy in mechanical aptitude for performing any experiment requiring special equipment.

Parsiminophobia: the fear of coming up with too simplistic an idea.

Calculatophobia: the fear of needing to perform any mathematical calculation more complex than counting on one's fingers.

Imperfectaphobia: the fear that his or her experimental idea will be imperfect in some detail.

Pseudononphonoscientiaphobia: the fear that they do not express their experimental idea in the proper "scientific jargon," and therefore it does not sound scientific.

Ergophobia: the student fear of doing work.

Martin explains that all of these fears may be cured, except possibly the last one.

Things to Consider When Selecting a Problem

Several practical issues must also be considered when selecting a research problem. These include time limitations, project difficulty, subject availability, testability, equipment availability, and relevance.

Time Limitations.   A major problem faced by a student carrying out a class project is time constraints. A psychologist working in his or her field may devote whatever time it takes to successfully complete a psychological investigation. The student is always limited by the length of the course. The project needs to be turned in by the end of the term. Suppose you were interested in determining whether a student learns more from a course when weekly rather than monthly exams are given. Such an objective is a worthy research project, but one that time would not allow. It would take at least one term to prepare course material and a second term to run the experiment. Be sure to consider how much time your project may need. Seek the counsel of the instructor. He or she can more efficiently predict the time your project may require.

Project Difficulty.   Another major source of difficulty for student projects is that students often select a project that is beyond their capabilities. A student taking wood shop for the first time does not start out making a chest of drawers. Smaller, simpler projects are done first. The same is true in psychological experimentation. Pick a simple but sound experiment to develop your skills. Getting advice from your instructor may save you several headaches and an incomplete experiment.

Subject Availability.   Be sure the type of subject your experiment requires is available. Many universities have animals (pigeons, rats, etc.) available for student projects while others do not. College students are generally available. Public schools are often a good source of subjects. Be sure to consider the special problems different types of subjects may cause. Many student projects are stifled because college students are unreliable and do not show up when they say they will. Children get sick and stay home from school. The number of animals needed may not be available. (Be sure to consider the ethical treatment of subjects also. See Chapter 5.)

Testability.   A student may select a general topic of research that later is very difficult to turn into operationally definable or measurable terms. Having been exposed to a course in personality, a student may wish to study how different personality types react to a given situation. With no experience in the use of personality tests, one might have a next to impossible task of properly categorizing the subjects to be used. If one is interested in studying whether sleep-learning works, one needs objective means (i.e., a polygraph) of determining when the individual is in fact asleep (and possibly what stage of sleep.)

Equipment Availability.   Many types of research projects require specialized equipment, and almost every psychology department has several pieces of equipment, including demonstration equipment that may be employed to carry out an experiment. Find out what is available at your school.

Relevance.   It has often been said that many published experiments simply pile trivia upon trivia. This is a criticism that the seasoned experimenter needs to consider when designing an investigation. His or her peers may conclude that the months of work do not justify being communicated to others. The student should not be too concerned about the relevance of a first attempt at experimentation. He or she should be more concerned with what will be gained personally from the experiment rather than what others will gain.

SUMMARY

Psychology as a separate discipline came about as an attempt to analyze human behavior in a scientific way. The scientific method is based on four rules: (1) the investigator carries out measurable observations (empiricism); (2) the relations between events are lawful (determinism); (3) the simplest plausible explanation of the relationships found is accepted (parsimony); and (4) only situations in which some test can be made that includes taking all the data into consideration are explored (testability).

Since their beginnings, people have believed in determinism; empiricism was not originally accepted as the best means to obtain knowledge. Parsimony and testability were not initially accepted either. As time went on, people began turning away from a philosophical explanation of their actions and toward empiricism, testing, and parsimony in solving problems of everyday existence. Some philosophers and medical men did likewise. With some philosophers asking for a stronger empirical analysis of humanity, and with greater emphasis on testing assumptions in physiology, psychology emerged from a fusion of the two positions.

After the formation of psychology as a separate discipline, different schools of thought arose—structuralism, functionalism, psychoanalysis, behaviorism, and gestalt psychology—each suggesting what psychology's subject matter should be and how it should be analyzed. The methods of analysis they proposed included introspection, systematic observation, clinical analysis, experimentation, and phenomenology. Psychology sifted through all the methodological approaches, taking the good points of each. The net result has been the application of various methodological approaches, all of which are based on the scientific method.

The experimental methods adopted by psychology from the natural sciences were inadequate to control background variables in the social sciences so an internally valid experimental paradigm was developed in the 1920s. This large-N approach added three important ingredients to experimentation: (1) provide control groups in the experiment by increasing the number of subjects in the investigation, (2) randomly select subjects and randomly assign them to groups, and (3) determine significance of results by employing statistical tests on the data.

A second internally verifiable experimental paradigm which requires few subjects has recently been adopted by psychology. This small-N experimental paradigm: (1) employs few subjects, (2) uses control "conditions" rather than control subjects, and (3) does not require the use of statistical tests.

I. Controlled Laboratory Experiments
   A. Definition
   B. An Example
   C. Steps
   D. Reasons for Controlled Laboratory Experiments
   E. Advantages and Disadvantages
II. Field Experiments
   A. Definition
   B. An Example
   C. Steps
   D. Reasons for Field Experiments
   E. Advantages and Disadvantages
III. Ex Post Facto Field Studies
   A. Definition
   B. An Example
   C. Steps
   D. Ex Post Facto Studies and Controlled Experiments
   E. Reasons for Ex Post Facto Field Studies
   F. Advantages and Disadvantages
IV. Ex Post Facto Laboratory Studies
   A. Definition
   B. An Example
   C. Steps
   D. Reasons for Ex Post Facto Laboratory Studies
   E. Advantages and Disadvantages
V. Summary

Types of Investigations

Chapter Three is important because it lays the foundation for all the following chapters. To determine how a particular situation should be analyzed, a psychologist must be familiar with the alternative ways of carrying out a scientific investigation and realize their distinguishing characteristics. Psychological investigations are divided into four basic types according to two factors. The four types of investigations are discussed in terms of (1) how they are defined, (2) the steps involved in carrying them out, (3) the main reasons for using a particular investigation, and (4) the advantages and disadvantages of each. Special care should be taken to understand the similarities and differences among the four types of investigations.

It is apparent from the last two chapters that the area of investigation carried out by experimental psychologists varies from one researcher to another. A physiological psychologist may devote most of his or her talent to analyzing the role of nucleic acids in learning, while spending little time investigating the shopping habits of housewives. Marketing psychologists may do just the opposite. Though they are both involved in extending humanity's knowledge of itself and its environment by means of experimental investigation, each has selected a different area of content according to individual interests.

Psychologists differ not only in areas of investigation but also in types of investigations carried out. To cite examples of the various types, much recent attention has been drawn to Masters and Johnson, who as researchers have carried out studies dealing with the sexual mores of our society. They have employed questionnaires and personal interviews to obtain information such as how people of varying socioeconomic levels differ in their attitudes on premarital relationships. John Watson (1878–1958), an early founder of behavior-oriented psychology, was interested in the development and expression of emotional behavior. The investigatory procedures he used, however, did not include questionnaires. With his famous Albert experiment, he applied a particular stimulus (a loud noise) to a child's environment and noted deviations in the child's behavior that followed. In many instances the area of investigation one selects will restrict the type of investigation one can employ; Watson would not have been very productive in his research by having babies fill out questionnaires, and Masters and Johnson would meet with strong opposition if they attempted to manipulate all of society's sexual behavior in an effort to see the effect on a person's values. It may be helpful, then, to try to classify some of the more common types of investigations used in experimental psychology.

There is a common misconception that a scientific inquiry must involve the manipulation of variables for the express purpose of causing some variation in a second variable. Actually, this is only one type of scientific investigation. There are others, less prestigious perhaps but much more common in the social sciences. With the increased diversity in psychological problem areas, psychologists have had to rely more heavily on nonmanipulating (ex post facto) investigations. All scientific approaches may be dichotomized as either experimental or ex post facto. Before elaborating on the differences between these two approaches, their points in common should be covered.

A scientific investigation is initiated because of an unanswered problem. A range of variation is observed in some empirical phenomenon. Noting this variation, the potential investigator asks, "Under what conditions will this variation occur?" "What event (the IV) is responsible for the observed variation (the DV)?" All scientific inquiries, manipulatory or nonmanipulatory, involve the investigation of situations in which variation has occurred in an effort to explain the reasons for that variation. What is the importance of maternal love in child development? Why is the suicide rate for prisoners of war higher than for those who have not been prisoners of war? What effect does delay of feedback have on learning? All these questions can be scientifically investigated. For some cases, the variation may have already occurred, while the investigator induces variation in the others. All involve an analysis of variation in which a relationship between some IV and some DV is sought. Scientific inquiry, then, involves the search for conditions to account for variations.

In any situation, a multitude of variables can and may be inducing changes in a DV. A fourth-grade child is doing poorly in class. The school psychologist sets out to determine why. Alternative explanations include poor intellectual ability, family problems, peer pressure, lack of motivation, language problems, and inadequate training in educational skills. What the psychologist is initially confronted with is a DV—poor scholastic records—and innumerable variables that may be responsible for these records. The task facing the school psychologist is to weed out all plausible variables that are incorrect and isolate the variable or variables responsible. How is this accomplished? Like all other scientific investigations, the analysis will rest on the systematic manipulation and control of the variables involved. There are several methods of scientific inquiry to choose from. All involve the reorganization and, where possible, the rearrangement of the events involved in order that a relationship between the DV and some other variable may be identified. By systematically combining and rearranging the events involved, an explanatory relationship is precipitated. The methods of scientific inquiry differ according to the strategy employed with the type of systematic manipulation chosen. Each method is based on a different way of organizing and rearranging the variables involved. The way events in any investigatory situation are organized determines the type of investigation to be carried out and, concomitantly, the type of analysis to be performed.

Using an *experimental* approach, the investigator sets out to determine causal relationships by actually manipulating an IV and measuring resultant changes in a DV. He or she becomes actively involved in the sequence of events. Not all conditions a psychologist wishes to investigate allow this type of direct involvement: many conditions are historical in nature; others restrict the psychologist's manipulations due to ethical issues or impracticability. What causes the high suicide rate of released prisoners of war? How has increased time for recreation influenced an individual's self-concept? Can children raised by animals be rehumanized?

In contrast to experimental investigations, *ex post facto* investigations do not include IV manipulation. Whereas experimental procedures identify relationships by directly manipulating IVs and the conditions in which the IVs are presented, an ex post facto approach identifies relationships more indirectly. The ex post facto strategy involves demonstrating causal relationships by deductively eliminating alternative explanations, and applying mathematical techniques to bring out possible correlations between changes in the DV and some other event. Though the ex post facto type of investigation is somewhat restricted by an inability to manipulate situations directly, it is a valuable tool available to the investigator.

Whether the investigator does or does not manipulate an IV is not the only dimension on which investigations may be categorized. A second functional dimension is the situation in which the investigation is carried out. Investigations may be classified according to whether they are carried out in a natural environment (the field) or in an unnatural setting (the laboratory). The situation in which investigation is carried out may influence the investigator's conclusions. With the increasing demands of society for the psychologist to carry out investigations in more applied situations, the field-laboratory dimension becomes more relevant to the budding psychologist.

Table 3–1 represents these two dimensions and shows the four types of investigations possible when they are superimposed. The remainder of

TABLE 3–1 *Types of Investigations*

		IV	
		Manipulated	*Not Manipulated*
Setting	Unnatural	Controlled laboratory experiment	Ex post facto laboratory study
	Natural	Controlled field experiment	Ex post facto field study

the chapter is devoted to a comparative analysis of these four types of investigations.[1]

CONTROLLED LABORATORY EXPERIMENTS

Definition

After the treatise on the basic assumptions of science you may wonder why the subject of controlled experimentation is being covered here. Are not science and controlled experimentation synonymous? Are we not just restating points described in Chapter One? Scientific inquiry need not involve the manipulation of an IV. Investigations that do involve the direct manipulation of an IV are only one type of scientific inquiry. Scientists who use this method may be referred to as control experimentalists.

A scientist deals with the world in terms of empiricism (measurable observations are carried out), determinism (relations between events are believed to be lawful), testability (only relationships that have the possibility of being proven true or false are considered), and parsimony (the simplest plausible explanation for lawful relationships is accepted). The control experimentalist, a special type of scientist, not only accepts these four bylaws of scientific investigation but adds one other—the direct manipulation of the IV. (The reason for the extra bylaw will be discussed in the next section of this chapter.) Now let us define control experimentation. *A controlled laboratory experiment is a scientific laboratory investigation in which the IV is directly and systematically manipulated.*

[1] There are other ways to classify types of investigations besides the two listed. Investigations may be categorized, for example, according to the type of subjects used (animal or human), the area of psychology involved (developmental, social, etc.), or the type of task involved. The two dimensions on which investigations are categorized in this text were chosen because they are based on methodological differences, and methodology is the central issue here.

An Example

To determine whether learning could occur without performance of an instrumental response, Dodwell and Bessent [1960] carried out a controlled laboratory experiment in which a water maze with eight choice points was used (see Figure 3–1). The sixteen rats serving as subjects were randomly assigned to two groups, experimental (E) and control (C) rats and were taught to swim through the maze to the criterion of three errorless trials.

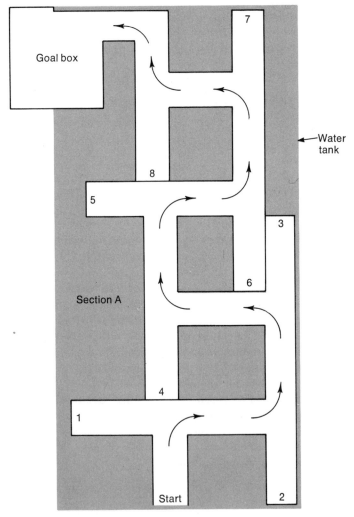

FIGURE 3–1 Diagram of the water maze used by Dodwell and Bessant
(Adapted from Dodwell and Bessant, 1960, Figure 1.)

The experimental animals were initially propelled through the maze on a trolley. They then learned the maze by swimming through it. The number of swimming trials required to reach the criterion and the number of errors made were recorded. An error was defined as making an incorrect turn at any of the eight choice points. On the average, group E subjects took 5.6 trials to reach criterion, wheres group C averaged 9.6. Groups C and E averaged 96.4 errors and 18.9 errors, respectively. It was concluded that learning could occur without an instrumental response being made.

Steps

For an investigation to be considered a controlled laboratory experiment, six basic steps must be included:

1. Formulate a hypothesis.
2. Select appropriate IVs and DVs.
3. Control alternative explanations for variation.
4. Manipulate the IVs and measure the DVs.
5. Analyze the variation in the DVs.
6. Make predictions regarding the relationship between the IVs and the DVs.

The following is an elaboration on these six steps using the previous example of a controlled laboratory experiment as a reference.

Formulating a Hypothesis.   Prior to the actual carrying out of their experiment, Dodwell and Bessent were confronted with a question to which they had no answer. The question was, "Can learning occur without some observable behavior being emitted by the learner?" For them to answer this question, they had to formulate a statement that could be shown to be either true or false.[2] To do this, it was necessary to formulate a statement that would meet two requirements. First, it had to be testable. It had to be stated in terms of operational definitions, that is, stated in measurable and manipulable terms. For example, to formulate a hypothesis dealing with the mind, you would have to define the mind in terms of some measurable unit such as location and rate of electrochemical transmission in the brain. Second, the hypothetical statement must involve a potential relationship between variables. Any hypothetical statement cannot be absolutely true or absolutely false, but has the potential of being one or the other. "I am on the moon or I am not on the moon" is an absolutely true statement. It has no physical possibility of being false, so it cannot be tested. It inherently

---

[2] No statement can actually be proved absolutely true or absolutely false. Instead, a statement is demonstrated to be more probably true or more probably false. Chapter Six deals with this fact in greater detail.

includes all alternatives. "I am on the moon and I am not on the moon" is an absolutely false statement. It logically cannot be; therefore, it is untestable. Notice that both are not hypothetical statements, although they deal with operationally definable variables (*I* and *moon*), because they are untestable. In contrast to these two statements, a testable statement would be "I am on the moon." At present, it is possible to take measurements to determine whether I am there or not; therefore, the last statement can be a hypothesis. A hypothesis, then, can be defined as a testable statement of a possible relationship between two or more variables.

Insight
Types of Hypotheses

Psychological investigations actually involve more than one hypothesis. On the one hand, there are *scientific hypotheses*. Scientific hypotheses are what the text has been discussing so far. There are two forms of scientific hypotheses: a *general hypothesis* and an *explicit hypothesis*. The general hypothesis for Dodwell and Bessant [1960] was, "Learning can occur without some observable behavior being emitted by the learner." As the name implies, a general hypothesis states the "general" reason for conducting the investigation. To transform this general testable statement into a workable investigation, the terms are then more "explicitly" stated in the explicit hypothesis in terms of operational definitions. An explicit hypothesis typically identifies the type of subjects to be employed, the IV to be employed, the procedural format to be employed, and the intended DV. Dodwell and Bessant's explicit hypothesis was that rats (the subjects) being pulled through a multichoice point water maze on a raft (the IV) will make fewer errors (the DV) while learning to traverse the maze than rats not pulled through the maze. The explicit hypothesis tells, in a nutshell, what the investigation will entail.

A second type of hypothesis is the *statistical hypothesis*. A statistical hypothesis is included in any investigation where analysis of the collected data includes the use of statistical tests. *A statistical hypothesis is a statistically testable statement concerning the relationship between the comparison conditions used in an investigation*. Typically, the comparison conditions are the scores of the experimental group subjects versus the scores from the control group subjects. It is generally expected in such investigations that the subjects have been assigned to the control and experimental groups in such a manner, most often by randomization, that the groups should be the same in terms of background variables. It is assumed then that there should be "no difference" in the behavior of the two groups of subjects until the IV is given to one of the groups. Once the IV is administered the investigator states two statistical hypotheses: the *null hypothesis* and the *alternative hypothesis*. The null hypothesis states, "There is no statistically significant difference between the behavior of the experimental and control groups." Conversely, the *alternative hypothesis*, states, "There is a statistically significant difference between the behavior of the experimental and control groups. Once the investigator outwardly states (most often it is merely mentally stated) these two statistical hypotheses, he or she sets out to statistically determine which is correct. The confirmation of the alternative hypothesis allows the investigator to say that the general and explicit hypotheses are correct. The confirmation of the null hypothesis indicates the scientific hypotheses were probably incorrect.

Selecting Independent and Dependent Variables.   After a hypothesis has been formulated, the experimenter begins specifying the IVs and the DVs in terms of events that can be manipulated and measured. In the example, Dodwell and Bessent selected the movement of rats through a water maze without any physical exertion on their part as the IV. The number of trials it took for a rat to swim through the maze three consecutive times without making a mistake and the total number of mistakes a rat made until the criterion was met were the two DVs selected. In more general terms, and to review, the IVs chosen are those variables manipulated by the experimenter acting upon the subject, whereas the DVs chosen are those variables manipulated by the subject itself. IV control occurs when the experimenter varies the IV in a specified course or action to a degree already known. Most psychological experiments measure only one DV, though it is not uncommon for an experiment to measure more than one.[3]

Actually, Dodwell and Bessent could have selected other IVs and DVs to test the same hypothesis. Two alternative IVs could have been (1) putting rats on an elevated platform and letting them watch other rats swim through the maze and (2) feeding RNA brain extract from sacrificed rats who had previously learned the maze to naive rats. There are certain problems to overcome, however, if one were to use either of the IVs proposed.[4]

Many things should be taken into consideration when the IV and DV are being selected. For example, if you plan to carry out an experiment with shock as the IV, how long should it be applied, or how intense should it be? The following are some questions Dodwell and Bessent had to deal with in their investigation when selecting their IV and DV: (1) what will be considered an error; (2) how many trials should the group E rats have on the trolley; (3) how fast should the group E rats be drawn through the maze; and (4) are three errorless trials in a row too easy or too strict a criterion? Chapter Five deals in greater detail with the types of problems encountered when selecting the IV and DV. At this point, it is sufficient to say that selection of appropriate IVs and DVs is a crucial step in experimentation and often spells success or defeat in terms of positive results.

Controlling Alternative Explanations for Variation.   In carrying out an experiment, the researcher must determine whether manipulation of some

---

[3] Various areas in psychology differ on the average number of DVs measured in an experiment. Psychophysical experiments most often measure one DV, whereas physiological studies dealing with the polygraph frequently measure four or more DVs (EEG, EAG, GSR, and EMG).

[4] For example, if you had rats on the elevated platform, how could you make sure they attended to the rats swimming the maze? In the second IV situation, how could you be sure the extract you fed naive rats could, in fact, influence them any differently than extracts taken from rats who had not previously been taught to swim the maze correctly?

variable, *A*, has any effect on the DV, *B*. It should be kept in mind, however, that there is always more than one variable influencing behavior at any given time. Examine an illustration in which a fisherman wants to know which type of bait is best for catching trout. Bait is the IV and number of fish caught in four hours is the DV. While on vacation, the fisherman goes to Lake Powell and fishes from 8 A.M. to 12 noon on a Sunday using flies as bait. The following day the fisherman goes to White Lake and fishes with worms from 2 P.M. to 6 P.M. He caught one fish at Lake Powell and six fish at White Lake. Should it be concluded that worms are the best bait to use? Obviously, variables other than bait could also be the cause of the difference in the number of fish caught. Plausible alternative causes for the variation in number of fish include (1) there are more fish in White Lake, (2) the weather was different on the two days of fishing (weather conditions are known to influence the feeding behavior of fish), and (3), the time of day could have caused the difference. It should not be too difficult for the student to suggest changes in the experiment to remove the alternative explanations or at least the possibility of their influencing the number of fish caught.

In an ideal experimental situation, all the variation in the DVs between the group not receiving the IV and the group receiving the IV should be due to the application of the IV. For an experiment to be ideal, however, both the control and the experimental group should be exactly the same except for the application of the IV. But an ideal experiment is a physical impossibility, for comparison groups will never be exactly the same. Ages of subjects will vary, temperature and lighting will fluctuate, the time each subject is run will vary, and so on. Each variable that fluctuates between the control and the experimental group will influence the DV variation between the groups and, obviously, the amount of influence will vary according to the significance of the variable. In the water maze experiment, temperature of the water, light intensity, and the time each rat was run were not exactly the same for each subject. As you would expect, the amount these variables did fluctuate was so small that their effect on the DV was relatively minor. Variables that could have a much larger influence on the number of trials it took to swim the maze with no mistakes would be past experience with water and past experience with mazes. Notice that Dodwell and Bessent controlled for these two variables by randomly assigning the rats to either the experimental or the control group.

The influence an IV has on the DV in an experiment is often called the primary, or systematic, variation; the influence any or all other fluctuating variables in the experiment has on the DV is called secondary and error variation. The objective of this step of controlled experimentation is to decrease secondary and error variation. One of the values of controlled laboratory experiments is the researcher's superior ability to deal with sources of secondary and error variation. (Chapter Four identifies major sources of secondary and error variation; Chapters Eight through Eleven deal with various means of controlling them when experimental investigations are used.)

Manipulating the Independent Variable.   At the beginning of this chapter types of investigations were categorized in terms of two dimensions, one of which concerned the direct manipulation of an IV. It was also mentioned that this dimension is actually a continuum rather than a sequence of discrete events. Although it is true that there are investigations carried out in which only partial control of the IV is possible, generally one can categorize research investigations in terms of whether the IV was actually manipulated or not. This is one of the most common bases for categorizing research investigations. Cronbach [1957] divides scientific psychology into two main parts: experimental and correlational psychology. He restricts experimental psychology to investigations that actively manipulate an IV; correlational psychology includes all studies in which an IV is not directly manipulated. I have chosen the term ex post facto over correlational because many scientific investigations not manipulating some IV similarly do not carry out any type of correlational analysis. An example is a type of investigation Maxwell [1970] calls straightforward fact-finding types of studies. The example he cites involved determining the whereabouts and present posts of psychiatrists who had trained at either the Institute of Psychiatry or the Maudsley-Bethlem Hospital. Maxwell noted where these graduates ended up. He then continued his study by asking why some graduates born in one country traveled abroad whereas those born abroad went to other countries to stay. Also investigated was the type of eventual post held by each graduate and the leanings of each (toward teaching, research, and so on) over the years. Thus, Maxwell used a minimum amount of statistical manipulation and no complicated methodology.

The distinction between investigations that directly manipulate variables and those that do not is important for several reasons. First, if one is unable to manipulate a variable in order to note its effects on some DV, there is a greater possibility that changes in the DV were, in fact, due to some other variable that varied simultaneously with the one originally being studied. In medicine, to give an example, it was originally suggested that the red spots present along with measles were the cause of the illness. The simultaneous occurrence of two events in time does not necessarily imply a cause and effect relationship. The ability to present and remove a variable at will decreases the probability that there is some concomitant variable causing the effect on the DV.

Second, when one is able to manipulate variables, certain powerful research techniques and types of statistical analysis are available that are inapplicable with nonmanipulative procedures. An elaborate explanation of this point is beyond the scope of this book, but a thorough explanation may be found in texts by Hays [1963], Keppel [1973], and Winer [1971].

Measurement and Analysis of Fluctuation in the Dependent Variable.   The measurement of change in some variable is an integral part of any type of investigation, from a relatively simple fact-finding type of study to a complex experimental investigation involving a sophisticated statistical analysis. Some events must be measured and recorded before any type of data analysis can be run.

There is a strong misconception about data analysis that is shared by most students interested in doing research: they believe that the more complex the statistical analysis involved, the more controlled the experiment. Actually, the correlation is just the reverse. If an experimenter can directly control sources of secondary variation, generally a simpler form of statistical analysis can be employed, because the complexity of the statistical analysis increases as the need to control secondary variation by statistical means increases. Chapter Four deals with this point at greater length; a point to be made here is that students often increase the statistical complexity of their data in an effort to compensate for their lack of adequate experimental control. No amount of statistical manipulation can make up for a poorly conducted project.

Drawing Conclusions about Relationships between Variables.   Step 6 is the most important of any experimental investigation; all five previous steps were taken so that an inference could be made about some relationship between the variables involved. First, a testable relationship was formulated between variables. Second, appropriate representatives of these variables were selected. Third, one decreased the possibility of other relationships interfering with the one of intended study. Fourth, intentional manipulation of one of the variables caused fluctuations in the other variables, which in turn could be noted and analyzed in the fifth step. All this was done so that a statement of some cause and effect relationship between two variables would be possible along with the necessary empirical proof to back it up. The basic premise of any scientific investigation involves demonstrating relationships between variables. The kind of relationship can range from no relationship at all to a strong cause and effect relationship. Controlled experiments are not carried out to find some correlational relationship between variables; rather, they are procedures designed to identify cause and effect relationships. In correlational studies one is limited to showing that variable A simultaneously occurs with variable B to a certain degree. In other words, with a higher correlation between A and B, the more one knows about A the greater one can predict about B. Correlational studies, however, do not enable the researcher to make a strong case for a cause and effect relationship between A and B.

In the water maze experiment previously examined, step 6 dealt with making some statement regarding the cause and effect relationship between learning and the necessity of instrumental responding for learning to occur. After carrying out the experiment, Dodwell and Bessent could state that instrumental responding is not necessarily required for learning to occur. The case for a cause-effect relationship is much stronger in a manipulatory investigation.

Reasons for Controlled Laboratory Experiments

Why do psychologists conduct laboratory experiments? The standard answer to this question has traditionally been "to test a theory." Theorizing was the main function of psychologists in the past when few principles of behavior were known. It was felt that evaluating a theory was the only acceptable reason for conducting psychological investigations. Over the years that view has changed, however, and now there are several acceptable reasons for conducting experiments. Laboratory experiments are performed for all five of the reasons listed in Chapter 2: satisfaction of curiosity, evaluation of a theory, demonstration of a new method, demonstration of a behavioral phenomenon, and for investigating the conditions influencing behavioral phenomena.

Advantages and Disadvantages

A major advantage of controlled laboratory experimentation over non-manipulatory investigations is the ability to control the application and withdrawal of the IV. One of a magician's basic tactics when attempting a sleight-of-hand deception is to carry out and accentuate certain irrelevant behaviors while performing the responses required to make a penny disappear. The observer perceives a cause and effect relationship between the accentuated behaviors and the disappearance of the penny. The deception becomes apparent when the observer imitates the magician, only to find the penny unwilling to dematerialize. Nature frequently presents us with similar situations. In 1866, Gregor Mendel carried out one of the first controlled experiments in genetics when he intentionally controlled the cross-fertilization of certain sweet-pea plants and obtained expected colors in the blossoms. The scientists of that day were so duped by nature's sleight of hand that it took until 1900 before previous conclusions drawn from ex post facto research were discarded. Because of the frequency of persons' misperceiving untrue relationships between variables in everyday situations, experimental manipulation of the IV is strongly advocated wherever possible.

A second advantage is superior ability to control secondary variation. There are two ways this is accomplished. First, control procedures may be used in a controlled laboratory situation that are unavailable in ex post facto studies. A variable (which in natural situations would compete with the IV to influence some DV) could be (1) completely removed from the experimental situation, (2) made an IV itself with its effects recorded, or (3) neutralized by randomly assigning subjects to either the control or the experimental group. With randomization, the effects of the variable are equated between the groups, thereby removing the possibility that any difference noted between the groups was a function of the variable in question. Second, control procedures are more precisely applicable in a controlled laboratory experiment.

A third advantage of the controlled laboratory experiment over other types of investigation is the ability of the experimenter to record the DV more precisely. In field investigations there is greater chance for error in measurement. It may not be possible to record some DVs at all outside the laboratory. Brain recordings, for instance, require a polygraph to sense changes that are not visible to the human eye. Also, many responses may occur faster than a person can record them. In addition, individual perceptual differences between experimenters would be a disadvantage in the ex post facto study, whereas in the controlled situation, precise, unquestionable, and agreed-upon measurements are taken by accurate instruments.

Let us now look at some of the disadvantages of a controlled laboratory experiment. First, some situations—such as mass riots—may not be carried out in the laboratory because of sheer physical impossibility. Second, certain situations may not be carried out because they are not socially acceptable; for example, it is not permissible to purchase human infants and raise them in extreme deprivation situations. Third, laboratory experiments may not be carried out because of time limitations. Even if it were socially acceptable to carry out genetic studies on humans, the time required to carry through just a few generations would be much too long. Fruit flies are much more suitable for genetic experimentation in the laboratory since tens of generations can be propagated in a month or so. A fourth disadvantage of controlled laboratory experimentation is cost. Usually, other types of investigation are less expensive to carry out because laboratory experimentation requires precision instruments of calculation. It is less expensive to send out questionnaires and ask people what they do than to place them in a situation and note their actions.

FIELD EXPERIMENTS

Definition

A field experiment may be defined as a scientific investigation carried out in the field which involves the direct manipulation of some IV or IVs. The field experiment is a scientific investigation carried out in real life. It is similar to a controlled laboratory experiment in that an IV is manipulated, and it meets the criterion of being a scientific investigation. Differences between the field experiment and the laboratory experiment lie in the fact that the field experiment is carried out in a realistic, everyday situation. The importance of this difference is further delineated by the ability of the experimenter to control secondary variation. The controlled laboratory experiment provides the most optimum conditions for control of secondary variation. Field experiments differ from controlled laboratory experiments in degree. Field experiments vary in their ability to control. Some are quite similar to laboratory experimentation and have almost complete control; others occur in a very loose experimental situation that allows little control.

An Example

In today's urbanized society, with its great city populations, response to police or law enforcement agencies has seldom been passive or readily obliging. The unspoken implication that police are the instrument of power generates a general intolerance of any of their efforts by the populace at large. Yet these agencies, by their very nature defenders of the status quo, are forced into a disadvantageous position as society struggles with disruption and change.

In an effort to understand and possibly avert the tide of citizen resentment, an experiment was recently conducted in which the parameters of police functioning within a common but extremely dangerous situation—the family disturbance—were examined. The project attempted to find out if within an area population of 85,000, a specially trained unit of police (eighteen men, only a fraction of the usual force) could effect changes in the rates of homicide and assault, two of the most widely found incidents of aggression in present urban society.

The eighteen officers were trained in a concentrated course of study that attempted to make the men more psychologically sophisticated, with highly technical skills, while still retaining their basic identity. They then were assigned to work in pairs to provide 24-hour coverage of the area in one radio car for a 22-month period. The core of the program consisted of a consultation period for the officers on a weekly basis with advanced doctoral students in clinical psychology, and in group discussions, also on a weekly basis, in which professional psychologists served as group leaders.

In the final evaluation, dramatic findings were noted. The unit processed 1,375 interventions with 962 families, and indirect sources indicated response to the unit was overwhelmingly positive. It is most interesting that while homicide rates in New York City increased during the period of the project, there was not a single homicide in a family known to the unit. A sharp reduction in assaults in the demonstration area was evidenced, as well as a drop in arrests for assaults. Furthermore, there were no injuries to any of the officers in the unit—a surprising fact since an unusually high risk is involved for officers in an emotionally charged and potentially violent family crisis.

In this investigation one can readily observe the most apparent IV manipulated, the education of the officers as applied to the reactions of that segment of society. The DVs measured included overall reaction of the population as evidenced in homicide level, the number of assaults, attitudes toward police intervention, and injury to the officers. In carrying out a field rather than a laboratory experiment, the researcher had less control over secondary variation, so there was an increase in the possibility of explaining any observed change in the DVs in terms of some variable other than the IV. For example, the increased effectiveness of the officers could have been a result not of their psychological training, but of the fact that they tried harder since they knew they were in an experiment.

Steps

The steps in a field experiment are the same as those employed in laboratory experiments: a hypothesis is formulated; IVs and DVs are selected; alternative explanations are controlled for; IVs are manipulated; DVs are measured and analyzed; and conclusions are stated about the relationship in question. The differences in these two types of investigations revolve around the ability of the experimenter to control the steps. In many instances the laboratory setting allows more accurate measurements in the application and recording of the IVs and DVs, thereby increasing analytical precision. It is also true that there are usually more control procedures for secondary variation available in the laboratory. In field experiments it is often difficult to hold sources of secondary variation constant or to completely remove them. The investigator must consider the myriad of conditions that affect subjects in the field situation more than in a laboratory experiment.

Reasons for Field Experiments

The reasons for carrying out field experiments are essentially the same as those for carrying out laboratory experiments. Field experiments can be devised to test theories, satisfy one's curiosity, try out new methods, demonstrate behavioral phenomena, and explore the conditions under which a phenomenon occurs. Of the five reasons, the third and fourth are the most common. Field experimentation is more often concerned with problems of practical application than with extensions of theoretical positions. New methods are frequently applied to deal with current problem areas. The previously mentioned study using autism as an area of experimental research is a situation in which little success had been achieved in the past. Field experiments which demonstrate results that have previously been unattainable are also common. For example, Shelley, Keysor, and Robinson [unpublished] demonstrated procedures that can be employed to develop pitch discriminations in people who previously could not tell to what degree two musical tones differ—whether one musical tone is higher, lower, or the same as the one presented before it. After pairing a light with each tone in one octave and then fading out the lights, the accuracy of discrimination improved from 50 to 94 percent.

Advantages and Disadvantages

In considering one of the values of field experiments, we discover one of the faults of laboratory experiments. With all of laboratory experimentation's advantages of control, it has one great potential defect—the inability to generalize the results obtained in the laboratory setting to real-life situations. This is commonly known as lack of *externl validity*. A scientific investigation may be *internally valid* (properly controlled to the extent that any change in the DV can be safely assumed to be caused by the IV), but not be externally valid (although the IV is demonstrated to hold a positive relationship to the DV in the experimental setting, the relationship does not hold in everyday situations because conditions in the experimental setting are not analogous to those outside that setting). A juvenile delinquent found guilty of breaking a law may be quite repentant before the judge and vow never to commit the act again. Once outside the courtroom and back in his previous environment, however, he or she commits the crime again. The pressures on that individual in the courtroom are not the same as those outside; therefore, the behavior emitted in the courtroom is not a valid indicator of behavior outside.

With a little reflection on previous comments regarding superior ability to control secondary variation in laboratory situations, it should be apparent that although laboratory experiments may control for internal validity better than any other type of investigation, this restriction of secondary variation may cause the experimental situation to vary from the real-life situation to such an extent that the experiment has little external validity. A main value of field experiments, then, is that they involve the manipulation of an IV in a situation that is more true to life than the laboratory setting. So, although the control of secondary variation (internal validity) is less than in laboratory experiments, there is greater possibility that the relationships found are truer demonstrations of what happens in real-life situations (external validity). This attribute of increasing external validity makes field experimentation the favorite procedure for social psychologists, clinical psychologists, sociologists, and educators.

Field experiments offer several advantages over ex post facto research. First, the IV can be actively manipulated. Second, control procedures for secondary variation that are unavailable to ex post facto studies (e.g., subject randomization, holding sources of secondary variation constant) can be applied.

EX POST FACTO FIELD STUDIES

Definition

Psychologists believe we can gain better understanding of ourselves not only by investigating present and future events, but also by analyzing events of the past. Something good or bad may have occurred, and we are not sure why, so we investigate the past in an attempt to identify the cause of the change. Acts of vandalism on college campuses were noted to be higher prior to World War II than after. The way to study the causes of the increased vandalism would be to carry out an ex post facto investigation. There are two reasons why this problem could only be investigated using this approach. First, it would be impossible to return to the prewar era to carry out a controlled experiment; second, society would not allow us to intentionally manipulate variables that would induce vandalism. This situation contains the two major reasons for the founding of the particular type of scientific investigations called ex post facto (EPF) research: if an unexpected event occurred in the past, it is obviously impossible to use a controlled experimental approach, and it is too late to manipulate a variable to see if it was the cause of the event. And because society stipulates certain moral codes that cannot be violated regardless of reason or interest, variables that so violate those codes cannot be used—much less manipulated. With this in mind, we can define ex post facto research as any systematic empirical inquiry in which the IVs have not been directly controlled because they have already occurred or because they are inherently not manipulable.

An Example

Pettigrew [1959] carried out a field study testing whether the widespread belief that white southerners are typically more prejudiced against blacks than are whites in the north was based on (1) more externalizing personality potential for prejudice among southerners, (2) the effects of different cultural norms and pressures, or (3) both of these. Basically, he was contrasting sociological and psychological explanations of prejudice. His test involved administering authoritarian, anti-Semitic, and anti-black scales to randomly selected white adults in four northern and four southern cities.

Pettigrew found that there was no significant difference between northern and southern adults in relation to the authoritarian scale used to measure externalizing personality potential. On the anti-black scale, however, it was found that there was a significant difference between the two regions. Hence Pettigrew reasoned that the anti-black prejudice was based on sociological factors rather than psychological ones.

Notice that no IV was manipulated in this study. Just as a detective might measure the amount of gunpowder residue on various suspects' hands in an effort to relate them to the firing of the gun, Pettigrew took measures of social and personality factors. These measures were taken along with measures of the anti-black attitudes of northern and southern white adults. The issue was whether anti-black prejudice was related more closely to social or to personality factors. If this were a controlled experiment, the social and personality factors would be the IVs to be manipulated and the prejudice would be the DV. Any prejudice that occurred as a result of manipulating social and personality factors would be said to be caused by those factors. Because Pettigrew could not actually manipulate those factors, all he could extrapolate was that when prejudice was found, social factors were "related" to anti-black prejudice.

Steps

Without the opportunity to manipulate an IV, the functions of the researcher shift to some extent. The role an investigator plays in EPF research is similar to that of a detective who attempts to solve a crime. The event has already occurred, so the opportunity to manipulate some variables and control others has been removed. Instead, one must deal with the situation as it is. All the facts that have any possible bearing are gathered. By a process of elimination, least possible causes are progressively discarded until one explanation is left. The last remaining choice is concluded to have caused the event because it had the greatest probability of being responsible from among all the possible alternative explanations.

In some cases, there is a prime suspect, and the procedure involves gathering data to determine the probability that the prime suspect was the cause. Pettigrew's study is a good example of this type of situation. There were two prime suspects for causing anti-black attitudes, social and psychological. Measurements were gathered and recorded. An analysis was then carried out to determine how strong the connection was between anti-black attitudes and psychological or social factors. The analysis dealt with taking any changes found in the two factors and noting any corresponding changes in anti-black attitudes. The ability to determine causal connections is limited, then, because all that can be shown is that one event occurs at the same time the other event occurs. When an IV can be manipulated, you can show the relationship when X follows Y. Showing X can bring about Y is a stronger basis for concluding a causal relationship than simply showing Y is present when X is present.

The steps in EPF research are the same as those for experimental research except that two steps have been eliminated. It is not possible to control actively for sources of secondary variation (step 3) and no IV is manipulated (step 4). The investigation does include forming a hypothesis, defining the possible IV (X) and the actual DV (Y), collecting and analyzing data, and drawing conclusions about the possible relationship of X to Y. Now the most important step for both EPF and manipulatory research is the one dealing with determining a probability that the change in the DV was, in fact, a function of the change in the IV. Actually, neither EPF nor manipulatory research can tell you for a fact that the manipulation of X *caused* the changes in Y. All either procedure can do is increase confidence that X did by decreasing the possibility that some other variable caused the difference.

Ex Post Facto Studies and Controlled Experiments

The difference between an ex post facto and a controlled approach becomes more apparent by looking at the application of both to the question of whether cigarette smoking causes cancer. In the well-known post hoc study on cigarette smoking and cancer, the smoking habits of a large number of people were studied. The investigators probed the backgrounds of the people to find out whether they smoked cigarettes and, if so, how many for how long. The study included (1) people presently living who did not have cancer, (2) people presently living who did have cancer, and (3) people who had died. The IV and the DV were the numbers of cigarettes smoked and the occurrence of lung cancer, respectively. It was found that the incidence of lung cancer rose with an increase in the number of cigarettes smoked. The conclusion reached in the study was that lung cancer was caused by cigarette smoking.

A controlled approach to a similar question was followed by Essenberg at the Chicago School of Medicine. Essenberg sought to reproduce in mice the conditions to which human smokers subject themselves. Two glass enclosures were constructed to serve as the controlled environment in which laboratory-bred mice were placed. Attached to the enclosures was a special device that "smoked" a cigarette an hour and sent the smoke to the mice inside. Mice in the second enclosure received ordinary air. Within the year, twenty-one of the original twenty-three mice living in the first enclosure had lung tumors. Essenberg concluded that the smoke of the cigarettes contributed to, if not directly caused, cancerous growth in tissues.

Reasons for Ex Post Facto Field Studies

Ex post facto field studies can be devised to test theories, satisfy one's curiosity, evaluate new methods, identify behavioral phenomena, and explore the conditions under which a phenomenon occurs. These reasons are similar to those for carrying out controlled laboratory experiments, though the approach and the results obtained may vary. The difference lies in the fact that experiments provide greater confidence in any causal relationships found. Ex post facto research is a more indirect approach for testing a hypothesis.

Advantages and Disadvantages

If the reasons for carrying out all investigations are the same and controlled experiments give one more confidence in one's conclusions, why carry out EPF field studies? There are several reasons. The major ones are found in its definition: The situation happened in the past or an IV cannot be manipulated because of physical or social restrictions. In addition, one may carry out EPF research with limited funds, for controlled experiments generally cost money. EPF research, on the other hand, can be carried out with pencil and paper. Time is another factor. For example, a school board wants to know whether it should hire teachers with bachelor's or master's degrees. Teachers with master's degrees are more expensive. The board could look at past histories of the success rates for both kinds of teachers rather than hire a couple of each and compare. Many times EPF situations will allow more subjects for analysis to be included. In the teacher example, it may not be physically possible to hire more than a few teachers and actually evaluate their ability, whereas past records may provide valuable comparative data upon which to evaluate the teachers.

The limitations of EPF research center around four points, the third of which is a function of the first two. First, no IV can be manipulated; second, there is less ability to control secondary variation sources; third, an incorrect interpretation of the results is more probable; and fourth, complicated statistical analytical procedures developed for controlled experimentation cannot be employed.

EX POST FACTO LABORATORY STUDIES

Definition

An EPF laboratory study may be defined as a scientific laboratory investigation in which the IVs have not been directly controlled due to the fact that they have already occurred. Often some event that occurs in a controlled laboratory setting is unexpected or noticed for the first time. The investigator may then formulate a hypothesis to explain that event, analyze any data regarding this event, and draw conclusions.

An Example

In the 1950s Joseph Brady carried out a research project at the Walter Reed Laboratories. Some long-term experiments being carried out on monkeys included the application of shock to the subjects, and Brady was finding a high mortality rate among his subjects. No explanation for the deaths was evident, so he attributed the losses to unavoidable circumstances. One day an ulcer specialist, R. W. Porter, asked if he might perform a post mortem examination on the next few monkeys that died. He found small perforated ulcers in the stomachs of the subjects. Since Porter had not found ulcers in hundreds of other monkeys not experiencing the conditions to which Brady had been subjecting his monkeys, an EPF laboratory study was carried out to determine which experimental conditions were most strongly related to the ulcers and the deaths of the subjects. A high correlation was noted between the use of certain types of schedules of reinforcement employing shock and the ulcers.

Steps

The steps in an EPF laboratory study are similar to those carried out in EPF field studies. A hypothesis is formed, IVs and DVs selected, data recorded and analyzed, and a conclusive statement made regarding the relationship found. EPF laboratory studies do not manipulate any variable or control for secondary variation sources as is the case with controlled experiments. As a consequence of these two steps being omitted, the type of statistical analysis employed in EPF research will substantially differ from that employed in controlled experimental research.

Reasons for Ex Post Facto
Laboratory Studies

Laboratory studies are often carried out as a means of selecting an appropriate controlled experiment. After carrying out a particular study, an investigator may feel there seems to be a relationship between some variable that is not controlled and fluctuations in the DV. The investigator then analyzes the data for this previously unthought-of relationship and finds a strong correlation. This variable is then selected to be an IV for a controlled experiment. In one particular situation, I was trying to teach kindergarten children a red-green color discrimination using a fading procedure so that the children would not respond to the wrong color. Some children were making many mistakes, while others were making none. With an EPF analysis of the situation, it was noted that the child made mistakes when he or she was left in the testing room alone with the testing equipment but not when an adult stayed in the room. Later, a graduate student decided it would be interesting to carry out a controlled laboratory experiment to investigate the effects of adult presence on discriminations with children.

In many cases EPF laboratory studies are carried out as a troubleshooting device in controlled experiments. During one semester in an introductory psychology class an individual instructional program was used. Students were allowed to go at their own pace throughout the course, and certain days were set aside for testing. Students were to come in and take each chapter exam when they felt prepared to do so. One hour each day the testing lab was open for them to take the exams. After two weeks of class, it became apparent that many students were frustrated. One afternoon, fifteen students approached the assistant and said they were "fed up" with the way the course was being run. They were questioned, and after a while it became apparent that the trouble centered around the fact that many times a student would study to take a test, go in, and wait for his or her turn, and not be able to take it because too many other students had come the same day. After the students left, the teaching assistants were called together and an analysis of the situation was made. It was decided that sign-up sheets would be posted so that a student could sign up in advance for the day and time to take an exam. In this way a student would be sure of taking the test when he or she wanted to. This EPF analysis directed us to a seemingly trivial variable in the program that was severely disrupting our experiment. After posting the sign-up sheets, the frustration dissipated. At the end of the course, seven of the students who initially came in and protested said the course turned out to be one of the best they had ever taken.

Advantages and Disadvantages

EPF laboratory studies may be carried out as rigorously as other types of investigations. They are commonly employed as a troubleshooting device for controlled experiments to save time and money in simply trying to find sources of trouble in other controlled experiments.

The limitations of EPF laboratory studies are many. First, no IV can actually be manipulated. Second, secondary variation is not directly controlled. Third, it is not generally considered a publishable type of investigation by itself. The information gleaned from it is usually closely related to a later controlled experiment that is of more interest to other scientists. Fourth, some experimenters do not consider it a true investigation, for it is not usually carried out by itself; instead, it is employed in connection with some other experiment that malfunctions. Other experimenters, however, believe one should analyze malfunctioning investigations rather than simply discard them.

Though EPF laboratory studies are not usually covered in experimentation texts, it is an important type of investigation, for its success is related to the skill of the investigator. Applied psychologists differ with respect to their skill in identifying the past sources of problems for which a patient seeks an answer. Those who set up graduate programs in applied psychology have had difficulty determining the exact steps by which this skill is obtained, so they have not yet been able to devise a course the student may take to acquire these skills in cookbook fashion. Instead, students proceed through an intern program in which they work side by side with applied psychologists in an effort to acquire them indirectly by some sort of imitation process.

The same problem is encountered in experimental psychology graduate programs. Some experimentalists are more skillful in their controlled research than others. Many researchers would not have been as perceptive as Brady and Porter in visualizing the potential relationship between the shock situations and the ulcers. Though the exact procedure for developing this senstivity to potentially relevant relationships in ongoing research is unknown, it is strongly related to the ability to carry through EPF laboratory studies. Many EPF laboratory analyses are in fact carried out only in the mind of the investigator. Nothing is written. An investigator may "eyeball" the data in ongoing research, mentally note the simultaneous fluctuations in the DV and some potential cause of that fluctuation, evaluate the possible strength of the relationship, and decide whether to carry out a controlled laboratory experiment to increase his or her confidence that there is in fact a cause-effect relationship there.[5] Most EPF laboratory studies are not published, for whenever there seems to be a strong relationship, it is generally followed up with a controlled laboratory study, the results of which are then published.

SUMMARY

All psychological investigations may be divided into four categories according to whether an IV is manipulated or not, and whether the investigation is carried out in a laboratory or in an everyday situation

---

[5] "Eyeballing" is a laboratory term for evaluating the importance of the changes in the DV by simply looking at the data. No formal statistical analysis is carried out. More is said about eyeballing in Chapter Eight.

(field). Psychological investigations that include the manipulation of an IV are called experiments, whereas nonmanipulatory investigations are called ex post facto studies. There are six steps involved in carrying out psychological investigations: (1) formulate a hypothesis; (2) select appropriate IVs and DVs; (3) control for alternative explanations of DV variations; (4) manipulate the IV and measure the DV; (5) analyze the variation in the DV; and (6) make predictions regarding the relationship between the IV and the DV. Controlled laboratory experiments include all six steps. Field experiments also include all six steps, but do not allow for controlling secondary sources of DV variation as effectively as laboratory experiments. Ex post facto studies differ from experiments in steps 3, 4, and 5. EPF studies cannot control secondary sources of variation as well as experiments, do not include the active manipulation of an IV, and require a different kind of variation analysis than experiments. Laboratory situations are more effective in step 3 than field situations, while field situations are more generalizable to other everyday situations.

There are at least five reasons for carrying out psychological investigations: (1) evaluation of a theory, (2) satisfaction of curiosity, (3) demonstration of a new method or technique, (4) demonstration of a behavioral phenomenon, and (5) investigation of conditions influencing a behavioral phenomenon.

The advantages of laboratory experiments include the ability to manipulate an IV, superior ability to control secondary variation, and precision measurements. Disadvantages include the facts that they cannot be used in certain situations because of physical impossibility, that they may not be socially acceptable in some situations, and that they may take too long and be too costly.

Field experiments are inferior to laboratory experiments in terms of measurement precision and ability to control secondary sources of variation. They are superior to EPF investigations in precision, control of secondary variables, and ability to manipulate an IV. EPF studies may be used to analyze past situations and nonmanipulable situations.

I. **What is Variance?**
  A. *Division of Variation*
  B. *Systematic Variation*
  C. *Within Variation*
  D. *Division of Variance in an Experimental Situation*
II. **Methods of Controlling Secondary Variance**
  A. *Elimination*
  B. *Constancy*
  C. *Making the Secondary Variable an Independent Variable*
  D. *Randomization*
  E. *Statistical Control*
III. **Sources of Secondary Variation**
  A. *Internal Validity*
  B. *External Validity*
IV. **Summary**

Variance

4

Chapter Four gives the rationale behind carrying out an experimental investigation using two or more groups. Systematic variation and within variation are two of the most important concepts in the whole book. Because the ability to control secondary variables is the crux of all psychological investigations, the five methods for controlling secondary variables presented in this chapter should be memorized. The last section of the chapter deals with problem areas that could invalidate an investigation.

There are two behavioral trends in which psychologists are interested: what makes people similar and what makes them different. On the one hand, psychologists study what the average child of six can do, what the average homemaker does in her spare time, and so on. On the other hand, psychologists investigate what makes one person's personality different from someone else's, how psychotics differ from neurotics, and so on.

In dealing with these questions, the experimentalist collects two kinds of information, *averages* and *variations*. Averages, such as the mean score or the mean number of attempts to solve a problem, give the psychologist information regarding the similarity of people and events. Suppose an instructor wants to determine how many multiple-choice questions the typical college student can answer in one hour. For the first class exam a 150-question test is handed out, with instructions to the students to answer as many as they can. The number of questions answered (not just correct) by each of the fifteen students in the class are 71, 75, 76, 76, 70, 64, 68, 70, 72, 70, 66, 65, 84, 74, and 69. He takes these raw scores, adds them up, and divides by the number of students to get the mean number of questions a college student can answer in one hour.

$$\frac{1,070}{15} = 71.33$$

He may now use this information to determine the number of questions an exam should have. (Since most students have a fairly good understanding of how to calculate and use means, the point will not be elaborated here.)

There is a second statistical measure, just as important to the psychologist as the mean, which most students have difficulty in understanding. That measure is variance. Generally, a course in statistics is required before a student can enroll in an experimental psychology course. Variance, a basic concept in statistics, is thoroughly covered in such courses. Unfortunately, many students have difficulty in relating the concept of variance covered in the statistics course to the use of the same term in an experimental situation. They have trouble conceptualizing just what variance represents, and, consequently, most wonder why researchers are so concerned with it. For this reason, a section on the role of variance and its importance in experimental situations has been included. This section does not cover all types of variation measures; instead, two variance measures will be discussed so that the student gets a feeling for the role of variance in experimentation.

The first measure of variance to be covered, *average variation*, is not a very useful statistical tool, and is presented here only because it is easy to calculate and may aid the reader to understand the second measure by allowing a comparison of the two. The second measure, *variance*, is an extremely useful concept in experimentation. The reader should pay close attention to how it is calculated, for it is the very foundation of experimentation.

WHAT IS VARIANCE?

Technically speaking, variance is a measure of the dispersion of a set of scores. It shows how much those scores are spread out and their degree of difference from one another. The meaning of this may be somewhat hazy to the student at this point, so let us look at a particular situation. As mentioned before, the main interest of researchers is to find cause and effect relationships. To do this, they generally select two groups, experimental and control. The experimental group is administered an IV; the control group is not. The major purpose of the experimenter's efforts is to cause variation between the groups. He or she wants the IV to influence the experimental group in such a way that the DV measured in the experimental group will vary from that of the control group. The difference between the group scores may then be explained in terms of the influence of the IV initially administered by the experimenter.

Here is a case in point. Eight grade-school children were selected to throw a ball as far as they could. The number of feet each child threw the ball were 11, 10, 8, 7, 5, 4, 2, and 1. It is apparent that all the scores are not the same. Some children threw the ball farther than others. Most people would say that's natural and let it go at that. Not the experimentalists; to them the differences between the scores represent the differential influence of variables in the situation. For each child there were genetic factors (e.g., size, weight, sex, age) and environmental factors (e.g., restrictive clothing, wind, gravity, weight of ball, physical conditioning) that were all partly responsible for the distance the ball was thrown. The difference in distance the ball was thrown indicates to the experimentalist that the children were not all influenced by the same variables to the same degree. Different variables and/or the same variable having different values were influencing each child.

The experimentalist would then set out to get some measure of how much the children were differently influenced by variables related to the situation. He or she would seek some measure of the average amount of variation between the distance the ball was thrown, thereby getting some indication of how much variability there was in the factors that influenced the distances the ball was thrown. This would give an answer to the question of how much the genetic and environmental factors in the situation differentially influenced the children's behavior.

To get an idea of how much each score varied from every other, the experimenter could subtract each score from every other score, as shown below.

```
11 − 10 =  1
11 −  8 =  3  10 − 8 = 2
11 −  7 =  4  10 − 7 = 3   8 − 7 = 1
11 −  5 =  6  10 − 5 = 5   8 − 5 = 3   7 − 5 = 2
11 −  4 =  7  10 − 4 = 6   8 − 4 = 4   7 − 4 = 3   5 − 4 = 1
11 −  2 =  9  10 − 2 = 8   8 − 2 = 6   7 − 2 = 5   5 − 2 = 3   4 − 2 = 2
11 −  1 = 10  10 − 1 = 9   8 − 1 = 7   7 − 1 = 6   5 − 1 = 4   4 − 1 = 3   2 − 1 = 1
           ──          ──          ──          ──          ──         ──         ──
           40          33          21          16           8          5          1
```

$$\Sigma\,(X_{ig} - X_{it}) = 40 + 33 + 21 + 16 + 8 + 5 + 1 = 124$$

The sum total of these absolute differences could then be divided by the number of comparisons carried out to get an average of the amount each score differed from every other score.

$$\frac{\text{sum of differences}}{\text{number of differences}} = \frac{124}{28} = 4.43$$

After you total up the amount each score varies from every other score and divide that total by the number of scores, you have a measure representing the average amount of variation between a particular score and *all* other scores. The *average variation* is an informative statistic in that it is a measure of the dispersion of any set or group of scores that can be seen through simple mathematical arrangement. It tells us how much the scores differ from each other due to the differential influence of variables in the situation.

Another way of getting a measure of score variation may be more familiar to you. In this procedure you calculate a mean ($\overline{X}$) for the group, subtract the mean from each score (x), square the difference between the score and the mean (x^2), sum up these squared differences, and divide by the number of scores involved.[1]

$$\frac{\Sigma (X_{ig} - \overline{X}_G)^2}{N}$$

This procedure is shown using the children's scores.

X_{ig}	$\overline{X}_G$	x	x^2
11	6	5	25
10	6	4	16
8	6	2	4
7	6	1	1
5	6	−1	1
4	6	−2	4
2	6	−4	16
1	6	−5	25

$N = 8$ $\qquad\qquad\qquad\qquad\qquad\qquad x^2 = 92$

$$\frac{\Sigma (X_{ig} - \overline{X}_G)^2}{N} = \frac{(11 - 6)^2 + (10 - 6)^2 \dots (1 - 6)^2}{8} = \frac{92}{8} = 11.5$$

The first variation measure obtained is called the average variation. The second variation measure is called variance.[2] Each in its own right is a measure of how much the scores varied from each other.

It can be seen then that variance is a measure of variation between all the scores. It indicates the degree to which subjects in any experiment were differentially affected by factors present while the investigation was going on. Actually, so does the measure of average variation. The variance measure is preferred over average variation because it may be quicker to compute, and you may also end up with a measure of central tendency

---

[1] X_{ig} is a symbol standing for any score (i) in any group (g). If you wanted to be specific in a situation and specify the second score of the third group, the symbol would be X_{23}. $\overline{X}_G$ stands for the grand mean of all the scores in the experiment. In this case there is only one group; in later situations, the experiments will include many groups. The mean of a group within the experiment is symbolized as $\overline{X}_g$, while the mean of *all* the scores in the study is symbolized as $\overline{X}_G$. Σ stands for the sum of, and N is the total number of subjects in the experiment.

[2] The common symbolic notation for variance is s^2.

(the mean). This second procedure also allows for certain statistical tests that cannot be carried out with the first approach.

Division of Variation

A formula for total variance between scores could be written as follows:

$$V_T = V_W$$

Or the total amount of variation(V_T) between the children's scores is equal to the variation (V_W) caused by all variables influencing the children. This is a redundant formula so far, since responsibility for the variation cannot be related to any particular variable. We cannot say to what extent any particular variable caused fluctuations in the distance the ball was thrown. This is analogous to the situation in which a detective runs into a room where a gun was fired only to find one dead body, a gun on the floor, and twenty-five people. All he or she may know for sure is that a person or persons in the room did the killing. He or she is unable to state empirically how much each person in the room was responsible for the crime.

The psychologist, like the detective, also likes to be able to assign variations in actions to the responsible variables. To do this, the psychologist looks over the situation to determine which variables may be causing a large portion of the variation. After deciding on a variable, the psychologist may then carry out an experiment to find out how much influence any particular variable (e.g., weight of the ball) had on the distance the ball was thrown. In doing so, the formula is now modified to read

$$V_T = V_S + V_W$$

The total variation (V_T) is due to the weight of the ball (V_S) plus all other secondary variables present (V_W). The psychologist has now divided V_T into two parts, that due to the systematic manipulation of the IV (in this example, IV would be the weight of the ball) and that due to other variables not controlled for in the situation (see Figure 4–1). The psy-

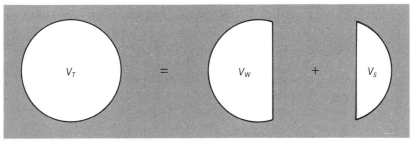

FIGURE 4–1   Division of variants in an experimental situation

chologist has divided the variation into systematic (V_S) and within variation (V_W). Now an experiment is set up in which the weight of the ball is the IV and the changes in the distance the ball is thrown are recorded. Before carrying out this experiment and demonstrating how this is done empirically, it may be advantageous to discuss the different types of variation in more detail.

Systematic Variation

The role of a professional baseball pitcher is similar to that of an experimenter in that his job involves manipulating variables in an effort to influence other variables. Most of his time is spent refining his ability to cause variations in the flight path of the ball being pitched. He throws fast balls, curve balls, sliders, risers, sinkers, changeups, and knuckle balls. Each type of pitch is related to behavioral variations in his delivery. The better his ability to systematically vary his deliveries, the better his control of the fluctuation in the ball's flight path.

The objective of the pitcher, then, is to choose from alternative ways of delivering the ball and apply that chosen approach in an effort to influence the ball's behavior. In this situation, the delivery used in pitching the ball is the IV; the behavior of the ball is the DV. It may be said that the pitcher is specifically varying his pitching behavior to cause a systematic variation in the ball's behavior. Whenever someone manipulates some IV and a resultant change in the DV is noted, the amount of DV change actually due to manipulation of the IV is called the *primary* or *systematic variation*. Notice that systematic variation is defined as that change in DV *actually due* to the manipulation of the IV, not as *all* the variation in the DV following the administration of the IV. In every experimental situation, variables (frequently referred to as secondary variables) other than the IV (also called the primary variable) are influencing the DV. In the present example, secondary variables would include dirt on the ball, how scuffed the ball is, and changes in the wind while the ball is being thrown. All three of these variables can influence the flight of the ball. Though the pitcher's delivery will be the cause for most of the variations in the ball's behavior, it certainly will not be responsible for all changes in the DV.

In many experiments, two groups are selected. One group is called the experimental group (Group E) and has the IV applied. The second group, called the control group (Group C), is not given the IV. Any variation found in the DV between the experimental and control groups is due mainly to the systematic manipulation of the IV by the investigator. In this situation, the systematic variation is also called *between-groups variation*. Between-groups variation reflects the effect of the IV; therefore, we say the numerical value of the between-groups variation represents the effect of (the difference due to) the IV.

Within Variation

As mentioned previously, any fluctuation of the DV in a controlled experiment is a function of the systematic variation of the primary variable, plus variations of the secondary variables involved in the experiment. The variation in a DV caused by variables other than the primary is termed *within variation*. Within variation is the amount of variation between scores due to variables "within" the experimental situation that have not been controlled for. Within variation may be divided into two parts, *secondary variation* and *error variation*. Secondary variation is the resultant fluctuation of secondary variables that could have been controlled by the experimenter but were not, because he or she did not know they were there, or was unable to control for them, or simply did not control for them. Variation in the distance the ball was thrown due to dirt on the ball or wind changes would be examples of secondary variation.

Error variation is a restricted category in which fluctuations in scores are due solely to chance. These are generally small, unsystematic changes in variables that occur in willy-nilly fashion and over which the investigator has no control. They are the reason no two situations are ever exactly the same.

It is important to note that in experimental situations the exact amount of within variation that is due to error variation cannot be identified and separated from the variation due to secondary variables that could possibly be controlled. For this reason, error variation and secondary variation are jointly represented by V_W in the variance formula. However, keep in mind that it is possible to reduce the effect of secondary variables and thereby decrease V_W.

One of the main jobs of an experimenter is to decrease within variation. Because within variation is the result of the influence of variables that were not controlled by the experimenter, it is undesirable. The main objective of any investigation, as you recall, is to demonstrate that manipulations of the IV cause the change in the DV. We can never technically prove some variable caused a fluctuation in some other variable, but we can manipulate the IV and show some high or low correlated change in the DV, and decrease the possibility that any other variable could have caused the change in the DV. Decreasing the influence of secondary variables automatically decreases within variation.

There are three reasons why an experimenter wants to decrease within variation in any project. First, secondary variables responsible for the within variation may interact with the IV in such a way that the change in the DV is not an accurate representation of what influence the IV would have on the DV by itself. To illustrate, a comedian may try out a new joke at a private party before telling it on television. He or she tells the joke (the IV) to see if people will laugh (the DV). After telling it at the party and receiving much laughter, the comedian tells it to a live TV audience and receives little laughter. In trying to figure out why the TV audience and the party guests "varied" in their amount of laughing, he or she realizes there was another variable in the situation that he or she forgot to take into consideration. The people at the party were fairly well inebriated when the comedian told the joke, so their reception of the joke was strongly influenced by a second variable. Often, failure to control the effects of secondary variables leads to incorrect conclusions regarding cause and effect relationships. Second, the effect of the IV on the DV may become more apparent by decreasing within variation. The situation is analogous to seeing the effect of a rock on a lake. The waves (the DV) caused by the rock (the IV) will be more apparent if the wind (a secondary variable) is not making the lake's surface choppy. Removing the secondary variable (wind) makes the lake smoother, so the effect of the IV is more visible. Third, decreasing within variation increases the possibility of demonstrating a cause and effect relationship. These last two points will become more apparent later.

Division of Variance in an Experimental Situation

Now that total variation has been divided into systematic and within variation, let us look at an experimental situation that includes both. We will take the ball-throwing example and turn it into an experiment. An investigator wants to know if the weight of a ball will influence the distance a ball can be thrown. He or she randomly selects eight children from a particular grade school and randomly assigns each child to either Group C or Group D, as shown.

Group C	Group D
11	5
10	4
8	2
7	1

Group C is given a ball weighing 10 ounces, group D, a ball weighing 16 ounces. Each child makes one throw.

Calculating Within Variance.   The calculations for within variance to determine how much variation in the scores in the experiment are due to the effects of uncontrolled secondary variation (within variance) are shown in Table 4–1. The variance between scores "within" each group is first calculated. The obtained value for both groups, in this case, is $V = 2.50$. This represents the variation between scores in each group being caused by uncontrolled secondary variables. (Remember, theoretically speaking, all subjects in any group should be the same and therefore have identical scores.) Notice that the within variance was the same for both groups, C and D. This should be the case if all subjects are randomly assigned to groups and have been randomly selected from the same population.

Insight
Variance is Not Equal to Variation

The present example of dividing variance into between and within variance has taken some statistical liberties. While the Total Variation in an experiment does equal the amount of variation between the groups plus the amount of variation within the groups, the *total variance* in an experiment *does not* equal the between groups variance plus the within groups variance. Variance and variation while synonomous are not exactly equal terms. As mentioned earlier in the chapter variance is only one of several statistical ways of representing variation. The present example has been done as though variation and variance are exactly the same. It has been presented this way to give the reader a logical rather than pure statistical understanding of what variance is, and how it relates to IV and secondary variable effects. Chapter Ten shows the exact statistical relationship of the different subparts of variance.

Calculating Between Variance.   After calculating the within group variance, the next step is to calculate the between group variance. This is done by figuring the mean for each group ($\bar{X}g$), treating each group mean as a separate score, and calculating a variance for the group means in the same manner you calculated the variance for individual subjects within a group. In essence, you treat each group mean as a specific score and then calculate a variance of group means (between-group variance). Table 4–2 illustrates how this is done.

With the amount of variance between the groups and within variance known, the next step is to determine whether the variance between the groups [variance due to the IV (V_B)][3] is larger than the within-group

---

[3] Remember that the variation between the groups was said to be due not only to IV but also to the uncontrolled fluctuation of secondary variables. The variation between scores within a group reflects random or uncontrolled variation occurring between one score and the next. The difference between the two means from which the between-group variance was calculated also is due in part to these random variations, for they are nothing more than two scores themselves.

TABLE 4–1 *Calculations of Within-Group Variances*

X_C	$\overline{X}_C$	x	x^2	X_D	$\overline{X}_D$	x	x^2
11	9	2	4	5	3	2	4
10	9	1	1	4	3	1	1
8	9	−1	1	2	3	−1	1
7	9	−2	4	1	3	−2	4

$$\Sigma X_C = 36 \qquad\qquad\qquad \Sigma X_D = 12$$

$$\overline{X}_C = \frac{\Sigma X_C}{n} = \frac{36}{4} = 9 \qquad \overline{X}_D = \frac{\Sigma X_D}{n} = \frac{12}{4} = 3$$

$$\Sigma x^2_C = 10.00 \qquad\qquad \Sigma x^2_D = 10.00$$

$$V_C = S^2_C = \frac{10.00}{4} = 2.50 \qquad V_D = S^2_D = \frac{10.00}{4} = 2.50$$

variance [variation due to random fluctuations of uncontrolled secondary variables (V_W)]. If the between-group variance is equal to the within-group variance, then we can say the weight of the ball had no effect, for the amount of variation between the groups would be equal to the amount of variation between any two scores in which the IV was not varied. To determine whether the IV had an effect, the variance between the groups is divided by the within-group variance. In this particular case, the ratio would be equal to 3.60:

$$\frac{V_B}{V_W} = \frac{9}{2.50} = 3.60$$

What we have just calculated is commonly referred to as the F ratio. We then look up 3.60 in the F table at the end of the book. The table will tell

TABLE 4–2 *Calculations of Between-Group Variance*

$\overline{X}_g$	$\overline{X}_G$	x	x^2
9	6	3	9
3	6	−3	9

$$\overline{X}_G = \frac{\Sigma \overline{X}_g}{n} = \frac{9 + 3}{2} = 6$$

$$V_B = S^2_B = \frac{\Sigma(\overline{X}_g - \overline{X}_G)^2}{n} = \frac{18}{2} = 9$$

The formula $V_T = V_B + V_W$ so far should read 11.50 = 9 + 2.50.

what the possibility is of obtaining this size F ratio by chance alone. Just as fluctuations in variables may influence the DV randomly, so it is possible to obtain an F ratio larger than 1. The more the F ratio differs from 1, the less likely the obtained ratio is due to chance. Generally, an investigator will consider the IV to have influenced the DV if the possibility of obtaining the F ratio could have occurred by chance 5 percent of the time or less. Sometimes researchers prefer the cutoff line to be a 1 percent possibility by chance.

Now that our illustration is complete, let us summarize what was involved. First, the investigator analyzes a situation to choose a particular variable, about which a hypothesis is made. Second, the operationally defined IV with which the investigator plans to bring about between-group variation in terms of some operationally defined DV. Third, secondary variables are controlled so that between-group variance can be attributed to the IV. This step also includes making sure that the within-group variance is due mainly to random fluctuations in variables so it can be used as a measure of within variance. Fourth, the IV is applied and the DV variations are recorded. Fifth, some measure of between-group variance and within variance is obtained. With these data the probability of the between-group variance being caused by chance is calculated. Sixth, a statement is made regarding a causal relationship between the IV and DV. If the size of the between-group variance could have occurred by chance less than 5 percent of the time, then the IV is said to have influenced the DV.

What has just been covered is the basic plan for almost every experiment the student will ever encounter. An investigator causes variation by systematically manipulating the IV to be evaluated. From the data obtained, the amount of between-group variance is calculated along with the within-group variance. The variance found between comparison groups is then divided by within variance to find out if the IV had an effect. No matter whether a t-test, a one-way analysis of variance, a two-way analysis of variance, or analysis of covariance is used, the principle behind the analysis is basically the same.[4] The following chapters will deal with alternative experimental designs. Take special care to notice the way the statistical analysis is carried out in succeeding chapters. You will realize that all are dealing with the same comparison (between-group variation versus within-group variation), although the statistical formulas appear to be quite different. Once the student visualizes the similarities between the procedures, the analysis of variance, no matter what type is used, will not seem so awesome and incomprehensible.

---

[4] All these statistical tests were probably presented in the statistics course generally required of the student before enrolling in the experimental course. Do not be alarmed if you do not recall how to carry these out. They will be presented and compared later on in the text.

METHODS OF CONTROLLING
SECONDARY VARIANCE

In addition to the IV and DV, which are the main concern of any investigator, all experimental situations include other variables that can influence the DV. These variables are often called nuisance variables, side variables, relevant variables, irrelevant variables, and secondary variables. In this book, all variables in an experimental situation other than the IV and DV have been termed secondary variables, with no distinction being made as to whether the secondary variables have a great or relatively little potential effect on the DV.[5] Secondary variables are undesirable sources of variation in an experimental situation that could influence the DV. Though these variables are of secondary importance to the investigator, their potential influence on the DV must be controlled for an accurate relationship between the IV and the DV to appear. An important step in any experimental procedure is controlling for potential sources of variation in the DV due to secondary variables. There are five basic procedures for controlling within variation:

1. Remove secondary variables from the experimental situation altogether.
2. Hold the effects of secondary variables constant for all groups.
3. Make the secondary variables IVs (manipulatory control).
4. Randomize the subjects and procedures being used.
5. Control secondary variables by means of statistical adjustment.

Each procedure has its advantages and disadvantages. The remainder of this section will deal with defining the control procedures in detail and indicating the value and limitations of each. In some instances this will include ranking them on effectiveness along certain dimensions. Keep in mind that, although it may be true that one control procedure is superior in one situation, it may not be superior in another.[6]

Elimination

One of the most straightforward methods of decreasing V_W is to remove secondary variables completely from the experimental situation. Since the V_W is the composite effect of all secondary variables, removing any

---

[5] Some texts label as secondary variables those that may have a large influence on the DV, whereas extraneous variables are those in the experimental situation that have little if any actual influence on the DV. Sometimes the terms *relevant* and *irrelevant* variable are used to make the same distinction.

[6] For example, eliminating secondary variables is generally better than controlling them by holding them constant. One exception to this statement would be when the cost of eliminating a variable (e.g., paying $10,000 to soundproof a room) may be more than it is worth.

secondary variables from having any possible influence in the experimental situation will automatically decrease the V_W. The amount the V_W is decreased depends on how influential the removed secondary variable could have been. A few years ago I was involved in a research project in which pigeons were conditioned to peck a key in total darkness. As the experiment progressed, it was noted that even faint sources of light infiltrating the test chamber seriously affected the pigeons' behavior. To eliminate this secondary variable, the test chamber itself was placed in a totally dark room. This resulted in a 40 percent reduction in what was initially thought to be random fluctuation in the birds' pecking. Faint amounts of light allowed in the chambers with pigeons being run with a houselight on have little, if any, observable effect on the birds. It is easy to conclude from this that eliminating the same variable in one situation may not have an equal effect on the V_W in another situation.

Controlled laboratory experiments are better able to employ this type of control on secondary variation than is any other type of investigation. The laboratory situation is often chosen to carry out an investigation mainly because of the ability to eliminate secondary variables. One of the major sources of V_W in scientific investigations is unexpected secondary variables: researchers frequently start their investigation only to find as it progresses that there are important secondary variables in their study which should have been eliminated. Undergraduate students in an experimental psychology course and graduate students carrying out field research are particularly afflicted with this problem. Wise student and professional researchers prefer laboratory situations over field situations where a choice between the two is possible. They realize that by simply moving their study into the laboratory most secondary variables are automatically left outside, and the possibility of being surprised by some secondary variable as the investigation progresses is greatly reduced.

Constancy

In many experimental situations, important secondary variables (e.g., time, gravity, body orientation, temperature, atmosphere) simply cannot be eliminated, while others (e.g., color, intelligence, shape, sound) may be so difficult to eliminate that it is considered impossible to do so. Since they may influence the amount of variation in the DV, the investigator must find an alternative way of controlling them. One possibility is holding them constant. Suppose you want to try a new abstract method of teaching math to grade-school children. You select two groups of children, one of which will use the standard method. Knowing that IQ is an important influence on the ability to learn, you want to make sure each group is equivalent in IQ. To do this, all the subjects selected for the study are ranked on IQ before being assigned group A or B, as shown in Table 4–3.

TABLE 4–3   *Illustration of Matching Groups on a Secondary Variable (IQ)*

IQ (ranked from highest to lowest)		GROUP A	GROUP B
128	103	128	127
127	101	121	120
121	100	118	113
120	100	108	107
118	97	106	106
113	97	103	101
108	93	100	100
107	92	97	97
106	87	93	92
106	86	87	86

Going down the ranking, the first subject is assigned to group A, the second to group B, the third to group A, and so on, until all twenty subjects have been assigned.[7] The experiment could then be carried out with more confidence that the difference in the DV between the two groups was not due to IQ. The terms *matching* and *blocking* when used in experimentation refer to holding a secondary variable constant by equating it among the groups.

Notice that the procedure of equating the two groups does not actually remove the effects of IQ from the investigation; it simply distributes it equally between the two groups so that the difference in the DV between the groups does not include IQ effects. The procedure of elimination, on the other hand, completely removes the effect of a variable from the experiment. Elimination has the effect of accentuating V_B by decreasing V_W. Normally, elimination is preferred to holding variables constant.

Making the Secondary Variable an Independent Variable

If a secondary variable cannot be eliminated, it can be *manipulated* and made an IV. By making a relevant secondary variable an IV, the formula for total variation becomes

$$V_T = V_{B1} + V_{B2} + V_W$$

The total variation in the DV (V_T) is equal to the variation caused by the initial IV you selected (V_{B1}), plus the variation of the secondary variable

---

[7] There are other ways of matching the group on IQ than the one shown that would be somewhat more equitable.

converted into an IV (V_{B2}), plus the variation due to all other secondary variables (V_W) in the experiment. A good question to ask is, "Where did V_{B2} come from?" Is it variation introduced into the experiment that would normally not be there, or did it come from V_{B1} or V_W? To answer this question, let us look at an example.

Harry Straightarrow is interested in carrying out an experiment dealing with the effects of alcohol on typing speed. He goes to a typing class at the university and asks for twenty volunteers willing to consume alcoholic beverages and willing to show up Saturday at 1 P.M. to participate in a typing experiment. One evening after designing the experiment he sits down and analyzes his experiment. It looks like the typical formula for an experiment with one IV. The systematic variation (V_B) in this experiment will be the effect of alcohol.

$$V_T = V_B + V_W$$

At noon on Saturday, Harry is busily working to get the typewriters set up when another student comes in and asks Harry what he plans to do. After listening to Harry's experimental plans, the other student notices that ten typewriters are brand X (electric) and ten typewriters are brand Y (manual). He then comments that the different kinds of typewriters might influence the number of correct words per minute a person can type. He suggests Harry control this secondary variable. Harry agrees, so he decides to divide the typewriters equally by brand between the alcohol and nonalcohol groups, thereby equating the effects of typewriter differences. The other student says, "That's a fine idea, but why don't you revamp your study to include the brand of typewriter as an independent variable? This could be done with little trouble, and you would not only find out the effects of alcohol, but also quantify the effects of typewriter differences." Harry takes the advice and changes the design of his experiment. Harry's design before and after his decision to make typewriter brand an IV is shown in Table 4–4.

TABLE 4–4   *Conversion of a Two-Group Design into a Four-Group Design*

BEFORE			AFTER	
GROUP A (no alcohol)	GROUP B (alcohol)		GROUP A (no alcohol)	GROUP B (alcohol)
10 subjects	10 subjects	TYPEWRITER — Brand X: 5 subjects $\overline{X}_{a1}$	5 subjects $\overline{X}_{a1}$	5 subjects $\overline{X}_{b1}$
		Brand Y: 5 subjects	5 subjects $\overline{X}_{a2}$	5 subjects $\overline{X}_{b2}$
$\overline{X}_a$	$\overline{X}_b$		$\overline{X}_A$	$\overline{X}_B$

Originally, Harry would have obtained two means, $\overline{X}_a$ and $\overline{X}_b$. The means would represent the difference between subjects having alcohol and those not. If he had made sure each group had an equal number of typewriters of each brand, he would not be able to tell what effect the difference in typewriters made. In his after design he is carrying out the experiment exactly as before, except that he is keeping track of which typewriter is given to each subject. He then can calculate a mean for each of the five subjects who are experiencing the same alcohol and typewriter condition. To determine the effects of alcohol, he can still contrast the mean of group A ($\overline{X}_A$) with the mean of group B ($\overline{X}_B$). To determine the difference caused by typewriter brand, the mean of the ten subjects using each typewriter could be compared ($\overline{X}_X$ versus $\overline{X}_Y$). Just by dividing his original ten-subject groups into groups of five, Harry is able to calculate the influence of a secondary variable.

With a secondary variable now a second IV, the variation formula reads

$$V_T = V_A + V_B + V_W$$

Total variation in typing speed equals the influence (V_A) of alcohol plus the influence of the typewriter, plus the influence of all other secondary variables. In Harry's first design, the difference due to the typewriter brands would have been lumped in V_W with all the other secondary variables.

Making a secondary variable an IV serves two functions. First, it decreases the size of V_W; second, it adds more to our scientific knowledge than the other two control procedures do. It tells us how much of the DV fluctuation is caused by the secondary variable that is controlled. It should be apparent that making a secondary variable an IV is preferable to eliminating it or holding it constant.

Randomization

Let us return to the example of demonstrating the effectiveness of an abstract method of teaching math. In that situation IQ was felt to be an influential secondary variable, so it was controlled by equating the control and experimental groups with respect to IQ. In this way, the effect of IQ was held constant. What would we have done if IQ scores were not available? How could we have controlled for this important secondary variable? *Randomization* is a procedure for controlling secondary variables by equating the control and experimental groups when no data are available for matching the groups on the particular variable. If the IQs were not available, the groups could have been equated on IQ by putting all the subjects' names in a hat, mixing them up, drawing them out one by one, and assigning every odd draw to group A and every even draw to group B. With this procedure each subject would have equal chance of being assigned to either of the groups. One theoretical principle underlying the concept of randomization states that, if subjects are randomly assigned to two or more groups, there is a high probability that all groups will be equated in terms of any secondary variable or variables that all the subjects have in common. As an example, suppose we were going to randomly divide 900 people, 50 percent of whom were females, into 10 different groups. Each group would probably end up being equated in terms of the ratio of men and women. Using randomization, the same 900 people made up of 300 caucasians, 300 blacks, and 300 Indians would end up equally proportioned in the 10 groups. Each of the 10 groups would most probably consist of 30 caucasians, 30 blacks, and 30 Indians (each having 50 percent women).

Randomization, then, is a procedure for equating groups with respect to secondary variables. It does not guarantee that all groups are equal, but groups in which subjects were assigned randomly have a greater probability of being equated than groups in which subjects were not assigned randomly. Another theoretical principle of randomization is, "The more subjects randomly assigned to groups, the higher the probability that the groups will be equated." In the previous example, 900 people were randomly assigned to 10 groups. There is a much greater probability that the 10 groups will be equated in this situation than in a situation in which only 30 people were to be divided into 10 groups.

Although eliminating a variable, holding it constant, or making it an IV are preferred methods of controlling a known secondary variable, randomization, with its equating effects through random assignment of subjects to groups, is considered to be the overall best tool for controlling many sources of secondary variation at one time. Randomization can equate groups for all secondary variables at the same time, including those not apparent even to the investigator while the investigation is in progress.

If we were to rank-order the control procedures covered so far in terms of effectiveness in controlling secondary variables, the order would be as follows: If you know of any secondary variable that may have a large effect on the DV, first try to make it an IV. If that is not feasible, eliminate it from the experiment. If that is not feasible, hold it constant. After applying the first three control procedures where possible, randomize the assignment of subjects to the groups involved in the experiment.

Statistical Control

The preceding four types of control to reduce variability caused by secondary variables are generally classified as *experimental* control procedures. An alternative approach to reducing within variation involves the use of a *statistical* control procedure. With this approach, no attempt is made to limit the influence of secondary variables; the procedure involves measuring one or more concomitant secondary variables (covariants) in addition to recording the DV. These concomitant secondary variables are potential sources of within variation that have not been controlled in the experiment. Through an analysis of covariance, the DV can be statistically adjusted to remove the effects of the uncontrolled sources of variation due to the concomitant secondary variables. Analysis of covariance is simply a statistical procedure involving the combined application of correlational analysis and analysis of variance. Changes in concomitant secondary variables are correlated with changes in the DV. The amount of variation in the DV (V_T) is then adjusted to remove the possible amount of variation in DV due to the variation in the concomitant secondary variables(s).

A better understanding of statistical control may come with an illustration of the use of the analysis of covariance in a situation involving one concomitant secondary variable. Suppose you wanted to compare two methods of teaching math to third-grade students in a school district made up of only two rural grade schools, each in a different town 50 miles apart. It would be impractical to randomly assign students from the towns to one or the other grade school.[8] It is also probable that the two third-grade classes would not be equated in terms of intelligence, an important secondary variable. If differences in learning ability or similar characteristics exist between the two third-grade classes prior to the administration of the two teaching methods, these secondary variables would bias the evaluation. Using statistical control, intelligence could be controlled by making it a concomitant variable. An intelligence test could be given to each student, and any difference in the DV between the two classes could be correlated with any difference in IQ. The DV would then be readjusted to take into consideration the effect of IQ differences on the DV.

Numerically, the use of statistical control goes like this: For class A, the mean IQ is 100 and the mean of the math exam (the DV) is 80; for class B, the mean IQ is 90 and the mean of the math exam (the DV) is 60. The statistically adjusted mean for class A is $\frac{9}{10} \times 80 = 72$. Using the math exam scores to compare the effectiveness of the two teaching methods, class A averaged 80, while class B averaged 60. The average IQ for class B was only $\frac{9}{10}$ that of class A. The mean of class A is readjusted ($\frac{9}{10} \times 80 = 72$).

---

[8] There is another alternative. We could try each technique in both classrooms by randomly dividing the students in each class into two different groups and then applying each method to one of the groups.

	Class A	Class B
Mean IQ	100	90
Mean score on math exam (DV)	80	60

Statistically adjusted mean of class A:

$$\frac{90}{100} \times 80 = 72$$

The comparison of 72 and 60 is a measure of the difference actually due to the teaching methods, rather than a comparison of 80 and 60.[9]

The exact statistical manipulations required to do this will be covered in a later chapter; here it is sufficient for the student to realize only that statistical control is possible and is one of the procedures for controlling within variation. It differs from the other four control procedures in that V_W is not reduced by actually manipulating secondary variables, but by statistically adjusting for them.

There are two types of situations in which a statistical control procedure may have to be employed. One is when subjects cannot be matched or assigned at random to the different experimental groups (field experiments in psychology, sociology, and education are frequently faced with this situation). The other is when groups in an ongoing experiment are found to differ with respect to some secondary variable not taken into consideration prior to the start of the investigation. As an illustration, an experiment may be carried out to determine the effects of alcohol on ability to recall previously learned lists of nonsense syllables. Initially, subjects are randomly assigned to one of two groups, and each group is required to memorize the same list of nonsense syllables. If the two groups require different amounts of training to be able to recite all twenty syllables with no errors, it is possible that differences in learning abilities between the two groups exist. The investigator may feel that the amount of time it takes to learn the list will influence the ability to recall the list later. He or she then makes the amount of time it took to learn the list a covariate (concomitant secondary variable) and employs an analysis of covariance to control the experimentally uncontrolled secondary variable. Analysis of covariance, then, allows the experimenter to control secondary variables whose influence may not appear until after the experiment has begun.

---

[9] The way the adjustment was calculated here is not statistically correct. It is actually much more complicated, but the principle is basically the same as shown. This example is simply to give the reader a general idea of how it is done.

SOURCES OF SECONDARY VARIATION

After defining secondary variation and alternative ways of controlling it, the next step is to identify the general sources from which it may appear. To present these sources adequately, the concept of *validity* needs to be introduced. Validity is an attribute possessed by all evaluation measures which relates to the ability that measure has to make a prediction regarding some event. Aptitude tests are good examples. A psychologist may administer a test of mental ability in order to better counsel a student on a vocation to select. The better the test can predict which vocation would be best, the more valid the test. Measures must have a certain degree of relevance to the point of interest being studied. The measure of a person's quickness would be a more valid measure of sports ability than a measure of degree of skin pigmentation.

Scientific investigations also involve validity. When carrying out a research project, the investigator is attempting to isolate and identify some relationships, usually between an IV and a DV. The more effective an investigation is in identifying a true relationship, the more valid the investigation. To increase validity, the psychologist carefully controls secondary variables. The more secondary variation that slips unnoticed into an investigation situation, the greater the possibility that the IV was not responsible for DV changes. Secondary variation may influence the situation to such an extent that an incorrect conclusion is drawn, or the investigator, realizing the results obtained would be erroneous, discontinues the investigation. In both cases the investigation is said to be invalid.

Experimenters generally divide validity problems into two categories, *internal* and *external* validity. Internal validity is concerned with making certain that the IV manipulated was responsible for the variation in DV so that a correct causal relationship can be stated. External validity is concerned with generality. An investigator is not usually satisfied to demonstrate the IV influence on the particular subjects used in an investigation; she or he also wants to be able to state that this IV will affect similar subjects in similar situations. External validity is therefore important to the investigator in generalizing the results obtained to other situations and persons.

Internal Validity

Nine major sources of secondary variation can produce internal invalidity in an investigation: proactive history, retroactive history, maturation, testing, statistical regression, experimental mortality, interaction effects, instrumentation, and experimenter bias. The first seven may be controlled by selecting the appropriate experimental design. The ability of different experimental designs to control for these seven different sources of secondary variation is one of the many reasons the use of experimental designs is considered such a basic issue in experimentation. The last two are only controlled for by the diligence of the experimenter as the investigation progresses.

Proactive History.   Proactive history refers to those learned and inherent differences subjects bring with them into the investigation. Sex, height, weight, color, attitude, personality, motor ability, and mental ability are all examples of variables on which subjects may differ. If the control and experimental groups differ on some variable, the difference in the DV measure between the two groups may be partly due to that unaccounted-for secondary variable. The validity of the investigation is then reduced. As an example, suppose you built two canoes that differed in design. To determine which is the best for running rapids in a river, you select two sixth-grade girls to paddle one and two sixth-grade boys to paddle the other. Both paddle down the same stretch of river. The boys and their canoe complete the course in half the time the girls and their canoe did. Should it be concluded that one canoe was better than the other? Obviously not, for the subjects differed in terms of some proactive history variables (sex, size, motor ability, etc.) that could easily have influenced the DV measure. This would not be considered a valid investigation

Proactive history is possibly the most important potential source of invalidity for two reasons. First, it represents more secondary variables than any of the other eight sources. More possibilities for within variance can show up here than in any other source. Second, it is relevant for all investigations, whereas others may be relevant only in certain investigations. For example, testing would be of concern only in research where the subjects are given pretests. All nine sources of invalidity are not equally influential in each situation. To illustrate, sex differences may be an important secondary variable in an investigation analyzing women's lib, whereas it is relatively unimportant in studies dealing with intellectual potential. The most common way of controlling for proactive history is randomization, although constancy and elimination are also frequently used.

Retroactive History.   Retroactive history refers to those changes in events and influences encountered in the course of the experiment or between a first and second testing time. As an example, if one were studying college students' political attitudes and two weeks into the study three campus radicals were unaccountably killed by police, obviously the subjects' attitudes would undergo some change and possibly render the original study internally invalid. Of the five previously mentioned control procedures, constancy and elimination are those generally used to control retroactive history. Certain experimental designs are also effective in controlling this source of invalidity. Retroactive history is especially liable to be encountered in a study using a lengthy time interval.

Maturation.   Maturation, commonly defined as systematic changes in the organism over a length of time primarily due to a biological and/or psychological growth or change, is mostly influential in lengthy studies, much like retroactive history. Let us take a look at a commonly employed, though invalid, situation (invalid because no control was used to compensate for the maturation factor). A five-year-old child is chosen and pretested for motor coordination control in manipulating blocks. A tutor then instructs the child in various exercises according to a new, scientifically based method. After one year the child is again tested and it is found that the score has improved. It is obvious that in this particular case changes caused by experience and maturation were not adequately controlled. Could the child have progressed to a similar degree if he had not been enrolled in the tutor's class? Without a control procedure, maturation may be as valid a reason for the changes as the new method. None of the control procedures covered are usually used to guard against this source of invalidity; maturation effects are generally controlled for by experimental designs that include a control group. Effects due to maturation will then show up in both groups, so that change between groups will not be due to maturation.

Testing.   Psychologists often administer pretests to subjects before the IV is applied in an attempt to carry out a before-and-after comparison. In some cases, however, the pretest may cause the subjects to score differently in the posttest than they would have if no pretest had been given. When an individual is administered an intelligence test or a similar test the second time, it is well known that there is a high probability the second score will be higher than the initial score. In such a situation, testing may be a source of internal invalidity and influence the DV measure when the test is administered the second time around. Though the second scores may be higher, it is improbable that subjects increased in IQ significantly over the period of time. Therefore, when the same or similar test is administered a second time without controls, the higher scores must be attributable or partly attributable to the repeated testing.

Pretests may also "sensitize" the subjects to the IV being given. Suppose you were carrying out an investigation to determine how attitudes toward violence change due to violent movies. Prior to having subjects watch a violent movie, you have them fill out a questionnaire dealing with attitudes on violence. This pretest may strongly bias what the subjects selectively attend to in the movie; any changes found in the before and after attitudes would not be a correct representation of the effect of the movie alone. Testing scores of invalidity are generally controlled for by using an experimental design that includes a non-pretested control group.

The Solomon four-group design, to be covered in Chapter Eight, is a popular design because of its ability to control for testing effects.

Statistical Regression.   In carrying out an investigation, the experimenter needs to consider yet another important characteristic of testing. A fundamental law of statistics is that in repeated testing both extremely high and extremely low numbers in the range of numbers will tend to be pulled toward a mean as the testing is repeated. Figure 4–2 represents a frequency distribution of scores on a particular IQ test. Each dot represents a subject's score; *represents the lowest scores; + represents the highest scores. If a retest were given immediately following the first, the distribution could change to the one shown in Figure 4–3. The retest scores of those subjects receiving the lowest and highest scores on the first test would be closer to the mean, although the ability of the subjects had not been modified by any external variables. In other words, subjects scoring high or low on a test will tend to score closer to a mean on a successive test. This tendency of migration of scores toward the mean is termed *statistical regression.*

Psychological researchers often deal with extreme cases for investigation. One frequent situation is the selection of subjects because of their extreme scores on some psychological test. An IV is then commonly administered in an effort to influence this extreme score. School districts many times isolate gifted and poor students with the intention of improving learning capabilities with the use of a new teaching method. At the end of the study, a common finding is that the poorer students, after much testing, improved their grades by several points, whereas the gifted children tended to level off and come down slightly in their scores with respect to the main body of the children. To control for this tendency, the investigator could divide the extreme groups into their own comparison groups, control and experimental, and observe resulting differences between them. The method would then be the only contributing change.

Experimental Mortality.   Loss of subject by death, accident, or simple discontinued performance during experimentation obviously can and will affect comparisons between groups. The loss of subjects may invalidate

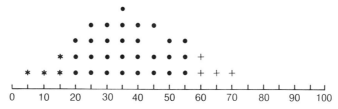

FIGURE 4–2   Frequency distribution of IQ test scores from a pretest measure

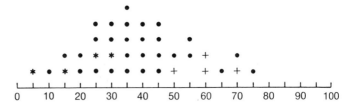

FIGURE 4-3 Posttest frequency distribution of IQ test scores demonstrating statistical regression

one's whole experiment. Where analysis of results is still possible, it becomes more difficult than usual because of statistical adjustments which have to be made.

Interaction Effects. Many investigations comparing two different elements or conditions will be limited in the sensitivity and validity of the method, depending on the order of testing. This order of testing or position in the sequence of effects is important when considering the interaction of those elements or conditions with one another. If an effect is experienced relating to the order of testing (e.g., going from drug A to drug B as opposed to going from drug B to drug A), variability of the results is greatly increased. Knowing there is a possible chemical reaction between two drugs, how would one examine the effects of the two drugs, A and B, in a single subject and control for possible interaction effects? A commonly employed procedure is the use of counterbalance design, in which subject 1 receives first drug A, then drug B, and then drug A. Reactions to the drugs are observed after each administration of the drug. Subject 2 is administered drug B, then drug A, and again drug B. Sequence of the drugs is thereby controlled, for a more accurate picture of the exact effects of each drug is obtained. Often interaction effects may be found when using a factorial design. Statistical calculations and certain experimental designs may be used for controlling for interaction. It should be apparent that interaction effects are not potential sources of invalidity if the investigation involves only one IV.

Instrumentation. In the use of vast and varied amounts of equipment, one may readily observe slight physical changes and impairments that accrue from day to day use. Not only does wear on equipment impair measurement, but the initial quality and calibration of the instrument is a measure that also affects results. A micrometer, for example, will measure distances much more precisely than a 12-inch ruler.

In measurement of social research studies, the instrument is the observer or interviewer. A natural change will occur as one's skill in noting pertinent and more complete information is increased. For example, an observation is made of children in a second-grade class, and the number

112

of their interpersonal interactions is noted. As the observers spend more time with the children, their skill in noting interactions will naturally increase, as will the validity of their observations. As the situation and techniques become more familiar, the ease and accuracy of the observations also increase. Instrumentation need not be complicated equipment; it can also be interview or questioning manner used by the interviewer. Instrumentation can also refer to the questions on the test as well as to the pencil and paper used by the subject. Changes in instrumentation may be a source of invalidity, especially if the experimenter acts as a recorder of "observed" data. Instrumentation is a function of the experimenter, not of the design used, and therefore cannot be controlled for by using a specific type of design.

Experimenter Bias.   More recently, concern has grown over the total effect of experimenter bias on an experimental situation. Rosenthal [1966] demonstrated that the experimenter's expectations of an outcome may significantly influence gathered data. Many times a teacher will be "tipped off " by a colleague or informed by a highly popular IQ test that a student in question is "dumb" and unable to learn as fast as the class. Then, true to the teacher's expectations, the child "follows" the recognized characteristics of the "dumb." Actually, recent studies have found that teacher expectations preclude and dictate actions toward the student. These actions in turn elicit the "expected" reaction from the student, and the student is thereby classified and labeled. Such is the case in many an experimental setting. It is well known that, though it may be unconscious and unintended, the expectations of an investigator may appreciably affect the collected data.

To control for this bias effect, a *double-blind* control situation is often employed. In a double-blind control procedure, the experimenter is not familiar with which subjects experience the intended IV and which do not. Thus, neither subject nor experimenter expectation can enter into the data outcome. In drug studies the double-blind procedure is done through the use of coded but otherwise unidentified drugs and by the use of placebos (harmless materials labeled as real drugs).

As we have previously mentioned, both experimenter bias and instrumentation are functions of the experimenter and not of any specific experimental design used. The experimenter must control for these sources of internal invalidity by physically holding them constant.

External Validity

We must be concerned not only with internal validity relating to the experiment but also with external validity. By *external* validity we mean how valid the results are when placed outside the experimental setting. Can we generalize from the experiment to real-life situations? The

experimenter is interested in relating findings with laboratory rat experiments not just to other rats, but to people in everyday situations as well.

It is important to realize that the more widely applicable the findings,
the greater the importance of the finding. Mendel in his experiment
provided us with insight into the genetic development of the sweet pea.
If his findings had ended there, it is doubtful he would hold the position
he does in science. His findings, however, had a wide range of application
to plants, animals and the human species.

In examining our ability to have external validity, we must realize
that there are sources of secondary variation which may influence the
ability of the experimenter to generalize findings. These secondary variations, therefore, are of great concern to the experimenter. Four of the
common ones are the Hawthorne effect, pretesting, selection bias, and
multiple treatment interaction effect.

Hawthorne Effect.   The Hawthorne effect is basically the effect that
experimentation has on subjects due to their awareness of being specially
treated. The discovery of this effect was made at the Hawthorne plant of
the Western Electric Company. Experimenters selected a group of workers
and introduced certain changes in their working conditions (e.g., decrease
in lighting, work hours, etc.). Regardless of the changes implemented,
production increased. They concluded that the changes in production
were due to the special treatment, because when similar IVs were used at
other plants where the workers did not feel themselves to be participants
in a study, work production did not change. The best way to control for
this effect is to limit whenever possible the knowledge of the subjects about
their special treatment.

Pretesting.   Pretesting is common in psychological research. Pretesting
effects are similar to those of the Hawthorne effect, and in fact may be
considered a subset of it. Pretesting may cause numerous reactions
including defensiveness; hardening of the subject's already held commitments, opinions or performance; reductions in attention; or even the
tendency of the subject to overreaction toward change in an effort to
please the experimenter. An example of this would be the predisposition
of the subject being heightened in one particular direction due to questions
the experimenter asks so that it later affects the subject's reactions in the
experiment.

To control for pretesting effects, the experimenter should find a
measure that does not call attention to the fact that the subject is being
assessed. If this is found too burdensome or impossible, the pretest should
be dropped completely.

Selection Bias.   Selection bias is another problem for external validity. If
a study is to be used to prove the necessity of teaching social values in
schools, it would be important to find a school district that would be a

good cross section of those to whom the need seemed applicable. If only lower socioeconomic area schools were chosen and the study was to apply to middle- or upper-class schools as well, we obviously would suffer from external invalidity. To prevent this, all that is really essential is a randomization of the subjects involved to make sure that they cover all pertinent variables.

Multiple Treatment Interaction Effect.   The final area needing control is that of the multiple treatment interaction effect. Here our problem is that, when more than one IV has been given a subject, the first IV's effect may still be affecting the subject and therefore our results will be unclear. One example is drug residue. By administering a particular drug to a subject we measure a DV; then an hour or so later we administer another drug, again measuring the DV. The question arises, however, whether the second measurement was solely a result of the second drug, included the residue of the first combined with the second, showed no effect, or was even due to some pretesting effect carried over from the first experience. This effect is important in psychopharmacological studies and also in learning experiments in which some learning "residue" remains. Certain experimental designs can be used to detect this (e.g., counterbalance designs), but if you feel interaction might occur, the use of different subjects is one means of control.

SUMMARY

Variance is a major concern of psychologists, for it represents the influence of different variables included in the situation on the DV being investigated. In any natural situation the total variation (V_T) is said to be equal to the influence of the relevant variables (V_W), none of which can be numerically isolated. In carrying out an experiment the investigator divides the subjects into at least two groups. In this way V_T may be divided into two parts—the difference in the DV between the groups (V_B) and the difference in the DV within a group (V_W). By carrying out such a procedure the investigator may determine how much a particular IV is responsible for causing changes in the DV, although other variables are present in the situation.

Variation is divided into two main categories: variation due to the effects of the IV (systematic variation, V_B), and variation due to all other variables that differentially influence the situation (V_W, or secondary variation). Within variation is also divided into secondary variable fluctuations in the situation that are potentially controllable and small fluctuations due to chance, which, practically speaking, cannot be removed.

The main objective of any scientific investigation is systematically to employ the five control techniques upon which all experimental designs are based in an effort to decrease the possibility that any differences in DV measures between groups are due to some secondary variable(s) instead of the IV. The five control techniques available to an investigator are elimination, constancy, randomization, making a secondary variable a second IV, and statistical control.

A distinction was made between internal and external validity. Internal validity refers to how well secondary variables have been controlled in the experiment, so that any difference noted between the experimental and control groups can honestly be attributed to the IV. External validity refers to how far the resutls of the particular experimental situation may be generalized to other situations. Although an investigation may be internally valid when it is not externally valid, the reverse is not possible.

There are nine main sources from which internal invalidity due to secondary variable effects may arise: proactive history, retroactive history, maturation, testing, statistical regression, experimental mortality, interaction effects, instrumentation, and experimenter bias. All nine may not be relevant in all experimental situations. They are, however, the main points an investigator should check to ensure that an investigation will yield valid results. There are four common sources of external invalidity: pretesting, the Hawthorne effect, selection bias, and the multiple treatment interaction effect.

I. Selection of Subjects
  A. Common Research Subjects
  B. Use of Nonhuman Species
II. Ethical Issues in Research
  A. Human Subjects
  B. Animal Subjects
III. Selection of the Dependent Variable
  A. Types of Dependent Variables
  B. Dependent Variable Measures
  C. Ways to Select a Dependent Variable
IV. Selection of the Independent Variable
 V. Elimination and Constancy as Nondesign Control Techniques
VI. Experimenter Bias
VII. Pilot Studies
VIII. Instrumentation
 IX. Summary

Nondesign
Experimental
Procedures

5

By looking over the Contents, the reader can see that much of the text will be spent on learning different types of designs. However, an investigator must take into account a number of things when planning an investigation that do not depend on the design employed. The objective of this chapter is to familiarize the reader with some of these nondesign issues.

One of the most important aspects in carrying out a psychological investigation is the selection of an appropriate design. An experimental design for an investigator is analogous to the house plans for a general contractor. The design indicates the basic structure and format upon which the whole experimental operation is based. An investigator may choose from literally hundreds of different designs, each having certain advantages over the others. Chapter Eight presents some of the more common designs used by psychologists.

An aspect of experimentation that is usually discussed briefly in most texts is the nondesign issues with which an investigator must deal. These include how to select subjects for an experiment, how to select and measure the IVs and DVs, and how to carry out a pilot study. One reason little attention is paid to the nondesign aspect is because it has become almost second nature to the person writing a text. Because the writer has carried out nondesign procedures so often (and they are less exciting than other parts of experimentation), he or she forgets to warn the novice investigator about them. Yet they are essential to any investigation. House plans are not enough to build a house. One must know how to nail, cut lumber, and do all the other tasks involved in building. The purpose of this chapter is to present the student with some of the things other than the experimental design that must be considered to perform an acceptable research project.

SELECTION OF SUBJECTS

The selection of subjects is important for two reasons. First, the subjects an investigator chooses for his experiment determine to a large extent how far he can generalize his results. An investigator is seldom interested in determining the effect an IV has on the particular subjects used in the investigation. He or she usually wants to make a general statement about some larger population. John Watson carried out research to understand emotion in all infants, not just a few. In order to generalize the results of an investigation to organisms other than those actually being treated, the investigator needs to choose his subjects in such a manner that they represent some larger group. Random selection is one of the best means of choosing subjects so that the investigator may generalize the results he obtains to a whole population. For example, if an investigator finds that subjects worked harder for social praise than for monetary reward and subjects have been randomly selected from the total population of girls at Brigham Young University, he or she may state in the conclusion that "Girls attending Brigham Young University work harder for social praise than for monetary reward." The investigator could generalize the findings to all students at Brigham Young University (and not just girls) if subjects had been randomly selected from all BYU students. If the investigator has randomly selected subjects from all the people in the world, the statement that "People of all ages all over the world work harder for social praise than for monetary reward," can be made. In each of these instances the investigator would carry out his investigation exactly the same way. The only difference would be the population from which subjects had been randomly selected, and that would determine how far he or she could generalize the obtained results. The reader should keep in mind the fact that if one is really randomly selecting subjects, all members of the population should have the same chance of being selected. One of the most common mistakes made by novice investigators is that they forget what population their sample subjects represent.

Recently, a student in an experimental psychology class wanted to find out how people of college age felt about premarital sexual relations. As a class project he randomly selected 200 students from the student body of 25,000 at Brigham Young University. Each was sent a questionnaire that included two questions:

1. Do you believe persons should engage in sexual intercourse before marriage? (Yes/No)
2. In which of the following yearly income categories do your parents fall?
   $3,000–$6,000
   $6,000–$12,000
   $12,000–$30,000
   Above $30,000

The student's purpose was to determine whether people of different economic levels had different attitudes about premarital relationships. He found from the results that approximately 70 percent of each of the four income categories did not believe in premarital sex. He concluded, "Most American people of university age do not differ on this point."

But he did not consider two main points. First, Brigham Young University is a religion-backed institution of higher learning, and therefore the attitudes, especially sexual or political, of the students may not adequately represent the views of all students across the country. Students attending Brigham Young University are more conservative on sexual issues than the average students because of their religious background. Second, the subjects were selected only from college students. Not all young people of college age (including those not attending college) had the same opportunity to be chosen to receive a questionnaire. The student carrying out the survey should not have generalized the results to all college-age people in the United States, only to students at Brigham Young University.

How do you go about randomly selecting subjects? First, define what population you want to make statements about. Second, give each member of that population an equal chance of being selected as a subject. This can be accomplished by assigning each member a number, putting all the numbers in a container, and drawing out the numbers until you have enough subjects to carry out the investigation. After the subjects have been randomly selected to participate in this project, they are then randomly assigned to the different groups in the investigation. Random selection of subjects for the experiment is used to allow the investigator to generalize the results to more than just the subjects used. Random assignment of the subjects to different groups in the investigation helps ensure equality of the groups so that any difference in the DVs between the groups is due to the IV and not some secondary variable.

The second reason choosing subjects is important in an investigation is because the type of subject an investigator uses may determine what type of investigation he or she can carry out. Rats, pigeons, human infants, children, adults, rabbits, and monkeys all have different characteristics. An investigator may capitalize on these differences to help in the study of different psychological problems. To illustrate this point, let us look at a situation I encountered several years ago.

In 1963, an article by H. S. Terrace was published that presented data suggesting an organism could learn without making mistakes. This discovery is one of the most significant in the area of learning in the last fifty years because it has been a commonly accepted idea that people must make mistakes in order to know what is wrong, so that they may then know what is correct. To demonstrate that errors were not necessary in learning, Terrace trained a pigeon to peck at a translucent plastic disc referred to as a key when it was illuminated red, and not to peck at the same key when it was green. By the time the experiment was completed, the pigeon would peck at the red key for food and stand quietly when the key was green, waiting for the red to come back on. It learned to do this even though it never had pecked the green key to find out it would not get a reward for doing so. Later, other psychologists [Moore and Goldiamond, 1963; Sidman and Stoddard, 1967] demonstrated children could learn to do things without making mistakes and without being told what not to do. This line of research became especially interesting when it was noted that animals and children who learn without making mistakes are not as frustrated or aggressive as those who learn by making mistakes.

As research continued on "errorless learning," the question was raised whether a person or an animal could really learn without making mistakes. After all, in all the experiments carried out, the subjects were either adult animals or children at least four years old. It was certain that all had made mistakes before coming into the experiment. It was suggested that the only reason the children and the pigeons could be conditioned to continually respond to one color and not another without mistakes was because they had made mistakes previously in their lives.

Since this issue stirred my curiosity, I wanted to devise an experiment that would shed some light on it. One possibility would have been to use younger children and younger pigeons. If they could be conditioned errorlessly, it would add support to the position that errorless learning does not depend on prior mistakes. There was a better alternative, however, and that was to condition a newborn subject. If a newborn organism could be conditioned errorlessly, it would give strong credence to the position that errorless learning is not a function of prior mistakes.[1] The problem in carrying out such an investigation is that newborn pigeons and newborn human infants have not developed enough at birth to perform a color discrimination task. In my undergraduate training, I had taken a course in comparative psychology that dealt with species differences. I recalled that some animals such as guinea pigs and chicks are mobile and conditionable at birth. Using this information, I was able to select a subject which, because of one of its unique abilities, made it suitable for the problem. I employed chicks in my investigation and found that they could be conditioned to peck at the red key and not at the green key without ever hitting green. From this experiment came information that supported the conclusion that learning a task without mistakes is possible when the subject has made few if any mistakes previously in its life.

---

[1] It would not definitely prove that prior mistakes are not necessary. For example, we know children can be conditioned in the womb before they are born. We would certainly have a strong case, however, that errorless learning is not a function of prior mistakes.

Certain types of investigations can be carried out better on some species than on others. After selecting a problem to analyze, the investigator should carefully consider the choice of subjects, which may determine to a large extent how to go about analyzing the problem. Some of the more common research subjects available are listed next along with some of the unique characteristics an investigator may wish to consider.

Common Research Subjects

Rats. The rat, the most common laboratory animal in psychological research, has many attributes that make it one of the best choices for a research project. It is small, inexpensive, and easily housed. It is also relatively resistant to disease and infection so that it can be deprived of food and water with less chance of getting sick than most animals. Rats are used in experiments dealing with heredity, perception, physiology, learning, and sensory processes. They are fairly easy to condition, slower than pigeons or guinea pigs in visual discrimination problems, but less flighty. They have an excellent olfactory system and can easily be conditioned to distinguish between different odors. One of the biggest advantages of using rats is that there are literally thousands of previous studies with which to compare data. Much is already known about the rat that may aid the student in carrying out a good investigation. By reviewing the literature, the student can find out such things as what type of response would be best to use as a DV, how to measure the response, how to present different types of stimuli to the rat, and what type of reinforcers can be used on the rat. Male rats give more consistent data in certain types of experiments than female rats because of the female's four-day estrous cycle. Information on the rat may be found in Barnett [1963] and Michael [1963].

Pigeons. Pigeons are also very good laboratory animals. They are small, inexpensive, and easy to care for and maintain. They do better on visual tasks than rats, but generally do worse on auditory and olfactory tasks. There is less difference in the behavior of male and female than is true for rats. Pigeons generally learn faster than rats, but are more easily distracted. Like the rat, much work has been done on the pigeon, so a student may review the literature to get ideas on what types of DVs and experimental conditions are appropriate. Information on the pigeon may be found in Ferster and Skinner [1957] and Reese [1971].

Other Nonhuman Species. Although rats and pigeons are the most common nonhuman subjects used in psychological research, many other species can be used that have unique characteristics making them more suitable for certain types of research. Monkeys are good experimental subjects, especially because of their higher intellectual capacity. They are frequently used in experiments on problem solving, concept formation, delayed response and language development. Chicks and guinea pigs may be used in developmental studies because they are mobile at birth. They are easy to house and are just as good as pigeons in visual discrimination tasks. Chickens are easier to work with than pigeons or guinea pigs, for they do not startle as easily, and they do not have to be deprived down to 80 percent of their normal body weight. They are easily conditioned when deprived of food for only 24 hours. This makes them an especially fine laboratory animal for undergraduate psychology course work. Many times students will "accidentally" put someone else's pigeon back on free feed, after which it requires about five days of deprivation to get the pigeon back to 80 percent of its normal weight so it will work. This can severely hamper the progress of any class experiment.

Rabbits are excellent subjects for drug studies because they have unusually large blood veins in their ears. Drugs may be easily injected into these veins, and blood may be easily extracted for analysis. Goldfish are becoming popular as experimental subjects. They are easy to keep and inexpensive to buy. They can be conditioned with shock to make visual discriminations within 1 or 2 hours using swimming from one end of the chamber to the other as the response.

Humans. Humans are the most common type of experimental subject used by students for class projects. As subjects, they have several advantages over nonhumans. They are easy to obtain and do not have to be housed or fed. Many experiments that take very little time may be carried out on them. They may simply be asked to answer questionnaires. They can be worked on in groups because they can respond to verbal instructions. Generally, one must experiment on one animal at a time, and in most cases each animal requires several weeks of training. Verbal reports can be used as DVs with human subjects, and they can also be used in a greater variety of analytical situations.

There are also disadvantages to using humans. Some types of investigations cannot ethically be carried out using humans as subjects (e.g., brain lesion work, certain shock situations). The past history of the subjects is not as easily controlled as with nonhumans. Human subjects frequently invalidate investigations by trying to "outguess" the investigator. Humans may change their behavior drastically when they know they are subjects in an investigation.

There has been growing concern in recent years about the ethical responsibility and obligations of investigators toward the use of human subjects. The issues of deception, invasion of personal privacy, and personal welfare have recently received much attention [Conrad 1967; June, 1971; Kelman, 1967; Lovell, 1967; Ruebhausen and Brim, 1966; Sasson and Nelson, 1969; Seeman, 1969; Walfensberger, 1967]. Students should be particularly careful in ensuring that experimental practices are ethical.

In some situations the psychologist has no choice as to which subjects will be involved in the investigation. This is especially true in applied settings, where the psychologist is asked to solve a particular problem. How can I increase the product output of my employees? What effect does a mistake during learning have on mentally retarded children? Why is little Johnny so destructive? In applied situations such as these, the psychologist is asked to deal with a particular subject or type of subject. When an investigator is in this position, the first step is to make note of all the subjects' attributes that could have a bearing on the problem to be solved. These could include sex, age, mental capacity, physical abilities, union membership, ethnic origin, and socioeconomic background. If, for example, the psychologist wants to increase the output of factory employees, he or she may find out whether or not they are union members. Unions generally have a strong say in what kind of incentive programs may be implemented and if the working conditions of the worker may be changed. Whether the workers are unionized or not may restrict the procedures the industrial psychologist can use to stimulate production. Identifying the attributes of the subjects is especially important when the investigator has no choice of subject, because they may determine to a large extent how the problem can be solved.

Use of Nonhuman Species

Two questions frequently asked by undergraduate psychology majors are, "Why are animals used in psychological investigations?" and "Do the behavioral principles found with animals hold true for, or can they be generalized to, humans?" These are important questions, ones to which a student should have answers before starting graduate training. In answering these questions, let us take the second one first: "Can you generalize behavior principles found with animals to humans?" One of the cardinal rules of behavioral research is *generality is the rule rather than the exception.* Past experience has taught behavioral scientists that what holds true for one behavior generally holds true for other behaviors. The controlling factors of behavior for one species are generally the controlling factors of behavior for other types of animals.[2] The processes of conditioning, extinction, and spontaneous recovery, for example, are essentially the same for most species. The means by which an organism develops phobias and fears are basically the same for rats, dogs, and humans. When Pavlov identified the principles of classical conditioning using a dog

[2] It is obviously not true that what is true for one species is always true for others. Breland and Breland bring this out in their article "The Misbehavior of Organisms" [1963].

salivating to a tone, he and most of the other behavioral investigators of the day saw no difficulty in generalizing those behavioral principles to humans. The behavioral principles identified by B. F. Skinner using rats and pigeons as subjects have been found to have wide interspecies generality. The factors that he found to influence key pecking and bar pressing in the laboratory have also been shown to influence a wide variety of human behaviors (e.g., crying, attention, cooperation, concept formation, talking, showing affection) in everyday situations.

What is learned in terms of animal behavior can usually be generalized to humans. However, the reverse is not as true. Humans obviously have greater mental capabilities than lower species and have developed many sophisticated behaviors (e.g., elaborate language) not found in mental subordinates. Most of the basic principles involved in learning behavior are the same for humans and nonhumans.

Why are animals used in psychological research? The most common reply is, "Because you can do things to animals that you cannot do to humans." Although true, this statement is not the major reason. Psychologists employ rats, pigeons, and the like in research mainly because they allow the investigator better control of secondary variables. In Chapter Four, sources of secondary variation were listed that could make an investigator draw incorrect conclusions about the effect of an IV on some DV. The differences in the proactive history of human subjects can often invalidate an investigation. An investigator can easily control for this by using naive animals who are much more homogeneous in terms of past experience. Retroactive history is also a more likely source of invalidity when humans are used. People's moods shift more from day to day. Some may have been up late the night before an experiment; some may have attitude changes during the course of an experiment because of problems in their personal lives. Animals are seldom bothered by changes going on outside the experimental contingencies. Generally, their attention is wholly directed toward what is involved in the experiment.

Animal investigations are not as susceptible to invalidity due to testing. Animals do not see themselves as being in or out of an experiment, and therefore their actions are more "natural" than is the case for humans in many types of experiments. Experimental mortality is higher with human subjects. They are also not as dependable.[3] With animals, the investigator knows they are always available when needed. Because proactive history, retroactive history, testing, and experimental mortality are responsible for 85 percent of the sources of invalidity, it is no wonder that behavioral researchers employ animals as subjects so often. The investi-

[3] Keep this point in mind especially if you have decided to use college students as subjects. Always request more subjects than you actually need, for approximately 30 percent will not show up if they are to participate in the project outside class time.

gator has a much greater chance of determining what effect an IV actually has on behavior and a much smaller chance that the investigation has been infiltrated by confounding secondary variables.

How many subjects should be used in an investigation? This is one of the most frequent questions asked of an instructor in research courses. With the skill of a politician, he or she generally says, "Well, that depends." Though students find this an unsatisfactory answer, it is the truth, for some experiments can be carried out on two or three subjects while others require several hundred. The variables that determine how many subjects you need include how many groups are involved in the investigation, how much control of secondary variables one has, and how large an effect the IVs will have. For example, fewer subjects are necessary if one has more control of secondary variables and if the IV effects are strong.

Not being familiar with all the ramifications of investigatory analysis, the student may still feel shortchanged with the preceding answer and want some figure with which to start. One answer to this could be to use five to fifteen subjects in each group involved in an experiment. If only two groups are involved, one should lean toward having fifteen in each group, whereas five subjects would be more appropriate if six or eight groups were involved. One of the best ways of determining how many subjects are needed is to review the literature and note how many subjects were used in similar projects.

ETHICAL ISSUES IN RESEARCH

Human Subjects

Do clothes make the man? Several years ago three students at Brigham Young University decided to base their research project on this social tenet. They approached their course instructor (a graduate student who had completed all his Ph.D. requirements) and received permission to develop an appropriate experiment. Due to communication problems the students believed they had the instructors permission to start an experiment, while the instructor meant they should now design a specific experiment and then clear it with him.

The students sat down and formally laid out the experiment. It was to be a relatively simple two-condition experiment. The objective of the experiment was to see if the clothing attire influenced drivers' tendency to pick up hitchhikers. They selected six days out of a two-week period (two Wednesdays, two Saturdays, two Sundays). For three of the six days (a randomly determined Wednesday, Saturday, and Sunday), all three were to dress in jeans, white t-shirts, and tennis shoes and try to hitchhike, holding a two-gallon gas can, for two hours each day. On the remaining three days they were to dress in sportcoat, slacks, and tie while hitchhiking with gas can in hand. The number of successful attempts in each of the two dress conditions were then to be compared. Two days into the experiment (on a Saturday) the course instructor received a call from the county sheriff's office. "We have a student of yours" the officer said, "that says you gave him permission to hitchhike as part of a class assignment. You are aware, are you not, that hitchhiking is against the law?"

Psychology departments receive a variety of phone calls concerning unethical conduct in psychological investigations. A woman calls to protest a telephone survey being conducted by a psychology student that includes some very personal and intimate questions. A student's father calls protesting that his daughter was coerced to be a subject in a psychology experiment involving hypnosis. A mother calls asking why a psychology student administered an IQ test to her eight-year-old son at the public school without parental consent. In many cases, pranksters are at the bottom of some of these problems, conducting phone calls and the like in the name of psychological research without any authority. All too often, however, unethical conduct was performed by a psychologist or psychology student who failed to demonstrate proper concern for the subjects used. In most cases the ethical violations committed by psychology students are unintentional, and are the result of students not taking the time to realize the unethical implications that are involved with what they require of their subjects.

To remedy this problem, there are the *ten containments* of ethical conduct a student should consider when conducting an experiment.

Do Not Commit Illegal Acts.   One should not conduct an experiment that breaks a law, even if the act is a minor offense. In some situations, people feel the value of the data to be collected outweighs the offense, and people will realize the offense was done for a good reason. Society perceives almost any law violation in the name of "science" as an indication that experimenters, and by association the field they are working in, hold themselves above the law. Be cautious about using the telephone or the mail to gather data. In many instances you may be violating the law without knowing it. Investigators often want to compare school records (e.g., student GPA's, single-married status). Such use can be illegal without consent. In some instances you may obtain information without consent if the data being requested do not identify individuals. Past records are an excellent source for research data. Just be sure it is collected legally.

Do Not Collect Sensitive Data.   Information concerning sexual habits, divorce, age, ability, and attitudes may be considered sensitive and personal information that should not be shared. It is not uncommon for a subject to answer personal questions during an experiment and later feel very uncomfortable that someone else knows. They then feel their rights have been violated. Sensitive data should only be dealt with in a highly professional and controlled situation.

Do Not Misinform or Deceive Subjects.   Openness and honesty between the experimenter and subject are considered by psychologists to be essential characteristics of any experiment. While instructional deception may be necessary in some types of psychological investigations, those investigations should only be performed by professional researchers who are familiar with the five conditions for deception that the American Psychological Association (APA) says may be acceptable [1973, p. 37]. Deception may have a long-term detrimental effect in that people learn of psychologists' use of deception and become wary when entering future experiments.

Do Not Pressure for Participation.   Principle 5 of the APA *Code of Ethics* says it is ethically unacceptable to coerce a subject to participate in research. Students enrolled in a psychology course cannot be required to participate in an experiment unless the requirement was announced. A student must have the right of choice to participate or not. One problem psychology students often fail to see is that undergraduates may feel they are in a power relationship [Kelman, 1972] where there is pressure, possibly indirect pressure, to participate. Make sure your subjects realize they may refuse the opportunity to participate in an experiment without fear of any type of reprisal.

Respect the Privacy of the Subject.   Whenever data are collected that are confidential in nature, the privacy of each individual subject must be maintained. Questionnaires may be filled out anonymously; subjects may be given impersonal numbers, with the information gathered being paired only with a particular number. In some cases the identity of each subject needs to be maintained as the data are analyzed. (Students should shy away from this last type of situation.) In 1975, for example, Robinson and Higbee sent out a questionnaire to 175 authors of psychology texts and asked some rather personal questions, such as (1) what royalty rate do you receive on your book, (2) how many copies has your book sold, (3) what do you like and dislike about your publisher? The subjects were told they would receive a summary of what we found out if they would send us their personal information. Many authors wrote on their questionnaire that they definitely did not want to be identified with comments they made about their publishers. We later received many requests asking what was specifically said about certain publishers and by whom. As we collected our data we had to make sure that even our secretaries did not have access to the questionnaires.

Treat the Subject with Respect. It is easy for a student to get so involved, or uninvolved, with an experiment that he or she fails to treat the subjects respectfully. A subject may be told to hurry up or be at a certain place at a certain time, may be given incoherent explanations, or may not be told what he or she was a party to after the experiment is over. Show every subject the courtesy you expect. Ask if they have any questions. Ask if the instructions were clear. Debrief them after the experiment, and thank them for taking the time to participate. You may even take the time to let "control subjects" experience the IV condition after the experiment is over so they have a better understanding of what was involved.

Make the Subject Aware of Any Harmful Experiences. One of the rights of any subject is that of deciding whether they are willing to participate in a situation that may include physical or mental discomfort. This is a ticklish issue in certain types of research because such information may bias the subject sample. However, subjects have the right to be forewarned of discomforts that may occur. The exact information given and how it is given is at the discretion of the experimenter. It is possible in most situations to generally inform the subjects and produce little bias in the results. A good rule for student projects is simply to stay away from experiments that include harmful experiences.

Consider Experimental Effects on the Subject. Can I use a less aversive subject experience in my experiment? Can I redesign the experiment to make the subject more relaxed and comfortable? Can I provide some sort of remuneration for my subjects for their inconvenience? An investigator should take all steps possible to minimize subject stress in the experimental situation.

Obtain Subject Consent. An investigator is expected to establish a clear and fair agreement between herself or himself and the subject (Principle 6, APA *Code of Ethics*). A good idea is to have the subject sign a note of consent that states what is expected of him or her. If children are to be used as subjects, parental consent should be obtained.

Obtain Instructor's Consent. Every student project should be cleared through the instructor. Preferably, each student hands in a two- to three-page proposal outlining what is to be done. Most psychology departments have a special committee or one particular faculty member who clears questionable student projects.

These ten containments are rules designed to reduce ethical problems encountered by undergraduate students. In the past, scientists have also been found guilty of intentional and unintentional violation of subject rights. Few people are unaware of some of the experimental atrocities that were carried out by the Nazis in the name of science. All manner of drugs were studied on prisoners. Nerves were severed, glands removed, and appendages amputated; then behavior was studied. Society has come to the realization that a person's rights can be violated in experiments that do not reach such extremes. Since the 1960s, psychologists have shown great concern over ethical problems in research. The emphasis on human rights led to the publication of *Ethical Principles in the Conduct of Research with Human Participants* (1973) by the American Psychological Association.

Insight
Ethics in Human Research

Ethical Principles in the Conduct of Research with Human Participants includes ten principles of conduct. The following is taken directly from the APA monograph:

The decision to undertake research should rest upon a considered judgment by the individual psychologist about how best to contribute to psychological science and to human welfare. The responsible psychologist weighs alternative directions in which personal energies and resources might be invested. Having made the decision to conduct research, psychologists must carry out their investigations with respect for the people who participate and with concern for their dignity and welfare. The Principles that follow make explicit the investigator's ethical responsibilities toward participants over the course of research, from the initial decision to pursue a study to the steps necessary to protect the confidentiality of research data. These principles should be interpreted in terms of the context provided in the complete document offered as a supplement to these principles.

1. In planning a study the investigator has the personal responsibility to make a careful evaluation of its ethical acceptability, taking into account these Principles for research with human beings. To the extent that this appraisal, weighing scientific and humane values, suggests a deviation from any Principle, the investigator incurs an increasingly serious obligation to seek ethical advice and to observe more stringent safeguards to protect the rights of the human research participant.

2. Responsibility for the establishment and maintenance of acceptable ethical practice in research always remains with the individual investigator. The investigator is also responsible for the ethical treatment of research participants by collaborators, assistants, students, and employees, all of whom, however, incur parallel obligations.

3. Ethical practice requires the investigator to inform the participant of all features of the research that reasonably might be expected to influence willingness to participate and to explain all other aspects of the research about which the participant inquires. Failure to make full disclosure gives added emphasis to the investigator's responsibility to protect the welfare and dignity of the research participant.

4. Openness and honesty are essential characteristics of the relationship between investigator and research participant. When the methodological requirements of a study necessitate concealment or deception, the investigator is required to ensure the participant's understanding of the reasons for this action and to restore the quality of the relationship with the investigator.

5. Ethical research practice requires the investigator to respect the individual's freedom to decline to participate in research or to discontinue participation at any time. The obligation to protect his freedom requires special vigilance when the investigator is in a position of power over the participant. The decision to limit this freedom increases the investigator's responsibility to protect the participant's dignity and welfare.

6. Ethically acceptable research begins with the establishment of a clear and fair agreement between the investigator and the research participant that clarifies the responsibilities of each. The investigator has the obligation to honor all promises and commitments included in that agreement.

7. The ethical investigator protects participants from physical and mental discomfort, harm, and danger. If the risk of such consequences exists, the investigator is required to inform the participant of that fact, secure consent before proceeding, and take all possible measures to minimize distress. A research procedure may not be used if it is likely to cause serious and lasting harm to participants.

8. After the data are collected, ethical practice requires the investigator to provide the participant with a full clarification of the nature of the study and to remove any misconceptions that may have arisen. Where scientific or humane values justify delaying or withholding information, the investigator acquires a special responsibility to assure that there are no damaging consequences for the participant.

9. Where research procedures may result in undesirable consequences for the participant, the investigator has the responsibility to detect and remove or correct these consequences, including, where relevant, long-term aftereffects.

10. Information obtained about the research participants during the course of an investigation is confidential. When the possibility exists that others may obtain access to such information, ethical research practice requires that this possibility, together with the plans for protecting confidentiality, be explained to the participant as a part of the procedure for obtaining informed consent.[4]

Animal Subjects

There are several reasons for employing nonhuman subjects in psychological research, two of which are most important. First, greater control of the subjects is possible with nonhuman subjects. Such subjects may be maintained in a well-controlled animal colony room at a university. Their diet, room temperature, lighting, and even their experiences can be well regulated. Second, things may be done to nonhuman subjects that are considered unethical in human research. Dangerous drugs may be administered, shock may be applied, brain lesions may be induced, stress situations may be created, and fighting may be permitted between subjects, to name just a few.

[4] From *Ethical Principles in the Conduct of Research with Human Participants.* American Psychological Association Committee on Ethical Standards in Psychological Research (Washington, D.C.: Author, 1973.) Copyright 1973 by the American Psychological Association.

While both reasons are justifiably employed in nonhuman psychological research, undergraduate class experiments and professional psychological researchers have been guilty in the past of unethical use of rats, pigeons, and the like. In such cases animals have been poorly housed, needlessly starved, and in general not shown the respect due any living animal. In many cases the mistreatment has been unintentional. In response to a growing concern about this problem the American Psychological Association has published a set of laboratory guidelines for the proper care and handling of animals in psychological research (in the *American Psychologist*, 1972, vol. 27, p. 337). These guidelines include the following points:

Legislation and guidelines for specific care and handling of all animals do exist. Students, teachers, and supervisors must be cognizant of such legislation and guidelines. Copies of appropriate humane laws are available by contacting the local humane organization and the American Humane Association, P.O. Box 1266, Denver, Colorado 80201. Each state also has specific animal health regulations that must be considered. Copies of animal health regulations are obtainable from the state veterinarian or state public health office.

No student shall undertake an experiment that includes the use of drugs, surgical procedures, noxious or painful stimuli such as electric shock, extreme temperature, starvation, malnutrition, ionizing radiation, and the like, except under extremely close and rigorous supervision of a researcher qualified in that specific area of study.

Students using animals must ensure for the proper housing, food, water, exercise, cleanliness, and gentle handling of such animals at all times. Special arrangements must be made for care during weekend, holiday, and vacation periods. The comfort of each animal, by meeting its basic daily needs, shall be of prime concern. Caution must be taken to avoid the animals being teased or harmed by other students.

When the research project has been completed and the student does not wish to maintain the animal(s) as a pet, arrangements shall be made for proper disposition by the supervisor. Under no circumstances should the student be allowed to provide "experimental" euthanasia.

Specifications for the detailed treatment of animals are available from the American Psychological Association, Office of Scientific Affairs, 1200 Seventeenth Street, N.W., Washington, D.C. 20036. A copy of these guidelines shall be posted conspicuously wherever animals are kept and projects are carried out.

SELECTION OF THE DEPENDENT VARIABLE

After an investigator chooses some problem to analyze and decides upon the IV, a variable on which to measure the IV's effect must be chosen. In psychological investigations, this variable, the dependent variable (DV), is generally a measure of behavior. There are two aspects an investigator must take into consideration when selecting a DV: (1) what type of behavior will serve as the DV, and (2) how that behavior will be measured.

Types of Dependent Variables

There are literally hundreds of different types of behaviors an investigator can use in an investigation. Included among the choices are physiological behavioral measures such as EEG recordings, galvanic skin response, and respiration; overt behavioral motor actions such as rats running through a maze, pigeons pecking a key, children answering written math questions, housewives choosing grocery products, biting, bedwetting, hitting, hugging, walking, and sleeping; and verbal reports such as opinions, attitudes, feelings, and observations. Which should an investigator select? That depends on the nature of the problem and the IV being used.

Dependent Variable Measures

If someone were to ask, "How do you quantify a behavior?" the reply would probably be, "Measure the number of times it occurs." An experimental psychologist may measure how many times the pigeon pecks the key or the number of correct turns a rat makes while traversing the maze. The applied psychologist may measure the number of times a patient loses his temper, while the industrial psychologist may measure the number of tasks the worker completes. In all these situations, the psychologist may measure the number of tasks the worker completes. And in all these situations the psychologist has measured the DV in terms of frequency of occurrence. Although frequency is the most common way of measuring DVs, it certainly is not the only way. Behavior can be measured in terms other than frequency, a possibility that most novice investigators fail to consider when planning an investigation. There are many measures of behavior. Five of the most common are frequency, latency, response duration, amplitude, and choice selection. To give the reader a better idea of how each of these may be employed, situations in which they have previously been used are presented along with an explanation of what they involve.

Frequency.   There are two reasons for the popularity of frequency as a unit of measure. First, it is one of the easiest ways of recording data. Response duration and latencies, for example, involve the use of timers and require the investigator to keep an eye on time as well as the behavior. Second, most of our everyday behaviors are measured in terms of frequency: how many compliments we get, how many answers we get right on a test, how many customers we wait on, how much money we have, how many friends call us, and so on.

Frequency is a well-used measure in basic research. It is especially useful in research involving memory and retention. Murdock [1962], for example, was interested in determining whether the ability of a person to recall individual items from a list was a function of the position of the item on the list. Murdock presented a list of English words, one at a time, to a subject. After the presentation of the complete list, the subject was asked to recall as many of the words on the list as possible. Murdock also varied the number of words in the list to see what effect the number of words given had on recall. Figure 5–1 shows the results of his study. He found that the words at the ends of the lists were recalled most frequently, while the words in the middle of the list were recalled least often.

Frequency is also an important dimension in applied psychological investigations. Sulzbacker and Houser [1968] devised and implemented a psychological investigation designed to decrease the frequency of an often encountered but seldom discussed classroom behavior emitted by youngsters. The behavior in question was the use of the "naughty finger" (raised fist with middle finger extended), and any reference to it or comments made by class members about it. The investigation was divided into three parts, as shown in Figure 5–2. First, the frequency of the undesired behavior in a class of fourteen educable mentally retarded children was recorded for ten days. In the second phase, the students were told they would all be given a special ten-minute recess at the end of the day. However, anytime the teacher saw or heard about the naughty finger, one

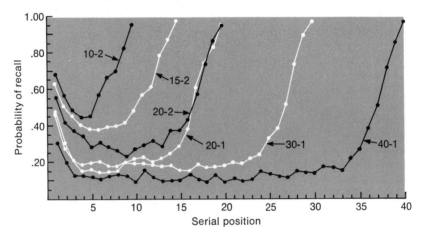

FIGURE 5–1   Probability of recall in free recall as a function of serial position of items in the original test
(Adapted from Murdock, 1962, Figure 2. Copyright 1962 by the American Psychological Association. Reprinted by permission.)

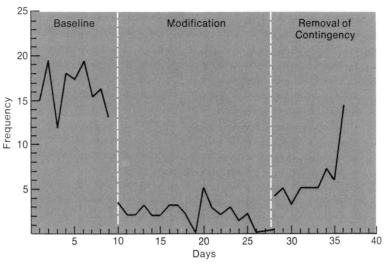

FIGURE 5–2 Frequency of occurrence of the undesired behavior under three contingency conditions
(Adapted from Sulzbacher and Houser, 1966, Figure 1. Reprinted by permission.)

minute would be subtracted from the recess time. After seventeen days of this procedure, a third phase was instituted in which the class was informed that the special recess and the group contingency were no longer in effect. As can be seen in the figure, the rate of the undesirable behavior was drastically reduced when the contingency of losing recess time was in effect. Note that the undesired behavior returned when the contingency was removed.[5]

Latency. There are many instances of behavioral analysis in which the investigator is concerned with how long it takes for a behavior to be emitted. This is called *response latency*. How long it takes a child to solve the problem, how quickly a drunk reacts when driving a car, how long it takes for a rat to traverse the maze are all behavioral measures involving latency. Employers are interested not only in whether an employee can perform a task, such as typing, but also in how long it takes. Latency is also a factor in determining a person's IQ, for some of the behaviors evaluated in intelligence tests involve determining how long it takes for the person to complete certain tasks. In recent years, latency of responding has taken on increased significance in research on emotion and motivation. It is even used as an indicator of fear and anxiety.

---

[5] This type of experimental design, commonly called an ABA design, is a very good design. The first and third stage are integral parts of the investigation and are included to check whether the IV (loss of recess time due to bad behavior) was actually the cause of the change in behavior. Chapter Twelve covers this type of design in detail.

Response Duration.   If an investigator records the length of time in which a subject responds, the measure is called *response duration*. Measures of response duration include the time it takes for the effects of a drug to wear off, how long a subject persists at a particular task, how long the infant cries, and how long the student does homework. Response duration is often used as one indicator of the mental development of a person. The attention span of mentally retarded children, for example, is much shorter than that of the average child, and many times they emit a behavior over and over again.

Response duration can also be used as a measure of anxiety level. The use of shock in psychological investigations generally raises the anxiety level of the subjects. In escape conditioning of rats, the subjects may have to learn to push a lever down several times in succession to turn off the shock. This is a somewhat difficult behavior to develop, for the rat will often hold the bar down rather than let it back up so it can be depressed again. The duration of holding the bar down in shock investigations is generally much longer than when the rat is taught to depress the lever many times to get food or water.

Although response duration is used as a DV in basic research, it is more frequently the DV in applied settings. Often people are guilty of emitting behaviors that are especially annoying to others because they persist for so long. A good example of this was Mary, an attractive sophomore at a western university who became the subject of an investigation. Mary was having difficulty keeping friends and getting dates because she talked so much. Although most young people find it hard to initiate conversation on a date, Mary had just the opposite problem. Being a bright young girl and an avid reader, she could expound for hours on such exciting topics as the high tariff on prune juice. Unfortunately, her dates and roommates did not enjoy her extended conversations. Space does not allow a complete presentation of what was involved in this investigation. Suffice it to say that the objective was to decrease the length of time she talked when around others. The procedure involved having her keep a written record of how often and how long she talked in her apartment, and having her intentionally decrease the length of her statements. At the end of two months, she was talking only one tenth as long as before the investigation was instigated. At last report her dating life and relationships with roommates were much better.

Amplitude.   Any measure of response strength that can vary along some dimension of intensity is termed *amplitude of response*. Response amplitude may be measured in a number of ways, depending on the response involved. The amount of force a subject uses in pressing a lever could be an amplitude measure. Response manipulanda may be purchased which indicate how much force is being applied to depress them. A handy device frequently used in basic research involving shock is a bite bar. The intensity with which the rat bites the bar may be recorded and used as a DV.

In physiological research, amplitude is often used as a measure of response strength. Brain wave activity may fluctuate in terms of cycles per second or height of the wave. The galvanic skin response (GSR) commonly used in lie detector tests is an amplitude measure of emotional responsiveness. Depth of breathing is an amplitude measure. The effects of a drug may be measured in terms of how deep a stage of anesthesia it develops, or in terms of the amount of constituents in the blood that change after its administration. The severity of epilepsy and rigidity of a patient in a catatonic state are also measures of response amplitude a clinical psychologist may encounter.

Measures of response amplitude are often employed in survey research. Subjects are frequently asked to respond in terms of some scale from one to seven on how effective they feel a product is or how intense a stimulus seems to be. Clinical psychologists are working with response amplitude in treating phobias when attempting to reduce fear and anxiety in their patients. Parents deal with response amplitude when they want their child to talk "quieter." Even quality of comments is a measure of response amplitude. An investigation may involve modifying the verbal behavior of juvenile delinquents to use less crude words in their vocabulary.

Choice selection.   Subject preference is also a way of measuring the effects of some IV. The TV viewer is constantly reminded of this type of research. The housewife samples three brands of coffee and is asked which one she prefers. One toothpaste is chosen over another, one car is selected more than another. Making choices is an integral part of everyone's daily routine, and is therefore a behavioral measure that concerns most psychologists.

Choice is a response measure frequently used in psychological testing. Intelligence tests include sections in which the child is given four or five articles and asked to choose the one that does not belong (e.g., shoe, stocking, glove, bowl). Aptitude tests include sections in which the person chooses one situation over another (e.g., which would you rather do, work on a car or hammer nails). Subject responses on psychological tests are often used as DVs, especially in educational research. The effectiveness of different methods of teaching may be evaluated in terms of how the students respond on an achievement test.

The use of choice as a response measure is more common in field research than it is in laboratory investigations. When an investigator has a choice as to the kind of response measure to employ in an investigation, frequency and amplitude are generally preferred because they allow a wider range of statistical tools to be used. Choice as a response measure is one of the more common DVs used in undergraduate course projects.

Ways to Select a Dependent Variable

How does one decide on a particular DV? It depends. In some situations the problem selected by the investigator automatically sets the DV to be used. If the investigator is concerned with getting rid of bedwetting in junior high school subjects, the problem defines the behavior to be employed as the DV. Generally, the DV is automatically set in psychological investigations carried out to solve the practical problems that confront clinical, educational, school, and industrial psychologists. In applied situations the psychologist is frequently restricted in terms of the subjects used and the DV to be studied in an investigation. In such cases, the psychologist does not have to worry about selecting the DV, but only with objectively defining the behavior so it can be measured.

When carrying out basic research, the investigator is not restricted in terms of the DV to choose or the subjects to use. This is an important advantage the research psychologist has over the applied psychologist. Because the research psychologist is not restricted, there is greater latitude in how a problem may be approached. The optimum type of subject and DV may be chosen for analyzing a particular psychological principle. People often have difficulty in understanding why psychologists employ pigeons in their research rather than humans and why they use key pecking (a seemingly irrelevant behavior) as a DV measure. The reason psychologists use behaviors such as key pecking and bar pressing is quite simple—they are easy to quantify. The more exactly a DV can be measured, the easier it is to detect the influence of an IV. It is more difficult to measure other behaviors such as head scratching, yawning, head turning, vocalization, and love.

Will relationships found between an IV and bar pressing or key pecking hold true for other behaviors and other species? This is an important concern for most novice psychologists. Students are often worried about whether psychological principles found when studying key pecking and bar pressing hold true for (or can be generalized to) human behaviors, or even other behaviors of the same species. The rule about subject generality mentioned earlier is also true for DVs. What is true for one behavior is more often than not true for another. The novice usually has difficulty in accepting this idea, and as a result sets up an investigation involving a more practical type of behavior as a DV rather than selecting a DV that is easy to measure and quantify.

One of the best ways for the student to go about selecting a DV is to review the literature. Going to *Psychological Abstracts*, looking up previous investigations dealing with a similar problem, and seeing what was used as a DV, will save a great deal of work in the long run and help to design a better investigation.

SELECTION OF THE INDEPENDENT VARIABLE

Once an area of investigation has been decided upon, the psychologist must select an appropriate IV to represent the issue of concern. Suppose one wishes to study the effects of family love on a child's academic achievement in grade school. What variable would be selected to represent family love in the investigation—hugs and kisses from the parents, verbal praise by parents and siblings, smiles? What variable should be selected as the IV in a study aimed at determining the effect of punishment on a child's self-concept—spankings, verbal reproof, electric shock?

Selecting an IV that truly represents the interests of the psychological investigator is one of the major problems. Other scientific disciplines do not have such a difficult time in selecting an IV. In biochemistry, for example, the scientist may be interested in studying the effects of acidity on enzyme action. Now, the terms "acid" and "enzyme" are fairly easy to define objectively, so the investigator has little difficulty in selecting as an IV a physical compound that most would agree represents the concept acid. She or he simply applies the selected IV, notes its effect, and concludes acidity has such and such an effect. The psychologist, on the other hand, has a much more difficult time of it because the terms dealt with are much more subjective. The variables that concern the social scientist are much more intangible than those dealt with in the physical sciences. Psychological terms such as love, motivation, emotion, anxiety, and self-concept cannot be quantified as easily as physical terms such as light, heat, acidity, and color. The inability to operationally define psychological terms was the main stumbling block when psychology was trying to become a science. A scientific approach required that psychological terms be defined in terms of things that were observable and recordable. If one is interested in studying an issue such as emotion, the literature should be reviewed to find what operational measures have been accepted to represent it.

Even after an acceptable measure of a term has been chosen as an IV for some particular investigation, one must not forget that different quantitative and qualitative values are possible. How much IV, what type of IV, how long should it be given are all questions the investigator may have to answer. If, for example, a drug is the IV, too little may have no effect, while too much may have a terminal effect. In the first chapter, Sid employed a drug called apomorphine in his investigation. Small doses of apomorphine elicit compulsive gnawing behavior in subjects, yet in large doses it is commonly used in hospitals to induce vomiting. If Sid had not reviewed the literature and become aware of the characteristics of the IV he had chosen, he could have been unpleasantly surprised by the reactions of his subjects. An investigator should be sure to review the literature of his IV before initiating experimental procedures. An operational definition includes defining a selected variable in terms of both quality and quantity.

ELIMINATION AND CONSTANCY AS NONDESIGN CONTROL TECHNIQUES

The reader will be shown in later chapters how experimental designs can be set up to make use of four control techniques for secondary variables—randomization, constancy, making a second IV, and statistical control. Secondary variables, however, may be controlled by means other than experimental designs. There are nondesign procedures that may help control for the effects of secondary variables in an investigation. These nondesign procedures include elimination and constancy.

After an investigator defines the IV, DV, and potential secondary variables, the next step involves setting up an experimental situation in which the secondary variables are controlled as much as possible. One of the best ways to make sure a secondary variable is not responsible for the difference between the control and experimental groups is to eliminate that variable completely from the experimental situation. Suppose, for example, that you were evaluating the ability of children to put certain puzzles together. If parents are present in such situations, it is not uncommon for the child to take cues from the parent. The child becomes aware of small changes in the parent's behavior (an unintended subtle frown when the child picks up the wrong piece) and solves the problem by cueing on the parent rather than attending to cues in the puzzle. In such cases, the parent is an important secondary variable. The investigator could easily control for this secondary variable by not allowing the parent in the room with the child while engaged in the experiment.

This secondary variable of cueing off people in the situation is also something to watch out for when animals are used as subjects. In Europe during the 1800s there was a horse (called Hans the Wonder Horse) that seemed to have extrasensory perception. Hans was used in an act in which he supposedly read a person's mind. The act involved having someone in the audience come forward and think of a number between one and ten. Hans, using his hoof, would then count off the number. Initially, many felt the trainer was somehow cueing the horse, but it was found that Hans could do it even if his trainer was not there. Later, it was shown that Hans could only do it if he could see the person, and not when the person was shielded from view. It was found that somehow the horse was able to sense the small behavioral changes a person would make whenever he had counted off the right number. Sensing these subtle changes, the horse would then stop.

Like randomization, elimination can easily be used to control more than one secondary variable in an investigation. By eliminating secondary variables, the investigator increases the possibility of showing his IV has an effect. Every secondary variable causes some fluctuation, though minor in many cases, between the DV measures of different subjects. The more secondary variables eliminated, the less non-IV variability between subjects. This allows the variability between subjects due to the IV to become more apparent. Elimination, then, is an important control procedure that can and should be used in every experimental situation.

Constancy is another control technique that can be applied irrespective of the design. Although it is true that constancy may be incorporated into a design (e.g., matching and blocking designs) to control for secondary variables, it may also be applied no matter what design is used. An experimenter may feel temperature variation might influence the behavior of the rat subjects in the experiment, so the temperature is held constant. An investigator may give verbal instructions to subjects; differences in the way the instructions are given may cause variations in subject's results. To cope with this problem, the experimenter may type out the instructions and read them off a card so that instructions are held constant in terms of what is said. If the investigator is worried about behavior mannerisms (e.g., voice inflection) unconsciously given with the instructions, the instructions may be presented by means of a tape recorder to hold them constant.

In some situations, a secondary variable may be held constant indirectly. There are times when the investigator may not be able to hold a particular variable constant, but can mask its influence by presenting another variable that overrides the first. For example, animals being run in test chambers are usually sensitive to small fluctuations in sound. Sounds from a person walking past the test chamber, a relay buzzing on a piece of equipment, a bell sounding in the adjoining hall, or a rat squeaking in a nearby chamber may disrupt the subject. To override the effects of these uncontrollable variables, a white noise (a rasping sound held at a constant intensity) is continuously presented inside the chamber at a high enough intensity so that the fluctuation in the other sounds cannot be heard. In this way, the secondary variable of extraneous noise is held constant. This procedure is called *masking* and is frequently applied in psychological research.

EXPERIMENTER BIAS

One of the biggest sources of internal invalidity in a psychological investigation is experimenter bias. While conducting an investigation, a researcher may unknowingly confound the results of the project by not dealing with the subjects uniformly. An investigator may ask questions in a different manner to the control group than to the experimental group. If the experiment involves observing the subjects' reactions, the investigator may have certain expectancies as to how they should act and read into their behavior things that are not really there. If, for example, the investigator has been told the drug given will cause a subject to become more aggressive, neutral statements made by the subject while injected may be interpreted as being aggressive and obnoxious in nature.

There are ways an investigator may go about reducing the possibility of experimenter bias. If a drug or capsule of some sort is to be given to the subjects, a double-blind technique may be used. In a *double-blind* situation, neither the person giving the capsule nor the subject receiving it knows whether the person is in the experimental or control group, and each is unaware whether the subject received a placebo or the real IV. This decreases the possibility of experimenter bias or subject expectancy invalidating the results. If surveys are being taken, interviews given, or observations of subjects' behavior being recorded by an experimenter's helper, the helpers should not be made aware of the objective of the investigation if such knowledge could cause their behavior to bias the results. Experimenter bias is an especially potent source of invalidity in class projects because the novice experimenter becomes overly intent on supporting a hypothesis rather than on keeping an open mind to any results obtained.

PILOT STUDIES

One of the best ways for the novice researcher to develop a firm experimental investigation is to first run a pilot study. A pilot study is one in which the investigator carries out what could be called a mini-experiment in which the IV is administered to a subject or two for only a short time. The experimenters use this practice run to try different levels of the IV or check out any of a dozen other things he or she may be unsure of. This dry run can give a basic feel as to what will happen and may reveal important secondary variables that might have been overlooked. One of the most common statements made by students after completing their projects starts out: "If I were to do it over, I would. . . ." That sentence is most often completed by mentioning a particularly poor aspect of the investigation that would have been identified if a pilot study had been run.

INSTRUMENTATION

In psychology's attempt at becoming a more exact science, greater emphasis has been placed on the use of more objective means of applying the IV and monitoring the DV. The internal validity of almost every type of psychological investigation can be increased by using mechanical and electronic instruments. The application of the IV can be done more exactly and consistently by decreasing fluctuations in amount of the IV given, the latency of its administration, and the duration of administration. Error variance in an investigation is reduced by the use of some instrument to measure the DV more uniformly. The types of behavioral research equipment available to the investigator are so numerous that a systematic coverage of them would require a book by itself. There are literally dozens of different ways electronically and mechanically to apply IVs, including slide projectors, tape recorders, light sources, and mechanized syringes. Every type of DV measure (frequency, latency, etc.) can be monitored by devices such as counters, timers, polygraphs, and printout counters. In reviewing the literature, the investigator generally pays close attention to how the IV and DV were measured in related investigations.

SUMMARY

There are a number of experimental issues an investigator must deal with that are not related to the design. Choosing the right subjects is important because the type of subject chosen often determines what type of investigation may be performed. Second, the way subjects are chosen determines how far the results of the investigation may be generalized. Different species are more suitable for certain types of experiments. The similarities and differences an investigator may consider when setting up an investigation are presented, along with two arguments for the use of nonhuman species by psychologists.

There are *ten containments* of ethical conduct a student should consider when designing an experiment with human subjects. These ten include: do not commit illegal acts, do not collect sensitive data, do not misinform subjects, do not pressure for participation, respect the privacy of the subject, treat the subject with respect, make the subject aware of any harmful experiences, consider experimental effects on the subjects, obtain subject consent, and obtain instructor's consent.

When animal subjects are used in experimentation, the student: should be supervised if drugs, surgery, or painful stimuli are used; should ensure proper housing and maintenance; should have used animals properly disposed of by a supervisor.

Five measures of DVs are frequency, latency, duration, amplitude, and choice. Each of these five is used in psychological investigations. DVs that are easy to quantify and adequately represent the issue under investigation should be selected. The investigator may find the best DV measure of the IV by reviewing the literature.

Selecting an appropriate operationally defined IV is more difficult for psychology than other sciences because psychological terms are more subjective in nature. The psychology investigator must then be more careful to make sure the IV used is operationally defined and therefore reproducible.

Two secondary variable control techniques may be applied irrespective of the design used. These are elimination and constancy. The experimenter should be careful not to bias results because of what he or she does. A pilot study should be carried out to give the investigator experience and to aid in selecting appropriate IVs and DVs. Wherever possible, an experiment should be instrumented to increase its validity.

I. Threshold Measurement
   A. Use of Threshold Techniques
   B. Types of Thresholds
   C. Calculation of Thresholds
   D. Stimulus Presentation
II. Scaling Techniques
   A. Types of Measurement Scales
   B. Classification of Scaling Methods
   C. Examples of Scaling Procedures in Use
III. Interviews
   A. Structured and Unstructured Interviews
   B. Selection of Questions
IV. Psychological Tests
   A. Types
   B. Uses
   C. Development
   D. Misuse
V. Application of Data-Collection Methods
VI. Summary

Methods of Data Collection

In many areas of research, standard ways of collecting data have been agreed upon. Not being familiar with these, the novice investigator frequently is unaware of the accepted procedures and employs a less acceptable data collection procedure. This chapter presents several methods of data collection commonly used in psychology. Note that the first three sections of the chapter emphasize how to go about collecting data, while the section on psychological tests emphasizes what kinds of tests are available and how to use them correctly.

There are literally hundreds of different ways of collecting data. Some are objective, others are subjective; some are quite reliable and valid, others are less so. Once the investigator has selected a DV, an acceptable way of measuring it is decided upon. For example, how does one go about determining how well a child can hear? This may sound simple; just increase the volume of sound until the child indicates hearing it. How do you carry out an interview? Just ask questions. Unfortunately, it is not as simple as it sounds.

The search for more objective, valid, and generalizable data has stimulated researchers to systematize their data-collection procedures. Over the years, standard DV measures have been agreed upon in particular research areas as being more acceptable than others.

Our objective here is to present some of the more standardized data-collection procedures used in psychological research. This is not an all-inclusive presentation, for each special research area has its own standards to some extent, and there are hundreds of special research areas. The data-collection procedures presented here, however, are some of the more general and well-known ones. Almost every psychologist during his or her training or professional practice will come in contact with them. There are two main reasons for including a discussion of data-collection procedures in this text. First, in case the reader decides to carry out investigations that require these methods, the presentation may help in selecting an appropriate procedure. Second, even if the reader never carries out such investigations, he or she should still be aware of the proper procedures for doing so because the results from such investigatory procedures are used by all professionals in psychology. When reading a psychology text or journal, a person may come across a statement such as, "the method of limits was used . . .," with no explanation of what the method of limits is. The author gives no explanation because the method of limits is a common data-collection procedure, and it is assumed that readers would have learned the main types of data-collection procedures as undergraduates.

THRESHOLD MEASUREMENT

Use of Threshold Techniques

The measurement of psychophysical thresholds has been one of the prime research concerns since the formation of psychology as a separate discipline. The analysis of a person's sensory thresholds was psychology's first step toward an evaluative measure of people in an attempt to identify the internal physiological and mental processes they employ in dealing with their surroundings. One needs a means of interacting with the brain if an understanding of brain mechanisms is to be accomplished. The only known means of input is through the sense systems, and the only means the brain has of expressing its functions are through muscular and glandular reactions. Many investigators have carried out threshold investigations simply to determine a subject's range and sensitivity to various stimuli. Questions such as what sounds can people hear, to what wave lengths are people sensitive, and so on, have been and are continually being researched in psychology by means of threshold investigations.

In many instances a person's threshold is used as a DV to determine the effects certain IVs have. What effect do alcohol or other drugs have on a person's ability to sense change? Is a person more or less sensitive to stimuli when angry or embarrassed? Can one "sharpen" his or her senses through training? Investigations seeking answers to these types of questions require the investigator to be familiar with the standard means of collecting threshold data.

Types of Thresholds

Psychological investigations involving thresholds may be divided into two groups, *absolute* threshold investigations and *difference* threshold investigations. Absolute threshold investigations entail determining the least amount of energy that some particular sense system or systems require before that stimulus is detected. What is the lowest intensity of sound you can hear, how bright must a light be before you can see it, and how much pressure must be exerted on some part of your body before you "feel" something are all questions that are dealt with by absolute threshold investigations.

The ability of an organism to sense a change in the magnitude of some stimulus is what a difference threshold investigation determines. Suppose two lights were simultaneously presented to a subject. How much brighter would one have to be than the other before the subject could perceive a difference in brightness between the two? If a man is holding a 250-ounce weight in one hand and a 253-ounce weight in the other, can he sense that the weights are not the same? What if he had a 5-ounce weight in one hand and an 8-ounce weight in the other? These types of questions could be answered with difference threshold investigations. Difference thresholds are the minimum amount of change in stimulus magnitude some particular sense system or systems require before a change can be detected.

Past difference threshold investigations have shown that the difference threshold tends to be a constant fraction of the stimulus magnitude. To illustrate, let us look at whether a person can tell the difference between a 5-ounce weight and an 8-ounce weight. Previous investigations have found that the fraction a weight must change in magnitude for one to sense a change is $\frac{1}{7}$. That means a person can detect the full difference between a 6-ounce weight and a 7-ounce weight, yet cannot distinguish between a 166-ounce weight and a 167-ounce weight. We would rightfully conclude, then, that a person could tell the difference between a 5- and an 8-ounce weight, but not between a 250- and a 253-ounce weight. Difference threshold investigations have shown that different sense systems have different fractions (meaning differences in sensitivity). Table 6–1 presents the fraction constants for several sense modalities. In difference threshold investigations, the minimum amount of stimulus change required to detect a change is referred to as a *jnd* (just noticeable difference). The *jnd* is commonly used for scaling the steps of sensation corresponding to increases in stimulus magnitude.

TABLE 6–1   *Fraction Constants for Difference Thresholds of Four Senses*

SENSE	FRACTION CONSTANT
Vision	$\frac{1}{62}$
Hearing	$\frac{1}{11}$
Smell	$\frac{1}{5}$
Pressure	$\frac{1}{7}$

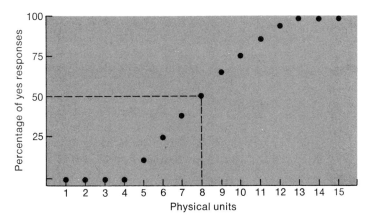

FIGURE 6–1 Illustration of a psychophysical curve: plotted on the ordinate is the percentage of times a person answered yes when asked to detect the presence of a stimulus. In this case the threshold would be defined physically as unit 8.

Calculation of Thresholds

Determining a person's absolute threshold for a stimulus (e.g., a tone) might initially seem rather simple and straightforward. If asked to perform such a task, you would probably begin increasing the volume of the tone after telling the subject to speak out when it was first heard. You would then want to define the absolute threshold of this person as the value that elicited a response. It is not quite that simple, however, for if you repeated your procedure a second time, you would find that the subject did not respond to exactly the same tone value as being the minimum heard. Past threshold investigations have taught researchers that a threshold is not a fixed and invariant level. Actually, one's threshold for stimuli fluctuates from one second to the next. This fact has required researchers to agree on what should be defined as threshold. The agreement reached was that threshold should be defined as that physical stimulus value at which 50 percent of the time the subject reported detecting it and 50 percent of the time a subject reported he or she could not detect it. This meant the stimulus should be presented many times over a range of values with each subject responding many times. The threshold would then be statistically determined by averaging the responses made. Figure 6–1 shows what a graph of the results of such an investigation might be like. The curve in Figure 6–1 is called a psychophysical function because it shows the relationship between a psychological variable (perception of a stimulus) and a physical variable (intensity of a stimulus).

The procedure for determining difference thresholds is basically the same as for determining absolute thresholds. There is no one single intensity value or jnd value that represents the "true" threshold of a person for some stimulus. Both types of thresholds are statistically determined. When calculating either an absolute or difference threshold, the investigator needs to present each physical level of the stimulus several times to be able to calculate the threshold value.

Stimulus Presentation

Four methods are commonly used to present stimuli in threshold investigations: the *method of limits*, the *method of constant stimuli*, the *method of average error*, and the *method of signal detection*.

Method of Limits.   This procedure entails presenting the subject(s) with a large number of stimulus values, with each value being presented several times. The stimuli are presented sequentially, according to their magnitude (as shown in Figure 6–2). The investigator begins by presenting the stimulus at an intensity that is well above the threshold of the subject. (The experimenter could also start out below threshold and go up.) After the subject's response is noted, a second stimulus of lower intensity is presented. This continues with successive presentations of the stimulus at lower intensity values as long as the subject continues to detect the stimulus. After the subject says that he or she cannot detect the stimulus for a certain number of presentations (defined by the investigator), the descending

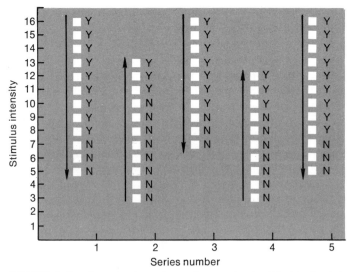

FIGURE 6–2   Sample data sheet the method of limits. Each box represents the presentation of a certain stimulus intensity. The letters indicate whether or not the subject could detect the stimulus (Y, yes; N, no). The arrows indicate whether the sequential presentation of stimulus values went from high to low or from low to high.

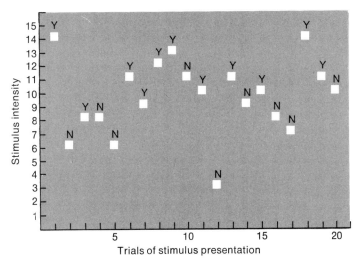

FIGURE 6–3   Sample data sheet for the method of constant stimuli. Each box represents the presentation of a certain stimulus intensity. The letters indicate whether or not the subject could detect the stimulus (Y, yes; N, no).

series is terminated, and an ascending series is begun. Starting with a stimulus value well below threshold, the experimenter continues increasing the intensity of the stimulus by predetermined increments until the subject responds positively for several presentations. Several ascending and descending stimulus presentation series are carried out until a threshold estimate can be made. Notice that the responses of the subject determine to an extent which stimulus values will be presented when the method of limits is used. The cue for terminating the ongoing sequence is when the subject changes his or her response. This also gives the experimenter an idea of the volume with which to start the next sequence.

Method of Constant Stimuli.   The method of constant stimuli is similar to the method of limits in that each includes presenting the subject with a large number of stimulus values, with each being presented several times. The method of constant stimuli, however, does not present the stimulus values in order of ascending or descending intensity values. Instead, they may fluctuate greatly from one trial of presentation to the next. Figure 6–3 illustrates how the values may be presented. Fifty, one hundred, or more trials may be used with the method of constant stimuli. Each square indicates the stimulus intensity applied, while the letters indicate subject responses.

The method of limits does not require any previous knowledge of threshold values. The investigator can simply continue up or down the series, letting the responses of the subjects determine the range of stimulus intensity values. With the method of constant stimuli, the investigator needs much more prior knowledge of the possible threshold values of the sense modality he or she is working with because the values and their range must be set prior to testing the subjects. The predetermined increments selected by the investigator using constant stimuli procedures may be too great or too small. Because the method of limits may employ a sliding scale rather than just discrete changes in stimulus intensity, this method can easily provide a much more accurate threshold measure.

With the method of limits, however, the investigator must be more concerned with the possibility of the subjects' giving incorrect replies. Because the intensity of the stimulus is systematically increased or decreased in sequence, the subject may *anticipate* the next response. For example, it is more common for Yes responses to be given at lower intensities when using a descending series than when an ascending series is being given. These false positives and false negatives, as they are called, may be controlled for to some extent by the random injection of blanks (no stimulus given) throughout the presentations.

The method of limits is considered a more flexible procedure than the method of constant stimuli because the values of the stimulus do not have to be predetermined. In many instances this allows the investigation to be carried out in less time, for certain levels of stimulus would not have to be presented once it was noted that the threshold was not close to those values.

In some situations the successive presentation of several stimulus values at one time may interrupt the ongoing behaviors of the organism.[1] The method of constant stimuli allows the investigator more easily to introduce only one stimulus value at a time over longer periods of time. This makes it an especially effective procedure in analyzing stimulus-response generalization gradients [Guttman & Kalish, 1956].

Can the method of limits and the method of constant stimuli be used on nonhuman subjects? Yes, they certainly can. The responses used in the illustrations so far have been verbal, but animals can be conditioned to make a response (e.g., press a bar, peck a key, squeal) if a stimulus is present or absent. Blough [1966] surveys a number of responses that can be used for animal threshold experiments.

Yes-no responding is not the only type of response human subjects can make. A second type of indicator response is called the *forced choice* response. The subject responds in such a way as to actually select a stimulus value from among several choices. One trial may consist of four successive intervals in which the stimulus was applied in only one of the four. The subject not only has to detect the stimulus, but also identify which of the

---

[1] In some cases the investigator may want to measure the threshold while the subject is involved in some task. The method of constant stimuli usually works better in such cases. Also, certain types of subjects (e.g., mentally retarded children, animals) may be easily distracted and lose their power of concentration when long periods of time are used to present stimuli sequentially.

FIGURE 6–4   An illustration of a subject using the method of average error. The method of average error has the subject manipulate the stimuli being compared.

four choices it occurred in. The forced choice method is commonly used in eye chart tests in which a dot is missing in one of four choices and the person has to identify which of the choices has only three dots (see the diagram). The size of the stimulus is then varied to determine visual distance threshold.[2]

Method of Average Error.   The two methods previously mentioned have the experimenter control the stimulus values and the subject simply responds verbally. The method of average error makes the subject a more active participant by requiring him or her to manipulate one of two stimuli. (Sometimes the experimenter adjusts the stimuli for the subject.) Suppose, for example, the experimenter was interested in studying distance perception. Using the method of average error, the subject would be placed in front of the elongated box illustrated in Figure 6–4. Through an opening in the end of the box, the subject can see two sticks at some distance. One stick (A) is called the standard and its distance from the subject is set by the experimenter. The subject holds two strings, which can slide stick B either forward or back. The task requires the subject to

[2] A more in-depth coverage of threshold measurement techniques can be found in the following texts: D'Amato [1970, Chapter Five]; Dember [1963, Chapter Two]; Kling and Riggs [1971, Chapters Two and Three].

align stick B exactly alongside stick A. The subject is required to repeat the task a number of times. The point of subjective equality (PSE), the value at which stick B is perceived to be the same distance from the subject as stick A, is determined by taking the average distance that stick B was adjusted to over all the trials. Table 6–2 illustrates how the PSE would be calculated if fifteen trials were run. The difference between the standard and the PSE is called the constant error (CE). The CE is an important measure, because the actual distance of stick A (the standard) is often varied from trial to trial, although it was not in the example given in Table 6–2.

Method of Signal Detection.   Of the three methods already presented, the signal-detection method is most like the method of constant stimuli. Two unique characteristics distinguish it. First, a substantial portion of the test trials are *catch* trials; that is, they do not include the stimulus. Fifty percent, or any percent the experimenter desires, of the trials include the signal, while 50 percent do not. Second, the subject is informed that the signal, be it a light, tone, or other type of stimulus, will only be present on a certain percentage of the trials in some random fashion.

In a signal-detection experiment, then, the subject's responses may actually be placed in four categories on any particular trial; the subject may (1) say *yes* correctly when the stimulus is actually present, (2) say *yes* incorrectly when the stimulus is not presented, (3) say *no* correctly on a catch trial, and (4) say *no* incorrectly when the stimulus is actually presented.

TABLE 6–2   *Determination of Distance Perception Using the Method of Average Error*

TRIAL	JUDGED DISTANCE OF THE STANDARD (STICK A), CM	DIFFERENCE BETWEEN STICK A AND STICK B, CM
1	123	23
2	118	18
3	122	22
4	119	19
5	110	10
6	117	17
7	106	6
8	123	23
9	122	22
10	109	9
11	108	8
12	110	10
13	108	8
14	104	4
15	107	7
	Average = 113.73 cm Difference (PSE)	Average = 13.73 cm Difference (CE)

TABLE 6–3   *Four Different Categories of Response Possible with the Signal-Detection Method and the Proportion of Responses to Each Category by a Hypothetical Subject*

	SUBJECT'S RESPONSE	
	Yes	No
Signal present	Correct identification (0.50)	Incorrect identification (0.50)
Signal absent	Incorrect rejection (0.20)	Correct rejection (0.80)

Table 6–3 illustrates what the four choices are, plus the percentages of responses emitted by a hypothetical subject.

Since its first application by Tanner and Swets in 1954, this method has had a predominate effect on psychophysical research. This method allows the investigator to do something none of the three previously discussed methods can do. It allows the investigator to separate out the *sensitivity factor* and the *response criterion factor*. In any threshold testing situation the measure obtained from the subject is a result of two major factors. First is the actual sensitivity of the subject's sensory receptors. (This is typically the main interest of the investigator.) Second is the judgment dimension of the subject, the criterion by which the subject decides to respond in the situations where he or she is not sure if the signal is present or absent. It is well known that people differ on the criterion they choose for responding on uncertain trials. Some subjects are more overly concerned about saying the signal is there when they are not sure. In such cases that subject will seldom say "yes" on uncertain trials. Another subject may have more of a devil-may-care attitude and, therefore, make a high level of incorrect rejections (say "yes" on those uncertain trials when the signal is not present). The inclusion of catch trials allows the investigator to isolate and identify that aspect of the subject's responding which is due to the response criterion factor, and therefore to obtain a more valid measure of sense receptor sensitivity than possible with the method of limits, constant stimuli, or average error.

The use of the method of signal detection can be illustrated by addressing the question, "Does a driver under the influence of alcohol have the same sensory sensitivity as a nondrinking driver?" Theoretically, it would be possible to study the visual sensitivity with the method of limits on drunk and on nondrunk drivers and obtain results indicating that nondrunk individuals have a lower (better) visual threshold than drunk individuals. Using the method of signal detection, you could obtain a finer analysis which would show that the "visual sensitivity" of the two types of individuals is actually the same, and that the previously found difference is actually due to judgment differences between subjects as to if they should respond or not. The issue against the drunk driver could be that judgment capabilities are impaired, causing greater susceptibility to accidents, rather than a loss of receptor sensitivity.

Insight
The Development of Psychophysical Methods

The reader may get a better understanding of the psychophysical methods, what they entail, and when to use them by looking at how and when they came about.

It is generally agreed that field of psychophysics was begun with the publishing of *Elements der Psychophysik* in 1860 by Gustav Theodor Fechner (1801–1887). Fechner's purpose was to find a means of integrating mental life with the physical environment.

Due to a miraculous recovery from illness, Fechner turned from physicist to religious philosopher. He attempted to turn science away from its materialistic course to one more considerate of the idea of consciousness. He devised three empirical methods for studying the mind-matter (psycho-physical) relationship. These methods, published in 1860, were called the method of limits, method of constant stimuli, and method of average error (also called the method of adjustment). With his empirical methods for determining absolute and difference thresholds, he succeeded in getting the study of psychophysics accepted as one of the most scientifically exacting experimental areas in psychology. Fechner's work formed the basic concepts on which the *classical theory of psychophysics* was based. The *phi-gamma hypothesis* put forth by Urban [1910] along with Fechner's work became the classical theory of psychophysics.

In 1954, Tanner and Swets proposed a new theory of psychophysics, commonly called the *theory of signal detectability* (TSD). This theory brought with it a new method of studying psychophysics. The most significant feature of signal-detection theory is that it provides a means for the sensitivity factor and response criterion factor in psychophysical research to be separated. This was not possible with previous psychophysical methods.

SCALING TECHNIQUES

Threshold measurement investigations involve comparing judgmental responses of subjects to physical scales such as intensity and brightness. There are situations, however, in which the investigation requires the subjects to compare stimuli along dimensions that are more qualitative than quantitative. Scaling techniques have been devised to measure such relationships. "Rank these makes of cars according to prestige," "Rate how happy you feel on a scale from one to seven," "Who will make the best president?"—questions such as these require the person responding to make a value judgment. People's preferences, attitudes, and beliefs are common DVs in psychological investigations. They usually present a problem to the novice investigator because she or he is not sure how to deal with responses that involve comparing value judgments.

In psychophysical investigations the investigator is relating psychological responses to a "quantitative" physical dimension—brightness, heaviness, length, and so on. In some cases, however, the interest of the psychologist is to compare stimuli, objects, or events on a dimension that is inherently "qualitative" rather than inherently "quantitative." Rank the top five girls in the beauty contest. List job occupations according to your likes. Rate the excellence of ten different roses. Rate the professors in the psychology department according to their effectiveness as teachers. In all these situations you are asking your subject(s) to judge the stimuli according to some qualitative dimension. Over the years, psychological research that deals with rating stimuli in terms of qualitative dimensions has come to be known as *psychophysical scaling*.

Psychophysical scaling is the problem of developing a form of measurement for qualitative stimulus dimensions. Measurement is formally defined as the assignment of symbols, usually numbers, to properties of objects and events according to rules. Students may be asked to rank five teachers in terms of teaching effectiveness. Instructors may be required to assign numerical scores to student essays. In both cases the task is to assign numbers to the stimuli. In the first instance, students assign numbers to the instructors, identifying teacher 1, teacher 2, teacher 3, teacher 4, and teacher 5. Such number assignment is called ranking, and it indicates the rating of teachers from first to fifth. The second instance requires the teacher to not only rank the student essays, but also to indicate by numbers how much one paper differs from the other. This type of scoring requires a different type of measurement scale.

Types of Measurement Scales

Four basic measurement scales may be used to assign numbers to objects and events: the nominal, ordinal, interval, and ratio measurement scales. The nominal scale is the simplest measurement scale and entails nothing more than the mere assignment of an identifying number to each stimulus. The numbers on football players' uniforms exemplify nominal scaling. Nominal numbers may categorize stimuli but say nothing about how they are ordered (first, second, etc.), how different they are from each other, or how big they are. In ordinal scaling, the stimuli are ordered or ranked in some fashion. The ranking of the instructors is an example of ordinal scaling. Such numbering tells the order of the stimuli, but says nothing about how much or how big the differences are between the stimuli. Interval scaling is the assignment of numbers to stimuli using a number

TABLE 6–4   *Illustration of the Four Types of Measurement Scales*

PLAYER	NOMINAL (number on jersey)	ORDINAL (order at finish line)	INTERVAL (time on a wristwatch used at finish line)	RATIO (seconds to run 100 yards)
A	22	1	4:15-30″	10
B	32	2	4:15-32″	12
C	44	3	4:15-36″	16
D	14	4	4:15-38″	18

scale with equal intervals. Grades on a multiple choice test exemplify this scale. A score of 83 on an exam is 3 units less than a score of 86. The scores of 53 and 56 differ in the same three unit amount. Numbers on a yardstick exemplify a ratio scale, but also have an absolute zero point. While the difference of an absolute zero point between an interval and ratio scale may seem unimportant to the reader, it makes a big difference in terms of what statistical operations may be performed. (This point is discussed more fully in Chapter Thirteen).

Table 6–4 illustrates the use of each of the four measurement scales. Four football players are running windsprints during practice to see how fast they can run. Player A has the number 22 on his jersey, player B is number 32, player C is 14, and player D is 44.

A second illustration the reader may more easily relate to is shown in Table 6–5. Six students took an exam in an experimental psychology class. As each turned in an exam paper, it was assigned an identification number (column 1). The second column indicates how the students ranked, with number 1 being the highest scoring paper. Column 3 indicates the actual scores obtained in terms of an interval scale. Notice that the interval scale scores provide more exacting information than the ranking does. Students typically want to know more than just where they

TABLE 6–5   *Nominal, Ordinal, and Interval Scales on Student Exam Papers*

STUDENT NUMBER	RANK ON THE EXAM	INTERVAL SCORE ON THE EXAM
4	1	97
1	2	91
6	3	86
3	4	80
2	5	63
5	6	42

ranked in the class. They want to know how well they did in terms of answering the questions.

There are a considerable number of scaling methods employed in psychological research. Due to the fact that a complete coverage of scaling methods would require a whole book, such a coverage is beyond the scope of this book [see Guilford, 1954; Stevens, 1958; Torgeson, 1958]. Only a basic classification system of scaling methods is presented here, with a few examples, to give the reader a rough idea as to what is involved in conducting a psychological scaling experiment.

Classification of Scaling Methods

One means of classifying scaling procedures is by *response measure* used and the *measurement scale* used. Recall that Fechner used two different response measures. With the method of limits and the method of constant stimuli, the subject gave a *verbal response*. With the method of average error, the subject gave an *adjusted* response; the subject physically adjusted the stimulus. In psychological scaling, the verbal response is termed an *estimation*, while the adjusting response is called a *production* (the subject physically manipulates or "produces" the response).

By considering all four possible measurement scales with both types of response measures, one comes up with eight different scaling methods. Table 6–6 illustrates the scaling methods possible using the proposed classification system. Notice that actually ten rather than eight scaling methods are indicated. The ratio scale dimension has been subdivided in Table 6–6 below into ratio versus magnitude dimension. This was done because magnitude scaling methods are actually a type of ratio scaling method although they are carried out in a somewhat different manner.

TABLE 6–6   *Ten Basic Scaling Methods Determined According to Response Measure and Measurement Scale*

MEASUREMENT SCALE	RESPONSE MEASURE	
	Estimation	*Production*
Nominal ⟶	Category estimation	Category production
Ordinal ⟶	Ordinal estimation	Ordinal production
Interval ⟶	Interval estimation	Interval production
Ratio ⟶	Ratio estimation	Ratio production
	Magnitude estimation	Magnitude production

(Ratio methods require the subject to judge *ratios* between two or more presented stimuli, while magnitude methods require subjects to make *proportional* judgments to a set of stimuli. Often the term *category* is used interchangeably with the term *nominal*, because nominal scaling typically involves having the subject place stimuli in categories.

Examples of Scaling Procedures in Use

Nominal Estimation. Do teen-agers perceive statements in the same way parents do? To answer this question an investigator could employ a nominal (category) estimation scaling procedure. Teen-agers could be given a list of fifty statements (such as pick up your coat, help me mow the lawn, pass me the salt and pepper, be quiet, shut up, stop that) and asked to indicate whether each is one of four types of statements: an acceptable demand, an acceptable request, an unacceptable demand, or an unacceptable request. Parents could then be asked to do the same. Once the subjects in both groups have nominally scaled the statements, a statistical test (i.e., a chi-square test) could be run to see if parents and teen-agers differ on how they perceive such statements. (An example of category production would be to have the subjects make up statements fitting into each category.)

Magnitude Estimation. Magnitude estimation is one of the simplest and most widely used procedures for employing ratio scaling. Such a procedure was employed by Stevens and Guirao [1962], who were studying the perceived loudness of tones with college students. Each subject was told that a series of tones were going to be presented, and the task involved having the students assign numbers to each of the tones according to how loud each was. The subject could assign any number desired to the first tone. From tone 2 on they were to assign numbers proportionally to their subjective impression. For example, if the second tone sounded twice as loud as the first, they were to assign it a number two times as large as the number given to tone 1. If tone 3 sounded half as loud as tone 1, they were to assign the number $\frac{1}{2}$ to tone 3. Seven tones varying in intensity were presented twice to each of ten subjects. A mean was then calculated for the twenty judgments of each stimulus intensity and plotted on log-log coordinates.

Magnitude Production. Stevens and Guirao (1962) also employed a magnitude production scaling procedure. Using ten other students, they told them

> I am going to present a tone whose loudness will be called 10. Then I will present a series of numbers one at a time. Your task is to adjust the tone until its loudness seems to you proportionate to the numbers I give you, remembering that the first stimulus was called 10 . . . [Stevens and Guirao, 1962, p. 147].

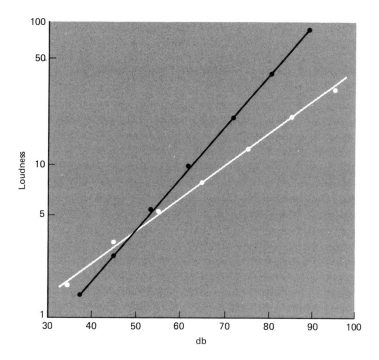

FIGURE 6–5 Loudness scales of a 1,000-Hz tone produced by the method of magnitude estimation (open circles) and the method of magnitude production (filled circles). Since the linearly spaced units on the abscissa refer to decibels, in terms of the physical stimulus itself they correspond to log coordinates. Consequently, in both scales loudness is a power function of stimulus intensity. (*Source:* SS. Stevens and M. Guirao. Loudness, reciprocality, and partition scales. *Journal of the Acoustical Society of America*, 1962, **34,** 1486–1471. Used by permission.)

The results of their investigation are plotted in Figure 6–5. It was apparent that the two scaling procedures can produce somewhat different results (although both obtained functions were power functions).

Insight
Hedonic Scaling-Comparing Response Rate to Value

H. L. Miller [1976] has employed a ratio production procedure to get pigeons to indicate the value they place on different types of foods (i.e., buckwheat, hemp, wheat). Keeping deprivation level and other secondary variables constant, it was found that pigeons will reliably respond at different rates for different foods. Which of these grains do pigeons most prefer? By comparing the value of pairs of grains via pigeons response rates (i.e., hemp vs. buckwheat, hemp vs. wheat, and wheat vs. buckwheat), Miller was able to determine that pigeons prefer wheat to buckwheat and wheat to hemp. The important finding of this study, however, was not that pigeons prefer one grain to another, but that through the use of ratio production Miller was able to use the ratio of responses during the first two choice conditions to accurately predict pigeons preferences for wheat and buckwheat in the final condition. At Brigham Young University, H. L. Miller and Bill Buskist employed the same ratio production on college students to scale Twinkies, chocolate cupcakes, and pecan rolls. Placing students in front of a multidoor vending machine in which the choices were visible, they intermittently reinforced the subjects for pulling on the three different doors in front of the three choices. From such experiments the investigators found out not only which of the three was most valued by the students, but also to what magnitude.

Ratio and interval scales allow an investigator to not only rank stimuli, but also determine the distance between each stimulus. Besides finding out which of two tones is louder, the investigator may also find out how much louder one is than the other. The goal of many psychologists is to be able to assign quantitative numbers to sensations and perceptions. Scaling is the means for doing this.

Insight
Stimulus Presentation Techniques Used with Scaling

There are three ways investigators commonly present stimuli to their subject. They may present all the stimuli to be scaled at the same time, or present them two at a time, or one at a time. When two stimuli to be compared are presented on each trial, it is called a *paired comparison* stimulus presentation procedure. When all the stimuli are presented simultaneously to the subject, the technique is referred to as *rank-order sealing*. Examples of each of these two techniques are illustrated with the use of an ordinal estimation procedure.

Paired Comparison

Which of the contestants is most talented? Which film did you enjoy most? In which situation are you most fearful? All these questions can be answered by randomly presenting pairs of stimuli to the subject and asking that one or the other be selected according to some attribute. Suppose a psychologist was interested in determining how prestigious people felt different occupations were. Seven occupations (milkman, store clerk, gas station attendant, plumber, carpenter, truckdriver, bricklayer) might be selected and presented two at a time, and the subject asked to indicate which of each pair presented is most prestigious. Each alternative is paired with every other alternative. The pairings are not presented in the sequence shown, but randomly. With seven stimuli, there are twenty-one pairings:

  milkman-store clerk
  milkman-gas station attendant
  milkman-plumber
  milkman-carpenter
  milkman-truck driver
  milkman-bricklayer
  store clerk-gas station attendant
  store clerk-plumber

store clerk-carpenter
store clerk-truck driver
store clerk-bricklayer
gas station attendant-plumber
gas station attendant-carpenter
gas station attendant-truck driver
gas station attendant-bricklayer
plumber-carpenter
plumber-truck driver
plumber-bricklayer
carpenter-truck driver
carpenter-bricklayer
truck driver-bricklayer

The investigator then records the number of times each alternative is chosen. Figure 6–6 shows how the data may look.

The result of a paired comparison procedure is a ranking of alternatives. Why might a psychologist want such a ranking? First, he or she might simply want to find out how a society might rank certain stimuli on some attribute. This would be considered simply a fact-finding or descriptive type of investigation. In such cases the investigator would present the findings as in Figure 6–6. The objective is not to analyze cause-effect relationships, only to report comparative findings. Second, two groups of subjects could be compared according to how they ranked the alternatives. How does ranking by children of different socioeconomic levels correlate with the rankings of their parents? This could give psychologists an idea as to whether attitudes are changing from one generation to the next. The statistical test employed to analyze such data is called the coefficient of consistence K. An example of such an analysis may be found in Ferguson [1973, pp. 228–231]. Third, the rankings may be used to determine the effectiveness of some IV. The government is now trying to influence more high school graduates to enroll in trade schools. To achieve this, several vocational films have been produced to influence the potential graduate's attitude about certain vocations. The effectiveness of these films can be determined by showing

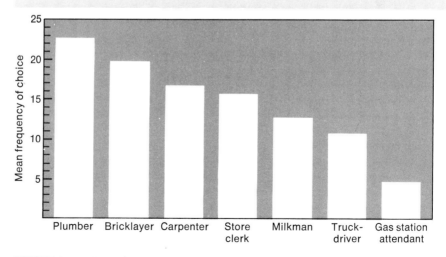

FIGURE 6–6   Paired comparison results.

them to one group and not another and then comparing the group rankings to see if they differ significantly. The paired comparison scaling technique, then, can be used to obtain three kinds of information: description of facts, analysis of trends, and cause-effect relationships.

Rank-Order Scaling

A third procedure for presenting stimuli according to some judgmental dimension is called the rank-order procedure. As might be expected from its name, its objective is the same as that of a paired comparison procedure. Both give an investigator a means of ranking stimuli on some dimension, but the way of obtaining the ranking differs. In the rank-order procedure a subject is presented with all the alternative stimuli at one time and asked to rank them from high to low or low to high according to some attribute. I once asked students in an introductory psychology class to rank five teaching procedures. They were given the following instructions:

> At the end of the course you will be given a final exam. The exam will be the only means by which you will be graded. Rank the following class procedures in terms of which you would prefer to be employed in this class for preparing you for the final exam. Rank them with 1 as your first choice.
>
> A. Lecture three times a week
> B. One lecture and two question-answer periods during the week
> C. Lecture twice a week with one no-count exam given each week
> D. No formal lectures; instructor just comes and answers questions
> E. No class held at all

The results tabulated for ten students are presented in Table 6–7. A graph similar to Figure 6–6 could also be drawn with the data in Table 6–7. The results of such an investigation are usually statistically analyzed using a rank correlational method called the coefficient of concordance. An illustration of the statistical com-

TABLE 6–7   *Illustrative Data from Rank-Ordering of Teaching Procedures*

SUBJECT NUMBER	TEACHING PROCEDURE				
	A	*B*	*C*	*D*	*E*
1	3	2	1	4	5
2	5	1	3	2	4
3	2	3	1	4	5
4	1	2	3	4	5
5	3	1	2	5	4
6	5	3	4	2	1
7	1	2	3	4	5
8	3	4	5	2	1
9	1	2	3	4	5
10	4	3	5	1	2
$X =$	28	23	30	32	37
Overall rank	2	1	3	4	5

putations required to calculate the coefficient of concordance may be found in Ferguson [1973, pp. 225–227].

Both paired comparison and rank-order procedures give the investigator a means of analyzing judgmental responses. These rankings do not indicate how much the subject prefers or judges one stimulus above the other; it simply puts them in order. Paired comparison scaling is generally more time consuming than rank-order, but the results are considered somewhat more reliable. Young children especially do better with paired comparisons where only two stimuli must be evaluated at a time.[3]

INTERVIEWS

The interview method of data collection involves a face-to-face situation in which the investigator (or an associate) extracts verbal responses from subjects by asking questions. It may be employed in both experimental and EPF investigations. There are three main purposes for employing interviews. First, the interview can be used as a probing device to identify variables and relationships of which an investigator may have no prior knowledge. Someone who has committed murder may be interviewed in an attempt to identify the psychological conditions under which that action occurred, or a psychologist may ask a child how he feels to get an idea of what is wrong. From comments of the child the psychologist may determine which variables should be dealt with to solve the child's behavioral problems. Second, it may be used as an information-gathering device in its own right for research purposes. Questions may have been selectively chosen to shed some light on a particular hypothesis or assumption. The responses of the subjects, for example, could be used as a measure of hostility or preference indicating personal bias. Third, it can be used as a checking system in conjunction with other research procedures. It is not uncommon for an investigator to obtain unexpected results from subjects. Rather than completely redesigning the experiment, the investigator may add an interview step with the subjects, asking why they did certain things or were they aware of certain things going on which they should not have been aware of.

Structured and Unstructured Interviews

Interviews may be grossly divided into two catetories—*structured* and *unstructured*. In a structured interview, the questions, their sequence, and their wording are fixed. This type of interview is generally carried out for the second of the three purposes—as a data-gathering device in its own

---

[3] A more in-depth coverage of scaling techniques may be found in the following texts: Underwood [1966, Chapter Six; good coverage with many examples], Dember [1963, Chapter Three], and Kling and Riggs [1971, Chapter Three].

right. Its function is to provide a psychometric measurement similar to an aptitude test on an attitude scale. A particular sequence of questions is asked dealing with an issue of interest to the investigator. The questions are arranged in such a manner that the responses will indicate the subject's position or ranking on some psychological dimension such as emotion, attention, apathy, or interest, Opinion polls are good examples of situations in which structured interviews are required.

The unstructured interview is generally used as a probing device. It is best illustrated by client-centered approaches used in the more applied clinical and counseling psychology situations. Although the interview is defined as being unstructured, the interviewer generally has some specific objectives in mind as she or he proceeds through the sessions. The questions, their sequence, and their wording are determined by the investigator, however, as the interview progresses. The additional flexibility allows the interviewer to let the responses of the subject being interviewed determine to a large extent the direction the interview may take. But the questions are asked in a manner intended to lead the respondent toward giving information related to the objectives of the investigation. Although the unstructured interview allows the investigator a great deal of latitude, preplanning of the basic interview format is still essential. Unstructured interviews are considered the optimal approach to data collection in situations in which the type of information sought is difficult for the subjects to express or is psychologically distressing. The flexibility of this type of data-collection procedure allows the investigator to modify the structure of the interview in progress.

Selection of Questions

Most structured interviews include three types of information: face sheet (identification) information, census-type or sociological information, and problem information [Parten, 1950, pp. 162–176]. Identification information refers to information, such as subject number, that identifies the subject being interviewed. In cases where different sequences of questions or different questions are used, identification information would also include which form was administered. Census information such as sex, age, education, income, and religious affiliation is also generally collected at the onset of the interview. The investigation usually involves measuring the correlation between this census information and the responses to the problem questions that are the main concern of the investigator. The questions concerning why the interview is being carried out make up what is called the problem information.

Structured interviews may be divided into two groups according to the types of problem questions employed: *fixed alternative* or *open-end* items. With fixed-alternative items the subjects are asked to respond by selecting one of several choices supplied. An example of a fixed-alternative item is this:

> Are you in favor of the President of the United States having unlimited powers in matters of international conflicts or war? (Yes/No)

Fixed-alternative interview questions have several advantages. They are more uniform in terms of measurement, have greater reliability, and are easier to score and compare. They are, however, more restrictive and may not provide a response the subject considers most appropriate. This problem may be dealt with in two ways. First, one of the choices given is "other." This allows the subject an alternative response that he or she feels appropriate. Second, the subject may be allowed to make a response in terms of a continuum; for example,

> Rate TV as an entertainment activity on a scale from 1 to 7 in which 1 represents very poor and 7 represents excellent.

Open-end interviews add an important dimension to data-collection procedures by putting a minimum of restraint on the subjects' answers. In many instances, this allows the investigator to get a better picture of the respondents' actual beliefs and attitudes. It also has a somewhat relaxing effect on the respondents by allowing them to put answers in their own words. A combination of fixed-alternative and open-end items is commonly used in educational research because such a format generally provides both more objectivity and more depth than is possible with either type alone.[1]

PSYCHOLOGICAL TESTS

Since one's abilities and mental capacity are potentials for behavior and are not directly observable, they are assessed indirectly with psychological tests. The idea of psychological tests is certainly not new to the reader; in fact, almost everyone has taken such tests at some point in life.

In the three previous sections we emphasized how stimuli were presented and how the response was measured when scaling, threshold, or interview methods are employed. This section emphasizes what types of measures can be obtained. The scores may be analyzed using the same analytical tools available when other similar types of measures are involved.

[1] A more in-depth coverage of how to conduct interviews may be found in Kerlinger [1973, Chapter Twenty-Eight provides an excellent and easy-to-understand coverage] and Kornhauser and Sheatsley [1959].

The important question an investigator contemplating the use of psychological tests needs to answer is, "Does the test measure what I want it to measure?" Psychological tests can measure such things as achievement, aptitude, and personality traits.

Types

Achievements Tests.   The most common type of psychological test given is the achievement test. Achievement tests are designed to measure what a person has actually learned, not what he or she is capable of learning (aptitude tests). Achievement tests may be divided into two categories: *standardized* and *unstandardized.* Standardized achievement tests are those that have been designed for and tested on a large number of subjects. In this way the scores on the achievement test can be interpreted in terms of how a particular subject rates according to the populace in general. Many standardized achievement tests are available to the investigator. Some are designed to measure knowledge of specific facts, whereas others attempt to measure the student's conceptual understanding and mastery of basic principles pertaining to the subject matter. Standardized achievement tests generally consist of a battery of tests. The California Achievement test (CAT), for example, contains tests in reading, language, and mathematics. The Sequential Tests of Educational Progress (STEP) include tests on essay writing, listening comprehension, reading comprehension, writing, science, mathematics, and social studies. The CAT takes only $1\frac{1}{2}$ hours to administer; the STEP requires 9 hours.

Unstandardized achievement tests are those that have not been given to a national sample. The tests given in college and other school classes at the end of the term are good examples of unstandardized achievement tests.

When selecting an achievement test for a research project, the investigator should first decide what areas of achievement are to be measured. Most investigations are designed to analyze only one area of achievement, so an investigator may select only one of the many test subsections in a battery. Achievement test batteries such as the CAT and the STEP were designed more for diagnostic reasons (e.g., to determine whether a student is behind in certain areas) than for research. Although unstandardized achivement tests are frequently used in research, standardized tests are generally considered better.

Aptitude Tests.   Whereas achievement tests are used to determine what a person knows now, aptitude tests are designed to predict how a person will do in the future. Aptitude tests, then, are used to determine one's potential abilities. How is it possible to determine one's future abilities? Because the person has not performed future actions yet, the aptitude test, like the achievement test, must be based on past actions and perform-ance. The questions in an aptitude test are actually samples of the person's past achievements. Since a person's ability to perform some future task depends to a large extent on present abilities, aptitude tests measure present abilities. A person's aptitude is usually measured by combining a number of different achievement measures.

Tests are available to measure all types of aptitudes, including artistic, musical, mechanical, physical, foreign language, and mathematical. Apti-tude tests that measure a wide range of abilities related to success in different occupations are also available. These are especially helpful in vocational counseling. The basic principle behind aptitude tests is the comparison of people's profiles (their scores on different categories of the test) with those of people who have previously been found to be successful. The General Aptitude Test Battery (GATB) measures a person's abilities in ten areas, including verbal aptitude, numerical aptitude, motor speed, and clerical perception.

Personality Tests.   There are a number of different types of personality tests that include personality inventories and projective tests. An inventory obtains information about personality by asking questions or requiring the person to respond to statements. Due to the fact that the questions employed in the inventory are direct, the subject can often guess the areas the investigator is attempting to measure. Personality inventories available to the investigator include the Minnesota Multiphasic Personality Inventory (MMPI) and the Objective Analytical Test Battery. These inventories are considered more appropriate for research because the objectives of the questions are not as easy to detect.

Projective personality tests were developed based on the idea that one's personality is projected into one's perceptions. The Rorschach Test, the Thematic Apperception Test (TAT), and the House-Tree-Person Test fit into this category. The advantage of projective tests over inventories is that the subject does not know what is expected. It is less likely that the subject can falsify responses, though it is still possible. By forcing the person to use imagination in responding to ink blots and pictures, or drawing particular objects, some psychologists believe they are forcing the subject to reveal the unconscious factors that make up her or his person-ality.

To illustrate the use of a projective test, let's look at the Rorschach. Ten ink blots in different shades of grey, black, or some other color are used. The subject is asked to describe what he or she "perceives" the ink blot to be. The scoring of the Rorschach is complex and difficult; examiners must undergo in-depth training to score the test properly. Different aspects of the subject's responses are interpreted to reveal different personality characteristics. The validity of this test, like other personality tests, varies to some extent according to the examiner.

Uses

There are two main uses of psychological tests in research. First, they may be used to assign subjects to groups. An investigator may be interested in trying a special training technique on underachievers, intellectually gifted children, or people with certain personality disorders. To obtain subjects, psychological tests need to be administered. Aptitude and personality tests are most frequently used for this purpose. Second, psychological tests can be used as DVs in investigations. Educational psychologists are constantly determining the effects of variables by means of psychological tests. What effect does social praise have on achievement? Do children learn better in groups? Can older people learn languages as easily as children? Questions such as these are investigated using psychological tests. As previously mentioned, achievement tests are the most common type of psychological test used in research as a DV measure. Though aptitude and personality tests may be used as DVs, they are more often used for subject selection.

There are three main purposes for psychological tests: prediction, diagnosis, and research. As might be expected, aptitude tests are more commonly used for predicting abilities than as a research tool. Personality tests are primarily concerned with diagnosis. They are designed to uncover the characteristics a person has.

When asked to carry out a class experiment, most undergraduates think first of dealing with a topic concerning people's abilities, aptitudes, or personality dimensions. To carry out such projects, the investigator has to be able to select and administer the appropriate psychological test. This is not a simple matter, for it requires the investigator to have a good understanding of the tests, plus special training in how to administer them and evaluate the results. Because the undergraduate investigator does not usually have these skills, psychological tests in class projects should be avoided unless there is someone available trained to select and administer them. The use of psychological tests is a sensitive issue in psychology at the present time, because most people do not understand what they are and how they can be misused. Even some practicing psychologists are guilty of inappropriately using psychological tests. In the next sections of this chapter we shall consider how psychological tests are devised and how easy it is to use them incorrectly.

Development

Psychological tests are frequently treated as if they were exact measures. These tests are designed to measure the mental abilities and processes of people, abilities and processes that are unobservable in their own right and therefore are only indirectly measured and inferred from related observable responses. A child's mathematical ability, for example, is determined according to how many mathematical problems she or he can solve. A college student's achievement in class is often defined according to the score obtained on the final exam.

Sometimes, however, the score on the final exam does not reflect a student's achievement. The student may know the material, but be unable to interpret the questions; or the questions may not represent a valid measure of what is supposed to be measured. For example, a final exam consisting of algebra problems would not enable a professor to get a valid measure of what a student knows about abnormal psychology. Once an instructor for a social psychology course apparently rummaged through test files and inadvertently selected a final exam designed for a course in personality. The mistake was not brought to his attention until the final exam period by students taking the exam. Much to his embarrassment, they were excused from taking a final exam because the only test available at that time would not have been a valid measure of what was discussed in the class.

How do psychologists go about developing valid psychological tests? This is a difficult problem and one that investigators should understand. There is no magic formula for selecting items for a test. The main ingredients for selection seem to be deductive reasoning plus large helpings of trial and error. Let us take a look at how the first successful intelligence test (a type of aptitude test) was developed.

In the early 1900s, the Paris school system was facing an important problem: How could it differentiate students needing special instruction from those who should go into the regular school system? What was needed was some measure of academic limitations and potential. In 1904, a commission whose members included Alfred Binet was formed to design methods for distinguishing between bright, average, and dull children. One reason Binet was chosen was because he had been actively involved in such projects for many years. He had his formal training as a lawyer and also had become a playwright. His interest in intelligence stimulated him to pursue a doctoral degree in psychology and to open the first psychology laboratory of the Sorbonne.

Binet's first attempts at devising an intelligence test included the analysis of handwriting and palm reading. Although these two approaches were unsuccessful, he continued testing as many factors as he could think of that might reflect intelligence. Using trial and error, he discarded methods that did not work and kept those that seemed to have possibilities. One of his problems in finding a measure of intelligence was the fact that the term had never really been defined. His job, then, also included defining intelligence. Binet never directly stated what his intelligence test was to measure, but he felt it needed to include three factors:

1. Direction: the ability to set up a goal and work toward it.
2. Adaptation: the ability to adapt oneself to the problem.
3. Self-evaluation: the ability to evaluate one's own performance.

The approach they finally came up with was to present various items and types of problems for the child to solve. The tasks in the test included (at the easiest levels) naming parts of the body and having the child select and hand objects to the examiner. Older children were asked such questions as which number was not in its correct position: 12, 9, 6, 3, 15. A more difficult task included verbally presenting seven digits (e.g., 8, 4, 5, 7, 2, 9, 1) and asking the examinees to repeat, in order, as many as they could. How were specific items determined to be representative of certain age abilities? Simple. If all children of age five, for example, could answer it, it was tested on six-year-olds, then seven-year-olds, and so on. Eventually, a test was developed that consisted of items for each age level from three through fifteen years.

How was a person's intelligence determined? After administering the test to a large sample of the population, norms were determined for the various physical ages. Binet proposed the term *mental age* (MA). A person's mental age was to be worth a certain number of months' credit of MA. The total MA score obtained by the person was then compared to the mean score obtained by people of the exact same chronological age (CA). If a six-year-old child has been tested and found to have an MA of 6, this information is used with the formula:

$$\frac{MA}{CA} \times 100 = IQ, \qquad \frac{6}{6} \times 100 = 100$$

A six-year-old with an IQ of 100 on the Binet test is said to be of average intelligence because he or she knows as much as the average six-year-old.

Misuse

Unfortunately, most psychological investigators are not psychometricians (experts on psychological tests). The results of investigations using such tests are often overgeneralized because the investigator is not as familiar with the test as he should be. One should keep in mind the fact that the results of psychological tests are open to interpretation. They are not hard physical facts. Rather, they are responses from which internal processes and abilities are inferred. Too often the results of such tests are used as "proof" of the presence of mental abilities or personality characteristics. The code of ethics urges psychologists to behave in a reasonable manner when interpreting test data. Some psychologists, however, act as if the results of such tests are completely valid and beyond question. An example of this problem was reported by Jeffry [1964] concerning the issue of whether a psychologist may be considered an expert witness in criminal cases involving insanity:

Psychologist A testified that she had administered the following tests to Kent: the Wechsler Memory Scale, the Bender-Gestalt, the Rorschach, the Thematic Apperception Test, the House-Tree-Person Test, and the Szondi Test. From this evidence she diagnosed the defendant as schizophrenic, chronic undifferentiated type, characterized by abnormal thoughts, difficulty with emotional control, deficient in common-sense judgement, and lacking in close relationships with other people. She considered these as indicative of psychosis and that the crimes of housebreaking, robbery, and rape, of which the defendant was accused, were products of the mental disease. The cross examination of the psychologist went as follows:

Q. What did the House-Tree-Person Test reveal?

A. The major finding was a feeling of withdrawal, running away from reality, feelings of rejection by women.

Q. And the results of the Szondi?

A. This showed a passive, depressed person who withdrew from the world of reality, with an inability to relate to others.

Q. Wasn't the Szondi Test made up around 1900, or the early 1900 period? And wasn't it made up of a number of pictures of Europeans who were acutely psychotic?

A. Yes, that is true.

Q. And this tells you something about his personality?

A. Yes, you can tell something about the person from his responses to the photos.

Q. And the House-Tree-Person Test—you handed the defendant, Kent, a pencil and a blank piece of paper, is that right, Doctor?

A. That is correct.

Q. And you asked him to draw a house?

A. Yes.

Q. And what did this tell you about Kent?

A. The absence of a door, and the bars on the windows, indicated he saw the house as a jail, not a home. Also you will notice it is a side view of the house; he was making it inaccessible.

Q. Isn't it normal to draw a side view of a house? You didn't ask him to draw a front view, did you?

A. No.

Q. And those bars on the window—could they have been Venetian blinds and not bars? Who called them bars, you or Kent?

A. I did.

Q. Did you ask him what they were?

A. No.

Q. What else did the drawing reveal about Kent?

A. The line in front of the house runs from left to right. This indicates a need for security.

Q. This line indicates insecurity! Could it also indicate the contour of the landscape, like a lawn or something?

A. This is not the interpretation I gave it.

Q. And the chimney—what does it indicate?

A. You will notice the chimney is dark. This indicates disturbed sexual feelings. The smoke indicates inner daydreaming.

Q. Did I understand you correctly? Did you say dark chimneys indicate disturbed sex feelings?

A. Yes.

Q. You then asked Kent to draw a tree. Why?

A. We have discovered that a person often expresses feelings about himself that are on a subconscious level when he draws a tree.

Q. And what does this drawing indicate about Kent's personality?

A. The defendant said it was a sequoia, 1500 years old, and that it was diseased. This indicates a feeling of self-depreciation. Also, the tree has no leaves and it leans to the left. This indicates a lack of contact with the outside world—the absence of leaves.

Q. Don't trees lose their leaves in winter, Doctor? If you look out the window now, in Washington, do you see leaves on the trees? Perhaps the defendant was drawing a picture of a tree without leaves, as they appear in the winter.

A. The important thing is, however, why did the defendant select this particular tree. He was stripped of leaves, of emotions.

Q. You then asked him to draw a person?

A. Yes.

Q. And he drew this picture of a male?

A. Yes.

Q. And what does this drawing indicate about Kent?

A. The man appears to be running. This indicates anxiety, agitation. He is running, you will notice, to the left. This indicates running away from the environment. If he had been running to the right this would indicate entering the environment.

Q. How about the hands?

A. The sharp fingers may indicate hostility.

Q. Anything else?

A. The head and the body appear to be separated by a dark collar, and the neck is long. This indicates a split between intellect and emotion. The dark hair, dark tie, dark shoes, and the dark buckle indicate anxiety about sexual problems.

Q. You then asked Kent to draw a person of the opposite sex. What did this picture indicate?

A. The dark piercing eyes indicated a feeling of rejection by women, hostility toward women.

Q. Are you familiar with the occasion upon which a Veteran's Administration psychologist gave this House-Tree-Person Test to 50 psychotics, and then gave 50 normal subjects the same test, and then a group of psychologists rated them?

A. No, I am not familiar with that research.

Psychologist B testified that he administered the Wechsler-Bellevue, the Graham Kendall, the Rorschach, and the Symonds Picture Story Tests. He also testified that he had diagnosed the defendant as schizophrenic, undifferentiated type, and that mental illness had produced the alleged crimes. The cross examination went as follows:

Q. Did you administer the Szondi Test, Doctor?

A. No, I don't happen to think much of it. The test assumes a schizophrenic looks a certain way, and we have evidence this isn't so.

Q. What responses did you receive from Kent on the Rorschach, the ink-blot test?

A. Wolf, butterfly, vagina, pelvis, bats, buttocks, etc.

Q. And from this you concluded the defendant was schizophrenic?

A. Yes, that and other things.

Q. You gave him the Wechsler Adult Scale?
A. Yes.
Q. On the word-information part of the test, the word "temperature" appears. What question did you ask the defendant?
A. At what temperature does water boil?
Q. You gave him a zero. Why?
A. Because he answered 190° and that is the wrong answer. The right answer is 212°F.
Q. What question did you ask about the Iliad?
A. I am not sure; I believe I asked him to identify the Iliad or who wrote the Iliad.
Q. And he answered "Aristotle?"
A. Yes.
Q. And you scored him zero?
A. That's correct.
Q. Now you asked the defendant to define blood vessels, did you not?
A. Yes.
Q. And his answer was capillaries and veins. You scored him zero. Why? Aren't capillaries and veins blood vessels?
A. I don't know. The norms don't consider the answer acceptable.

A third psychologist testified he saw the subject once at jail or the receiving home for an hour and a half, that he administered the Rorschach, and started the Human Figure Drawing Test. The testing was interrupted when the defendant's father was announced, and Kent became very upset, highly emotional.

He diagnosed the defendant as schizophrenic, undifferentiated type. He thought productivity existed; that is, the schizophrenia produced the house-breakings, robberies, and rapes. The test showed severe thinking disturbance, an inability to control impulses, and disturbed sexual feelings. His cross examination went as follows:

Q. Why did you see the defendant, Kent?
A. Because of a call from Mr. Arens.
Q. Are you a member of the Washington School of Psychiatry?
A. No.
Q. The defendant made one drawing for you, right, Doctor?
A. Yes that is right.
Q. After the announced arrival of his father?
A. Yes.
Q. Do you use the House-Tree-Person Test?
A. Never.
Q. Does it have validity?
A. Yes.
Q. You do use the Szondi?
A. Five or six times.
Q. When did you stop using it?
A. At the fifth administration, about nine years ago.
Q. What does this drawing that Kent made for another psychologist indicate to you?
A. The transparency of the picture—that is, seeing through the figure to something beneath—suggests pathology.

Q. Do you usually use an extensive battery of tests before reaching a diagnosis?

A. Yes.

Q. Do you usually arrive at the diagnosis on the basis of one Rorschach administered twice within an hour?

A. Frequently.

Q. What else in the drawing is significant psychologically?

A. The irregularity or sketchiness of the lines may suggest tension and anxiety. The attention paid to details—to the belt-bow-tie, and pockets—indicate a little-boy-like quality about the defendant.

Q. Is it significant that the figure is running to the left, and not to the right?

A. To some people, yes. I don't place any significance on it.[5]

Notice how the psychologists called as expert witnesses contradicted each other by claiming the results of the tests to be exact and above interpretation. An investigator should be especially careful when using psychological tests as DVs, particularly when personality tests are used. Most psychologists agree that achievement tests are usually more valid than aptitude tests, which are also more valid than personality tests. When conducting an investigation involving the use of a psychological test, the investigator should take special care to select the appropriate test. Because the validity of most aptitude and personality tests can be influenced by who administers them, a psychometrician should be used to give the tests.

APPLICATION OF DATA-COLLECTION METHODS

How are data-collection procedures employed? Psychologists emphasize the use of data-collection procedures for identifying cause and effect relationships so much that their other uses are often overlooked. Psychological tests, scaling methods, and threshold techniques have several important uses, four of which are presented here:

1. Descriptive research
2. Subject selection
3. Prediction
4. As DV measures

Descriptive Research.   What is the range of human hearing? Which athletic event is most popular in the United States? How many schoolchildren are hard of hearing? Research conducted to answer such questions is termed *descriptive* because its objective is to gather information that "describes" or reports the frequency of occurrence of some event. No cause-effect

---

[5] From Jeffry [1964, pp. 838–843]. Copyright 1964 by the American Psychological Association. Reprinted by permission.

relationship is sought in such projects, simply the presentation of information. Descriptive research is common in our society and includes political polls, attitude surveys, and marketing surveys. Almost every descriptive research investigation that deals with psychologically related factors involves the use of one of the data-collection methods presented in this chapter. Generally, descriptive research investigations are not considered appropriate as undergraduate class projects because they do not involve much in the way of data analysis.

Subject Selection.   Psychological tests, interviews, scaling methods, and threshold measurement techniques are frequently used by investigators to select subjects for research projects. What effect does high anxiety have on the ability to learn of mentally retarded, normal, and gifted children? Before applying an anxiety-provoking IV to mentally retarded, normal and gifted subjects, an investigator must have a means of identifying subjects who would fit in these categories. Psychological investigations frequently involve determining the differential effects of some IV on psychotic versus neurotic subjects, tone-deaf versus normal-hearing children, introvertive versus extrovertive subjects, and high achievers versus low achievers. The data-collection procedures previously discussed are used in such projects for selecting subjects to serve in the different groups. This use of data-collection techniques for subject-selection purposes is often overlooked in texts dealing with methods of data collection.

Prediction.   Data-collection procedures such as aptitude tests are often given in an effort to predict future behavior. Vocational aptitude tests are employed by counseling psychologists to help predict at which type of work a person could succeed. Scholastic aptitude tests are given to most students applying for admission to universities in an effort to predict their chances of success. The predictive aspect of data-collection procedures is used more by applied psychologists in dealing with patients than as a research tool.

Dependent Variable Measures.   Most psychological investigations involve the use of the data-collection procedures presented here as DV measures. The effects of different IVs may be determined by comparing the subject's responses with these methods. All psychological subfields, including physiological, social, perceptual, learning, and clinical psychology, employ these methods of data collection as DV measures. As previously mentioned, these methods all require the subject to make some sort of evaluative judgment. Whether attempting to identify an absolute threshold or applying a personality test, the investigator is indirectly trying to identify certain nonobservable capacities or mental abilities. In such situations, the psychologist needs to pay special attention to the issue of whether the data-collection method employed will give a valid measurement.

SUMMARY

Several data-collection methods are commonly used in psychological research. These include threshold measurement techniques, scaling techniques, interviews, and psychological tests. Threshold measures are employed to determine both absolute and differential thresholds and attempt to establish a *psychological function* (the relationship between a psychological variable such as perception and a physical variable such as intensity of a stimulus). Four procedures are frequently used to determine thresholds: the method of limits, method of constant stimuli, method of average error, and method of signal detection.

Scaling techniques are employed to compare subjects' behavior on a more qualitative than quantitative basis (e.g., better than, more prestigious). Ten procedures one may use for scaling psychological stimuli include category estimation, category production, ordinal estimation, ordinal production, interval estimation, interval production, ratio estimation, ratio production, magnitude estimation, and magnitude production.

Interview methods of data collection require the user to set up questions and interview in certain ways. Structured or unstructured interviews with fixed or open-end items can be used. Three types of information are gathered in each: identification, sociological, and problem information.

Several types of psychological tests were discussed, including achievement, aptitude, and personality tests. Achievement tests can be employed to determine what a person actually knows or can do. Aptitude tests are designed to measure potential ability. Personality tests are designed to measure personality characteristics and attributes. How well a psychological test validly measures what it reports to measure varies from one test to another. Generally, achievement tests are more valid than aptitude tests, which are more valid than personality tests.

There are four main uses of the data-collection methods presented here: for descriptive research, subject selection, prediction, and as DV measures.

I. Quasi-Experimental Designs
II. Correlational Designs
   A. Types of Correlational Techniques
   B. Application of Correlation
III. Contrast Designs
IV. Case Study Designs
V. Advantages and Disadvantages of Nonexperimental Designs
VI. Summary

Nonexperimental Designs

7

As mentioned in Chapter Three, not all psychological investigations are experimental. Although experimental designs are of central importance in psychology, there are nonexperimental designs a psychologist may also use, and the reader should be familiar with them. It would be unfortunate if the reader thought that experimentation was the only avenue of investigation the psychologist could choose. Pay special attention to the correlation section, for it tells how an investigator may try to determine the degree of relationship between variables rather than a cause-effect relationship.

Scientific investigation is almost always thought of as a process of finding lawful relationships between variables or parameters that one finds in nature. Because these relationships are often obscured by being too complicated or too numerous, the experimental method was devised to simplify and clarify systematically one variable's relationship to another. The experimental method involves direct experimenter manipulation of situations to create parameters and variables that can logically be related only in certain ways. Such active manipulation of what scientists call independent variables has proved to be a powerful tool in science. Although many psychologists carry on basic research to clarify some theoretical principle of psychology, most psychologists are involved in solving practical everyday problems. Should couples have children early or late in their married life? Can children live normal lives after being raised in a closet for years by disturbed parents? What causes people to commit suicide or murder? All these are practical problems for which society turns to psychologists for answers.

Unfortunately, however, psychologists are often asked questions that either should not, or cannot, be investigated by experimental manipulation. It would be unethical, for instance, for a psychologist to manipulate a situation to create all the parameters and variables he or she believes would produce a murder and then wait to see if a murder occurs. Some experiments are physically impossible to carry out. One requiring an earthquake to study the effects of stress in an emergency situation would be impossible (as well as unethical) for a psychologist to arrange. Another kind of impossible experiment would be one in which a psychologist would have to travel back in time to change a variable here and there so that the present situation could be more readily clarified.

It is possible to carry out a scientific investigation without manipulating an IV. Relationships can be found between events without such manipulation. Ex post facto investigations allow an investigator to gather information without manipulating an IV. These investigations are just as sound as experimental investigations, but less powerful in terms of identifying causal relationships. The objective of nonexperimental investigations is to provide an appropriate way of analyzing problems not amenable to experimental investigation.

Nonexperimental designs can be divided into four categories:

1. Quasi-experimental designs
2. Correlational designs
3. Contrast designs
4. Case study designs

QUASI-EXPERIMENTAL DESIGNS

An EPF quasi-experiment is carried out exactly like a true experiment, except for two important variations. First, the investigator does not have the ability to assign subjects randomly to either the control or experimental groups. Rather than actively arranging an experimental situation consisting of a control and an experimental group, the investigator searches for a group of subjects that has been exposed to the particular IV of interest, and a second group, similar to the first in other relevant respects, that has not experienced the IV. Being unable to select subjects randomly greatly increases the possibility that secondary variables may contaminate the investigation. Suppose, for example, you wanted to see if giving elementary school children grades increases achievement. Using a quasi-experimental approach, you find two classes, one in which grades are given and one in which grades are not given. You then compare the two classes on an achievement test given to both at the end of their last year. Because you did not randomly select your subjects and set up your groups, the differences could be due to IQ, socioeconomic level, home training practices, and many other important secondary variables.

Second, the investigator cannot apply the IV whenever and to whomever she or he wishes. This also decreases the ability to draw a valid causal relationship. With these two variations restricting the control of secondary variables in quasi-experimental approaches, the investigator must rely more heavily on the control technique of constancy and exert more effort in trying to match groups on important secondary variables. The better the matching of groups on relevant secondary variables, the closer a quasi-experimental approach comes to being as good as a true experiment in identifying cause and effect relationships.

A good example of an EPF quasi-experiment was carried out in 1961 by Jo Taylor Auld. For years a controversy had been brewing over whether students within a class should be grouped according to ability and worked with by the teacher in this manner, or whether the teacher should work with the whole class as one unit. Auld's study set out to determine whether grouping or nongrouping was more effective. She searched until she found two schools, one that grouped its students and one that did not, which were identical in terms of relevant secondary variables. Two elementary schools in South Carolina were used in the study. The neighborhoods served by the two schools were alike in terms of housing, community facilities, churches, and so on. The numbers and experience of the teachers from both schools were approximately the same. The classroom, library, and recreational facilities of the two schools were similar. Being in the same school district, the schools operated under the same policies and followed the same testing procedures.

In terms of socioeconomic status, the families were much alike for the two schools, although more fathers associated with the nongrouped school were engaged in professional occupations and slightly more mothers with children in the grouped school were employed outside the home. The median IQ of the children in the grouped school (school A) was 107; the median for the nongrouped school (school B) was 110. Fifth-grade students at school A had been divided into three intraclass groups, high, average, and low, after their first grade. They had been worked with in these groups for grades two through five. Auld than obtained the first-grade records of the fifth-grade students at school B and categorized those students into three groups, high, average, and low, in the same manner that they would have been grouped for instructional purposes if they had been enrolled in school A.

Auld thus established equivalent groups in the two schools and compared the two classes on the results of the Metropolitan Achievement Test given to all students of both schools at the end of their fifth-grade year. The results she obtained from the study were that (1) there were no statistically significant differences in performance of the students in schools A and B who were in the high and average categories; and (2) students in the low category from the ungrouped school (school B) achieved significantly higher than the low group students from school A.

Notice that the purpose of the EPF quasi-experiment is the same as that of a true experiment—to isolate a cause-effect relationship. The initial steps involved in an EPF quasi-experiment are essentially the same as those employed with experimental designs. First, a problem must be identified and a hypothesis spelled out in detailed and specific terms. The IV and DV are defined, and relevant secondary variables are identified. Random assignment of subjects to groups is not possible with EPF quasi-experiments and is therefore a handicap in control of secondary variables. The investigators are not able to apply the IV to whomever they please in this situation, and that also increases the possibility that the study may be internally invalid. The investigator is limited as well because he or she often must rely on past records whose thoroughness and accuracy are unknown and because he or she had no control over the measuring of the DV. The statistical tests involved in analyzing the data are the same as those used to deal with data in true experiments.[1] The investigator cannot have as much confidence in drawing conclusions with EPF quasi-experimental designs because some of the assumptions (e.g., randomization) underlying the statistical tests have been violated, and the investigator had less control over secondary variables. With the exception of randomization, all the control techniques available for large-N experimental designs are also available to the EPF quasi-experiment, including statistical control. It is even possible to perform an analysis of covariance on the data of such investigations, as long as a covariate measure is available.[2]

EPF quasi-experimental investigations do have some advantages over experimental investigations. It is possible to seek answers to certain kinds of questions about past or unethical situations that could not be dealt with using experimental designs. Time can be saved by dealing with records that have been kept over the years rather than starting fresh. School, educational, social, and industrial psychologists may especially benefit from using EPF quasi-experimental investigations because schools, businesses, and government agencies generally secure and preserve records over many years.

CORRELATIONAL DESIGNS

Psychologists are constantly confronted with situations in which they are required to determine whether two or more variables are related in any way. Is the success of a person in later life related to the type of family training received as a child? Is cigarette smoking related to lung cancer?

---

[1] No statistical example is given here because the statistical procedure is carried out exactly as in a true experiment. If the reader wishes an example to follow in calculating data, turn to the chapter that presents the type of design used (e.g., two-group, one-way ANOVAR, etc.) and follow the steps shown there.

[2] The statistical analyses used on quasi-experimental designs are discussed more specifically in the experimental design chapters to follow because they are employed in exactly the same manner in both experimental and quasi-experimental situations.

Are there any particular behaviors a person contemplating suicide emits prior to committing the act that might warn us of the impending plan? In such cases the psychologist takes measures of each of the variables in question and correlates their presence or absence in given situations. These types of investigations are called correlational studies, and they include all research projects in which an attempt is made to discover or clarify relationships using correlational statistical methods. Experimental research compares different groups of subjects in which an IV is either present or absent; correlational studies usually compare members of a single group in which the variables under scrutiny are present in varying degrees.

The basic design of correlational research is quite simple, involving nothing more than the collecting of two or more scores on the same group of subjects and computing a correlation coefficient from those scores. The objective of a correlational statistic is to index the degree of covariation that can exist between two variables. It may be seen by observation that when variable X increases, variable Y generally increases also, and some measure is needed to index the relationship that might exist between X and Y. By manipulating the data it can be shown, and proved mathematically, that the sum of the cross products between variable X and Y, XY, becomes larger when the variables are compared in order of magnitude than when they are not. For example, if $X = (3, 2, 1)$ and $Y = (2, 1, 0)$, then $\Sigma XY = 6 + 2 + 0 = 8$. Now, if the order of magnitude is changed, $X = (3, 2, 1)$ and $Y = (1, 2, 0)$, then $\Sigma XY = 3 + 4 + 0 = 7$; or, if X (3, 2, 1) and $Y = (0, 2, 1)$, $\Sigma XY = 0 + 4 + 1 = 5$. This example shows that ΣXY increases with the increase in covariation between X and Y, reaching a maximum when X and Y are in corresponding order. Using this mathematical relationship, researchers have devised statistical methods for determining how closely the variations in one variable are related to variations in a second variable. To illustrate how this is done, let us take a look at a situation that arose several years ago.

Is the amount of time a student studies related to the scores received on a class exam? A psychology major enrolled in a senior seminar was not sure a strong relationship existed between these two variables and asked if she might carry out an investigation. Such an investigation would require the investigator to have control over the materials to be studied for the class, so it was not carried out until the next semester, when ten students enrolled in another senior seminar. At the beginning of the class the students were told that the material to be covered in the class was not available in text form and could not be purchased. Copies of the material would be available, however, in the reserve section of the library and could be checked out and used only in the reserve room of the library. They were told to do all the studying for the class in that room, and they were to sign in and out of the room so that a measure of the amount of studying they did could be kept. The amount of time each student studied during the semester was recorded in number of hours and the total number of points earned on the four 50-point exams given during the term was also recorded. Table 7–1 shows the results of the investigation.

A number of statistical methods are available for determining a correlation. The best-known correlational coefficient measure is the Pearson r correlation, which was chosen to analyze the data obtained here. The exact steps involved in calculating the correlation are presented so that the reader may follow them exactly if interested in carrying out a correlational analysis.

The computational formula for calculating a Pearson r correlation coefficient is

$$r = \frac{N \Sigma XY - (\Sigma X)(\Sigma Y)}{\sqrt{[N \Sigma X^2 - (\Sigma X)^2][N \Sigma Y^2 - (\Sigma Y)^2]}}$$

The next step is to calculate all the numbers (N, XY, X, Y, and so on) required in the formula. This is done in Table 7–2. With these figures calculated, one simply plugs them into the formula to come up with the correlation coefficient.

The size of a Pearson r correlation coefficient that a person may obtain from data ranges from $+1$ through 0 to -1. The two important aspects of the correlation coefficient are its numerical size and its sign value. The larger the number, the stronger the relationship between the two variables. A correlation of 1.0 indicates a perfect relationship between the variables. A perfect relationship means one can exactly predict the numerical value of X, for example, if Y is known. A zero correlation means one cannot predict what X is if Y is known. The sign value indicates whether the relationship found is *directly* or *inversely* related. Figure 7–1

TABLE 7–1   *Results of Study Time Investigation*

SUBJECT NUMBER	NUMBER OF HOURS STUDYING (X)	TOTAL NUMBER OF TERM POINTS EARNED (Y)
1	88	18
2	60	16
3	76	21
4	68	18
5	56	12
6	180	36
7	76	12
8	104	16
9	140	47
10	192	32

TABLE 7-2 *Calculation of a Pearson r Correlation*

SUBJECT NUMBER	X	X^2	Y	Y^2	XY
1	88	7,744	18	324	1,584
2	60	3,600	16	256	960
3	76	5,776	21	441	1,596
4	68	4,624	18	324	1,224
5	56	3,136	12	144	672
6	180	32,400	36	1,296	6,480
7	76	5,776	12	144	912
8	104	10,816	16	256	1,664
9	140	19,600	47	2,209	6,580
10	192	36,864	32	1,024	6,144
$N = 10$	$\Sigma X = 1{,}040$	$\Sigma X^2 = 130{,}336$	$\Sigma Y = 228$	$\Sigma Y^2 = 6{,}418$	$\Sigma XY = 27{,}816$

$$r = \frac{(10)(27{,}816) - (1{,}040)(228)}{\sqrt{[10(130{,}336) - (1{,}040)^2][10(6{,}418) - (228)^2]}}$$

$$= \frac{278{,}160 - 237{,}120}{\sqrt{(1{,}303{,}360 - 1{,}081{,}600)(64{,}180 - 51{,}984)}}$$

$$= \frac{41{,}040}{\sqrt{(221{,}760)(12{,}196)}}$$

$$= 0.79$$

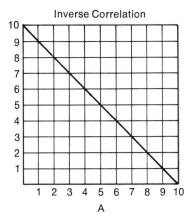
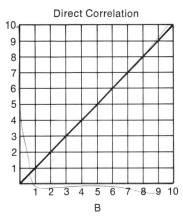

FIGURE 7–1   An inverse and a direct relationship.

gives an example of both an inverse and a direct relationship that has a numerical value of 1.0. If we had obtained a −1.0 from our data (as shown in A), it would mean that the person studying the fewest hours would score highest on the exams, the second least studier would do second best, and so on right on down the line for the rest of the students.

A direct correlation of +1.0 (represented by B) would again mean that there was a perfect correlation between studying and exam scores, but in this case it would show the person studying the most would do best on the exam, and so on down the list of subjects. The +0.79 obtained indicates that study time is highly correlated with achievement on exams, but not perfectly so. It tells us that, if we knew how much a particular student studied in relation to classmates, we could predict pretty closely how the student will do in the course in comparison with the other students.

Correlational studies can and have been used to investigate almost the entire range of problems of psychological interest. Matheson, Bruce, and Beauchamp [1970] give a brief illustration of the range of correlational studies by listing several investigations in various areas of interest. They list correlational studies used to show that there are fewer erotic inscriptions (graffiti) in women's rest rooms than in men's (the difference was less in the Philippines than in the United States); that crackdowns on speeding did not result in any significant decrease in the number of traffic fatalities; and that scare promotional ads for seat belts had less effect than an ad featuring a professional race driver appealing to masculinity. Another area of interest that has been studied using the correlational method is the relationship between Down's syndrome (Mongolism) and the age of the mother giving birth to the retarded child. It has been known for some time that the risk of having a Mongoloid child varies greatly with the age of the mother. The chance of a mother between the ages of fifteen and twenty-four having a Mongoloid child is only one in 1,500 births, but for a woman older than forty-five, the risk is one in 35 births [Robinson and Robinson, 1970]. Collmann and Stroller [1962] investigated the rates of Mongolism in Melbourne, Australia, for many years and found an exponential relationship between age and rate of Down's syndrome. The correlation between the two variables was almost perfect.

It should be noted that although the correlational method points out a relationship between two variables, it does not specify the cause of the relationship. Is age of the mother the "cause" of Mongoloid births? Later studies have shown that Down's syndrome is the result of a chromosome abnormality—in fact, two abnormalities. In younger women it is usually a hereditary abnormal chromosome, but with older women the abnormality is usually the result of a failure of meiosis, and the condition is not hereditary. Is, then, the "cause" of the abnormality the age of the woman? Stroller and Collmann [1965] did a later study and found a correlation of 0.81 for the incidence of Mongoloids per 100,000 live births and those of infective hepatitis per million cases. They then postulated that the virus-human interaction could well be the basis of the genetic abnormality. Recent data indicate that this may not yet be the full answer; first-born children of older mothers do not have the same chance of being retarded by Down's syndrome as do later siblings. The studies of Mongolism and mother age offer an excellent example of what a correlational study can and cannot do. The method readily shows if a relationship exists between variables and the strength and direction of the relationship, but it does not show the cause of the relationship.

Although correlation does not technically show that one variable causes the occurrence of another, psychologists often treat correlation as if it does. With human subjects, for example, past records have been analyzed and have shown a high correlation between certain people being dead and the presence of arsenic in their gastrointestinal tract. Although law enforcement agencies have not carried out experiments to show a cause and effect relationship, most conclude such is the case. In the past, correlational studies showing a high relationship between cigarette smoking and lung cancer have been used to indicate cigarette smoking causes cancer.

On the other hand, there are many instances in which high correlations are found between variables, yet psychologists would not conclude causal relationships. There is, for example, a very high correlation between foot size and academic achievement. If a person would take into consideration people of all ages (from birth to adulthood) and calculate the correlation coefficient between foot size and achievement, a high correlation would be obtained. No cause relationship could be drawn, however. When is it permissible to draw conclusions about a cause-effect relationship using correlation? Generally, a correlational study is not considered sufficient for drawing causal inferences. If, however, there are other types of supportive data that agree with the correlational findings, then correlational results are more acceptable when making such suggestions. Studies that correlate smoking with the incidence of lung cancer in humans are more accepted as showing cause-effect relationships because experiments on nonhuman species support such conclusions. Correlational investigations are not generally considered a proper type of investigation if one is seeking to find causes, unless the problem is not amenable to experimental manipulation. In such cases it may be permissible to use correlation to imply causation.

Types of Correlational Techniques

In the last chapter the reader was introduced to the idea that there were four basic types of measurement scales one could employ when conducting psychophysical scaling research. Actually, the role of measurement scales in science transcends its use in psychophysical scaling. As stated earlier, measurement scales are the assignment of numbers to any object or event along some dimension; and this is done in many scientific areas. The four measurement scales (nominal, ordinal, interval, and ratio) are considered basic number scales, which form the basis of all statistical manipulations. They are the four main ways scientists go about relating variables. With this in mind, it seems only natural that psychologists would have devised correlational techniques for each of the four types of measurement scales. And they have. Keep in mind, however, that a correlation is the relationship between *two* (or more) variables. Therefore, psychologists had to take into consideration the idea that an investigator may in fact try to "relate" some variable measured in terms of one measurement scale (e.g., nominal) with a variable measured in terms of a different measurement scale (e.g., interval). Table 7–3 lists nine correlational techniques commonly used in psychology. It also indicates the types of measurement scales the particular correlational technique is designed to handle, along with an indication as to when and where it may be employed. To better understand how different correlational techniques actually calculate correlation coefficients, let us look at how a Spearman rho and point-biserial correlation is calculated.

Spearman Rank-Difference Correlation (rho).   Suppose we took the data from Table 7–1 concerning a subject's hours of studying and term points earned and changed the subject data to ranked (ordinal) information rather than ratio information. We could still calculate a correlation coefficient by using a correlational technique designed to handle two variables measured ordinally rather than with a ratio measurement scale. The Spearman rank-difference correlational technique is specifically designed to do this.

TABLE 7–3 *Appropriate Correlational Techniques For Different Forms of Variables*[1,2]

TECHNIQUE	SYMBOL	VARIABLE 1	VARIABLE 2	REMARKS
Product-moment correlation	r	Continuous	Continuous	The most stable technique
Rank-difference correlation (rho)	ρ	Ranks	Ranks	Often used instead of product-moment when number of cases is under 30
Kendall's tau	τ	Ranks	Ranks	Preferable to rho for numbers under 10
Biserial correlation	r_{bis}	Artificial dichotomy	Continuous	Sometimes exceeds 1; has a larger standard error than r; commonly used in item analysis
Widespread biserial correlation	r_{wbis}	Widespread artificial dichotomy	Continuous	Used when you are especially interested in persons at the extremes on the dichotomized variable
Point-biserial correlation	r_{pbis}	True dichotomy	Continuous	Yields a lower correlation than r and much lower than r_{bis}
Tetrachoric correlation	r_t	Artificial dichotomy	Artificial dichotomy	Used when both variables can be split at critical points
Phi coefficient	ϕ	True dichotomy	True dichotomy	Used in calculating interitem correlations on multiple choice or two choice items
Contingency coefficient	C	Two or more categories	Two or more categories	Comparable to r_t under certain conditions; closely related to chi square

[1] Borg, Walter R., *Educational Research: An Introduction*, David McKay Co., New York, 1963, p. 157. By permission.
[2] Concerning the Variable 1 and Variable 2 categories, a *continuous* variable is one representing an underlying continuum tending to be normally distributed. Examples include such variables as height, weight, and ability or achievement as measured by standardized tests. *Artificial dichotomies* can be constructed by arbitrarily dividing continuous variables into two groups,

TABLE 7–4   *Illustration of the Use of a Rank Order Correlation Technique (Spearman Rho)*

SUBJECT NUMBER	NUMBER OF HOURS STUDYING (X)	TOTAL NUMBER OF TERM POINTS EARNED (Y)	RANK X	RANK Y	DIFFERENCE d	DIFFERENCE d^2
1	192	32	1	3	-2	4
2	180	36	2	2	0	0
3	140	47	3	1	2	4
4	104	16	4	7	-3	9
5	88	19	5	5	0	0
6	76	21	6	4	2	4
7	75	12	7	9	-2	4
8	68	18	8	6	2	4
9	60	15	9	8	1	1
10	56	11	10	10	0	0

$$\Sigma\, d^2 = 30$$

$$\rho = 1 - \frac{6\,\Sigma\, d^2}{N(N^2 - 1)} = 1 - \frac{(6)(30)}{10(100 - 1)} \qquad \Sigma\, d^2 = 30$$

$$= 1 - \frac{180}{990}$$

$$= 1 - 0.18$$

$$= 0.82$$

Table 7–4 shows the original data, its conversion to an ordinal measurement, and the analysis.

Generally speaking psychologists would not convert interval data into ordinal data. It has been done in this situation simply to show how a Spearman Rho correlation coefficient is calculated. Typically the investigator would only have the rank (X and Y column) data when using a Spearman Rho correlational approach. From the analysis done here the investigator would conclude there is a .82 Spearman Rho correlation between study hours and term points earned.

usually about the center of the data. Examples include such classifications as achiever-nonachiever, above average-below average, pass-fail, and warm-cold on an attitude scale. *True dichotomies* involve relatively clear-cut (though not necessarily absolute) differences, allowing the data to be categorized into two groups. Examples include such dichotomies as male-female, living-dead, teacher-nonteacher, dropout-nondropout, and smoker-nonsmoker. Other variables that can be treated *as if* they were true dichotomies for the purposes of computing, for example, a point-biserial correlation coefficient, include color blind-noncolor blind, alcoholic-nonalcoholic, and right-wrong responses with respect to a particular test item in item analysis (see example, page 192). The distributions underlying true dichotomies, if not absolute differences, tend to be bimodal and/or relatively discontinuous. For a more complete discussion of these problems, see the references cited previously.

Point Biserial Correlation. As indicated in Table 7–3, the point-biserial correlation technique is designed to determine the relationship between two variables, one that is continuous (on a ratio or interval scale) and one that is on a nominal scale, in this case having only two possible categories. Suppose a certain psychological test was being devised to help psychologists detect whether a person was "psychotic" or "normal." The test could be administered to both psychotic and normal individuals. A point biserial correlation coefficient could be calculated to determine how well scores on the test relate to a person being psychotic or normal. Table 7–5 presents hypothetical data on fifteen subjects, and shows how the point biserial correlation coefficient (r_{pbis}) is calculated, using the following formula:

$$r_{pbis} = \frac{\overline{X}_p - \overline{X}_q}{S_t} \sqrt{pq}$$

where S_t = standard deviation of all scores on the continuous variable defined as $\sqrt{\Sigma (X - \overline{X})^2 / N}$

p and q = proportions of individuals in the two categories of the nominal variable

$\overline{X}_p$ and $\overline{X}_q$ = mean scores on the continuous variable of the individuals within the two categories

TABLE 7–5   *Calculation of Point Biserial Correlation Coefficient (r_{pbis})*

SUBJECT NUMBER	TEST SCORE	CLINICAL DESCRIPTION
1	7	Normal
2	9	Psychotic
3	9	Normal
4	12	Normal
5	17	Psychotic
6	26	Normal
7	28	Normal
8	32	Psychotic
9	32	Psychotic
10	40	Normal
11	45	Normal
12	51	Psychotic
13	57	Psychotic
14	69	Psychotic
15	70	Psychotic

Mean score for psychotics: $\overline{X}_p$ = 42.13
Mean score for normals: $\overline{X}_q$ = 25.29
S_t = 20.59, p = 8/15 = 0.533 q = 7/15 = 0.467

$$r_{pbis} = \frac{42.13 - 25.29}{20.59} \sqrt{0.533 \times 0.467} = 0.41$$

From the previous analysis it would be concluded that there is a .41 point biserial correlation between a person's test score and whether he or she is psychotic or normal.

Insight
Historical Look at Correlation

When considering the applications of correlation, it is important to keep in mind what correlation is. Recall from Chapter Two that application of correlational techniques to psychological research came about 50 years before the development of large-*N* experimental designs with their statistical tests. By combining certain mathematical concepts (developed by Adolph Quetelet) with recorded observations, Francis Galton devised a way of determining to what extent two (or more) variables were related. Galton's correlational methods were quantitative methods, which gave some idea of interdependence between two variables. In 1869, Galton published *Hereditary Genius*, a biographical study of the tendency of genius to run in family lines. He pointed out that eminent men tend to have had eminent fathers. His conclusion was that, due to the high correlation between intelligent offspring and intelligent parents, intelligence was determined by heredity. Somewhat infatuated with the idea that mathematical values relating variables could be reliably obtained using correlational techniques he devised, Galton spent a major portion of his career calculating the correlation between objects and events such as height, weight, and mental abilities. All psychological research efforts involving correlational techniques collectively became known as individual psychology.

During the formative years of individual psychology, the idea began to develop that by studying the relationship between variables, one can determine cause-and-effect relationships. This belief that causality could be identified with correlation was based on the work of John Stuart Mill, who in 1843 published a book entitled *Logic*, which pointed out several logical ways a scientist could determine causal relations. One of the ways mentioned by Mills was the method of *concomitant variation*. Basically, the idea of concomitant variation is that it is possible to conclude variable A causes fluctuations in variable B if variable B is found to fluctuate when variable A fluctuates. Some experimental critics, however, argued that correlation could not be used to determine causality because observations of concomitant variation could not tell the investigator whether variable A caused variable B to fluctuate or whether variable B caused changes in variable A. The time relationship of two correlated variables, according to the critics, could not be determined through correlation. Therefore, correlation could only indicate the degree relationship, if any, not cause.

A second and well-founded argument against the use of correlation to determine causality was based on the idea that many relationships between variables are obviously not causal. For example, over the last 40 years there has been an increase in both juvenile delinquency and the amount of fresh vegetables used in our society. Also with the rise in delinquency is a correlated rise in the number of bathrooms in houses. Do fresh vegetables or bathroom usage cause delinquency? The answer to this question is obvious.

One of the main retorts by psychologists employing correlational methods was that the "experimental" methods of that day were no better than the correlational approach in identifying causes. Keep in mind that at this time the use of control groups, randomization, and statistical tests were not part of experimentation. With the absence of an internally verifiable experimental paradigm for determining causes, many social scientists could see possibilities in trying the quantitative correlational approach to identify causes.

As the Fisherian large-*N* experimental approach came about in the 1920s, stronger stances against the correlational approach to causation were taken (e.g., Burt, 1940, argued against such use of correlation). With the refinement of such research areas as survey analysis and factor analysis, however, there has been a resurgence in the idea that there are times when correlation may be used to study causes (e.g., Eysenck, 1953; Rosenberg, 1968; Rosenthal and Rosnow, 1975).

Application of Correlation

There are several ways correlation is presently being used in psychological research. Some of these require the user to be relatively sophisticated in statistical techniques. Correlational analyses play such an important role in psychological investigations that it is unfortunate space does not allow a more complete coverage in this book. The interested reader can get a more in-depth understanding of correlation from the many books and courses devoted exclusively to that topic.

Basically, correlational analysis finds application in four main types of research. First, it is employed in dealing with causality problems when experimental methods are inappropriate. Second, it may be used in a descriptive and predictive capacity. For example, personality traits and sociological characteristics associated with suicide cannot be studied with the experimental approach. After a person commits suicide, the researcher can only look at the historical records of the person's life, ex post facto. An example is offered by a study of suicide performed by Sainsbury and Barraclough [1968]. They found that the suicide rates in 1959 of foreign-born U.S. citizens correlated 0.87 with the suicide rates in their country of birth. You could predict, given the suicide rates of their native lands, which of two immigrants was more likely to commit suicide. (Austrian immigrants, for example, were more likely to commit suicide than a person from Mexico.)

A third application of correlation is to control for secondary variables by means of the statistical control method. The analysis of covariance suggested earlier as a statistical control technique for removing the influence of some unwanted variable from the data is nothing more than a statistical formula made up by combining the principle of analysis of variance (V_B V_W) with correlational principles (Σ XY). This has been a useful tool for research, mainly because it allows the investigator to adjust for secondary variables after an experiment is completed.[3]

The fourth application of correlation relates to the issues of reliability and validity. The correlational method is an excellent way to check on how close judges are in their ratings, one with another. For example, the coefficient gives a measure of how much alike two different judges rated or ranked some variable in an experimental situation. Such data can add to the internal validity of an investigation. This is an especially important concept in field research, where the DV is often measured by some observer rather than by a mechanical recorder in a laboratory. Suppose you wanted to study the effects of reinforcement on cooperative play. The DV would be cooperative play, a somewhat subjective term. A more objective, and reliable, measure of cooperative play could be obtained by first operationally defining what the term meant (e.g., playing in a game involving more than two children), and then having three or more observers, rather than one, record the DV. Later, the observers' records would be analyzed to see how well their judgments of cooperative play correlated.

CONTRAST DESIGNS

Like correlational designs, the contrast, or comparative, design, as it is sometimes called, may be a substitute for experimentation. It is used primarily in the analysis of historical data, the number of cases of which are too small to permit meaningful statistical manipulation. The contrast design is often required in the comparative analysis of national units, which of course are few in number, or when comparing regions, cities, and other subnational units. Warwick and Osherson [1973] illustrate the method with a contrast study of suicide reported by Durkheim. One of Durkheim's central findings was that Protestants have higher suicide rates than do Catholics. The variable he used to explain the finding was the difference in the tenets and traditions of the two religions. Durkheim noticed, however, that in every country from which he investigated the data, Catholics constituted a minority group. Could it be, he asked, that the difference in suicide rates was due to minority status rather than to religion? To answer this question, Durkheim expanded his study to include regions such as Austria and Bavaria, where Catholics are a majority. In such regions he noted some diminution of the religious differences between Catholics and Protestants, but the Catholic rates were still lower. Durkheim was then able to conclude that the lower suicide rate of Catholics as compared to Protestants was not solely a matter of minority status. Durkheim used no statistical methods, yet he was able to approximate

---

[3] The way in which correlation is used, combined with the analysis of variance to statistically control secondary variables, is treated in detail in Chapter Ten.

their use by means of a systematic contrast between one group and another.

The task of any investigator is to reduce the number of conditions that can influence the DV, isolate one condition from another, and make precise the role of each condition. Contrasting one group with another is necessary to accomplish this when the groups are small and statistical analysis is inappropriate. In sociology and developmental psychology, the effects of family size can be determined by contrasting the behavior and development of children from small families with those from large ones. Such studies have isolated differences from dependency behavior in nursery school to adult alcoholism rates. For example, children from small families have a higher activity level and seem to be more poised and self-confident with adults than do children from large families [Johnson and Medinnus, 1969].

The contrast design finds particular application in anthropologically oriented psychological studies. Much can be learned about the origins and development of human behavior by comparing one society with another, for differing social and physical environments often produce radical differences in acceptable behavior from one society to another. Of more telling interest, perhaps, are not the differences but the similarities that can be found between divergent and isolated groups. These differences and similarities make excellent contrast studies. For example, in some societies brides are not courted, they are bought. Is marriage in these societies more a matter of economics and less one of love than in societies where brides are courted? To test the proposition that a bride price (the price a man pays for his bride) is economic, an observer might undertake to see if the society being studied perceives the transaction in the same way an economic transaction is perceived in our own society. Walter Goldschmidt [1973] set out to do exactly that with the Sebei, a Southern Nilotic people who live in Uganda. Among the Sebei, kinship is reckoned by male descent and clan relationships are of great psychological importance. One of their basic beliefs is that immortality is dependent upon having descendants. It is understandable, therefore, that the essence of Sebei marriage is the husband's concern with procreation. Goldschmidt studied the amount of bride price negotiated by seventy-nine men between 1910 and 1960 and found the price paid was consistent with economic trends. The lowest price paid over the 50-year period was $33, while the highest price was $420. Cattle were always exchanged and varied from one to seventeen.

Polygamy was a common practice among the Sebei, second and third wives being highly prized, which made single women of marriageable age rare. The Sebei believed, therefore, that second wives were very expensive. Goldschmidt found this was not the case. The first wife was usually more expensive than the second, and the third wife was the most expensive of all. However, the groom's parents usually help pay for the first wife, whereas the husband is on his own for the second. By the time he can afford a third, he is generally better off economically. All this paints a rather bleak picture for Uganda Valentine makers. The fact that the Sebei bride price is susceptible to economic analysis tells much about the Sebei. However much sentiment or emotion may enter into a Sebei man's desire to marry, he must at the same time face the economic realities of Sebei society and make his choice in an economic context.

CASE STUDY DESIGNS

Whereas the correlational design may be used to investigate the relationship between variables with large groups and the contrast design allows investigation of small groups, what of the individual case? The study of individual cases has always been an important undertaking for numerous specialists, ranging from journalists and biographers, policemen and judges, to social workers and psychoanalysts. Professional journals serving clinical and other applied psychologists abound in case reports of individuals being treated for some form of mental illness, or, at least, maladaptive behavior. All these reports are essentially like the case study design.

Deviant Case Analysis. Case studies do not manipulate an IV and look for change, but simply observe conditions as they unfold, whether in real time or ex post facto. An important subdivision of the case study is the deviant case analysis. This analysis attempts to take instances that are exceptions to the general trend and to locate IVs that set the instance off from the general. The investigator takes two groups or individuals that differ in outcome and attempts to locate differences in conditions between them. One group or individual is comprised of the deviant cases and the other by the majority of cases expressing the general finding. The method of deviant case analysis can be thought of as "reading backward" to approximate the experimental situation. In the experimental method, the IV is varied between experimental and control groups to produce different outcomes. In deviant case analysis, the starting point is the difference already found, and the investigator's task is to read backward to deduce the condition that produced the difference [Warwick and Osherson, 1973].

Isolated Clinical Case Analysis. This is another important subdivision that is nothing more than an investigation of individual units with respect to some analytical problem. The method has been predominant in psychoanalysis. Freud's study of little Hans is well known, as are many other case studies. Freud's theories of human psychic response were formulated through the accumulation of many case studies of individuals. Many of the problems an analyst faces are unique or are found in a very small population. An excellent example is Wixen's [1973] study of the special problems of the children of the very rich. Wixen found that many children of the very rich suffer from lack of role image and goals, and a lack of normal social and psychological development that Wixen calls "dysgradia." Wixen's study of Brewer offers an interesting example of the case study.

> Brewer's grandfather, by working hard and investing wisely, amassed a respectable fortune in an automobile franchise and TV interests. His son, Brewer's father, had inherited the total and married a girl from a well-known family after she had become pregnant with Brewer. There was not much love in the marriage. After Brewer's birth, she was completely frigid towards Brewer's father and drank heavily. After being found in bed with one of the servants, she was divorced by Brewer's father and he was awarded custody of Brewer. The father seemed to genuinely be fond of Brewer, but left his upbringing completely to servants, especially to Elsie, a large, warm black woman of around fifty. Her entire life revolved around her ward, with whom she played out many of her own fantasies.
>
> Brewer did well in school, his grades were good, he was popular and did well in sports. All this changed when he got into college. He was sent off with a large party and was given $1,000 a month allowance plus having his tuition paid along with the upkeep of his Porsche. Brewer was involved in accident after accident until he became an insurance risk. He was failing his classes, smoked a lot of marijuana, drank heavily, and began putting on weight. He contracted gonorrhea twice and had to pay for a girl's abortion. He could not handle his money and even with $1,000 a month would many times finish out a month living on bread and grape jelly. Brewer's father would become angry, write out a new budget, which Brewer would dutifully resolve to keep, and then continue in his ways. He finally dropped out of school and returned home. He was offered a job at his father's business. The first day he arrived two hours late, made a pass at a married personnel clerk and engaged in behavior termed "clearly self-destructive." In therapy, Brewer wept, "I don't know what got into me! I just wasn't thinking. I didn't want to embarrass Dad—or did I?"[4]

Wixen worked with Brewer for two and a half years and solved some of his basic neurotic problems generated by his deep distrust of all women and his conflict with his father. Brewer still lacked goals or any reasonable purpose in life. There was never any real need for him to work. He had all the money he would ever need to live on. From this experience, Wixen learned more about the special problems of the very rich and how to treat their problems.

[4] Paraphrase of case study from *Children of the Rich*, by Burton N. Wixen. © 1973 by Burton N. Wixen. Used by permission of Crown Publishers, Inc., New York.

The case study lends itself to naturalistic studies. Animals generally learn through repetition, often requiring many trials before a behavior becomes an established part of the repertoire. Exceptions are rare, and when observed, they offer a good example of the usefulness of the case study. Recently, a green heron at the Miami Seaquarium was observed to possess a complicated set of apparently self-learned behaviors. The heron had learned that by placing a bread pellet, sold for a nickel a handful at vending machines to visitors desiring to feed the fish, into the water, fish would be drawn to the spot and the heron had an easy meal. Robert F. Sisson, a photographer from the *National Geographic*, was called in to take pictures and record what he saw (Figure 7–2). Sisson states:

> I am barely set with my camera when the heron picks up a dry pellet from the island and carries it in his bill down to the edge of the water. As he comes closer, his walk takes on the slow stealthy-sneaky manner typical of most herons. Reaching the channel, he pauses and seems to survey the water for the best fishing spot. Then slowly his neck stretches out and out, as if made of elastic, and ever so gently he drops the bait in the water.
>
> Now the fisherman in him really takes over. Hunkering down between two rocks he stays as still as a statue; his eyes never leave the pellet as it bobs in the water. [Sisson, 1974, pp. 144–145.]

As the fish comes to the bait, the heron strikes and seldom misses.

At least two other herons (the mother and a brother) at the same seaquarium have apparently learned much of the same behavior, and one wonders if the heron's fishing behavior might be passed on to future generations. Sisson continues:

> One afternoon I found my heron intently watching a school of fish. He was the picture of despair. He would feint with his bill, but they were just out of range. I threw a pellet on the ground just to his left. He turned, looked at the pellet, looked at the fish, then picked up the bait. He carefully placed it in the water just short of the fish. In their rush for the food, they inadvertently pushed it and themselves shoreward toward him. Like lightning, he struck. After gulping down his catch, he retrieved the bait, which had drifted downstream, and placed it once again within his range. (p. 146)[5]

It is interesting to contemplate how psychologists would have reacted to this phenomenon if it had been observed in the wild. Would we have concluded it was another example of instinctual behavior?

The case study can be a very valuable tool in research, for a single instance can lead to new knowledge. There are many situations that can happen only once or on rare occasions. Penfield showed that stimulation of the exposed brain could evoke fine details of memory in patients during

[5] This and the above quote from Sisson [1974]. Copyright National Geographic Society. Reprinted by permission.

FIGURE 7–2   A heron fishing with bait at the Miami Seaquarium (clockwise from upper left corner): heron taking a piece of bread to the stream; heron crouching in the rocks after dropping the bread in the water; fish coming up to the surface to eat the bread; heron lunging for the catch; heron holding his catch.
(All photos copyright National Geographic Society)

open brain surgery [Halacy, 1970]. The rarity of surgery of this kind combined with a surgeon with the interests of Penfield necessitates studies involving only one or two persons. In such situations, the case study becomes a valuable method of organizing and analyzing knowledge.

ADVANTAGES AND DISADVANTAGES OF NONEXPERIMENTAL DESIGNS

The major advantage of quasi-experimental investigations is that they may be applied in situations that do not lend themselves to experimental analysis. Even in situations where experimentation is possible, quasi-experiments may be run because they may be carried out in a relatively brief time. The investigator may simply analyze existing records rather than take the time, years in many cases, required to carry out a more powerful experimental analysis. Less money is usually required to carry out a quasi-experiment. Experimental situations do not have to be set up, hiring of people to carry out the procedures is not necessary, and so on.

The major limitation of quasi-experimentation is that it cannot provide safeguards as effective as those available with a true experimental design. The four major reasons for this fact include inability to assign subjects randomly to the control and experimental groups, less control over secondary variables during the course of the experiment, no direct manipulation of an IV possible, and no control over the recording of the DV. Lack of control over the recording of the DV is important because it may not be accurately recorded, and the recorder may have been biased in the recording (e.g., scores of certain students recorded higher than actually occurred because they "would fail anyway").

The correlational method has several advantages over other approaches. It provides information concerning the degree of relationship between variables that cannot be obtained by any other analytical approach. This is particularly important in the social sciences, where few things have an all-or-none effect. A correlational approach permits a number of variables to be simultaneously measured and correlated, whereas experimental approaches are geared mainly toward dealing with one or two variables at a time. Multiple correlational studies are especially pertinent in personality research. Correlational analysis may be employed as a control technique and as a check for reliability and validity. It may also be used where experimentation is physically or ethically impractical. Experimental methods often introduce a high level of artificiality into behavioral research situations. In contrast, correlational analysis usually permits the studying of behavior with less disruptions in the analytical setting.

The major disadvantage of correlational investigations is that they are not as effective in determining cause-effect relations as more experimentally oriented investigations. They do not provide the amount of situational control normally encountered with experiments. It is important for the reader to remember that correlational studies are not just a means of seeking cause-effect relationships. They should not be thought of just as a less powerful type of investigation for identifying cause, but as the most effective means of determining degrees of relationship between variables.

Contrast investigation has little advantage over other approaches except that it can be applied in situations not conducive to experimental, quasi-experimental, or correlational analysis. It is generally not acceptable for independent class projects in undergraduate psychology courses because it requires the investigator to devote a lot of time to developing experience in analyzing such situations. Because neither statistical nor manipulatory procedures are available to the investigator, as is the case in large-N and small-N investigations, the researcher must rely more on inductive reasoning ability. This requires greater experience and background, yet does not ensure as powerful a means of drawing cause-effect conclusions as is true with the experimental designs.

The case study is essentially descriptive or exploratory in nature and is in the same predicament as the contrast method because help through statistical or manipulatory procedures is not available. In some cases, however, it is the only option for obtaining information, and a basic principle of research is that some information is better than none. The case study is usually more effective in isolating relationships than a contrast design, however, because there are not as many secondary variables involved in a situation with only one person as there are when more people are involved. One case study approach is similar to the small-N approach in that it is based on verification and generalization by means of interinvestigatory affirmation. Unfortunately, a case study approach is often erroneously equated with a small-N approach in terms of power in determining cause-effect relationships, mainly due to a lack of understanding of the principles and procedures underlying small-N research. A small-N experiment provides tools for establishing baseline IV manipulation, monitoring the control of secondary variables, and obtaining a reliable cumulative record analysis not possible with the case study. Small-N designs (discussed in Chapter Twelve) are extremely powerful in determining cause-effect relationships, even better than large-N analysis in some situations, whereas case study is severely limited and must be used with caution if conclusions about causes are to be drawn.

SUMMARY

Chapter Seven presents the four main categories of EPF designs. The first is the quasi-experimental design, which is carried out exactly like an experiment except for two differences: subjects are not randomly assigned to groups, and an IV is not directly manipulated. Two or more groups that are found to vary on the IV in question are compared. The quasi-experimental design relies heavily on the control technique of constancy. Correlational designs are a second type of EPF analytical approach. They differ from all other types of investigations (both EPF and experimental) in that they are designed not to determine cause and effect relationships between variables, but to determine the degree of relationship between variables. Correlational analysis finds application in four general types of research: (1) in dealing with causality issues when experimental methods cannot be used, (2) in descriptive and predictive capacities, (3) as a statistical means of controlling secondary variables, and (4) in determining the reliability and internal validity of measures.

Contrast EPF designs are primarily used in the analysis of historical data that has too few measures to permit a meaningful statistical manipulation. They find particular application in anthropologically oriented psychological studies. The case study method does not involve the manipulation of an IV, but is an observational approach to analyzing ongoing or past situations. The three principal subdivisions of the case study method are deviant case analysis, isolated case analysis, and naturalistic observation.

The major advantage of EPF investigations is that they can be applied in situations where experimentation cannot be used because of ethical considerations, physical restrictions, or the prior occurrence of the event.

I. **What Are Experimental Designs?**
   A. *Control Procedures*
   B. *Number of Groups*
II. **Types of Experimental Designs**
III. **One-Group Designs**
   A. *One-Group Posttest Design*
   B. *One-Group Pretest-Posttest Design*
   C. *Time-Series Design*
IV. **Summary**

Experimental Designs

Chapter Three divided research investigations into two groups—experimental and ex post facto. The objective of this chapter is to give the reader a comparative overview of sixteen designs from which to choose when carrying out an experiment. Sixteen designs may seem like an overwhelming number at this point, but they are elaborated on in the following three chapters. The most important concepts presented in this chapter are the two factors upon which all experimental designs are based and how the investigator may combine aspects of these two factors to come up with the sixteen designs. Also presented here is the difference between exploratory and analytical designs. The last section of the chapter describes in detail three of the sixteen designs. Not all the sixteen designs presented are good; some poor designs are included because they are commonly used.

WHAT ARE EXPERIMENTAL DESIGNS?

Chapter Four dealt with variance, where it comes from, and basic ways of controlling it. The main objective of this chapter is to provide the student with the procedures required for applying those control techniques. This comes under the heading of experimental designs.

The term *experimental design* has two different though interrelated meanings. In a general sense, experimental design represents the six basic activities required for carrying out an experiment. All the procedures involved in an experimental investigation, from formulating a hypothesis to drawing conclusions, are considered by many researchers to be the experimental design of an investigation. A second definition of experimental design is more restrictive. In this sense, it is a procedure for assigning subjects to experimental conditions and selecting an appropriate statistical analytical procedure. The second definition is emphasized here, for it is the most common. When someone asks which experimental design you employed, generally a reply such as a randomized two-group design or 2 × 3 factorial design is expected, rather than a discourse on all the steps you carried out in your experiment. Procedures that would be classified as part of an experimental design in the general sense, such as selecting appropriate IVs and DVs, deciding how many sessions to run, and which equipment to use, were covered in Chapter Five.

When carrying out an experiment, an investigator wants to maximize the effect of systematic variance. Next secondary sources of variance must be controlled for. Third, error variance should be minimized. The first and third objectives are for the most part dealt with by procedures other than assigning subjects to groups. For example, maximizing the effect of an IV may be done by increasing the magnitude of the IV, while error variance may be reduced by increasing the accuracy of measuring the DV. These two objectives and procedures for accomplishing them are mostly done by means other than the selection of the experimental design.

The major function of experimental designs is to meet the second objective, that of controlling for secondary variation. Experimental situations vary with respect to the ability of different sources of secondary variation to have an effect on an IV under investigation. Not all nine sources of internal invalidity influence each experimental situation to the same extent. For instance, subject sensitization due to pretesting may strongly influence some experiments and not be even potentially relevant in others. Different experimental situations are challenged by various combinations of relevant secondary variables. To help them cope more effectively with the large number of alternative sources of secondary variation that could invalidate an investigation, experimenters have developed designs that employ various combinations of the five basic secondary variation control procedures. Each of these experimental designs has its advantages and disadvantages. A particular design may provide the optimal control of secondary variation in one situation, and be hopelessly inadequate in others. It may allow cause-effect relationships to be drawn in some situations, yet not allow adequate inferences in others.

All experimental designs can be categorized by the type of control procedure employed and the number of groups involved. The type of control procedure employed is important in determining how reliable and valid the conclusions drawn from the experiment are, and may be used to restrict the opportunity of secondary variables to bias the results. The number of groups involved in an experiment is important not only for determining which control procedures may be employed in an experiment, but also for determining what types of research problems an investigation may answer.

Control Procedures

Of the large number of designs from which an investigator may choose when carrying out an experiment, some are relatively basic, whereas others

TABLE 8–1   *Control Procedures and Designs*

CONTROL PROCEDURE	DESIGN
Randomization	Randomized
Constancy	Blocked, matched
Second IV	Factorial
Statistical control	Covariant
Elimination	—

Note: Elimination is used irrespective of the type of design.

are more specifically designed for a particular type of research problem. In the next three chapters the reader will be introduced to sixteen experimental designs with which the undergraduate psychology student should be familiar.[1] Experimental designs to be covered may be categorized functionally according to the types of control procedures involved. Table 8–1 shows the five control procedures and the types of designs that employ each one. Experimental designs are generally labeled according to the type of control procedure involved. For example, an experimental design that employs randomization is called a randomized two-group design, randomized three-group design, and so on. A particular experimental design may employ more than one control procedure. In such cases, the name of the design is made up of a composite of the control procedure labels. A three-group design employing randomization and blocking would be called a randomized, blocked three-group design. Generally, then, the name of the design is composed of the type of control procedure involved, plus the number of groups in the investigation. Some designs, however, have picked up second names due to their frequent use in particular situations and certain academic areas. Time series and Solomon four-group designs are good examples. The Solomon four-group design is actually a special type of 2 × 2 factorial design. It is used so extensively in educational research to check for the effects of pretesting that it is presented here as a specific design. In social research circles it is considered one of the finest designs available.

Notice that there is a dash following the control technique of elimination in Table 8–1. Elimination as a control procedure is not restricted to any particular experimental design. It is a nonexperimental design control procedure for eliminating secondary sources of variation that the experimenter carries out irrespective of the design employed. An investigator may want to eliminate variation due to sex differences, so either all males or all females are selected. An experiment may be carried

---

[1] The student should have a basic understanding of the similarities and differences of these designs. Only the major similarities and differences are described in this text. More extensive coverage can be found in Winer [1963] and Kirk [1970].

out on a nonwindy day if the influence of the wind is not desired. In either case, the investigator removes the unwanted secondary variable, regardless of which design is used.

One other control procedure may also be employed irrespective of the experimental design used, and that is constancy. An investigator may feel temperature will influence the DV so room temperature is held constant, no matter what design is employed. However, secondary variables can be held constant by using certain designs. Matching or blocking may be added to a design in an effort to hold a variable constant.[2] An investigator may employ different races of people as subjects. To hold the race variable constant, he or she will make sure each group has equal proportions of each race. The investigator has not eliminated the race variable, only equated the groups on that variable. (The use of elimination and constancy as control procedures not related to experimental design was covered in Chapter Five.)

Number of Groups

A second factor to be considered in classifying experimental designs is the number of groups involved. Experiments may be carried out using one, two, three, up to an infinite number of groups. The number of groups employed will to an extent determine what kind of control procedure an investigator might use. Table 8–2 classifies experimental designs according to type of control procedure and number of groups. Dashes within columns indicate that a particular control technique is not applicable to the group with which it is correlated. For instance, there is no such thing as a randomized one-group design.[3]

One-group designs are not considered a good experimental approach for determining the effect of IVs. As has been emphasized in previous chapters, experimentation involves manipulation, comparison, and evaluation. Manipulation entails applying an IV and noting its effect on the subjects' behavior. The manipulated subjects' behavior is then compared to the behavior of subjects who have not experienced the IV. An evaluation of the influence of the IV on behavior is then carried out, based primarily on the comparison data.

Unfortunately, one-group experimental investigations do not generally allow comparison, for there is no second group with which a comparison can be made. Therefore, although manipulation is involved

---

[2] *Matching* and *blocking* are terms used to identify certain procedures experimenters use to equate groups in an experiment on a particular secondary variable.

[3] Actually, it would be possible to select randomly one group of subjects from a population of subjects without having to divide randomly the chosen subjects into two or more groups. However, this is not a very practical situation.

TABLE 8–2   *Experimental Designs by Control Procedure and Number of Groups*

CONTROL PROCEDURE	ONE-GROUP	TWO-GROUP	ONE-WAY ANOVAR	FACTORIAL
Randomization	—	Randomized two-group design	Randomized three-group design	Randomized factorial
Constancy	Pretest-posttest one-group design	Matched two-group design	Blocked three-group design	Blocked factorial
Second IV	—	—	—	Any factorial
Statistical control	—	Analysis of covariance, two-group design	Analysis of covariance, three-group design	Analysis of covariance, factorial

in one-group investigations, the lack of comparative data decreases the possibility that any valid conclusions will result. The investigator has no way of knowing how much the IV influenced the behavior, for there is no measure of the behavior without the IV. The investigator has not been able to divide V_T into V_B and V_W. Measures of the DV for the subjects in a one-group comparison indicate only that the scores varied. The investigator cannot isolate the influence of the IV from that of any other variables present in the situation.

One-group experimental investigations can, however, be carried out in such a way as to allow comparison. To illustrate this point, let us first look at how an experimental situation would be dealt with using two groups. Suppose you wanted to carry out a two-group experiment to determine whether taking an introductory psychology course increases students' knowledge about psychology, a question asked by many psychology majors who survive such courses. You could select a number of subjects, divide them into two groups, have one take the course, and then give both groups a test on psychological terms and principles. The two groups would give you a measure of the DV (knowledge of psychology) with and without the IV (taking an introductory psychology course). The effect of the IV could then be isolated as the difference between the two.

A one-group design could also be used as an alternative approach to answering the same question about introductory psychology by using a pretest-posttest one-group procedure. Subjects could be selected and given a test (pretest) made up of psychological terms and principles. This would give the investigator a measure of what the students know about psychology without the influence of the IV. After taking an introductory course, all subjects would then be given a posttest. Next, all the subjects' scores on the posttest minus the pretest could be used as a measure of the influence of the IV.

One factor about one-group designs is emphasized by Table 8–2. Only one of the four control procedures possible with experimental designs is available for one-group investigations. Random assignment to IV and non-IV groups is not possible, for there is only one group. No secondary variables may be controlled by making them a second IV, for each IV would require a separate group.[4] Statistical control is also not available due to lack of comparative measures. The technique of constancy is a viable control procedure with one-group designs where more than one measure is taken for each subject, as is the case with time series and pretest-posttest one-group designs.

By setting up an experimental design involving two groups, the investigator has arranged conditions so that V_T may be divided into V_B and V_W, thereby allowing the effect of the IV to be isolated. The investigator also automatically increases the number of usable control techniques. It becomes possible to equate the effects of potentially confounding secondary variables by randomly assigning subjects to either the control or the experimental group. Other secondary variables may be controlled by matching or balancing the groups on these variables.[5] A second group also makes statistical control possible.

By adding a third group and employing a one-way ANOVAR design, the investigator does not increase the number of control procedures available for use, but he or she does add an important dimension. Two major questions in research are, "Does the IV have an effect?" and "How much of an effect does the IV have?" Analogous to these two questions are two types of experiments: *exploratory* and *analytical* experiments. Exploratory experiments generally involve only two groups, one to be a control and the second to receive the IV. This type of experiment answers the question, "Does the IV have an effect?" It does not answer the question of what levels of IV are required to get different amounts of change in the DV. The answer to the second question requires many groups, each receiving a different level of IV. These are analytical experiments. When an investigator ventures into an uncultivated area of research, the first question to answer is, "Does the IV have an effect?" To answer this, an exploratory investigation is launched. Later, if that question has been answered in the affirmative, the researcher carries out an analytical (also called *parametric*) investigation to determine how much effect different values of the IV have.

Good examples of exploratory and analytical investigations are found

---

[4] It is possible to study more than one variable with one group using a small-N design and analysis by means of repeated measures. An excellent investigatory approach is based on different assumptions than those in the large-N statistical approach (see Chapter Twelve).

[5] *Balancing* involves making sure each group has the same amount of a particular variable in each group, for example, making sure each group has the same number of males and females. The terms *matching* and *blocking* indicate designs using balancing.

in historical experimentations in the medical field. Before the 1840s operations were extremely painful ordeals in which the surgeon worked in great haste to shorten the patient's agony. Amputations, for example, were carried out in a few seconds. In the early 1840s, William Morton, a medical student at Harvard, started carrying out surgery on cats, dogs, and rats. After administering ether to some of them, he noted that those who received ether prior to surgery felt no pain during the operation, whereas those who did not suffered greatly. From these exploratory investigations, Morton concluded that ether could alleviate pain.

Having seen a demonstration by Morton, a venturesome doctor, Horace Wells, attempted to demonstrate the use of this anesthetic. During an exhibition at a large eastern hospital, the demonstration failed. Unfortunately, the patient woke too soon, screaming in pain. Although Morton's exploratory experiment had demonstrated ether was effective, it was not known what dosages were most effective or how long the drug would last. Parametric investigations were then carried out to answer the question, "How much effect does ether have at different dosage levels?"

One-way ANOVAR experimental designs add a new dimension to experimentation by allowing more than one comparison to be carried out in one experiment. One-way ANOVAR designs are multigroup designs in which more than two levels of *one* variable are compared in one experiment. Although two-group experiments are generally used in exploratory investigations, one-way ANOVAR designs, like factorial designs, are generally used in analytical investigations.

One-group, two-group, and one-way analysis designs are alike in that all of them allow investigators to manipulate one IV. A factorial design is a multigroup design that allows the variation of two or more variables in an experimental setting. Factorial designs are especially important for psychological research because behavior is a function of many variables impinging on a person simultaneously. In many instances, factors simultaneously influencing behavior interact to produce results that do not occur when only one factor is free to vary. What a person will do in an emergency, for example, is determined both by the emotional state he or she is in and who else is in that situation. How a married woman will respond to various emergencies (e.g., fire, earthquake, physical harm) depends not only on the type of emergency, but also on whether her husband, children, and/or parents are present at the time. An investigation of how she would react in these situations could lead to misleading conclusions if the variable of "who is present" was held constant. Factorial designs allow investigations to be carried out to analyze the interaction effects of variables concurrently influencing an organism.

Table 8–2 indicates another advantage of factorial designs: they make more control procedures available than two-group or one-way ANOVAR designs. Not only can factorial designs use randomization, constancy, and statistical control, they can also allow a secondary variable to be converted into a second IV. The effects of this second IV can then be quantitatively extracted from V_T. The formula for a factorial design would be:[6]

$$V_T = V_{B_1} + V_{B_2} + V_W$$

The symbol V_{B_2} represents the isolation of the effects of the secondary variable that was transformed into the second IV.

The decision, then, of how many groups an investigation will have is an important step because the number of groups to some degree limits what the investigator may do and the types of information that may be obtained. The reader should not conclude that an experimental investigation consisting of many groups is inherently better than one having only two groups. Although a factorial design with its added groups provides a larger selection of control procedures than a two-group design, it may not be any more functional for certain situations. In fact, it may be detrimental because of the increased number of subjects and preparations necessary.

TYPES OF EXPERIMENTAL DESIGNS

By combining the experimental dimensions of a number of groups and control procedures plus a little imagination, one can come up with numerous experimental designs. Table 8–3 presents sixteen experimental designs, symbolically diagrams them out, and indicates which control procedures they employ. The sixteen listed are not the only ones possible, but are those commonly used in behavioral research.

In Table 8–3 the symbolic representation O represents the measurement of some DV, the X stands for the application of an IV, and R stands for randomization. A Y represents some measure of a covariate. Each row of symbols represents one group. To illustrate, take the following symbols:

A			B			
R	*X*	*O*	*R*	*Y*	*X*	*O*
R		*O*	*R*	*Y*		*O*

Column A states that there are two groups (*R X O* and *R O*); both have been randomly selected (*R*); one receives the IV (*X*) and the second does not. Column B is identical to A except for the inclusion of a measure of

---

[6] Technically, the formula should read $V_T = V_{B_1} + V_{B_2} + VI + V_W$. The term *VI* stands for interaction effects. V_I will be presented later to prevent confusion at this point.

TABLE 8–3 *Sixteen Experimental Designs*

TYPE OF DESIGN	SYMBOLIC REPRESENTATION	RANDOM-IZATION	CONSTANCY	SECOND IV	STATISTICAL CONTROL	ELIMINATION
One-Group Designs						
1. One-group posttest only	$X\ O$·					
2. One-group pretest-posttest	$O_1\ X\ O_2$·		+			
3. Time series	$O_1\ O_2\ O_3\ X\ O_4\ O_5\ O_6$		+			
Two-Group Designs						
4. Posttest control group	$X\ O$ / O					
5. Randomized posttest only control group	$R\ X\ O$ / $R\ \ O$	+				
6. Randomized matched posttest only control group	$RM\ X\ O$ / $RM\ \ O$	+	+			
7. Pretest-posttest control group	$O\ X\ O$ / $O\ \ O$		+			
8. Randomized pretest-posttest control group	$R\ O\ X\ O$ / $R\ O\ \ O$	+	+			
9. Randomized pretest-posttest control group, analysis of covariance	$R\ YO\ X\ O$ / $R\ YO\ \ O$	+	+		+	

TABLE 8-3 (Continued)

TYPE OF DESIGN	SYMBOLIC REPRESENTATION	RANDOM-IZATION	CONSTANCY	SECOND IV	STATISTICAL CONTROL	ELIMINATION
One-Way Anovar Designs						
10. Randomized ANOVAR	$R\ X_1\ O$ $R\ X_2\ O$ $R\ X_3\ O$	+				
11. Randomized blocked ANOVAR	$RB\ X_1\ O$ $RB\ X_2\ O$ $RB\ X_3\ O$	+	+			
12. Randomized analysis of covariance	$R\ Y\ X_1\ O$ $R\ Y\ X_2\ O$ $R\ Y\ X_3\ O$	+			+	
Factorial Designs						
13. Randomized factorial	(matrix below)	+		+		
14. Solomon four-group	$R\ O\ X\ O$ $R\ O\quad O$ $R\quad X\ O$ $R\quad\ O$	+	+	+		

Matrix for 13. Randomized factorial:

		IV_1 LEVELS		
		1	2	3
IV_2 LEVELS	A	X_{A1}	X_{A2}	X_{A3}
	B	X_{B1}	X_{B2}	X_{B3}

15. Randomized blocked factorial

	IV₁:	1	2	3	1	2	3
	IV₂:	A	A	A	B	B	B
BLOCKS	1	X_{A11}	X_{A21}	X_{A31}	X_{B11}	X_{B21}	X_{B31}
	2	X_{A12}	X_{A22}	X_{A32}	X_{B12}	X_{B22}	X_{B32}
	3	X_{A13}	X_{A23}	X_{A33}	X_{B13}	X_{B23}	X_{B33}

(LEVELS)

16. Randomized analysis of covariance factorial

		IV₁ LEVELS		
		1	2	3
IV₂ LEVELS	A	YX_{A1}	YX_{A2}	YX_{A3}
	B	YX_{B1}	YX_{B2}	YX_{B3}

some covariate (*Y*). Two randomly selected groups are involved, with one receiving the IV. The covariate measure *Y* could represent the IQ level of each group of subjects.[7] If the groups did differ on IQ, the investigator could statistically adjust the differences in the group *O*s to remove that portion of the difference between the group DV measures due to group IQ differences.

Notice in Table 8–3 that all designs involving more than two groups are diagramed with boxes rather than symbolized by *R*s, *X*s, and *Y*s. There are two reasons for this. First, the use of boxes makes the representation less cumbersome and gives the reader a more graphic illustration of what is involved. The symbolic representation of the randomized factorial design (13) shown in Table 8–3 would be

$$R \quad X_{A_1} \quad O$$

$$R \quad X_{A_2} \quad O$$

$$R \quad X_{A_3} \quad O$$

$$R \quad X_{B_1} \quad O$$

$$R \quad X_{B_2} \quad O$$

$$R \quad X_{B_3} \quad O$$

The box diagram makes it easier to see that two variables, one with two levels and one with three, are involved. The second reason for not using *R*s, and so on, is that it is generally assumed for studies involving three or more groups that each subject is randomly assigned to a group, and a DV measure *O* is taken. Few investigators would go to the expense of carrying out a multigroup investigation without employing the control technique of randomization. The *X* in the box indicates which IV condition that group experiences. The subscripts tell which level of each variable a group receives.

Insight
True versus Pseudo-experimental Large-N Designs

Technically, all sixteen large-*N* designs illustrated in Table 8–3 are not experimental designs. In Chapter Three an experiment was defined as an investigation in which the IV is directly and systematically manipulated. When a large-*N* experimental ap-

[7] A covariate is any other variable on which groups in an investigation differ other than the IV. Suppose you were going to carry out a two-group experiment to see which of two types of puzzles is easiest to solve. Each of the groups would be given one of the two types of puzzles. The groups would then "vary" on only one variable, the type of puzzle they tried to solve. If the two groups also varied in terms of IQ (i.e., one group's IQ was higher than the other), then IQ would be a covariate.

proach is used, there is, however, a second requirement for an investigation to be considered an experiment: assignment of subjects to groups must be done randomly. Recall from Chapter Two that random assignment of subjects to groups was one of the three design requirements that Fisher [1925] pointed out was necessary for a large-N experimental paradigm to be scientifically sound and internally verifiable. Notice that several designs listed in Table 8–3 do not include the use of subject randomization. Such large-N designs are not considered to be true experimental designs, and are often referred to as *preexperimental designs* or *pseudo-experimental designs*.

Why are nonrandomized large-N designs considered preexperimental designs when designs omitting the other three types of control procedures are not? What is so special about the control technique of randomization? It is important to remember that randomizing the assignment of subjects to groups does more than control for secondary variables. Randomization is considered necessary for an experimenter to employ analysis of variance statistical tests on the data and determine the significance of the data. The statistical tests originated by Fisher to determine whether between-group variance is significantly different from within-group variance are based on several requirements of the data collected. One of the most important of these requirements is that the data collected must be taken from subjects randomly assigned to groups in order for the tests of significance (i.e., t-test, F test) to produce valid results. More is said later (page 346) about these requirements for using tests of significance.

ONE-GROUP DESIGNS

So far, the intent of this chapter has been to give the student an overview of all the designs to be covered and how they compare in terms of the control procedures involved. The remainder of this chapter and the three that follow are devoted to an elaboration of each experimental design, its basic points, advantages, and disadvantages. An example of each is included so that the student may see how it is statistically analyzed.

One-Group Posttest Design (X O)

The city council of a town consisting of 30,000 people decided to set up a drug crisis center. Both youths and adults were encouraged to come to the center to obtain help with drug problems. Information regarding the effects of different drugs could be obtained at the center, and a group of people was available to provide social support for anyone desiring to deal with a drug problem. After the center had been operating for one year, the director of the program was requested to send information to the city council to demonstrate the program's effectiveness. In compliance with the request, the director sent the following letter:

Dear Sirs:

The drug center has been in operation in this town for more than a year now. At the end of the first year the staff of the center has carried out thoughtful discussions in an attempt to thoroughly and objectively appraise the effectiveness of the program. Empirical data were collected regarding the results of the program, as shown below:

TYPE OF PATIENT	NUMBER TREATED	NUMBER CURED
Marijuana smokers	158	96
LSD users	256	149
Glue sniffers	463	298
Opium addicts	23	10
Morphine users	18	6
Alcoholics	563	84

From the data it is obvious that the drug center has been effective in our area. We are looking forward to your continued support of this project. Do not hesitate to call on us for any further information.

Yours truly,

Alfred Schwartz
Director
Drug Crisis Center

The preceding is an example of a one-group posttest design. In actuality, this type of design is a forerunner of other present-day designs. It is commonly called a *pre-experimental design* or a *pseudo-experimental design*, for it is not generally considered to be a good experimental approach because a formal comparison is not performed. For a scientific investigation to be a true experiment, at least one comparison must be carried out. Generally, data from the one group experiencing the IV is compared to the data from a second group that did not experience the IV.[8] Note that in the drug center problem there was no control group to allow for a comparison. Although empirical observations are reported, the one-group posttest design has little power; that is, it provides little control with respect to ensuring that the IV and not some other secondary variable was the effective ingredient. Actually, the data presented could have been obtained without a drug center, for no information is presented showing how many cures would occur without a drug program available. It is possible that many people would have "cured" themselves without the center. The point to be made is not that the drug center had no effect, but that without

---

[8] Not all cases require a second group. Some experimental designs use one group for both control and experimental conditions. This is perfectly acceptable and allows a formal comparison to be made. The time series and ABA designs are examples of this procedure; more will be said of these designs in Chapter Twelve.

carrying out some type of comparison between a group having the program and one not having the program, little can be demonstrated about any cause-effect relationship. The type of investigation carried out here was not, technically, a true experiment. It might be better classified as an information investigation, for the data do provide descriptive information about what happened.

One-group posttest designs do not adequately control for any of the internal sources of invalidity. Let us look at how this particular design copes or does not cope with potential sources of invalidity. Proactive history has not been controlled for in any way, so the data obtained may be a function of a previous experience rather than the IV. Only certain people may have come to the center for help, and these people may have decided to change whether the center was there or not. Some of the change may have been due to time. It has been found, for example, that as glue sniffers, usually grade school children, get older they move toward more potent drugs. This could explain the reason for some of the decrease in glue sniffing. Some may have gone on to marijuana and other drugs. Testing does not apply to one-group posttest designs. No pretest was given; therefore, it could not possibly influence the results. Regression is not applicable either, there being no comparison with which to evaluate regression. There are no means for controlling retroactive history or mortality, both of which are usually involved in one-group situations. Maturation may not be a relevant source of variability if the length of time involved is relatively short. The longer it takes to carry out the study (weeks, months, years), the greater the possibility that maturational effects are present. Only one IV was applied, so interaction would not be a relevant factor. As mentioned previously, neither instrumentation nor experimenter bias is controlled by a particular design. Both sources of internal invalidity may fluctuate in an experimental situation irrespective of the design used; only the experimenter can make sure these are controlled.

It may seem puzzling that one-group posttest designs are included in this chapter on experimental designs. One reason for including them is that they are often used in social research [Campbell and Stanley, 1966] for drawing causal inferences, even though this is an incorrect use. Second, case studies that are in essence one-group posttest designs are frequently carried out in psychology. From therapeutic situations and the results obtained, cause-effect relationships are often inferred regarding therapeutic procedures and concurrent behavioral changes. The therapist may unwittingly conclude that she or he caused the change for the better when in fact the improvement was a result of something else.

The one-case study situation is not restricted to psychology. The same problems are encountered in other areas, such as applied medicine. A doctor may prescribe a certain drug to combat the flu or some other virus. If the patient gets better, it is sometimes concluded the drug was responsible, when the flu may just have run its course. The incorrect conclusions that may be drawn in therapeutic and medicinal situations are also analogous to an Indian doing a dance to bring rain. If it rains, the dance receives the credit. Although psychologists are most often restricted to the applied setting (one-case study situations), any conclusions drawn about the effectiveness of their techniques should come from experimental situations (either field or laboratory) rather than the actual case histories. Advances in field experimental procedures presently allow the clinical psychologist to carry out cause-effect analysis in most applied settings, even if only one subject is involved.[9]

One-Group Pretest-Posttest Design (*O X O*)

The one-group pretest-posttest design is also considered to be a rather poor design, though somewhat better than the one-group posttest design. Suppose you want to try a new type of exercise plan on third-grade students to see if it increases their coordination. A pretest is given at the beginning of the year. The exercise plan is employed during the whole school year. A posttest may then be carried out to determine whether the scores on the pretest significantly differ from those on the posttest.

Initially, this may seem like an adequate design, since a formal comparison can be carried out. The problem, however, involves inadequate control for internal and external validity. As can be seen, in Table 8–2, the one-group pretest-posttest design does little in the way of controlling secondary influences on the IV. All the arguments for lack of control for internal invalidity presented for the one-group posttest only design are also true for this design, with the following exceptions: pretest influences, not applicable in the posttest situation, may influence scores on the posttest; and persons frequently do better when taking a test the second time due to the experience of taking it the first time.

Proactive history is more effectively controlled with the pretest-posttest condition. Both the pretest and the posttest should be influenced by the past history of the subject to the same degree, thereby equating the effects of this secondary source of variation. Mortality is also controlled for by the fact that a loss of subjects during the experiment could be checked by dropping the pretest scores of the subjects lost (this could bias the results).

In summary, though the one-group pretest-posttest design is better than the one-group posttest only design, neither is advocated. Neither

---

[9] Chapter Twelve discusses procedures for carrying out cause-effect investigations in the applied setting.

design adequately controls for secondary variation. They may be appropriate if no other type of design is feasible, for some information is always better than none, but one must be careful in deducing cause-effect relationships with these designs. They are used all too frequently in situations in which more appropriate designs could be employed.

Time-Series Design (O_1 O_2 X O_3 O_4)

Social research frequently involves analyzing the influence of a variable or variables over relatively long periods of time. Educators may be interested in determining the effects of a certain type of educational curriculum on grade-school children over several years. A case in point involves an experiment carried out by Wolf, Giles, and Hall [reported in Whaley and Malott, 1971, p. 282]. Wolf, Giles, and Hall selected culturally deprived children who had advanced only 0.6 years on the Scholastic Aptitude Test (SAT) administered by the public school over the past few years. The SAT scores were obtained previous to the administration of a modified educational program (X), and are presented by the symbols O_1 and O_2. All sixteen fifth- and sixth-grade students involved in the study were at least 2.0 years below their grade level in reading achievement. The children were put on a token economy system in which they received trading stamps for completing class assignments and participating in academic endeavors. These trading stamps could be exchanged for opportunities to go on field trips including swimming, picnics, visits to the zoo, sporting events, and so on. During the first year the modified program was employed, the children typically gained 1.5 years on the scholastic aptitude test. The 1.5 would be O_3, with the next year's average O_4.

It is apparent that a time-series design is a better design than either of the aforementioned one-group designs. The repeated measure of the DV provides the investigator with information on the variability of the DV both before and after the IV is given. Like the other one-group designs, several sources of internal validity may not be controlled for, including retroactive history, instrumentation, and experimenter bias. Other variables may have simultaneously fluctuated to produce any effect noted in a time-series design, making invalidity due to retroactive history a real possibility. In some time-series experiments, retroactive history may be a plausible alternative explanation, whereas in others it may not.[10]

Notice how the time-series design controls the remaining sources of internal invalidity. If maturation or testing is influencing the DV, the variations will show up between $O_1 - O_2$ and $O_3 - O_4$, as well as between

---

[10] If some secondary variable fluctuated at the same time a variable was applied in a time-series design, the experimenter may not be as confident that any change occurring in the DV was actually due to the IV.

O_2 and O_3. Regression effects are implausible in this design and would also show up between $O_1 - O_2$ and $O_3 - O_4$ if they were present. Due to the fact the same subjects are used throughout, proactive history is held constant. The effect of any subject lost during the experiment can be isolated from the other scores, and therefore mortality is controlled for.

The statistical analysis of time-series designs is somewhat complicated and will be covered in more detail after some of the more common designs and simpler statistical analyses have been discussed. Here it is sufficient to say that carrying out a t-test between O_2 and O_3 is not considered an appropriate statistical treatment of this design.

The time-series design is used by researchers whose interest lies in changes occurring over time. Many educators, developmental psychologists, political scientists, and sociologists are dependent upon a time-series, for their topic may not lend itself to two-group analysis. Generally, two-group designs are preferred over one-group designs. There are single-group designs (e.g., ABA designs) that are considered more effective than two-group designs, but these will be covered in Chapter Twelve.

SUMMARY

An investigator has three main concerns when carrying out research: to maximize the effect of the IV, to control for secondary sources of variation, and to minimize error variance. The main responsibility of experimental designs is to control for secondary variation. Because the means for accomplishing this change from one situation to another, alternative experimental designs have been constructed. Experimental designs are based on two dimensions—the type of control procedure involved and the number of groups employed. Experimental designs are classified according to the control procedures being used and the number of groups required. More than one control procedure may be used in a particular experimental design. This allows greater control of secondary variable effects.

The number of groups employed in an investigation has two important effects on that investigation. First, it determines to some extent what control procedures may be employed. For example, controlling a secondary variable by making it a second IV cannot be done with only two groups; a factorial design is required. Second, the number of groups determines what types of experiments can be carried out. A distinction is made between analytical and exploratory investigations. Exploratory investigations consist of two groups; one group receives the IV and the other group does not, in an effort to determine whether or not the IV is effective. Analytical investigations require three or more groups and are carried out to analyze parametrically the effects of different levels of the IV.

Two-group designs may employ the control procedures of constancy, randomization, and analysis of covariance, and are restricted to exploratory investigations. One-way analysis of variance designs do not allow greater choice in control techniques over two-group designs, but they do give the added dimension of allowing the investigator the option of carrying out analytical investigations as well. Factorial designs allow both analytical and exploratory investigations to be carried out, plus adding an optional fourth control technique—making a secondary variable an IV. Alternative one-group designs are discussed. It is emphasized that most one-group designs are poor experimental designs and provide the investigator little or no control of secondary variables.

  I. Logical Analysis of Two-Group Designs
  II. Types of Two-Group Designs
   A. *Randomized Two-Group Design, Posttest Only*
   B. *Matched Two-Group Design*
   C. *Pretest-Posttest Control Group Design*
   D. *Static Group Design*
   E. *Nonrandomized Pretest-Posttest Control Group Design*
   F. *Analysis of Covariance Two-Group Design*
  III. Advantages and Disadvantages of Two-Group Designs
  IV. Summary

Two-Group
Designs

This chapter discusses the cornerstone of psychological experiments—two-group designs. More two-group experiments are carried out than almost any other type of experiment. Six types of two-group designs are presented. The last, the analysis of covariance two-group design, is generally not covered in an undergraduate experimental psychology course, probably because the statistical manipulations involved frighten even most graduate students. Remember, however, that understanding the statistical analysis is not as important here as understanding when and where different designs should be used. Whether your instructor requires you to learn the formulas involved will depend on what level course you are in and whether you have had a prior course in statistics. By the time you finish your graduate training you will be expected to know them. The formulas and specific numerical examples on how to use them have been included here so that the student may carry out the statistical analysis whether he or she understands the statistics or not.

LOGICAL ANALYSIS
OF TWO-GROUP DESIGNS

The mainstay of psychological experimentation is the situation in which the effects of an IV on some DV are determined using two groups. The investigator generally is interested in whether a particular variable will influence a particular behavior. To answer the question, only two groups are needed for carrying out the investigation: one to experience the IV and the second to act as a control. The control group should be as identical to the experimental group as possible so that any difference in behavior between the two groups can be attributed to the variable in question.

Most people assume that two-group comparisons have been the cornerstone of scientific inquiry for thousands of years. Although it is true that two-group comparisons have been carried out for centuries, they have come into their own only in the last 80 years or so. Prior to that time, systematic observation of ongoing behavior and comparative analysis[1] of past events were the rule in empirical investigations. Only the wealthy could afford to be scientists, and acceptance of a scientist's results was based primarily on his integrity and the social soundness of his previous statements. Because of the lack of statistical and manipulatory sophistication in experimentation, knowing what to look for, when to look, and how to report it concisely was considered more important than the ability to manipulate. Although manipulatory studies were carried out over the centuries, the importance of such research was not realized until the turn of the nineteenth century. Since that time, manipulatory and statistical procedures have continually been refined until both have become central figures in research circles.

The analytical foundation for two-group designs is based on the principle of variation presented in Chapter Four. With systematic natural observation, the investigation is based on the principle of causation due to temporal and spatial association. More simply, if some variable (*A*) was noted to change, any immediate change in some other variable (*B*) which was close to *A* noted immediately was said to be "caused" by *A*.

Scientists began to realize that if they manipulated variable *A* and a change in variable *B* occurred, there was less chance that the fluctuation of *B* was due to some other secondary variable. There are two main reasons for this assumption. First, if the investigator decides when *A* is to be varied, there is less chance that some secondary variable may "just happen" to fluctuate at the same time and cause the variation in *B*. Second, an argument was commonly invoked which held in essence that variable *B* was going to fluctuate anyway. By having the investigator apply the IV at will when so desired, any change in *B* following the application of *A* increases the probability that any fluctuation in *B* was due to *A* rather than simply to random fluctuation. The idea that experimental manipulation was valuable initiated the rise of one-group experimental designs.

After experimental manipulation was accepted, the next important concept to gain credence was the idea of *control data*. It became apparent that an investigator could strengthen the demonstration of IV effects by showing that a second group of subjects not experiencing the IV responded differently from those receiving the IV. Adding a second group, then, gave the researcher a measure of the specific effects of the IV. This would show up as the difference in DV scores "between" the two groups, for ideally both groups are equated on all secondary variables.

The additional control group is important for another reason. With a second group, the investigator has the ability to identify the effect of the IV by dividing the total variation among scores into two categories, V_B and

---

[1] Comparative investigations are similar to what is presently called ex post facto analysis. One main distinction, however, between comparative investigations and present EPF research is that many statistical procedures developed in the last eight decades have enhanced confidence in EPF investigations.

V_W. The difference in the DV between the two groups (V_B) represents the amount of variation due to the IV, and the difference between the scores in a particular group (V_W) gives a measure of the amount of fluctuation in the DV between subjects due to uncontrolled secondary variables. This measure of within-group variation gives the investigator something with which to compare the difference between the two group scores. As mentioned in Chapter Four, the question in experimentation is not whether the DV measures of the control group differ from those of the experimental group. We expect they will not be exactly the same, even if the IV has no effect on one of the groups. The question is whether the difference between the two groups is significantly larger than the amount of random fluctuation usually found between scores in the given situation with no IV present. To calculate this, the difference in DV between the groups is divided by the difference between the scores within the groups. This ratio then tells how many more times the variation in DV between the groups was larger than chance fluctuation between scores.

In a statistics course you are taught that it is possible for the DV measures of the IV group to be larger than the DV measures for the control group simply because of random fluctuation rather than because of any real influence of the IV. Therefore, a measure of V_B/V_W could be larger than 1 when the IV had no effect. The probability of this happening, however, varies according to the size of the value obtained. (For example, the probability of V_B/V_W equaling 1.25 by chance is higher than if the obtained V_B/V_W ratio is 4.30.) The student does not need to calculate the probability of receiving a certain V_B/V_W value due to chance; this has already been done for him in the t and F tables. He or she simply takes the value obtained, looks it up on an appropriate t or F table, and notes the probability.

In a two-group design situation, then, the investigator is interested in the following points:

1. Controlling secondary variables.
2. Applying an IV to the experimental group while not giving it to the control group.
3. Getting a measure of V_B and V_W.
4. Comparing V_B to V_W to determine the probability that the difference in scores between the two groups could be due to chance fluctuations.

Six different types of two-group designs are covered in this chapter. All six involve these four points. Generally, all carry out the last three points in exactly the same way. The differences center around the different way each carries out the first point—controlling secondary variables.[2]

---

[2] Actually, two-group designs using statistical control (analysis of covariance) do differ from the others on point 3 also. This should not bother the reader to the extent that the similarities are not perceived.

Each employs a different combination of the five control procedures presented earlier. The next six sections of the chapter present the types of two-group designs and examples of how each is carried out.

TYPES OF TWO-GROUP DESIGNS

Randomized Two-Group Design,

Posttest Only $\begin{pmatrix} RXO_1 \\ R\ \ O_2 \end{pmatrix}$

The randomized, posttest only, two-group design is the most common two-group design, and possibly the easiest to understand. Let us take a hypothetical case in which the effects of household pain relievers such as aspirin are tested on the ability to memorize a list of words. First, we formulate the hypothesis that household pain relievers decrease the ability to learn previously learned lists of words. Second, we specify what the IV and DV will actually be. Four aspirin tablets will represent the category of household pain relievers, and the time it takes to memorize fifteen nonsense syllables so that they can be repeated in order by a subject without making any mistakes is the DV representing the category of ability to remember. Third, we set about controlling secondary variables. We do not use the control procedure of making some secondary variable an IV because we have limited our investigation to a comparison between two groups. Isolating a secondary variable by making it an IV would require at least two more groups, so we skip this control possibility. We may then look for secondary variables that can be eliminated. We randomly select subjects from an introductory psychology class, eliminating any foreign students from the random selection because of possible language problems that would bias the results. Students afflicted with arthritis may also be excluded, for arthritis patients generally use large amounts of household pain relievers and thereby build up an unusually high tolerance for such drugs. Visual distractions (e.g., posters, pinups) may be removed from the room where the experiment is to be carried out. Next we look for secondary variables to hold constant. There may be sex differences, so we make sure there are as many women as men in each group. Both groups are tested in the same large room at the same time. This will equate the effects of temperature, time of day, noise, and visual secondary variables. The same instructions are given to each group in the same manner. Next we look for any measurable covariates possible in the situation. IQ is a potential covariate, but unfortunately we do not have any measure of it, so statistical control is not possible. Finally, we randomize the assignment of subjects to the two groups. This should equate both groups on IQ and any other secondary variable not eliminated or held constant.

Our fourth major experimental step is the actual carrying out of the experiment and the application of the IV. Each subject in group B is given four aspirin tablets and subjects in group A are given none. Thirty minutes later both groups of ten subjects are taken to a large classroom, where they are given the list of nonsense syllables to memorize. The time required for each subject to memorize the list to the point of being able verbally to repeat the list with no errors is recorded for each subject. The results obtained from the experiment are presented below. Each number represents the DV (number of seconds) for a particular subject.

GROUP A	GROUP B
178	191
175	202
187	183
170	196
175	195
173	193
163	207
171	198

The fifth major experimental step is the statistical analysis of the data. What empirical effect did the IV have on the DV? Is the effect significant? Did the IV cause the variation in the DV? Whenever an experiment involves two, and only two, groups, a statistical analysis called the t-test is carried out to determine if the IV did have an effect. A formula for determining t for two randomized groups is

$$t = \frac{\overline{X}_a - \overline{X}_b}{\sqrt{\dfrac{SS_a + SS_b}{(n_a - 1) + (n_b - 1)}\left(\dfrac{1}{n_a} + \dfrac{1}{n_b}\right)}}$$

Although this formula may seem somewhat awesome, it is actually rather easy to compute and understand. Remember that the numerator reflects the variation between groups and the denominator represents the variation within groups.

The first step is to compute the means for both groups. (The subscripts are added to indicate which group a particular statistic represents.) In the numerator, $\overline{X}_a$ represents the mean of group A and n stands for the number of subjects in a particular group. Any use of large-N in this text will represent *all* the subjects in a particular experiment (in this example N would equal 16). The Greek letter Σ (called sigma) will be employed to mean "the sum of" or "total." The mean for group A and group B can be calculated as follows:

$$\overline{X}_a = \frac{\Sigma X_a}{n_a} = \frac{178 + 175 + 187 + 170 + 175 + 173 + 163 + 171}{8}$$

$$= \frac{1,392}{8} = 174$$

$$\overline{X}_b = \frac{\Sigma X_b}{n_b} = \frac{191 + 202 + 183 + 196 + 195 + 193 + 207 + 198}{8}$$

$$= \frac{1,565}{8} = 195.625$$

After computing the means, the "sum of squares" for each group is computed with the following formula:

$$SS = \Sigma X^2 - \frac{(\Sigma X)^2}{n}$$

GROUP A

Subject Number	X_a	X_a^2
1	178	31,684
2	175	30,625
3	187	34,969
4	170	28,900
5	175	30,625
6	173	29,929
7	163	26,569
8	171	29,241

$$n_a = 8 \qquad \Sigma X_a = 1,392 \qquad \Sigma X_a^2 = 242,542$$

$$\overline{X}_a = \frac{1,392}{8} = 174$$

$$SS_a = \Sigma X_a^2 - \frac{(\Sigma X_a)^2}{n_a}$$

$$= 242,542 - \frac{1,937,664}{8}$$

$$= 334$$

GROUP B

Subject Number	X_b	X_b^2
1	191	36,481
2	202	40,804
3	183	33,489
4	196	38,416
5	195	38,025
6	193	37,249
7	207	42,849
8	198	39,204

$$n_b = 8 \qquad \Sigma X_b = 1,565 \qquad X_b^2 = 306,517$$

$$\overline{X}_b = \frac{1,565}{8} = 195.625$$

$$SS_b = \Sigma X_b^2 - \frac{(\Sigma X_b)^2}{n_b}$$

$$= 306,517 - \frac{2,449,225}{8}$$

$$= 363.88$$

We now have all the values required to compute the t. In summary, these values are

$$\overline{X}_a = 174 \qquad \overline{X}_b = 195.625$$

$$n_a = 8 \qquad n_b = 8$$

$$SS_a = 334 \qquad SS_b = 363.88$$

Substituting these values into the formula, t is then computed with the largest of the two group means always being put first in the numerator.

$$t = \frac{195.625 - 174}{\sqrt{\frac{334 + 363.88}{(8-1) + (8-1)}\left(\frac{1}{8} + \frac{1}{8}\right)}} = \frac{21.625}{\sqrt{12.46}} = \frac{21.625}{3.53} = 6.13$$

Now that t has been computed, a table of t is consulted to determine the probability of obtaining a t equal to 6.13 by chance. A t table may be found in the Appendix. On the left-hand side of the table is a column labeled df.[3] In a randomized two-group design $df = N - 2$. The df, for

---

[3] The term df stands for degrees of freedom. Degrees of freedom may be calculated differently for different types of experimental designs. If a student is unfamiliar with this term, consult a text on statistics for a more thorough explanation.

example, equals 14, $(16 - 2)$, so we run down the *df* column to 14, then read across the row correlated with *df* = 14 until we come to a value just smaller than 6.13. In this case, however, the largest number is 2.977. We now read up the column to the top where it says 0.01, which stands for the probability of 1 percent. Now if our *t* had equaled 2.977, the chart would tell us that the probability of getting *t* = 2.977 with 14 *df* by chance is 1 out of 100. Because the *t* obtained was larger than 2.977, this finding indicates that a difference between the two groups obtained in this experiment would occur by chance less than 1 time out of 100. Because a *p* = 0.05 is usually accepted as showing that the change was significant, we may in step 6 conclude that the aspirin did influence the time it took to learn.

Matched Two-Group Design $\begin{pmatrix} \text{RMXO}_1 \\ \text{RM } \text{O}_2 \end{pmatrix}$

Recall from Chapter Four that holding secondary variables constant was preferred over randomization for equating experimental groups on some particular variable. A matched two-group design is a modification of the totally randomized two-group design. With this design, both groups are matched in terms of some variable the experimenter feels would influence the DV. Suppose we want to carry out an experiment to determine whether words closely associated (e.g., bride, church, ring, white) are learned faster than words not so associated (e.g., tree, watch, hook, curtain, ruler). At the start of the project we believe that IQ will influence how well a person can retain words, so we match the two groups on IQ. We might have ten subjects available for the experiment with IQs as follows:

Subject Number	IQ
1	120
2	120
3	110
4	110
5	100
6	100
7	100
8	100
9	90
10	90

To divide the ten subjects into two matched groups of five subjects each, we initially rank-order the subjects on the matching variable, in this case IQ. We then divide the ten subjects into five pairs by going down the list making 1 and 2 the first pair, 3 and 4 the second pair, and so on. We then randomly assign one of each pair to either group A or group B by flipping a coin and saying that the odd-numbered subject of the pair goes to group A if heads comes up or to group B if tails comes up. The coin would be flipped a total of five times, once for each pair. The random assignment of matched subjects to either group is done as a means of equating both groups on *all* secondary variables other than the one controlled for by matching. After matching and randomly assigning subjects, the composition of the two groups would be as shown in Table 9-1.

After the groups have been made up, the IV (word lists) is applied. Each group is given five minutes to memorize their respective twenty-word list. One week later the subjects are asked to recall as many words as they can from their list. The results are given in Table 9-2.

To carry out a statistical analysis of matched groups, the randomized *t* formula is somewhat modified.

$$t = \frac{\overline{X}_a - \overline{X}_b}{\sqrt{\dfrac{\Sigma D^2 - \dfrac{(\Sigma D)^2}{n}}{n(n-1)}}}$$

The symbols are basically the same for this calculation as for those used before. The only difference is the *D* score, which is the difference between the recorded scores (DV scores) for each pair of subjects. To find *D* in a pair of scores, subtract the first member of the pair from the second number member. In the example, subjects 2 and 1 scored 8 and 10, respectively. *D* would therefore be $D = 8 - 10$, which equals (-2). The presence of the negative sign actually makes little difference in the final score, since our next step is to square that value. The only preference for

TABLE 9–1   *Matching Subjects on IQ for a Matched Two-Group Design*

NONASSOCIATED WORD GROUP Subject Number	IQ	ASSOCIATED WORD GROUP Subject Number	IQ
2	120	1	120
3	110	4	110
6	100	5	100
7	100	8	100
10	90	9	90
Total	520	Total	520

TABLE 9–2   *Raw Scores for Subjects in a Matched Two-Group Design*

NONASSOCIATED WORD GROUP		ASSOCIATED WORD GROUP	
Subject Number	Retention Score	Subject Number	Retention Score
2	8	1	10
3	6	4	9
6	5	5	6
7	2	8	6
10	2	9	5

---

using that particular order in subtraction is for consistency. Completion of the *D* calculation is shown below. The nonassociated word group is X_a, the associated word group X_b.

Subject Number	X_a	Subject Number	X_b	D	D^2
2	8	1	10	−2	4
3	6	4	9	−3	9
6	5	5	6	−1	1
7	2	8	6	−4	16
10	2	9	5	−3	9

$n_a = 5$ $\Sigma X_a = 23$ $n_b = 5$ $\Sigma X_b = 36$ $\Sigma D = (-13)$ $\Sigma D^2 = 39$

$(\Sigma D)^2 = (-13)^2 = 169$

$\overline{X}_a = \dfrac{23}{5} = 4.6$ $\overline{X}_b = \dfrac{36}{5} = 7.2$

Recall that *n* is the number of subjects in a group, not the total number of subjects in the entire experiment. The latter is noted as *N*. The numerator is the difference between the two DV means of the two groups, $\overline{X}_a$ and $\overline{X}_b$. The calculated means of the two groups are, respectively, 4.6 and 7.2. Substitute all those values in the equation and the results are as follows:

$$ t = \frac{7.2 - 4.6}{\sqrt{\dfrac{39 - \dfrac{(-13)^2}{5}}{5(5 - 1)}}} = 5.10 $$

To compute the *df* (degrees of freedom) for the matched *t*-test, calculate *df* = number of pairs − 1. Note the difference from the equation from the randomized two-group design. Upon consulting the *t*-test table, with a *t* of 5.10 and 4 degrees of freedom, we find that the *t* is significant at the

	GROUP I (CONTROL)	GROUP II (STRESS)
LITTER	NO. OF SUBJECTS	NO. OF SUBJECTS
1	3	3
2	3	3
3	3	3
4	3	3
5	3	3
6	3	3
7	3	3
8	3	3
9	3	3
10	3	3
Total	30	30

TABLE 9–3   *Two-Group Design Blocked on the Secondary Variable, Litter*

0.01 level.[4] We may then conclude that the groups differ to a significant degree. Our original hypothesis is confirmed.

It is important to keep in mind the fact that matching groups on a secondary variable does not improve the analysis of the data unless the secondary variable being matched is *correlated* with the DV being measured. For example, if the students were matched on shoe size instead of IQ, matching would not have improved the design at all because shoe size is not related to one's ability to remember things. IQ, on the other hand, is related to one's ability to memorize. The principle is *the more a secondary variable is correlated with the DV measure, the more important matching becomes.*

Insight
Matching or Blocking?

In the previous chapter the terms *matching* and *blocking* were introduced. Blocking is the procedure of equating groups in an experiment on one particular secondary variable. Suppose, for example, an investigator was interested in determining the effects of stress on the behavior of rats and explores this with a two-group design having thirty rats in each group. Realizing heredity may be an important secondary variable, the researcher decides to block the groups according to littermates. Taking six rats from each of ten different litters, three rats from each litter are then randomly assigned to the two groups. Table 9-3 shows the results of the blocking. Both groups have been equated on an important secondary variable.

Matching is a special form of blocking in which the experimenter "matches" the subjects in a two-group design into *pairs* according to some important secondary variable (as shown in the least example, where IQ was the secondary variable the

---

[1] The same *t* table is used for both matched and unmatched two-group designs.

subjects were paired on, see table 9-1). In the last example the pairing allowed the experimenter to use a *t*-test based on difference scores between the pairs, rather than the standard *t*-test for randomized two-group designs. In essence, the *t*-test for matched groups helps control for the secondary variable effect of IQ differences and makes the effect of the IV more detectable.

It is possible for the investigator to have equated (blocked rather than matched) the two groups on IQ without specifically pairing the subjects. The investigation would then have used the *t*-test for the randomized two-group design on the data as shown in Table 9-4.

Notice that the *t* value obtained from just blocking (not matching) is smaller and does not reach the 0.05 level of significance, while the *t* value obtained by matching the pairs was large enough to be significant. (Keep in mind that the size of the two *t* values is not directly comparable because the degrees of freedom are calculated differently for the two types of *t*-tests being compared here.)

The point made here is that matching (a special form of blocking) is often used with two-group designs to not only equate the two groups on an important secondary variable, but also to control the effects of that secondary variable in the test of significance. Blocking may be employed in any experiment to equate the groups on some secondary variable. (In the next chapter we will see that blocking, like matching, also may allow one to improve the statistical analysis run.)

Pretest-Posttest Control Group Design $\begin{pmatrix} RO_1XO_2 \\ RO_3\ \ O_4 \end{pmatrix}$

One of the most common experimental designs in human investigations is the pretest-posttest control group design. It is a popular design, for it not only neatly controls for seven of the nine sources of secondary variation, but also provides a measure of the DV for each group prior to the administration of the IV. This also allows the investigator to employ an analysis of covariance if the DV is originally different for the two

TABLE 9–4   *A t-test Calculated on the Data from Subjects Blocked Rather Than Matched on IQ*

GROUP A SCORES	GROUP B SCORES
8	10
6	9
5	6
2	6
2	5
$\Sigma X_a = 23$	$\Sigma X_b = 36$

$$t = \frac{\bar{X}_a - \bar{X}_b}{\sqrt{\dfrac{ss_a + ss_b}{(n_a - 1) + (n_b - 1)}\left(\dfrac{1}{n_a} + \dfrac{1}{n_b}\right)}}$$

groups, and provides a measure of effects due to retroactive history. The scores on the pretest and posttest for the control group would be almost identical, unless some unsuspected secondary variable influences the DV while the investigation is in progress. When this happens, O_3 will vary from O_4, giving a measure of the effect of the unnoticed secondary variable. Upon spotting this fluctuation, the investigator may statistically adjust for this effect on the DV score of the group experiencing the IV. The following example illustrates the use of a pretest and posttest control group design.

Paul Stevens received his bachelor's degree in business education with a minor in psychology. After graduation, Paul became a manager of a large meat packing plant dealing mainly with chicken processing. He was going over the books one day in an effort to find ways of cutting processing costs when certain figures caught his eye. Chicken pluckers were paid $1.80 an hour, and the average number of chickens plucked per hour was twelve. He recalled from the behavior analysis course that he had taken that the type of reinforcement schedule employed was shown to influence productivity. Remembering his instructor mentioned that people would produce more on a fixed ratio schedule, Paul decided to carry out an experiment to test this statement. From the list of 120 chicken pluckers applying for jobs, he randomly assigned 10 to one of two 5-man groups. After the 10 new men had been working a whole week for $1.80 per hour, Paul calculated the number of chickens plucked by each man per 8-hour shift. The results of this calculation are shown below.

GROUP A		GROUP B	
Worker Number	*Pretest Score*	*Worker Number*	*Pretest Score*
1	92	6	93
2	96	7	95
3	94	8	99
4	98	9	97
5	94	10	96

He then told group B workers that they would be paid 12¢ a chicken for each one plucked rather than $1.80 per hour. Group A workers remained on the hourly wage. After 4 weeks had passed, Paul calculated the number of chickens plucked per 8-hour shift by each worker for the past week. The results are shown below.

GROUP A		GROUP B	
Worker Number	*Posttest Score*	*Worker Number*	*Posttest Score*
1	96	6	112
2	98	7	116
3	97	8	108
4	101	9	110
5	98	10	114

Actually, there are a few ways to analyze this type of design statistically, though the most common is a *t*-test on gain scores.

The tables and equations below demonstrate how to line up your data. The procedure basically involves subtracting each worker's pretest score from the posttest score. The difference is called the *gain score*. Each gain score is then treated as a raw score for each subject, and a *t*-test is carried out using the same formula employed with the randomized two-group design.

Worker Number	GROUP A Pretest Score	Posttest Score	Gain Score	Worker Number	GROUP B Pretest Score	Posttest Score	Gain Score
1	92	96	4	6	93	112	19
2	96	98	2	7	95	116	21
3	94	97	3	8	99	108	9
4	98	101	3	9	97	110	13
5	94	98	4	10	96	114	18

Worker Number	GROUP A Gain Score (X)	X^2	Worker Number	GROUP B Gain Score (X)	X^2
1	4	16	6	19	361
2	2	4	7	21	441
3	3	9	8	9	81
4	3	9	9	13	169
5	4	16	10	18	324

$$n_a = 5 \quad \Sigma X_a = 16 \quad \Sigma X_a^2 = 54 \qquad n_b = 5 \quad \Sigma X_b = 80 \quad \Sigma X_b^2 = 1{,}376$$

$$\overline{X}_a = \frac{\Sigma X_a}{n} = \frac{16}{5} = 3.2 \qquad \overline{X}_b = \frac{\Sigma X_b}{n} = \frac{80}{5} = 16$$

$$SS_a = \Sigma X_a^2 - \frac{(\Sigma X_a)^2}{n} \qquad SS_b = \Sigma X_b^2 - \frac{(\Sigma X_b)^2}{n}$$

$$= 54 - \frac{(16)^2}{5} = 2.8 \qquad = 1{,}376 - \frac{(80)^2}{5} = 96$$

Next, the values are substituted into the *t* formula for two randomized groups. The rule is to put the largest mean first in the numerator so that the resultant number is always positive.

$$t = \frac{\overline{X}_b - \overline{X}_a}{\sqrt{\dfrac{SS_a + SS_b}{(n_a - 1) + (n_b - 1)}\left(\dfrac{1}{n_a} + \dfrac{1}{n_b}\right)}} = \frac{16 - 3.2}{\sqrt{\dfrac{2.8 + 96}{4 + 4}\left(\dfrac{1}{5} + \dfrac{1}{5}\right)}}$$

$$= \frac{12.8}{\sqrt{4.94}} = 5.76$$

Turning to the *t* table with *t* equaling 5.76 and *df* equaling 8, we find the change in pay schedule to have influenced output, for the probability of a *t* this size occurring by chance is less than 0.01, or less than 1 in 100.

It is not an uncommon thing for students to carry out an *incorrect* statistical analysis on a pretest-posttest design. Students frequently compute two *t*s, one for the pretest-posttest difference obtained with the experimental group and one for the pretest-posttest difference in the control group. If the *t* test for the experimental group is significant and the control group's *t* is not, they then conclude that the IV had an effect. The *incorrect* procedure is shown below.

Worker Number	Pretest Score	GROUP A Posttest Score	Difference (D)	D^2
1	92	96	4	16
2	96	94	-2	4
3	94	97	3	9
4	98	95	-3	9
5	94	98	4	16

$$n = 5 \quad \Sigma X_a = 480 \quad \Sigma X_b = 480 \quad \Sigma D = 6 \quad \Sigma D^2 = 54$$

$$X_a = \frac{474}{5} \qquad X_b = \frac{480}{5}$$

$$= 94.8 \qquad\qquad = 96$$

$$t = \frac{\overline{X}_b - \overline{X}_a}{\sqrt{\dfrac{\Sigma D^2 - \dfrac{(\Sigma D)^2}{n}}{n(n-1)}}}$$

$$= \frac{96 - 94.8}{\sqrt{\dfrac{54 - \dfrac{36}{5}}{5(5-1)}}}$$

$$= 0.76 \text{ (not significant)}$$

If the *t* for the experimental group is significant and the *t* for the control group is not, it is erroneously concluded that the IV had an effect.

Worker Number	Pretest Score	GROUP B Posttest Score	Difference (D)	D^2
6	93	112	19	361
7	95	116	21	441
8	99	108	9	81
9	97	110	13	169
10	96	114	18	324

$$n = 5 \qquad \Sigma X_a = 480 \qquad \Sigma X_b = 560 \qquad \Sigma D = 80 \qquad \Sigma D^2 = 1{,}376$$

$$\bar{X}_a = \frac{480}{5} \qquad \bar{X}_b = \frac{560}{5}$$

$$= 96 \qquad\qquad = 112$$

$$t = \frac{\bar{X}_b - \bar{X}_a}{\sqrt{\dfrac{\Sigma D^2 - \dfrac{(\Sigma D)^2}{n}}{n(n-1)}}}$$

$$= \frac{112 - 96}{\sqrt{\dfrac{1{,}376 - \dfrac{6{,}400}{5}}{5(5-1)}}}$$

$$= \frac{16}{\sqrt{4.8}} = \frac{16}{2.19} = 7.3$$

This analysis is incorrect because it may lead to significant *t*s when in fact there was no significance.

Insight
Related Measures Designs

While a randomized matched two-group design and a randomized pretest-posttest two-group design differ in some respects, there is one important dimension that they have in common. Both are *related measures* designs. Related measures two-group designs improve on the main randomized two-group design in that they both try to not only equate the two groups on all important secondary subject variables, but also to additionally reduce an important secondary variable, the between-subject differences (proactive history).

Matched Designs

Notice from the example previously given for a matched design that the subjects were paired on an important secondary variable, IQ. The data analysis, then, consisted of comparing the scores of the subjects *related* on IQ. The statistical test for the randomized matched two-group design is designed to inherently compare only the DV measures of subjects that are similar (related) in terms of IQ. For example, a subject with an IQ of 120 is compared with a related subject in the opposing group, not with a subject differing substantially on IQ (e.g., a subject with an IQ of 90). This greater control of an important secondary variable through matching gives the statistical test greater resolving power in detecting IV effects.

Pretest-Posttest Designs

The best way to reduce the problem of variability between subjects is to compare a subject with himself or herself rather than with a different subject. And that is what a pretest-posttest design allows the investigator to do. From the example earlier in this chapter, it is apparent that the gain score is obtained by subtracting a subject's pretest score from his or her own posttest score. The *gain* score from a pretest-posttest design, like the *difference* score from the matched design, is the result of subtracting related measures.

The pretest-posttest design is a special type of related measure design called a *repeated measure design*. Repeated measure designs are any designs where more than one DV measure is taken from each subject in the investigation. (In the following chapter a repeated measure design is illustrated in which each subject experiences several different levels of the same IV.)

Static Group Design $\begin{pmatrix} XO_1 \\ O_2 \end{pmatrix}$

The static group design is identical to the randomized two-group design with one important exception: subjects are not randomly assigned to groups. This one factor makes a large difference in Table 9-2 between the static group design and the randomized two-group design. The randomized two-group design is much preferred, for randomization allows one to control for secondary variables. The static group design is devoid of any of the five control procedures previously covered, and it therefore leaves any conclusion from the results open to misinterpretation regarding the influence of the IV. In some cases, however, the situation leaves one no alternative but to use the static group design. Here is an example.

Suppose that during wartime a new type of fighter plane is developed. The war office wants a study carried out to determine whether the new plane is more effective in dog fights than the one currently being used. It is not feasible to supply two present air squadrons with one-half new and one-half old planes, for special training is required of the pilots and each squadron has to have all planes alike for coordinated flying. The practical solution is to compare one whole squadron equipped with the new fighter.

The type of statistical analysis carried out on a static group comparison is the same as for randomized two groups. One must be careful, however, in using this analysis. To justify the use of the *t*-test in experiments involving the comparison between means, two assumptions are necessary:

first, the populations from which the subjects come should be normalized, and, second, the population variances should be homogeneous.[5] When a static group comparison is carried out, the possibility that these assumptions are not met is much greater than when a randomized group design is used. It is strongly suggested that students refrain from using this design whenever possible. It is not considered adequate, especially for theses or dissertation research.

Nonrandomized Pretest-Posttest Control Group Design

$$\begin{pmatrix} O_1 X O_2 \\ O_3 \ O_4 \end{pmatrix}$$

The nonrandomized pretest-posttest control group design is related to the randomized pretest-posttest design in the same way the static group design is related to the randomized two-group design. It is identical to the pretest-posttest control group design except that the groups have not been composed of randomly assigned subjects. Therefore, it is highly probable that the two groups have not been equated. As a result, the same type of statistical analysis difficulties encountered with the static group design hold also for the nonrandomized pretest-posttest design. Because the same statistical t-test is employed for the pretest-posttest control group design as for the randomized two-group design, the problem of meeting the underlying assumptions is again present. Although the nonrandomized pretest-posttest control group design is inferior to the pretest-posttest control group design, it has an advantage over the static group design. The pretest-posttest design may show differences in the groups prior to the administration of the IV. The experimenter may then adjust for this by using an analysis of covariance.

Analysis of Covariance Two-Group Design

$$\begin{pmatrix} RYXO_1 \\ RY \ O_2 \end{pmatrix}$$

So far all the two-group designs have used a manipulatory approach to decrease the influence of secondary variables. Analysis of covariance is a means for controlling secondary variables using a statistical rather than a manipulatory approach. Differences among observations in an experiment may be due in part to differences that existed among the subjects prior to

---

[5] By *normalized* we mean results will be more accurate the more symmetrical the population distribution curve. If there are too many deviances from the general trend, it is only logical that their presence would tend to skew the obtained results. By *homogeneity* we mean the within-group variances obtained should resemble, in degree variation, the within-group variation of the experimental group data. A complete explanation is found in Hays [1973].

the experiment and that persisted through the experiment. It is possible to adjust the observations for the purpose of eliminating these initial differences, if there are measures of these differences available.

In Chapter Eight the idea was put forth that variability in measures could be adjusted using regression analysis procedures. If an investigator had the numerical values of two different variables (X and Y) for each subject involved in an investigation, it is possible to determine how much of the fluctuation of either variable was related to changes in the other. If, for example, the IQ score (Y) and scores on a math exam (X) are known for each child in the class, it is possible to determine how much of the variation in the math scores of the class were related to differences in the students' IQ. As shown in the formula

$$V_T = V_{IQ} + V_O$$

the total variation in scores is equal to the variability due to IQ (V_{IQ}) plus variations due to all other factors (V_O).[6] By means of correlational procedures the amount of variability due to IQ could be numerically identified and removed.

In an ideal experimental situation the investigator has employed adequate control procedures so that both groups in a two-group design are equal in terms of all secondary variables potentially relevant in the experimental situation. Most investigations, however, are not ideal. In some instances a potent secondary variable may not be adequately equated in both groups although control procedures were employed. In other situations it may not be possible for the investigator to equate the groups on all important variables. In such cases the investigator combines correlational analysis procedures with the normal analysis of variance procedures. Here is an example.

Carol Davis, a creative grade-school teacher for twelve years, developed what she felt was a better method of teaching first-grade children to identify written words verbally. With the support of the school board and another first-grade teacher in a nearby grade school, Carol set up a two-group experimental design to compare her new method of teaching (method A) with a more common approach (method B). She was to be responsible for teaching words to the two different first-grade classes. With one class, group A, she used method A, and with the other, group B, she used method B. She and the other teacher traded classes each day at noon. After lunch each day Carol would drive to the second school, while the other teacher would drive over and take Carol's class for the last half of the day.

---

[6] Remember, the phrase *related* to IQ is used, for IQ may not actually be causing the variability. The variability may represent the influence of some other variable that concurrently influences both IQ and math behavior to the same degree.

At the end of the year, all the children of both classes were given a test to determine their ability to identify written words verbally. The results of this test are shown below.

GROUP A (METHOD A)		GROUP B (METHOD B)	
Student Number	Score	Student Number	Score
1	11	1	2
2	11	2	7
3	7	3	5
4	8	4	7
5	7	5	6
6	12	6	14
7	14	7	7
8	5	8	5
9	5	9	1
10	9	10	5

It was Carol's intent to determine the between-group variance and the within-group variance, and then calculate the t of the two to determine whether her new method was better. She then proceeded to do the following statistical analysis:

$$t = \frac{\overline{X}_a - \overline{X}_b}{\sqrt{\dfrac{SS_a + SS_b}{(n_a - 1) + (n_b - 1)}\left(\dfrac{1}{n_a} + \dfrac{1}{n_b}\right)}}$$

GROUP A

Student Number	X	X^2
1	11	121
2	11	121
3	7	49
4	8	64
5	7	49
6	12	144
7	14	196
8	5	25
9	5	25
10	9	81

$n_a = 10$ $\Sigma X_a = 89$ $\Sigma X_a^2 = 875$

$$\overline{X}_a = \frac{\Sigma X_a}{n} = \frac{89}{10} = 8.9$$

$$SS_a = \Sigma X_a^2 - \frac{(\Sigma X_a)^2}{n} = 875 - \frac{(89)^2}{10} = 82.9$$

GROUP B

Student Number	X	X^2
1	2	4
2	7	49
3	5	25
4	7	49
5	6	36
6	14	196
7	7	49
8	5	25
9	1	1
10	5	25

$$n_b = 10 \qquad \Sigma X_b = 59 \qquad \Sigma X_b^2 = 459$$

$$\bar{X}_b = \frac{\Sigma X_b}{n} = \frac{59}{10} = 5.9$$

$$SS_b = \Sigma X_b^2 - \frac{(\Sigma X_b)^2}{n} = 459 - \frac{(59)^2}{10} = 110.9$$

$$t = \frac{8.9 - 5.9}{\sqrt{\dfrac{110.9 + 82.9}{(10 - 1) + (10 - 1)} \left(\dfrac{1}{10} + \dfrac{1}{10}\right)}}$$

$$= \frac{3.0}{\sqrt{\dfrac{193.8}{18} \left(\dfrac{1}{5}\right)}}$$

$$= \frac{3.0}{\sqrt{(10.8)(1/5)}}$$

$$= \frac{3.0}{\sqrt{2.16}} = \frac{3.0}{1.47} = 2.04$$

In checking the files on the first graders, Carol noted that the IQ levels appeared to be different for the two classes. Realizing that IQ might be an important secondary variable, Carol then decided to carry out an analysis of covariance to adjust for any differences in the experimental results (scores on the word recognition test) related to differences in IQ. To carry out an analysis of covariance between the two groups, the

t formula had to be modified as follows:[7]

$$t = \frac{(1 - r^2)(\overline{X}_a - \overline{X}_b)}{\sqrt{\dfrac{SS_a + SS_b}{(n_a - 1) + (n_b - 1)}\left(\dfrac{1}{n_a} + \dfrac{1}{n_b}\right)}}$$

Notice the numerator has the added value $(1 - r^2)$. You may recall from Chapter Seven that r stands for correlation coefficient and can be used for determining the amount of variability in X related to some correlated variable (Y). The argument was put forth that if two variables were correlated the square of the correlation between the two (r^2) would indicate the percentage of variations in X that could be related to Y. The value of $(1 - r^2)$ would then represent the percentage of variability of X due to factors other than variable Y. In the two-group design, the objective was to equate the two groups on all secondary variables in the experimental setting so that the difference between the group means could be due only to the IV. In the present case, the groups were found to differ also on IQ, a secondary variable known to be an important determinant for academic achievement. The obtained variation between the means $(\overline{X}_a - \overline{X}_b)$ is then partially a function of IQ. The following formula shows that the total variation between the means (V_B) is equal to variation due to the IV (V_{IV}) plus the variation related to IQ (V_{IQ}).

$$V_B = V_{IV} + V_{IQ}$$

The variation related to IQ must then be extracted from the obtained difference between the means. If r^2 equals the percentage of V_B due to IQ, then $1 - r^2$ should equal the percentage of V_B due to the IV. With this fact in mind, the obtained $(\overline{X}_a - \overline{X}_b)$ is adjusted to obtain the predicted difference between the means if IQ had been held constant for both groups.

To accomplish the adjustment of $(\overline{X}_a - \overline{X}_b)$, the following calculations need to be made:[8]

---

[7] The analysis of covariance formula is a simplification of the exact formula. It has been modified here to make it easier for the reader to see what is involved in using analysis of covariance. Although this formula may be used for learning the logic behind analysis of covariance, one should employ the analysis of covariance using the F test for two groups when statistically analyzing data from a real experiment, thesis, or dissertation. This procedure is covered in the following chapter. If one is interested in employing the true formula for analysis of covariance using a t-test, it may be found in Keppel's *Design and Analysis: A Researcher's Handbook* [1973].

[8] Y in the calculations represents a measure of IQ. Low numbers have been used instead of actual IQ scores so that the calculations would be less cumbersome. The letter X represents the score of each subject.

GROUP A

Student Number	X	Y	XY	X^2	Y^2
1	11	5	55	121	25
2	11	5	55	121	25
3	7	3	21	49	9
4	8	3	24	64	9
5	7	3	21	49	9
6	12	4	48	144	16
7	14	9	126	196	81
8	5	4	20	25	16
9	5	4	20	25	16
10	9	5	45	81	25
$N_a = 10$	$\Sigma X_a = 89$	$\Sigma Y_a = 45$	$\Sigma XY_a = 435$	$\Sigma X_a^2 = 875$	$\Sigma Y_a^2 = 231$

GROUP B

Student Number	X	Y	XY	X^2	Y^2
1	2	4	8	4	16
2	7	3	21	49	9
3	5	4	20	25	16
4	7	3	21	49	9
5	6	5	30	36	25
6	14	6	84	196	36
7	7	5	35	49	25
8	5	3	15	25	9
9	1	3	3	1	9
10	5	3	15	25	9
$N_b = 10$	$\Sigma X_b = 59$	$\Sigma Y_b = 39$	$\Sigma XY_b = 252$	$\Sigma X_b^2 = 459$	$\Sigma Y_b^2 = 163$

$$r = \frac{N\,\Sigma XY - (\Sigma X)(\Sigma Y)}{\sqrt{[N\,\Sigma X^2 - (\Sigma X)^2][N\,\Sigma Y^2 - (\Sigma Y)^2]}}$$

$$= \frac{(20)(435 + 252) - (89 + 59)(45 + 39)}{\sqrt{[(20)(875 + 459) - (89 + 59)^2][(20)(231 + 163) - (45 + 39)^2]}}$$

$$= 0.66$$

$$r^2 = 0.44$$

After calculating r^2, the numerical value is plugged into the formula as follows:

$$t = \frac{(1 - 0.44)(\overline{X}_a - \overline{X}_b)}{\sqrt{\dfrac{SS_a + SS_b}{(n_a - 1) + (n_b - 1)}\,(1/n_a + 1/n_b)}}$$

$$= \frac{1.68}{1.46} = 1.15$$

Notice that the correlation between IQ and test scores is fairly high (0.66). By removing the differences in scores related to IQ, an adjusted *t* is obtained that is no longer significant. This result suggested that Carol's new teaching method was no better than the old method.

Two points should be emphasized. First, if the secondary variable is not highly correlated with the DV measures, then carrying out analysis of covariance adds nothing to the study, for it does not increase control of secondary variable effects in such situations. Second, if the covariate is highly correlated with the DV, then the experimental investigation has been enhanced and is better than carrying out the easier noncovariance analysis.

Insight
Related Measures or Covariance Designs?

By now the astute reader may have realized that there is an important similarity between the analysis of covariance two-group design and the related measures two-group designs. The randomized covariance design and the randomized related measures design improve on the basic randomized design by improving the resolving power of the investigation through better control of an important secondary subject variable.

Covariance and related measures designs are the same in that both require the secondary variable they are specifically controlling for to be measurable. The IQ scores were required in order for the subjects to be "matched" in the experiment on memory. There had to be pretest scores on the subjects for a gain score to be calculated with the pretest-posttest design. IQ scores again had to be available for Carol to employ an analysis of covariance design to study the superiority of teaching methods.

Covariance and related measures designs are also similar in that they only improve on a randomized design to the extent the secondary variable being controlled is correlated with the DV measure being recorded. The higher the correlation, the more covariance and related measures designs improve resolving power over randomized only designs.

The secondary variable, IQ, was intentionally used as the controlled variable in both the matching design and the covariance design to make a point. Both covariance and related measures designs may be employed on the same secondary variable (though obviously not in the same experiment). How then does an investigator decide whether to use a related measures design or a covariance design? Is one of these types of designs always superior to the other? Covariance designs are not always superior to related measures designs; and related measures designs are not always preferred to covariance designs. The answer as to "when" each type of design is more appropriate becomes evident when looking at the differing characteristics of the two types of designs.

Covariance designs, as previously mentioned, employ a statistical means of controlling a secondary variable and require no special means of assigning subjects to groups (other than randomization). The problem of accurately matching up subjects does not arise. The covariate scores are not required before the experiment begins; so analysis of covariance may be employed to control a secondary variable whose effect is not apparent until after the experiment is underway. Therefore, covariance designs allow greater flexibility in the time and means of obtaining the covariate measure. Covariance designs can also result in more powerful statistical tests [Lee, 1975]. It is also possible to control for multiple covariates in one covariance experiment; but it is not feasible to explicitly control for more than one secondary variable with a related measures design. Using randomization, the control of second variables is implicit.

For related measures designs, the analysis of the data is simpler than the analysis of covariance. There are also certain statistical assumptions required when the analysis of covariance is used, which, if not met, may distort the analysis. Related measures designs also allow for a more direct control of the secondary variable.

Most experimenters have a slight preference [e.g., Lee, 1975] to control a secondary variable with a related measures design rather than a covariance design. Keep in mind that one could employ both a related measure (to control variable A) and a covariance procedure (to control variable B) in the same experiment. Such an experiment would consist of a randomized matched analysis of covariance two-group design.

ADVANTAGES AND DISADVANTAGES OF TWO-GROUP DESIGNS

As mentioned, it is possible to reach valid conclusions in experimental situations that do not include a second group for control. Carrying out noncontrol one-group manipulating investigations is a step toward more valid investigations. Being able to determine when an IV would be applied does allow an investigator greater confidence in concluding that any succeeding change in the DV was a function of the IV. Adding a second group made two important contributions to scientific analysis. First, it greatly increased the internal validity of the investigation by allowing the investigator to employ more methods for controlling secondary variables. Second, it furnished the conditions necessary for a true comparison to be made. With the control group, the investigator has a measure of the DV without the influence of the IV. Not only does the control group allow the investigator to see if there is a difference due to the IV, it also provides data necessary for available statistical tests to determine the significance of any obtained group differences.

Two-group designs are generally considered to be excellent for carrying out exploratory investigations aimed at determining whether a particular variable has an effect. They may also be appropriately used to determine which of two alternative variables is better, as was the case with Carol Davis's attempt to compare two teaching approaches. One of the main advantages of two-group designs is simplicity. Later, the designs covered will involve more groups and more complex statistical procedures. The two-group designs are easier to conduct and analyze statistically, yet provide all the factors necessary for a scientific analysis. Too often students assume that the more groups involved and the more complex the statistical analysis, the better the project. Remember, you do not need a baseball bat to kill a fly. A flyswatter will accomplish the job just as well, and possibly faster.

It is difficult to rank-order two-group designs according to which one is best, for each has its good and bad points, and certain ones are more suited to specific situations. The analysis of covariance two-group design has the ability to control secondary variables better than the other two-group designs because it allows the investigator to apply a statistical control procedure in addition to elimination, constancy, and randomization. It also allows the investigator to adjust for the influence of a secondary variable that cannot be controlled experimentally, because randomization or constancy is not possible or the effects of the secondary variable were not apparent until after the investigation began. Disadvantages of two-group analysis of covariance designs are (1) a more complex statistical analysis must be carried out, and (2) a covariate measure must be available.

Randomized, matched two-group designs are also considered good designs, for they employ two control procedures—randomization and constancy. They are similar to randomized analysis of covariance two-group designs in that they can be used to adjust for the effects of a particular secondary variable, besides using randomization to control for all other secondary variables. The advantages of the matched design over the covariance design are in terms of the statistical analysis required. The matched *t*-test is much simpler and faster to calculate than an analysis of covariance. The covariant design is more advantageous in terms of when the control procedure can be applied. Matching for a particular secondary variable must be carried out prior to the beginning of the investigation, whereas a secondary variable may be adjusted for after the experiment begins when an analysis of covariance is used. Analysis of covariance of two-group designs may be used where matching is not feasible, such as in the investigation comparing teaching procedures. It was not feasible to match the two first-grade classes by making some of the students change schools.

Pretest-posttest designs are generally preferred over posttest only designs, mainly because the investigator obtains more information. Pretests may be used to ensure that both groups are equated in terms of the DV when the investigation begins. In some situations an investigator may administer a pretest before assigning subjects to either of the groups. In this way, the investigator may match the two groups on the DV to ensure that the groups are equated. Pretest-posttest two-group designs may "sensitize" the subjects to what is going on in the experiment, thereby biasing the scores they make on the posttest. In many situations, carrying out a pretest is either not practical or not functional for dealing with the problem being investigated. Randomized two-group designs are always preferred over nonrandomized designs, no matter whether they involve pretests, posttests only, matching, or analysis of covariance.

Two-group designs are generally preferred to one-way analysis of variance and factorial designs because they are relatively easy to set up and carry out, yet they are just as scientifically sound as the more complex designs. Though simplicity is the two-group design's greatest asset, it is also its main disadvantage. Due to its simple statistical analysis and its limitation to two groups, it does not allow more than one between-group comparison to be made. If the investigator desires to carry out a parametric study or compare more than two variables at one time, two-group designs are not suitable.

SUMMARY

Although two-group experimental designs have been around for centuries, their importance in scientific investigations has come about only in the last few decades. The basic idea behind adding a second group to an investigation is to provide some measure of a DV from subjects not experiencing the IV. The effect of the IV will then show up as the difference between the DVs of the two groups. Six two-group designs were presented: (1) the randomized two-group design, (2) the matched two-group design, (3) the pretest-posttest control group design, (4) the static group design, (5) the nonrandomized pretest-posttest control group design, and (6) the analysis of covariance two-group design.

 I. Logical Analysis of One-Way ANOVAR Designs Using an F Test
 II. Types of ANOVAR Designs
     A. Randomized One-Way ANOVAR Design
     B. Randomized Blocked One-Way ANOVAR Design
     C. One-Way Analysis of Covariance
     D. Repeated Measurements: One-Way ANOVAR Design
 III. Summary

Multigroup Designs with One Independent Variable

10

Obviously, experiments can be carried out in which three or more groups are employed. These are called one-way ANOVAR experiments. This chapter shows how such experiments are set up and carried out. The first section gives a logical explanation of what is involved in the statistical analysis of one-way ANOVAR designs. The explanation relates very strongly to the discussion of variance given in Chapter Four. The concept of sums of squares is explained. Although the student could simply follow the numerical illustrations given and carry out a statistical analysis without really understanding sums of squares, the explanation is provided for those interested in a more thorough understanding of what is involved in the statistical analysis. As was true with the last chapter, step-by-step examples showing exactly how the statistical tests are conducted have been included so that the student does not need a course in statistics to carry them out. Remember, knowing how to perform the statistical test is only one step in the investigation. The student should concentrate on understanding when one-way ANOVAR designs are used, how they differ from other types of designs, and the advantages and disadvantages of the different ANOVAR designs.

So far, the most complex types of experiments discussed have been those consisting of two groups, an experimental and a control. The objective of these two-group experiments is to determine whether some IV differentially influences the DV of the experimental and control groups. Although two-group designs are the most common in psychological research, they are somewhat restrictive. Events in nature do not always conveniently order themselves into two groups. Frequently, the ivestigator asks which of several alternative variables has the greater effect or wants to compare the effect of different values of the same variable. Which of five different types of teaching machines is most functional for a particular educational program? What dosage of a certain anesthetic is required for deep anesthesia? Obviously, the design necessary to answer these questions requires comparison of more than two groups. Such designs are called one-way ANOVAR designs.[1]

[1] ANOVAR stands for analysis of variance. Analysis of variance is commonly abbreviated as ANOVA to represent analysis of variance as a statistical test.

Suppose you are hired by a pharmaceutical company to find out which of three cough remedies is most effective. The zealous student may see no trouble at all in carrying out such an investigation. Diligently, the student starts through the six steps of experimental analysis involved in a laboratory experiment. Being rather perceptive, he or she realizes all the methods of control for secondary variables covered are just as applicable to experiments involving three or more groups as they are to two-group investigations. The student eliminates as many of the secondary variables as possible, holds others constant for all three groups, and randomly assigns subjects to the groups in an effort to equate all remaining secondary variables. The different cold remedies are then administered, one to each group. The number of minutes each subject goes without coughing over the next hour is then recorded as the DV.

So far the student has done very well. The procedure for carrying out one-way ANOVAR designs is the same as for two-group designs. The means of selecting a hypothesis, determining which IV and DV to employ, controlling for secondary variables, and actually carrying out the procedure are basically identical. The distinguishing feature between the two types of investigations is in the type of statistical analysis used. How do you compare three or more groups? The student may unhesitantly suggest that three *t*-tests be carried out—one between the first and second groups, one between the second and third groups, and one between the first and third groups. This analytical approach is generally considered to be unacceptable, however, and the reason involves the probability of drawing an incorrect conclusion about the results.

Remember, a scientist is very cautious about making a statement that some IV did affect the DV, so cautious, in fact, that he or she will not make such a statement unless there is only a 5 percent chance or less that the fluctuation of the DV occurring in an experiment could have been due to chance. The scientist wants to be at least 95 percent sure that the variation in the DV is due to the IV and not some other variable. An analogy might be betting on a horse race. The scientist would not bet on a horse unless the horse had a 95 percent chance of winning or, inversely, only a 5 percent chance of losing. Most people betting, however, would jump at the chance to bet on a horse if it had even a 60 percent chance of winning.[2] The scientist has a reputation to protect. Society looks to the scientist for direction in terms of what is effective and what will work. His or her statements of cause-effect relationships are respected, for scientists do not make outlandish claims. With precision comes confidence by the people in the conclusions. The scientist is cautious in claiming causes of

---

[2] Most gambling establishments in Las Vegas work on less than a 53/47 split (53 percent probability that the casino will win, 47 percent probability that the customer will win), yet people flock there to accept these odds.

a disease, cancer, mental retardation, and so forth, just as in claiming cures for such conditions.

Although the 5 percent significance level was somewhat arbitrarily selected, scientists revere it and look with disdain on investigators who do not adhere to it. This is the reason the suggested t-test analysis would not be acceptable. The effect of increasing the number of t-tests in an investigation is a correlated increase in the probability that an incorrect conclusion will be drawn. With one t-test the probability is 5 percent for concluding a cause-effect relationship incorrectly. With two t-tests the probability rises to 10 percent. Three t-tests raise it to 15 percent, and so on. From this you may rightly conclude that the probability of stating an incorrect causal conclusion is equal to the number of t-tests carried out times the 5 percent significance level of acceptance. Because of this fact, researchers are reluctant to carry out more than one t-test in an experiment. To cope with the analytical needs of a multigroup comparison, a different statistical technique is employed, an analysis of variance called the F test.

The F test is a statistical technique employed to deal with the problem of significant differences encountered when more than two groups are involved. It may be used in multigroup situations to determine statistically whether the IVs are actually producing differences in the various group DVs.[3]

LOGICAL ANALYSIS OF ONE-WAY ANOVAR DESIGNS USING AN F TEST

As previously mentioned, the six basic steps for carrying out two-group or more than two-group experiments are essentially the same. The only real difference between two-group and multigroup experiments is in the way the statistical analysis is carried out on the data. The main objective of this chapter, then, is to show the student how the statistical analysis can be carried out and to help the student understand the reasoning behind the statistical F test.

In Chapter Four it was stated that the objective of an experiment was to divide total variation into two parts, that which can be accounted for (due to the IV) and that which cannot be accounted for (due to unknown secondary variables and chance variations). We also saw that all experimental investigations involve dividing the variance between groups (V_B) by the variance within groups (V_W). Statistically, this is called an F test. It tells the investigator whether the variance due to the IV was relatively

---

[3] An F test may also be applied in investigations involving only two groups. The principle behind the F and t-tests is the same, and the t-test was a specially devised test for only two groups.

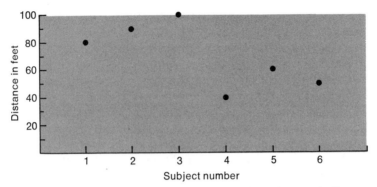

FIGURE 10–1   Theoretical distance six children threw a ball.

larger than the variance expected by chance fluctuation alone. We will now look at this variance idea more closely and see how it relates to the statistical analysis of two-group and ANOVAR designs.

Let us return to the ball-throwing example in Chapter Four. Suppose six children were asked to throw a ball as far as they could, with the results shown in Figure 10–1. As one would expect, the scores vary. The variation in scores would be due to the differential influence of both genetic and environmental factors. All the subjects were not equal in terms of height, strength, and so on. Also, environmental factors such as wind, wetness of ball, and exact weight of ball were not identical on each throw. If one were able magically to take all the genetic and environmental variables present in the situation and redistribute their effects equally among all the subjects, making them all the same height, strength, and so on, the distance each subject threw the ball would be exactly the same as shown in Figure 10–2. The result would be that each subject would throw the ball a distance equaling the mean of the original scores shown in Figure 10–1.

Now that all variables are equally distributed, suppose you took one variable (weight of the balls thrown) and intentionally redistributed it in

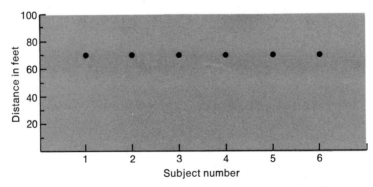

FIGURE 10–2   Theoretical distance six children equal in all respects threw a ball.

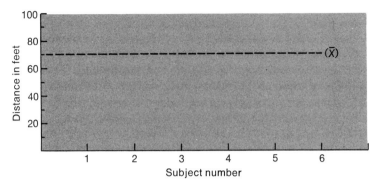

FIGURE 10–3   Theoretical distance six children equal in all respects threw a ball with the weight of the ball being different for each child.

such a way that each subject had to throw a ball of different weight. Figure 10–3 shows the results of such a situation. Each score is different again, with the difference of each score from the mean due to the varied weights of the balls. The cause of the differences in the throws could truthfully be said to be due to the weight of the balls, for the effects of all other variables were equally distributed among the subjects. The vertical distance of each score from the mean would represent the differential influence of the ball's weight.

Suppose the six equated subjects were now divided into two groups, again with the weight of the ball being the only variable unequally distributed. Now, instead of six balls of different weights, only two balls of unequal weight are thrown, one by group A and one by group B. With the results of Figure 10–4, it is not too difficult to conclude that the group B subjects threw the heavier ball. The mean for group A equaled 90 ($\overline{X}_A$ = 90), while the mean for group B equaled 50 ($\overline{X}_B$ = 50). The distance

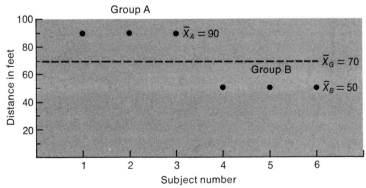

FIGURE 10–4   Theoretical distance six children threw a ball: all genetic and environmental factors were equal except the weight of the ball.

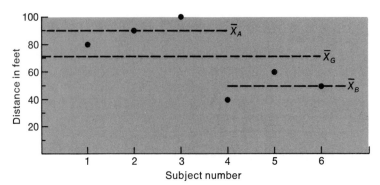

FIGURE 10–5   Theoretical distance six children threw a ball in a usual experimental situation.

from each group mean to the grand mean of all the throws put together ($\overline{X}_G = 70$) would represent the influence of the ball's weight. It could be said that the weight is what caused the difference between the group means and the grand mean.

   Figure 10–4 shows the results of what could be an ideal experiment in which an investigator wanted to determine what effect a ball's weight would have on the distance children could throw. Ideally, he would select six subjects identical in age, weight, strength, and so on. He would divide them into three-subject groups (A and B). Group A would throw a 4-ounce ball, while group B would throw a 5-ounce ball.

   Unfortunately, ideal subjects and situations are seldom found in research. We are stuck with the fact that all subjects are not equal and that environmental conditions are not exactly the same from one moment to the next. Being practical, an experimenter realizes all subjects in either group will not throw the ball the exact same distance as shown in Figure 10–4. The results shown in Figure 10–5 are more like what would be expected. Each subject would throw the ball a different distance, though the mean distance for the group with the lightest ball would be farther than that for the group throwing the heavier ball.

   Figure 10–5 diagrammatically represents the results of a typical experiment. An IV (weight of the ball) is systematically varied from one group to another. This causes scores to vary from the grand mean. A numerical measure of the effect of the IV is the difference of the group means from the grand mean. All the variation from the grand mean, however, is not due to the IV alone. The secondary variables (strength, size, etc.) and error fluctuations (e.g., inexact measurement of distance) are responsible for some. Figure 10–6 presents this point diagrammatically.[4]

[4] The symbol X_{ig} is used through the text to represent *any* subject's score. The subscripts (*i* and *g*) stand for the *i*th subject of the *g*th group. If we were talking about the score of the second subject of group A, the score would be stated as X_{2a}.

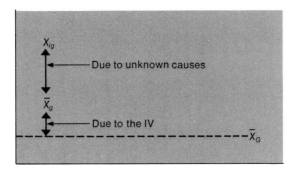

FIGURE 10–6   Diagrammatic representation of the reason any score differs from the mean.

The total distance any particular subject's score varies from the mean of all other scores ($\overline{X}_G$) is equal to (1) the variation caused by the IV, and (2) the variation due to *all* the other unknown or unmeasured variables in the situation. A measure of the influence of the IV on any subject's score may be represented by the difference between the mean ($\overline{X}_g$) of the group the subject was in, minus the grand mean ($\overline{X}_g - \overline{X}_G$). A measure of the effects of all the unknown variables is found by subtracting the group mean from the subject's score ($X_{ig} - \overline{X}_g$).[5] The total variation of any score can be divided as follows:

$$(X_{ig} - \overline{X}_G) = (X_{ig} - \overline{X}_g) + (\overline{X}_g - \overline{X}_G)$$

The total amount any score (X_{ig}) varies from the grand mean is equal to the variation of the score from the group mean ($X_{ig} - \overline{X}_g$) *plus* the variation of the group mean from the grand mean ($\overline{X}_g - \overline{X}_G$). The total variation of any score from the other scores then can be divided into two additive parts: that caused by the IV ($\overline{X}_g - \overline{X}_G$), and that caused by all the unknown variables ($X_{ig} - \overline{X}_g$).

Simple algebra may be used to demonstrate the point that the total sums of squares of all scores in an experiment is composed of two additive parts, the within-group sum of squares ($X_{ig} - \overline{X}_g$) plus the between-group sum of squares ($\overline{X}_g - \overline{X}_G$). The difference between any score (X_{ig}) and the mean of all the scores in the study put together ($\overline{X}_G$, the grand mean) can be represented as

$$(X_{ig} - \overline{X}_G) = (X_{ig} - \overline{X}_g) + (\overline{X}_g - \overline{X}_G)$$

This identity states that the deviation of any particular score from the grand mean is comprised of two parts, a deviation of the individual

---

[5] Remember, all scores in a group should be exactly equal, as in Figure 10–4. The differences between the scores in a group are due to unknown variable influences. A measure of the effects of these unknown variables is obtained by subtracting X_g from these individual scores (X_{ig}).

score from the group mean $(X_{ig} - \overline{X}_g)$, and the deviation of the group means from the total mean $(\overline{X}_g - \overline{X}_G)$. To get back to sum of squares, the previous identity is summed and squared to read:

$$\sum_{}^{N}(X_{ig} - \overline{X}_G)^2 = \sum_{}^{k}\sum_{}(X_{ig} - \overline{X}_g)^2 + \sum_{}^{k}\sum_{}^{n}(\overline{X}_g - \overline{X}_G)^2 + 2\sum_{}^{k}\sum_{}^{n}(\overline{X}_g - \overline{X}_G)\sum_{}^{k}\sum_{}^{n}(X_{ig} - \overline{X}_g)$$

This identity states that if you subtract the grand mean from each score, square the difference, and sum up those differences (in other words, calculate SS_T), the total will equal the difference of each score subtracted from the group mean squared and summed (SS_w) *plus* the summed squared difference of the grand mean subtracted from the group means (SS_B).[6]

The third portion of the right side of the equation will drop out, for it involves summing the difference between each score and its group mean $(X_{ig} - \overline{X}_g)$, and this will always equal zero. What has just been demonstrated is the fact that the total sum of squares is equal to the within-group sum of squares plus the between-group sum of squares.

$$SS_T = SS_W + SS_B$$

$$\sum_{}^{N}(X_{ig} - \overline{X}_G)^2 = \sum_{}^{k}\sum_{}^{n}(X_{ig} - \overline{X}_g)^2 + \sum_{}^{k}\sum_{}^{n}(\overline{X}_g - \overline{X}_G)^2$$

This point may be illustrated by substituting raw scores obtained in Figure 10-6. The following calculations show how.

GROUP A

Subject Number	X_a	$\overline{X}_a$	$(X_{ia} - \overline{X}_a)$	$(X_{ia} - \overline{X}_a)^2$
1	100	90	10	100
2	80	90	−10	100
3	90	90	0	0
	$\Sigma X_a = 270$			$\sum_{}^{n}X_{ia} - \overline{X}_a)^2 = 200$

GROUP B

Subject Number	X_b	$\overline{X}_b$	$X_{ib} - \overline{X}_b$	$(X_{ib} - \overline{X}_b)^2$
4	50	50	0	0
5	40	50	−10	100
6	60	50	10	100
	$\Sigma X_b = 150$			$\sum_{}^{n}(X_{ib} - \overline{X}_b)^2 = 200$

[6] Remember that each score is composed of $(X_{ig} - \overline{X}_g)$ plus $(\overline{X}_g - \overline{X}_G)$, so the second term on the right is actually the summation of the squared difference of the total mean subtracted from a group mean, for "every" score in the group. The "n" above the summation sign is placed there to remind the reader to subtract the grand mean from the group mean for *every* score in each group. The "K" reminds us to do it for all groups.

$$\overline{X}_G = \frac{\Sigma X}{N} = \frac{100 + 80 + 90 + 50 + 40 + 60}{6} = 70$$

$$
\begin{aligned}
SS_B &= \overset{n}{\Sigma}\,(\overline{X}_g - \overline{X}_G)^2 \\
&= (100 - 70)^2 + (90 - 70)^2 + (80 - 70)^2 + (50 - 70)^2 \\
&\quad + (40 - 70)^2 + (60 - 70)^2 \\
&= 30^2 + 20^2 + 10^2 + 20^2 + 30^2 + 10^2 \\
&= 900 + 400 + 100 + 400 + 900 + 100 \\
&= 2{,}800
\end{aligned}
$$

$$
\begin{aligned}
SS_B &= \overset{n}{\Sigma}\,(\overline{X}_g - \overline{X}_G)^2 \\
&= (90 - 70)^2 + (90 - 70)^2 + (90 - 70)^2 + (50 - 70)^2 + (50 - 70)^2 \\
&\quad + (50 - 70)^2 \\
&= 400 + 400 + 400 + 400 + 400 + 400 \\
&= 2{,}400
\end{aligned}
$$

$$
\begin{aligned}
SS_W &= \overset{N}{\Sigma}\,(X_{ig} - \overline{X}_g)^2 \\
&= (100 - 90)^2 + (80 - 90)^2 + (90 - 90)^2 + (50 - 50)^2 \\
&\quad + (40 - 50)^2 + (60 - 50)^2 \\
&= 100 + 100 + 0 + 0 + 100 + 100 \\
&= 400
\end{aligned}
$$

Substituting the obtained values into the formula, we find

$$
\begin{aligned}
SS_T &= SS_B + SS_W \\
&= 2{,}400 + 400 \\
&= 2{,}800
\end{aligned}
$$

What has just been mathematically demonstrated is the fact that the total variation of all scores from the overall mean in an experiment is composed of two additive parts: that due to the IV (represented by SS_B), and that due to all other unmeasured variables (represented by SS_W). This is a very important concept in experimentation, and one the student should understand thoroughly.

There is another procedure for calculating SS_B and SS_W that is much faster, for it does not involve the calculation of means and the subtraction of every score from the mean. Recall from Chapter Six the SS calculated for the groups in the randomized two-group *t*-test analysis were equal to

$$SS_T = \Sigma X^2 - \frac{(\Sigma X)^2}{N}$$

This is simply another way of writing

$$SS_T = \overset{N}{\Sigma} (X_{ig} - \overline{X}_G)^2$$

By employing the first of these two formulas, the total sums of squares could be calculated as follows:

Subject Number	X	X²
1	100	10,000
2	80	6,400
3	90	8,100
4	50	2,500
5	40	1,600
6	60	3,600
N = 6	Σ *X* = 420	Σ *X*² = 32,200

$$SS_T = \Sigma X^2 - \frac{(\Sigma X)^2}{N}$$

$$= 32,200 - \frac{(420)^2}{6}$$

$$= 32,200 - \frac{176,400}{6}$$

$$= 32,200 - 29,400$$

$$= 2,800$$

SS_W and SS_B may be calculated with the following formulas:[7]

$$SS_B = \left[\Sigma \frac{(\Sigma X_g)^2}{n} \right] - \left[\frac{(\Sigma X)^2}{N} \right]$$

$$SS_W = [\Sigma X^2] - \left[\Sigma \frac{(\Sigma X_g)^2}{n} \right]$$

[7] The brackets are not essential and are provided only to help the student follow what is involved.

Here are the calculations:

	GROUP A			GROUP B	
Subject Number	X_a	$X_a{}^2$	Subject Number	X_b	$X_b{}^2$
1	100	10,000	4	50	2,500
2	80	6,400	5	40	1,600
3	90	8,100	6	60	3,600
	$\Sigma X_a = 270$	$\Sigma X_a^2 = 24{,}500$		$\Sigma X_b = 150$	$\Sigma X_b^2 = 7{,}700$

$$SS_b = \left[\Sigma \frac{(\Sigma X_g)^2}{n} \right] - \left[\frac{(\Sigma X)^2}{N} \right]$$

$$= \left[\frac{(270)^2}{3} + \frac{(150)^2}{3} \right] - \left[\frac{(100 + 80 + 90 + 50 + 40 + 60)^2}{6} \right]$$

$$= \left[\frac{72{,}900}{3} + \frac{22{,}500}{3} \right] - \left[\frac{176{,}400}{6} \right]$$

$$= [24{,}300 + 7{,}500] - 29{,}400$$

$$= 31{,}800 - 29{,}400$$

$$= 2{,}400$$

$$SS_W = [\Sigma X^2] - \left[\Sigma \frac{(\Sigma X_g)^2}{n} \right]$$

$$= [10{,}000 + 6{,}400 + 8{,}100 + 2{,}500 + 1{,}600 + 3{,}600]$$

$$- \left[\frac{(270)^2}{3} + \frac{(150)^2}{3} \right]$$

$$= 32{,}200 - 31{,}800$$

$$= 400$$

Note that the SS_T, SS_B, and SS_W obtained by each procedure is the same. The second method is much faster. The formulas used in the second procedure are called the *computational* or *raw score* formulas for calculating the sums of squares.

TYPES OF ANOVAR DESIGNS

Randomized One-Way ANOVAR Design

Now that the relationship between SS_T, SS_B, and SS_W has been demonstrated, let us look at how this relationship is involved in the one-way analysis of variance. To illustrate, we will proceed with the cough remedies example. Table 10-1 shows the results of this hypothetical experiment.

Recall from Chapter Four that the analysis of variance in experimentation is carried out by calculating the between-groups variance, calculating the within-groups variance, and then substituting the results into the ratio V_B/V_W. To do this, V_B and V_W are calculated using the following formulas:

$$V_B = \frac{SS_B}{df_B} \qquad V_W = \frac{SS_W}{df_W}$$

These formulas state that the between-group variance is equal to SS_B divided by its degrees of freedom (df), while within-group variance is equal to SS_W divided by its degrees of freedom.

What is *degrees of freedom*? The term refers to the number of values that are free to fluctuate after certain restrictions have been made on a particular set of data. Suppose five scores were to equal 30. To meet the criterion, we may pick any four scores whose sum would be less than 30. Once we have picked four, however, the fifth score is automatically determined. If we chose the numbers 6, 8, 3, and 7, the last score would have to be another 6. In any one group, then, the number of degrees of freedom will equal $n - 1$, the total number of scores in the group minus

TABLE 10-1 *Raw Data for a Randomized Three-Group One-Way ANOVAR Design*

GROUP A		GROUP B		GROUP C	
X_a	X_a^2	X_b	X_b^2	X_c	X_c^2
4	16	12	144	1	1
5	25	8	64	3	9
4	16	10	100	4	16
3	9	5	25	6	36
6	36	7	49	8	64
10	100	9	81	5	25
1	1	14	196	3	9
8	64	9	81	2	4
5	25	4	16	2	4
$\Sigma X_a = 46$	$\Sigma X_a^2 = 292$	$\Sigma X_b = 78$	$\Sigma X_b^2 = 756$	$\Sigma X_c = 34$	$\Sigma X_c^2 = 168$

1. If you had a total of three separate groups, the degrees of freedom for all the groups together would equal $N - 3$, for all scores in each group could fluctuate except the last one. Since there are three groups, a total of three scores should have no freedom to vary. They would automatically be set when all the other scores had been chosen.

Why employ degrees of freedom? Originally, variance was calculated using the formula

$$V = \frac{SS}{N}$$

Variance was said to be equal to the sums of squares divided by the total number of scores involved. After this formula was originally devised and had been used for a while in statistical manipulations involving other formulas, it was noted that $V = (SS/N)$ did not adequately represent the variance of a group. This formula biased the variance measure in such a way that the variance calculated was consistently smaller than it should be. Remember, no formula is sacred. It has been devised to perform some function, and if it does not carry out that function as well as desired, it is then modified. In trying various modifications, researchers noted that a true variance estimate could be obtained if degrees of freedom was substituted in the denominator for the simpler term N.

From this brief discourse, it should be apparent that the variance formula was modified to read

$$V = \frac{SS}{df}$$

The variance equals the sum of squares divided by the degrees of freedom. This formula is true for all three variance measures: V_T, V_B, and V_W.

Calculation of V_B. The calculation of V_B involves two major steps: calculation of SS_B and the determination of the degrees of freedom for between-groups variance. The following material shows the data and calculations necessary for determining SS_B:

$$SS_B = \sum \frac{(\sum X_g)^2}{n} - \frac{(\sum X)^2}{N}$$

$$= \frac{46^2}{9} + \frac{78^2}{9} + \frac{34^2}{9} - \frac{(46 + 78 + 34)^2}{27}$$

$$= 1{,}039.55 - \frac{24{,}964}{27}$$

$$= 1{,}039.55 - 924.59$$

$$= 114.96$$

The sums of squares for between groups is calculated using the raw score formula. Keep in mind the fact that the SS_B represents subtracting the grand mean from the group means for all scores $(\bar{X}_g - \bar{X}_G)$. This represents the total amount that all the scores together varied from the grand mean because of IV influences.

With SS_B calculated, the degrees of freedom are determined. The degrees of freedom for between groups is equal to the number of groups employed in the study *minus* 1. Notice the procedure for determining the between-groups degrees of freedom is consistent with that used in the *t*-test. In the present case *df* equals $3 - 1$, or 2. Once SS_B and df_B are known, the calculation of V_B is straightforward, using the following formula:

$$V_B = \frac{SS_B}{df_B}$$

$$= \frac{114.96}{2}$$

$$= 57.48$$

Calculation of V_W. The calculation of V_W entails the same steps involved in determining V_B. SS_W is obtained, and the within-groups degrees of freedom are determined. Table 10–2 shows the data and calculations for determining SS_W.

The sum of squares for within groups is calculated using *all* the individual scores obtained in the experiment. In this example, twenty-seven scores are involved.

The within-groups degrees of freedom is defined as the total number of scores in the entire experiment *minus* the number of groups involved. In this case the df_W equals $27 - 3$, or 24. The calculation of V_W is then carried out as follows:

$$V_W = \frac{SS_W}{df_W}$$

$$= \frac{176.45}{24}$$

$$= 7.35$$

Calculation of the F Ratio. With V_B and V_W calculated, the F ratio is then computed:

$$F = \frac{V_B}{V_W}$$

$$= \frac{57.48}{7.35}$$

$$= 7.82$$

TABLE 10–2   *Raw Data and the Calculation of SS$_W$ for Randomized Three-Group One-Way ANOVAR Design*

GROUP A		GROUP B		GROUP C	
X_a	X_a^2	X_b	X_b^2	X_c	X_c^2
4	16	12	144	1	1
5	25	8	64	3	9
4	16	10	100	4	16
3	9	5	25	6	36
6	36	7	49	8	64
10	100	9	81	5	25
1	1	14	196	3	.9
8	64	9	81	2	4
5	25	4	16	2	4
$\Sigma X_a = 46$	$\Sigma X_a^2 = 292$	$\Sigma X_b = 78$	$\Sigma X_b^2 = 756$	$\Sigma X_c = 34$	$\Sigma X_c^2 = 168$

$$SS_W = \Sigma X^2 - \Sigma \frac{(\Sigma X)^2}{n}$$

$$= [(292 + 756 + 168)] - \left[\frac{(46)^2}{9} + \frac{(78)^2}{9} + \frac{(34)^2}{9} \right]$$

$$= (1{,}216) - \left(\frac{2{,}116}{9} + \frac{6{,}084}{9} + \frac{1{,}156}{9} \right)$$

$$= 1{,}216 - 1{,}039.55$$

$$= 176.45$$

In calculating the F ratio the investigator is asking, "How much larger is V_B than V_W?" The F ratio will state how many "times" V_B is larger than V_W. In the present example, the obtained F ratio states V_B is 7.82 times larger than V_W.

The next question the investigator needs to answer is, "Would an F equal to 7.82 occur by chance in conditions like this less than 5 percent of the time?" This question is answered by referring to an F table, where some statisticians have gone to the trouble of calculating what the F would be that would occur exactly 5 percent of the time. The F in the table is commonly called *critical* F. If the F obtained in the experiment is larger than the critical F, we know that the obtained F would occur by chance "less" than 5 percent of the time. It may then be concluded that the group DVs are significantly different.

Turning to the F table in the Appendix, we find that it is different from a *t* table. The *t* table listed degrees of freedom only down the side, whereas the F table lists degrees of freedom both down the side and along the top. There is a very good statistical reason for the difference in the tables.[8] Suffice to say here that the size of any F depends both on df_B and df_W. To read the F table, read across the top until you come to the number equal to df_B. Then read down the chart until you come to the number equal to df_W. The F shown in light type at that square is the critical F that would be obtained 5 percent of the time by chance.[9]

Notice that the critical F in this case equals 3.40. The F obtained in the experiment is larger than 3.40, so it may be concluded that the groups were significantly different in the experiment.

Review of Steps in the F Test. Now that the F test is completed, let us summarize the steps involved:

1. Calculate the between-groups sums of squares (SS_B).
2. Determine the between-groups degrees of freedom (df_B).
3. Compute the between-groups variance (V_B) by dividing SS_B by the df_B.
4. Calculate the within-groups sums of squares (SS_W).
5. Determine the within-groups degrees of freedom (df_W).
6. Compute the within-groups variance (V_W) by dividing SS_W by df_W.
7. Calculate the F ratio (V_B/V_W).
8. Compare the obtained F ratio to the critical F.

After calculating a few F tests, the student will realize the steps involved are not that difficult. Do not shy away from an F test because of the seemingly complex statistical manipulations involved. Remember, memorizing the statistical manipulations is not as important as understanding the rationale behind the F test. Though committing the formulas to memory would be helpful, most readers are not planning to be statisticians or experimental psychologists; instead, they will be educators, clinicians, counselors, and administrators. Like these professionals, you will have forgotten the specific formulas when you need them. What you should remember is when an F test would be appropriate. Then, when you need to perform such a test you can turn to your personal library of reference books, look up an example of an F test analysis in a text such as this, and carry it out in cookbook fashion.

The eight steps mentioned for carrying out an F test on a one-way analysis of variance are exactly the same for any experiment no matter how many groups are employed in the investigation. The procedure for carrying out an F test in a nine-group experiment would be just like that carried out in the cough remedies example. The calculations would be more cumbersome, however, due to the increased number of groups.

---

[8] Explanations may be found in Hays (1973) and Keppel (1973).
[9] The bold type indicates the F obtained 1 percent of the time by chance. This is included for some investigators who prefer to use a 1 percent significance level instead of a 5 percent significance level.

Multiple-Group Comparison Tests. It would be nice to say that the F test already presented here is all there is to a statistical analysis involving a one-way analysis of variance experimental design. Unfortunately, that is not so. There is one more statistical manipulation that needs to be covered—the statistical comparison of the groups within the experiment.

What does a *significant* F mean? If the F turns out to be significant, which means it is larger than critical F, the investigator now knows that the groups significantly differed in the amount of coughing (DV) after the three different cough remedies (IV) were administered. A significant F *does not* indicate which group coughed less or which group coughed most; all it tells the investigator is that the cough remedies did differ in their ability to influence coughing.

Now that it is apparent the remedies differed, the investigator must determine which was the most effective. To do this, a multiple-group comparison test is performed. There is a variety of multiple-group comparison tests available to the investigator. Because the reason for employing all the tests is basically the same, only one multiple-group comparison test will be presented here—the Scheffe test.[10]

With three groups there are three group comparisons that can be made: group A can be compared to group B, group A can be compared to group C, and group B can be compared to group C. There are three basic steps involved in carrying out a Scheffe test. First, a Scheffe F (F_s) is calculated, using the following formula

$$F_s = \frac{(\overline{X}_a - \overline{X}_b)^2}{(V_W/n_a) + (V_W/n_b)}$$

Then the three comparisons are made:

Comparison	Formula		F
A, B	$F_s = \dfrac{(\overline{X}_a - \overline{X}_b)^2}{(V_W/n_a) + (V_W/n_b)}$	$= \dfrac{(5.11 - 8.67)^2}{(7.35/9) + (7.35/9)}$	$= 7.77$
A, C	$F_s = \dfrac{(\overline{X}_a - \overline{X}_c)^2}{(V_W/n_a) + (V_W/n_c)}$	$= \dfrac{(5.11 - 3.78)^2}{(7.35/9) + (7.35/9)}$	$= 1.09$
B, C	$F_s = \dfrac{(\overline{X}_b - \overline{X}_c)^2}{(V_W/n_b) + (V_W/n_c)}$	$= \dfrac{(8.67 - 3.78)^2}{(7.35/9) + (7.35/9)}$	$= 14.67$

The second step involves calculating F′ (F prime). F′ is a critical F that is adjusted to work with Scheffe's formula for determining F_s. F′ is

[10] A complete review of multiple-group comparison tests may be found in Ryan (1960) and Kirk (1968). The Scheffe test was selected here not because it is necessarily the best, but because it may be the easiest for the reader to understand.

calculated by multiplying the original critical F (obtained from the F table) by df_B. F' in this case equals

$$F \times df_B = F'$$

$$3.40 \times 2 = 6.80$$

Third, the three F_s are compared to F'. If an F_s is larger than F', then the two groups involved are said to be significantly different. In the present example, group B is shown to significantly differ from groups A and C, while groups A and C do not differ significantly. The conclusion to be drawn from this investigation is that the cough remedy given to group B subjects was more effective than the other two remedies. After completing the multiple-group comparison test, the investigator has completed the statistical analysis. It is now known that the cough remedies differed in effectiveness *and* which one was most effective.

The F test and the F_s test provide two different though closely related types of information. The F test indicates whether there is any significant difference between *any* of the groups in the experiment. If the F is not significant, the investigator stops there, for carrying out an F_s test would have no value. If the F is significant, F_s tests are performed to provide information as to the comparative effectiveness of the different levels of the IV.

Randomized Blocked One-Way ANOVAR Design

With the randomized one-way ANOVAR design, the investigator relies solely on randomization to control the effect of secondary variables. It is possible to add a second control technique, constancy, by employing blocking. An investigator may be so strongly concerned about the potential influence of some particular secondary variable that she or he does not want to take the chance that randomization might not equate the groups for this variable. Instead, the investigator ensures that all groups are equated on this variable by intentionally distributing the variable equally among the groups. Blocking one-way ANOVAR designs is a common practice, especially in educational and social investigations in which the investigator may be concerned with the secondary variables of age, sex, intelligence, race, or socioeconomic status and is restricted in the selection of subjects (e.g., only the children in an already existing grade school class).

David Harris was interested in comparing three different instructional procedures at a regional Indian school. The student body consisted of Indian children who came from various tribal reservations in the western United States. Harris was interested in evaluating the educational progress of Indian students in a particular sixth-grade class. The class was to be divided into three subgroups for the year, with each subgroup experiencing a different instructional procedure. One group was taught math using teaching machines, the second group was taught math in a discussion group environment in which the logic of mathematical manipulations was emphasized rather than just exercises in calculations, and the third group was taught math in a regular individual desk classroom situation with the emphasis on written mathematical calculation exercises.

Realizing Indian tribes differ in terms of the training given the children, Harris blocked the three groups of subjects according to tribal origin. The subjects were first divided up according to tribe:

TRIBE	NUMBER OF SUBJECTS
Ute	12
Blackfoot	9
Pueblo	9
Ouray	12

Then the subjects from each tribe were randomly assigned to one of the three teaching groups in such a manner that each teaching group consisted of 4 Ute, 3 Blackfoot, 3 Pueblo, and 4 Ouray, as shown in Table 10–3. All three groups were equated on possible variation due to tribal background by blocking the subjects according to tribe prior to the randomization procedure. A strictly randomized one-way ANOVAR design would not have taken tribal background into consideration; it would be expected that random assignment alone would have automatically equated the groups.

The statistical analysis of the randomized, blocked one-way ANOVAR design is exactly the same as that carried out for a randomized one-way

TABLE 10–3   *Random Assignment of Subjects from Each Tribe to Three Groups Differing in Instructional Procedure*

	GROUP A (TEACHING MACHINES)	GROUP B (DISCUSSION GROUP)	GROUP C (WRITTEN MATHEMATICAL EXERCISES)
Ute	4	4	4
Blackfoot	3	3	3
Pueblo	3	3	3
Ouray	4	4	4

ANOVAR design. For an illustration of the statistical calculation of the blocked ANOVAR design, refer to the calculations on page 264.

Insight
Statistical Analysis of Blocked Designs

So far, blocking has been explained as a means for applying the control technique of constancy to equate all the groups in a one-way ANOVAR design on a particular secondary variable. It was stated that the statistical analysis of a blocked one-way ANOVAR design is identical to the statistical analysis of a randomized one-way AN-OVAR design. However, there are psychologists [and texts; e.g. Lee, 1975] who do employ a different statistical analysis for blocked designs. After blocking each group on an important secondary variable (Indian tribe in the preceding example), some psychologists would treat that secondary variable as a second IV, thereby converting the design into a factorial design having two IVs; in the preceding illustration the IVs would be teaching method and tribal origin. Using the preceding example, the ex-perimental design would be diagrammed as shown in Table 10–4.

The data are then treated as if the experiment involved a 3 × 4 factorial design. The statistical analysis run would then be different from the analysis of a randomized one-way ANOVAR design. Instead, a factorial type of statistical analysis (illustrated in Chapter 11) would be employed.

Why would anyone want to treat a blocked one-way ANOVAR design like a factorial design, thereby increasing the complexity of the statistics required? One reason is that the effect of that blocked secondary variable could be determined. Another important reason is to reduce the size of V_w. This automatically increases the investigator's ability to detect the effects of the first IV chosen as the basis of the experiment in the beginning. By reducing the amount of background secondary var-iable noise, the effect of any IV becomes more detectable. The relative power of the experiment is thereby increased in comparison to the initial IV experiment chosen.

One-Way Analysis of Covariance

Just as statistical control may be used with two-group designs, so may it be applied in one-way ANOVAR designs. The reasons for employing a covariance analysis with more than two groups are exactly the same for

---

TABLE 10–4   *Blocked One-Way ANOVAR Design Converted into a Factorial Design with Two IVs*

Tribal Origin	IV 2 Group A (teaching machines)	IV 1 Group B (discussion group)	Group C (written mathematical exercises)
Ute	4	4	4
Blackfoot	3	3	3
Pueblo	3	3	3
Ouray	4	4	4

investigations involving two groups: the groups employed in the study differ on some important secondary variable at the beginning of the investigation and cannot be equated, or it becomes apparent as the investigation progresses that a secondary variable is differentially influencing the various groups.

Statistical Computations for Analysis of Covariance.   The principle behind the analysis of covariance for multigroup experiments is the same as that discussed for two-group situations in the last chapter; it differs on only one point. The sums of squares are adjusted in the analysis of covariance to remove the differences between the groups that are related to some covariate. In an analysis of covariance the V_B/V_W ratio is still sought. The way the sums of squares is adjusted is shown in the following formula. The definitional formula for the sums of squares in an analysis of covariance is

$$SS_T = SS_B + SS_W$$

$$\left[\sum_{}^{N} (X_{ig} - X_G)^2 - \frac{\left\{ \sum_{}^{N} [X_{ig} - \overline{X}_G)(Y_{ig} - \overline{Y}_G)] \right\}^2}{\sum_{}^{N} (Y_{ig} - \overline{Y}_G)^2} \right]$$

$$= \left[\sum_{}^{k} \sum_{}^{n} (\overline{X}_g - \overline{X}_G)^2 - \frac{\left\{ \sum_{}^{k} \sum_{}^{n} [\overline{X}_g - \overline{X}_G)(\overline{Y}_g - \overline{Y}_G)] \right\}^2}{\sum_{}^{k} \sum_{}^{n} (Y_g - Y_G)^2} \right]$$

$$+ \left[\sum_{}^{k} \sum_{}^{n} (X_{ig} - \overline{X}_g)^2 - \frac{\left\{ \sum_{}^{k} \sum_{}^{n} [X_{ig} - \overline{X}_g)(Y_{ig} - \overline{Y}_g)] \right\}^2}{\sum_{}^{n} (Y_{ig} - \overline{Y}_g)^2} \right]$$

Note that SS_T, SS_B, and SS_W for analysis of covariance designs each have an additional component (indicated above by gray tint). The untinted parts of the formula are the same as in the illustration of a randomized one-way ANOVAR design. The tinted portions of the formula represent how one statistically removes the effect of some secondary variable. Note that these tinted portions are *subtracted* from the original SS_T, SS_B, and SS_W components, thereby making them smaller because the effect of the secondary variable is removed. Though this formula may seem mindboggling, keep one fact in mind—it also seems mindboggling to most professional psychologists.[11] It is not really necessary at this time for the student to understand exactly what is involved in the mathematical derivation of this formula, since most graduate psychology programs include courses that delve into this more thoroughly. The student should, however, have a general understanding of how this formula deviates from

[11] The n above each Σ is a reminder that calculations should be carried out for all the scores in the groups. The "K" reminds us to do it for all groups.

the sums of squares formula given in the preceding section. The sums of squares formula for analysis of covariance differs from the simpler analysis of variance sums of squares formula in that it includes a value being subtracted from each of the three parts of the formula. This subtracted value represents the amount of the variation between scores related to the Y covariate on which the groups in the investigations were not equal. Once the sums of squares are adjusted, the remaining statistical steps are identical to those carried out with the simpler analysis of variance.

To illustrate the statistical procedures involved in a one-way analysis of covariance, let us take the following situation. Three groups of mentally retarded children having a mental age of 5 to 6 years were used to compare three teaching procedures on their effectiveness in helping mentally retarded children learn the alphabet. Group A children were taught the alphabet with no verbal aids, and group B children were taught the alphabet using a rhyming jingle as an aid, group C children were taught the alphabet by pairing each letter with a word as they went along (e.g., A is for *apple*, B is for *bear*, C is for *cat*, and so on). The subjects were given the training for one week. The number of letters the children knew at the end of the week is shown below.

GROUP A	GROUP B	GROUP C
19	22	14
8	17	15
14	16	10
11	18	12
16	12	10
13	19	16
12	15	11
15	23	17
10	21	20

After the experiment was over, the psychologist carrying out the investigation was talking to one of the children's parents, who mentioned her child already knew five letters of the alphabet prior to the initiation of the experiment. Realizing a very important secondary variable had been overlooked, the psychologist checked with all the parents to find out how many letters each child knew before the week of special training. The findings are presented below. The Y columns indicate the number of letters each child knew before the training, and the X columns represent the number of letters known after the special training. The covariate (Y) picked here was the number of letters each subject knew prior to the experiment. These scores could also be used as pretest scores, thereby converting this example into a pretest-posttest design. A better covariate for illustrating analysis of covariance would be IQ. Using the number of letters previously known, however, gives a smaller number to use in the statistical analysis.

	GROUP A		GROUP B		GROUP C	
	Y	X	Y	X	Y	X
	5	19	8	22	0	14
	3	8	9	17	3	15
	1	14	4	16	5	10
	3	11	2	18	2	12
	6	16	7	12	4	10
	4	13	6	19	5	16
	4	12	5	15	3	11
	2	15	7	23	6	17
	5	10	4	21	3	20

From the data it was apparent that the groups differed in terms of the number of letters already known by the children. With these data the investigator then proceeded to carry out an analysis of covariance in an attempt to remove any differences in the DVs between the groups' final results due to preexperimental differences. Here are the statistical calculations carried out. The adjusted portions of the formulas and calculations are tinted gray to emphasize what new steps are required in an analysis of covariance as compared to the analysis of variance in a randomized one-way ANOVAR design.

	GROUP A Y	GROUP A X	GROUP B Y	GROUP B X	GROUP C Y	GROUP C X
	5	19	8	22	0	14
	3	8	9	17	3	15
	1	14	4	16	5	10
	3	11	2	18	2	12
	6	16	7	12	4	10
	4	13	6	19	5	16
	4	12	5	15	3	11
	2	15	7	23	6	17
	5	10	4	21	3	20
n		9		9		9
$\Sigma Y, \Sigma X$	33	118	52	163	31	125
$\bar{Y}_Y, \bar{X}_g$	3.67	13.11	5.78	18.11	3.44	13.89
$\Sigma Y_g^2, \Sigma X_g^2$	141	1,636	340	3,053	133	1,831
ΣXY	442		947		434	
$\dfrac{(\Sigma X_g)^2}{n}$	1,547.11		2,952.11		1,736.11	
$\dfrac{(\Sigma Y_g)^2}{n}$	121		300.44		106.78	

$$N = 27 \qquad \Sigma \frac{(\Sigma Y_g)^2}{n} = 528.22 \qquad \Sigma \frac{(\Sigma X_g)^2}{n} = 6{,}235.33$$

$$\Sigma Y = 116 \qquad \Sigma X = 406 \qquad \Sigma XY = 1{,}823$$

$$\bar{Y}_G = 4.30 \qquad \frac{(\Sigma X)^2}{N} = 6{,}105.4 \qquad \Sigma \frac{(\Sigma X)(\Sigma Y)}{n} = 1{,}805.01$$

$$\frac{(\Sigma Y)^2}{N} = 498.37 \qquad \Sigma X^2 = 6{,}535 \qquad \frac{\Sigma X \Sigma Y}{N} = 1{,}744.30$$

$$\Sigma Y^2 = 614 \qquad \Sigma X \Sigma Y = 47{,}096$$

$$SS_T = \left[\Sigma X^2 - \frac{(\Sigma X)^2}{N} \right] - \frac{\left[\Sigma XY - \dfrac{\Sigma X \Sigma Y}{N} \right]^2}{\left[\Sigma Y^2 - \dfrac{(\Sigma Y)^2}{N} \right]}$$

$$= [6{,}535 - 6{,}105.04] - \frac{[1{,}823 - 1{,}744.30]^2}{[614 - 498.37]}$$

$$= 429.96 - 53.56$$

$$= 376.4$$

$$SS_W = \left[\Sigma X^2 - \Sigma \frac{(\Sigma X_g)^2}{n} \right] - \frac{\left[\Sigma XY - \Sigma \dfrac{\Sigma X_g \Sigma Y_g}{n} \right]^2}{\left[\Sigma Y^2 - \Sigma \dfrac{(\Sigma Y_g{}^2)}{n} \right]}$$

$$= 6{,}520 - 6{,}235.33 - \frac{(1{,}823 - 1{,}805.01)^2}{614 - 528.22}$$

$$= 284.67 - 0.20$$

$$= 266.48$$

$$SS_B = SS_T - SS_W$$

$$= 376.4 - 266.48$$

$$= 109.92$$

$$F = \frac{SS_B / df_B}{SS_W / df_W}$$

$$= \frac{\dfrac{109.92}{2}}{266.68 / 23}$$

$$= \frac{54.96}{11.59}$$

$$= 4.74$$

$$\text{critical } F = 3.42$$

The procedure for an analysis of covariance is quite similar to that for an analysis of variance, the main difference being that the sums of squares in an analysis of covariance must be adjusted. Note that the adjustment involves making the sums of squares smaller by subtracting a value representing some statistical relationship between the covariate (Y) and the final results (X). This statistical relationship represents the differences between the final result scores due to the difference between the children present when the investigation began. There is one other minor difference between an analysis of variance and an analysis of covariance. The degrees of freedom for within groups (df_W) in an analysis of covariance equals $N - k - 1$ rather than $N - k$, which is the case in an analysis of variance. The letter k stands for the number of groups in the investigation.

Because the obtained F is larger than the critical F, the conclusion drawn from this analysis is "The three training procedures do significantly differ in terms of their ability to aid mentally retarded children in learning the alphabet." The next step would be to run the Scheffe multiple group comparison test.

Steps in the Analysis of Covariance.   The steps for carrying out an analysis of covariance are these:

1. Calculate two sums of squares—total sums of squares and the within sums of squares using the covariance formulas.
2. Calculate between the sums of squares by subtracting the within sums of squares from total sums of squares.
3. Divide the within and between sums of squares by their appropriate degrees of freedom (remember df_W equals $N - k - 1$).
4. Calculate the F ratio.
5. Check the obtained F with the critical F.
6. If the F is significant, calculate the F_s to determine which groups were significantly different.

Notice the steps for computing a one-way analysis of covariance are very similar to those for computing a one-way analysis of variance. One interesting difference is that the between sums of squares for a one-way analysis of covariance is calculated by subtracting SS_W from SS_T instead of being calculated directly. There are good statistical reasons for this which are beyond the scope of this book (see Kirk, 1968, p. 464).

Repeated Measurements: One-Way ANOVAR Designs

In Chapter 9 it was pointed out that a two-group experiment involving pre- and post-DV measurements from each subject was an example of a repeated measurement design. On occasion, psychological investigations are encountered that require more than one measure to be taken from each subject. The number of measurements an investigator may take from each subject in an experiment is limitless. Sometimes each subject may be tested with a number of different levels of one IV. Table 10–5 presents data from a hypothetical experiment involving ten subjects, each experiencing four different levels (amounts) of some IV. The data is collected in such a way that it can be grouped in *rows* (R) and *columns* (C). The four scores for each subject (e.g., $X_{C_1} + X_{C_2} + X_{C_3} + X_{C_4} = 21 + 32 + 4 + 70$) is added up and considered a row (ΣX_R).

Essentially, what one does when statistically analyzing a one-way repeated measurement ANOVAR design is to treat it as if it were a two IV factorial design with F_C indicating whether different levels of the drug had differing effects, and F_R indicating whether there were differences between subjects. Subject differences become the second IV. Recall from Chapter 4 that whenever a secondary variable (in this case subject differences) becomes a second IV, the V_W becomes smaller. This automatically increases the size of the obtained F. (Remember $F = V_B/V_W$; and if V_W decreases in size while V_B remains constant, the resultant F must be larger.) If one were to run the standard one-way ANOVAR statistical analysis on the data in Table 10–5 and treat each score as if it were obtained from a different subject, the F obtained when comparing the different drug levels would be substantially less than 3.92.

Notice that SS_I/df_I rather than SS_w/df_w is the denominator in the F formula when a repeated measurement design is employed. This is because there is only one subject per group when subject differences become a second IV. With only one score in each cell, there are obviously no differences between scores in a cell. With no V_W available, V_I becomes the denominator in the F formula. V_I stands for interaction variance and is explained in more detail in Chapter 11. At this point it is sufficient for the reader to note the differences in the statistical analysis between a one-way ANOVAR design and a repeated measurement one-way ANOVAR design.

At this point the reader may be justifiably overwhelmed, for this example of repeated measures design has in essence tried to explain in two pages how to statistically analyze a factorial experiment. Because the analysis of a one-way ANOVAR repeated measures design is exactly like a two IV factorial design, the reader will have a much better understanding of how to analyze repeated measures designs after the chapter on factorial designs has been covered.

ADVANTAGES AND DISADVANTAGES OF ONE-WAY ANOVAR DESIGNS

In comparison with two-group designs, one-way ANOVAR designs give the experimenter more latitude by allowing more than two groups to be compared at one time. Experimenters can carry out parametric investi-

TABLE 10–5 Data and F Calculations for a One-Way ANOVAR Repeated Measurement Experiment Consisting of Ten Subjects and Four Levels of the IV

DIFFERENT LEVELS OF IV (DRUG)

Subject Number	X_{C1}	X^2_{C1}	X_{C2}	X^2_{C2}	X_{C3}	X^2_{C3}	X_{C4}	X^2_{C4}	ΣX_R
1	21	441	32	1,024	4	16	70	4,900	127
2	32	1,024	16	256	15	225	96	9,216	159
3	74	5,476	11	121	9	81	73	5,329	167
4	16	256	50	2,500	26	676	59	3,481	151
5	4	16	25	625	34	1,156	38	1,444	101
6	6	36	70	4,900	18	324	66	4,356	160
7	19	361	39	1,521	70	4,900	29	841	157
8	22	484	28	784	66	4,356	74	5,476	190
9	35	1,225	55	3,025	5	25	81	6,561	176
10	30	900	61	3,721	72	5,184	29	841	192
ΣX_C	259		387		319		615		$\Sigma X_G = 1580$
	$\Sigma X^2_{C1} = 10{,}219$		$\Sigma X^2_{C2} = 18{,}477$		$\Sigma X^2_{C3} = 16{,}943$		$\Sigma X^2_{C4} = 42{,}445$		

$$SS_C = \Sigma \frac{(\Sigma X_G)^2}{n} - \frac{(\Sigma X_G)^2}{N} = \left[\frac{259^2}{10} + \frac{387^2}{10} + \frac{319^2}{10} + \frac{615^2}{10}\right] - \left[\frac{1{,}580^2}{40}\right] = 7273.6$$

$$SS_I = \Sigma \frac{(\Sigma X_{RG})^2}{n} + \frac{(\Sigma X_G)^2}{N} - \Sigma \frac{(\Sigma X_R)^2}{n} = 88084 + 62410 - 64122.5 - 69683.6 = 16687.9$$

$$SS_R = \Sigma \frac{(\Sigma X_R)^2}{n} - \frac{(\Sigma X_G)^2}{N} + \left[\frac{127^2}{4} + \frac{159^2}{4} + \frac{167^2}{4} + \frac{151^2}{4} + \frac{101^2}{4} + \frac{160^2}{4} + \frac{157^2}{4} + \frac{190^2}{4} + \frac{176^2}{4} + \frac{192^2}{4}\right]$$
$$- [62410] = 1712.5$$

$$df_C = (\text{columns} - 1) = (4 - 1) = 9$$

$$df_R = (\text{rows} - 1) = (10 - 1) = 9$$

$$df_I = (\text{rows} - 1)(\text{columns} - 1) = 27$$

$$F_C = \frac{SS_C/df_C}{SS_I/df_I} = \frac{7273.6/3}{16687.9/27} = \frac{2424.5}{618.1} = 3.92$$

$$F_R = \frac{SS_R/df_R}{SS_I/df_I} = \frac{1712.5/9}{618.1} = \frac{190.3}{618.1} = 0.31$$

gations not possible with two-group designs. One-way ANOVAR designs do not provide more control techniques to use in checking secondary variables, all the secondary variable control techniques available for one-way ANOVAR designs are also applicable with two-group designs. Two-group designs are superior in that they generally involve fewer subjects and groups, making them easier to carry out and analyze statistically.

The randomized one-way analysis of covariance design allows more control of secondary variables than either the randomized or randomized blocked one-way ANOVAR designs. It is preferred in situations where subjects may not be randomly assigned to different groups (a common problem in educational and clinical settings), where preexperimental group differences on some important secondary variable become apparent only after the investigation is in progress (e.g., groups found to differ on IQ after an experiment is completed), and where groups differ on some important secondary variable as the experiment progresses (e.g., groups differ in the number of hours they study while in an experiment evaluating the effect of a varying number of term tests on learning material).

Blocked designs are preferred over nonblocked designs when the experimental situation may include variations in potentially important secondary variables apparent before the experiment begins. Blocking is commonly used in field investigations in which the experimenter must select subjects from a heterogeneous group. Dimensions on which subjects are fequently blocked include sex, IQ, race, socioeconomic level, ethnic origin, and age.

There are three main advantages for employing the repeated measurement one-way ANOVAR design. First, the denominator in the F formula is reduced, making significance of results more probable. Second, it requires fewer subjects and may be more economical in terms of time and effort. Third, the nature of certain experimental investigations requires the use of repeated measurement designs.

There are two main disadvantages to employing a repeated measurement design. First, there may be *carry-over effects* from one level of the IV to a second level. Performance changes from one IV level to the next may be due to fatigue, experience, or residual IV effects rather than being due to the particular IV level being administered at the time. Second, there are more assumptions required about the data (e.g., homogeneity of covariance) that must be met before an F test may be run on the data.

SUMMARY

One-way ANOVAR designs are parametric investigations that provide a means for comparisons involving more than two groups. The statistical analysis is based on the same concept as for two-group designs: the variance between groups is compared to the variance within groups (V_B/V_W) to determine whether the IV (theoretically the only factor causing differences in group scores) causes differences between the groups that are larger than differences between scores within groups. It was mathematically demonstrated that $SS_T = SS_B + SS_W$, an important concept for the reader's understanding of the rationale behind the more common statistical tests employed to determine cause-effect relationships.

The statistical analysis of one-way ANOVAR designs involves the calculation of an F ratio rather than a t. After a significant F is obtained, a multigroup comparison test such as the Scheffe test must be carried out to determine which of the group(s) is/are significantly different. The statistical analysis of randomized and randomized blocked one-way ANOVAR designs is identical and similar to the analysis of covariance in one-way ANOVAR designs. The analysis of covariance was shown to vary in only one step: the sums of squares were adjusted statistically to remove the influence of some covariate.

In comparison with two-group designs, one-way ANOVAR designs increase the range of experimentation available to the investigator, but do not give the experimenter access to control techniques not also possible with two-group designs. A one-way ANOVAR design with analysis of covariance is generally preferred over a simpler one-way ANOVAR design, and randomization plus blocking is preferred over just randomization. An important point to remember however, is to *use the design most suitable for the particular situation*. Do not select a design simply because it includes more control techniques for secondary variables. If the situation does not include a variable that needs to be blocked or a variable that needs to be statistically controlled for, use a randomized one-way ANOVAR design. Always pick the simplest, most efficient design.

  I. Logical Analysis of Factorial Designs
  II. Randomized Factorial Designs
 III. Randomized Blocked Factorial Designs
 IV. Statistical Control with Factorial Designs
  V. Advantages and Disadvantages of Factorial Designs
 VI. Summary

Factorial Designs

11

Factorial designs are the most complex of general experimental designs, and they complete the list of experimental designs from which an investigator may choose. Like two-group and one-way ANOVAR designs, factorial designs are classified as randomized, randomized blocked, and statistically controlled. By carefully comparing the procedures of one-way ANOVAR and factorial designs, the student will see that the statistical analyses are almost identical. The same F test is used to analyze statistically both one-way ANOVAR and factorial designs. The only difference is that more F tests are performed in factorial designs (one for every IV involved). Interaction, a concept previously not covered, is introduced as an important part of factorial designs. Factorial designs are considered by some to be too difficult for most students to handle and are frequently omitted in undergraduate experimental psychology courses. They are included here as the last major type of experimental design with which the student and professional should be familiar, and if they were left out, the reader would not receive the total picture of experimental designs. The student should realize that factorial designs are not much more difficult to understand than one-way ANOVAR designs, yet they add much greater versatility to any scientific investigation.

Would college students learn more if they were not graded? Do examinations help the student learn? These two questions were the topic a group of psychology students chose to debate in a senior seminar presided over by the author several years ago. The issues were of such great concern that several students volunteered to help carry out an experiment on an introductory psychology class during the following term to answer those questions. Now, a number of different experimental situations could be devised to shed some light on these issues. After lengthy discussions on how to proceed, the following experimental plan was adopted. The class of approximately 200 students would be divided up into four groups, with each group experiencing one of the following conditions:

   I. Weekly exams that counted toward the student's grade
  II. Weekly exams that did not count toward the student's grade
 III. Monthly exams that counted toward the student's grade
 IV. Monthly exams that did not count toward the student's grade

TABLE 11–1   *Factorial Design Having Two Independent Variables, Each with Two Levels*

	iv 1 FREQUENCY OF EXAM	
	Weekly	*Monthly*
iv 2 EFFECT OF EXAM — *Graded*	Weekly exam, graded (Group I)	Monthly exam, graded (Group III)
iv 2 EFFECT OF EXAM — *Not graded*	Weekly exam, not graded (Group II)	Monthly exam, not graded (Group IV)

The investigation involved two IVs—frequency of exam and whether the students were graded or not. Each IV in the experiment had two levels. Diagrammatically, the investigation could be represented by Table 11–1. The results of the investigation are covered later in this chapter. For now, however, let us direct our attention to the design. What type of design is required to perform such an investigation? The reader should immediately rule out two-group and one-way ANOVAR designs, for they are employed in situations in which only one IV is involved.

Up to now, all the designs have involved the manipulation of only one IV. But psychologists are not always interested in analyzing the influence of one variable at a time. A person's behavior is actually a function of the simultaneous influence of many variables or factors. Consequently, psychologists require experimental designs that allow the simultaneous manipulation of more than one IV at a time. These designs are called *factorial* designs. The term factorial design does not stand for one design, but rather for a group of designs. There are two-factor factorial designs, three-factor factorial designs, four-factor factorial designs, and so on.[1] The number in the factorial design stands for the number of IVs involved; a two factorial has two IVs; a three factorial has three IVs. Symbolically, factorial designs are referred to in the following way:

DESIGN	SYMBOLIC REPRESENTATION
Two factorial	$A \times B$
Three factorial	$A \times B \times C$
Four factorial	$A \times B \times C \times D$
n factorial	$A \times B \times C \times D \times \cdots \times n$

[1] More appropriately, they are called two factorial designs, three factorial designs, and so on, rather than redundantly speaking of two-factor factorial designs, and so on.

Factorial designs vary on two dimensions: the number of IVs employed, and the number of levels for each IV applied. Suppose you were interested in determining how long it took for LSD to influence heart rate. You select room temperature and drug concentration as IVs, for you think that both variables may influence how long it takes for the drug to take effect. Your design may be diagrammed as shown in Table 11–2.[2]

You have selected an $A \times B$ design with three levels of drug and two levels of temperature. The design is also called a 3×2 factorial design.[3] This symbolic designation tells you that there are two IVs employed in the design; one having three levels and the other, two. If only two amounts of drug were used in the same experiment, the design would be classified as a 2×2 and diagrammed as follows:

	C_1	C_2
R_1	R_1C_1	R_1C_2
R_2	R_2C_1	R_2C_2

Each different cell in the diagram stands for a treatment. In the 3×2 factorial design, for example, the subjects selected for the R_1C_1 treatment would be given 10 milligrams (mg) of LSD in a room whose temperature was 72°F. The subjects experiencing the R_2C_1 treatment would also receive 10 mg of LSD, but in a 95°F room. A 3×2 design involves six different treatments; therefore, six different groups of subjects are required. Each treatment group could consist of only one subject, so as few as six subjects would be required. (It is preferable to have more than one subject per treatment, however.[4]) All treatment cells should have the same number of subjects. Equal numbers of subjects per treatment is not essential, but the statistical analysis is easier.

How many IVs and different levels of IVs can be employed in one factorial design? Theoretically, there is no limit; an experimenter may choose as many levels and IVs as desired. Practically, however, the experimenter is limited in terms of the statistical analysis to be carried out. Manually carrying out an analysis of larger factorial designs is a very time consuming job. The computer is a welcome tool in this respect, for many

[2] The letters R and C are used in the following tables to stand for column (C) and row (R). C_1 represents column 1, R_1 represents row 1, and so on. Each cell stands for a group. The R_1C_1 cell, for example, is the group of subjects that experience 10 milligrams of the drug in a room with a temperature of 72°F.

[3] The × stands for the word "by." A 3×2 factorial design is verbalized as "a 3 by 2 factorial design." The expression is analogous to calling a piece of wood measuring 2 inches by 4 inches a "2 by 4."

[4] With only one subject per group there is no within-group variation to represent error variance, so some other less preferable representative measurement must be used.

TABLE 11–2   *A 3 × 2 Factorial Design*

	IV 1 DRUG DOSAGE		
	C_1 (10 mg)	C_2 (20 mg)	C_3 (30 mg)
IV 2 TEMPERATURE R_1 (72°)	R_1C_1	R_1C_2	R_1C_3
R_2 (95°)	R_2C_1	R_2C_2	R_2C_3

more large factorial designs that an investigator would have avoided years ago are presently being carried out. This chapter will deal only with two and three factorial designs for two reasons. First, the highest percentage of factorial designs a student may encounter in the research literature are two and three factorial designs; second, the experimental and statistical procedures of factorial designs with more than three factors are basically the same as those for two and three factor designs. A student capable of analyzing a three factorial design would also be capable of analyzing an eight factorial design, though the statistical analysis would be much more cumbersome.

There are three main reasons for employing factorial designs. First, they allow the investigator to control for a secondary variable by making it a second IV. This is the most desirable of all control techniques, for it not only controls for that variable, but it numerically tells you how much variation in the DV is due to that variable. Second, it allows the experimenter to study the effects of more than one variable at a time. This gives a measure of the comparative effectiveness of the IVs, plus saving the time and money of two experiments. Third, factorial designs may be used to study interaction effects of IVs that are present at the same time. Interaction is an important concept in psychological research, although a somewhat difficult one to understand. It has not been discussed with prefactorial designs because it cannot occur unless two or more IVs are involved.

If the effect of an IV (let us call it *H*) on some DV is a function not only of its own value but also of the value of some other variable (*L*) in the situation, it is said that there is an interaction between the variables *H* and *L*. Suppose someone asked, "Does the wearing of lipstick increase the amorous advances a person receives from the opposite sex?" The answer would be, "That depends on whether the person wearing the lipstick was a guy or gal." In other words, the effect lipstick has on amorous behavior depends not only on its presence, but also on the sex of the person wearing it. If one wanted to carry out an experiment to determine whether lipstick

TABLE 11–3   *A 2 × 2 Factorial Design to Illustrate Interaction*

	IV 1 LIPSTICK	
	Present	*Absent*
Male	A	C
Female	B	D

(IV 2 SEX — left axis labels: *Male*, *Female*)

and sex of the person influenced amorous affection, a factorial experiment like the one in Table 11–3 could be set up. Four groups of subjects would be compared: males wearing lipstick (*A*), males not wearing lipstick (*C*), females wearing lipstick (*B*), females not wearing lipstick (*D*).

Assuming some measure of amorous advances was obtained (e.g., number of kisses each group received from the opposite sex), three possible results could be obtained, as shown in Table 11–4. The first set of data (I) shows more amorous behavior for females than males, for there are differences between the first and second row. The presence or absence of lipstick in this case has no effect, for there is no difference between the two columns. Data in situation II indicate just the opposite: lipstick is important, while sex is not. The data for situation III show interaction. It is apparent from these data that amorous behavior depends both on whether a person wears lipstick and on the sex of the person. In the first case you could predict that females get more kisses than males irrespective of whether lipstick is present or not. In the second case, the presence of lipstick gets more kisses than the absence of lipstick, irrespective of the sex of the person. In the third case, the effects of lipstick and sex interact. Lipstick and sex do not always have the same effect. The results from employing lipstick depend on whether the user is male or female.

TABLE 11–4   *Three Possible Results of a 2 × 2 Factorial Design, with III Showing Interaction*

	I			II			III	
	Present	*Absent*		*Present*	*Absent*		*Present*	*Absent*
Male	7	7	*Male*	14	7	*Male*	7	14
Female	14	14	*Female*	14	7	*Female*	14	7

Whenever you have to answer the question, "Does IV *H* have an effect?" by saying, "That depends on the value of *L*," there is interaction involved in the situation between the two variables. In the lipstick example, the effect of lipstick *depended* on whether the wearer was male or female.

Interaction is an effect on a DV that must be checked for whenever an investigation involves the manipulation of two or more variables. The statistical logic involved in determining its presence is hard for most undergraduates (and some graduates for that matter) to follow. The student should not feel anxious if she or he is unable to understand the mathematical logic behind its computation, for that will come later in graduate courses on experimental design.

LOGICAL ANALYSIS OF FACTORIAL DESIGNS

As you might expect, the six steps in carrying out two-group and one-way ANOVAR investigations are also employed with investigations involving factorial designs. In summary, these steps are as follows:

1. Formulation of a hypothesis.
2. Selection of appropriate IVs and DV.
3. Control for secondary variables.
4. Manipulation of the IV and the DV.
5. Analysis of variations in the DV.
6. Drawing of conclusions regarding the relationship between the IVs and the DV.

Recall that one-way ANOVAR designs differ from two-group designs only in terms of variations in the procedures for carrying out the statistical calculations. Both types of designs could include the use of three control techniques—constancy, randomization, and statistical control. Factorial designs allow the experimenter to use those three techniques plus one more—making a secondary variable a second IV. One should not be misled by this statement and conclude that factorial designs are only used in situations in which the investigator wants to make some secondary variable an IV. Although this is one reason, most factorial designs are carried out simply because the investigator is interested in two or more primary variables.

A second feature of factorial designs that distinguishes them from two-group and one-way ANOVAR designs relates to step 5 of carrying out an experiment—the statistical analysis of variations in the DV. With more IVs and groups involved, we could rightly predict that the statistical computation of factorial designs will be more complex. But if observant, the reader will soon realize the statistical analysis of factorial designs is strikingly similar to the analysis carried out on one-way ANOVAR designs. Little is new. Most of the calculations are simply more of what was done in one-way ANOVAR analysis: more sums of squares are calculated, and more F ratios are computed. For example, three sums of squares are calculated in a 2×2 factorial design compared to one in a one-way ANOVAR analysis (excluding any multigroup comparisons that might be necessary). In factorial designs at least three F ratios are calculated, in contrast to only one in a one-way ANOVAR analysis.[5]

The differences in one-way ANOVAR and factorial analysis in terms of sums of squares are shown with the following formulas:

$$\text{One-way ANOVAR:} \quad SS_T = SS_{IV} + SS_W$$

$$\text{Two factorial:} \quad SS_T = SS_{IV1} + SS_{IV2} + SS_I + SS_W$$

In one-way ANOVAR experiments the total sums of squares was divided into two parts, that related to the IV and that related to all other unknown variables.[6] In a two-factorial investigation, variations between the scores can be divided into four categories:

1. Variation due to IV 1.
2. Variation due to IV 2.
3. Variation due to any interactive effects between IV 1 and IV 2.
4. Variation due to unknown secondary variables.

Three of the sums of squares (SS_{IV1}, SS_{IV2}, SS_I) represent intended variations in the subjects' scores brought about by experimenter manipulation. Numerically, they show up as differences between groups in the investigation. The calculation of SS_{IV2} and SS_{IV1} is the same as for SS_B in previous designs. SS_I is a new concept and is calculated differently, as we shall see. SS_W is calculated the same as in one-way ANOVAR designs. To illustrate how the sums of squares are calculated, the sums of squares are computed for the data shown in Table 11–5. Eight rats were divided into four groups, each consisting of two subjects. The objective of the investigation was to determine whether dosage level of the drug and temperature of the room influence the time it takes for rats to become anesthetized. The two values in the four cells represent the number of minutes it took for the subjects to lose consciousness. The formula for the variation in this situation would be

$$V_T = V_{\text{dosage}} + V_{\text{temp}} + V_{\text{interaction}} + V_W$$

---

[5] The number of Fs mentioned here does not include Scheffe's F calculations, which can vary a great deal depending on the number of groups.

[6] One should keep in mind the fact that sums of squares represents variation between the scores due to variables present in the situation.

TABLE 11–5   *A 2 × 2 Factorial Design with Two Raw Scores in Each Group*

IV 1
DRUG DOSAGE

		C_1 (10 mg)	C_2 (20 mg)	
TEMPERATURE IV 2	R_1 (72°)	14 17	10 12	$\bar{X}_{R_1}$
	R_2 (95°)	11 10	5 7	$\bar{X}_{R_2}$
		$\bar{X}_{C_1}$	$\bar{X}_{C_2}$	

Calculation of Sums of Squares.   The sums of squares of this formula a calculated as follows:

$$SS_T = \Sigma X^2 - \frac{(\Sigma X_G)^2}{N}$$

$$= (14^2 + 17^2 + 10^2 + 12^2 + 11^2 + 10^2 + 5^2 + 7^2)$$

$$- \frac{(14 + 17 + 10 + 12 + 11 + 10 + 5 + 7)^2}{8} = 99.5$$

$$SS_{IV1} = SS_C = \Sigma \frac{(\Sigma X_C)^2}{n} - \frac{(\Sigma X_G)^2}{N}$$

$$= \left[\frac{(14 + 17 + 11 + 10)^2}{4} + \frac{(10 + 12 + 5 + 7)^2}{4} \right]$$

$$- \frac{(14 + 17 + 10 + 12 + 11 + 10 + 5 + 7)^2}{8} = 40.5$$

$$SS_{IV2} = SS_R = \Sigma \frac{(\Sigma X_R)^2}{n} - \frac{(\Sigma X_G)^2}{N}$$

$$= \left[\frac{(14 + 17 + 10 + 12)^2}{4} + \frac{(11 + 10 + 5 + 7)^2}{4} \right]$$

$$- \frac{(14 + 17 + 10 + 12 + 11 + 10 + 5 + 7)^2}{8} = 50.0$$

$$SS_I = \Sigma \frac{(\Sigma X_{RC})^2}{n} + \frac{(\Sigma X_G)^2}{N} - \Sigma \frac{(\Sigma X_C)^2}{n} - \Sigma \frac{(\Sigma X_R)^2}{n}$$

$$= \left[\frac{(14 + 17)^2}{2} + \frac{(12 + 10)^2}{2} + \frac{(11 + 10)^2}{2} + \frac{(5 + 7)^2}{2} \right]$$

$$+ \frac{(14 + 17 + 10 + 12 + 11 + 10 + 5 + 7)^2}{8}$$

$$- \left[\frac{(14 + 17 + 11 + 10)^2}{4} + \frac{(10 + 12 + 5 + 7)^2}{4} \right]$$

$$- \left[\frac{(14 + 17 + 10 + 12)^2}{4} + \frac{(11 + 10 + 5 + 7)^2}{4} \right] = 0$$

$$SS_W = \Sigma X^2 - \Sigma \frac{(\Sigma X_{RC})^2}{n}$$

$$= [(14^2 + 17^2 + 10^2 + 12^2 + 11^2 + 10^2 + 5^2 + 7^2)]$$

$$- \left[\frac{(14 + 17)^2}{2} + \frac{(12 + 10)^2}{2} + \frac{(11 + 10)^2}{2} + \frac{(5 + 7)^2}{2} \right] = 9$$

A comparison of the way sums of squares were calculated on page 263 for one-way ANOVAR designs with the calculation of sums of squares in this example shows the similarity of the two procedures. SS_T and SS_W are calculated exactly the same way. The SS_{IV1} and SS_{IV2} are also calculated the same way as SS_B in a one-way ANOVAR design, though it is not as apparent at first glance. SS_{IV1} is calculated as if there is no other IV and as if there are only two groups involved in the investigation. The data are treated as if only two groups (C_1, C_2) exist, group C_1 rats given 10 mg of drug and group C_2 rats given 20 mg. Temperature differences are ignored for the moment because the two C groups are equated on this variable.

IV 1

C_1 (10 mg)	C_2 (20 mg)
14	10
17	12
11	5
10	7
X_{C_1}	X_{C_2}

$$SS_C = \Sigma \frac{(\Sigma X_C)^2}{n} - \frac{(\Sigma X_G)^2}{N}$$

$$= \left[\frac{(14 + 17 + 11 + 10)^2}{4} + \frac{(10 + 12 + 5 + 7)^2}{4} \right]$$

$$- \frac{(14 + 17 + 11 + 10 + 10 + 12 + 5 + 7)^2}{8}$$

$$= 40.5$$

The sums of squares for the second IV is then calculated as if there were no IV # 1, and as if only two groups are involved.

$$
\begin{array}{c|cc|c}
 & \begin{array}{c} R_2 \\ (72°) \end{array} & \begin{array}{cc} 14 & 10 \\ 17 & 12 \end{array} & \bar{X}_{R1} \\
\text{IV 2} & & & \\
 & R_2 (95°) & \begin{array}{cc} 11 & 5 \\ 10 & 7 \end{array} & \bar{X}_{R2}
\end{array}
$$

$$
SS_R = \Sigma \frac{(\Sigma X_R)^2}{n} - \frac{(\Sigma X_G)^2}{N}
$$

$$
= \left[\frac{(14 + 17 + 10 + 12)^2}{4} + \frac{(11 + 10 + 5 + 7)^2}{4} \right]
$$

$$
- \frac{(14 + 17 + 10 + 12 + 11 + 10 + 5 + 7)^2}{8}
$$

$$
= 50
$$

Notice that the formula for calculating the sums of squares for the rows and columns is identical to the formula for SS_B except that $\Sigma \frac{(\Sigma X_C)^2}{n}$ or $\Sigma \frac{(\Sigma X_R)^2}{n}$ is substituted for the symbol $\Sigma \frac{(\Sigma X_g)^2}{n}$.

Calculation of the F Ratios.   With the sums of squares calculated, we turn to the computation of the F ratios. As previously mentioned, three F ratios are calculated with a two factorial design.

$$
F = \frac{SS_R / df_R}{SS_w / df_w}
$$

$$
F = \frac{SS_C / df_C}{SS_w / df_w}
$$

$$
F = \frac{SS_I / df_I}{SS_w / df_w}
$$

The first F listed would need to be calculated to determine whether temperature influenced the time it took for the drug to act. The second F would be used to determine whether dosage influenced the time it took for the drug to act. The third F is used to determine whether the time it took for the drug to act was influenced by the interaction of the two IVs. Table 11–6 summarizes the computation of the three Fs.[7]

[7] The reader should keep in mind the distinction between F_s and Fs. F_s represents Scheffe F, whereas Fs is simply the plural of F.

TABLE 11–6   *Summary of the Analysis of Variance for a Factorial Design*

SOURCE OF VARIABILITY	FORMULA	NUMERICAL VALUE	OBTAINED F	CRITICAL F
Dosage	$F = \dfrac{SS_c/df_c}{SS_w/df_w}$ =	$\dfrac{40.5/1}{9/4}$	18	7.71
Temperature	$F = \dfrac{SS_R/df_R}{SS_w/df_w}$ =	$\dfrac{50/1}{9/4}$	22.22	7.71
Interaction	$F = \dfrac{SS_I/df_I}{SS_w/df_w}$ =	$\dfrac{0/1}{9/4}$	0	7.71

$df_C = (\text{columns} - 1) = 2 - 1 = 1$

$df_R = (\text{rows} - 1) = 2 - 1 = 1$

$df_I = (\text{rows} - 1)(\text{columns} - 1) = (2 - 1)(2 - 1) = 1$

$df_W = N - (\text{rows})(\text{columns}) = 8 - (2)(2) = 4$

It is apparent that both dosage level and temperature significantly influence the time it takes for the drug to act, for both obtained Fs (18 and 22.22) are larger than the critical F (7.71) shown in the F table.

The steps involved in the statistical analysis of a two factorial design are as follows:

1. Calculate the sums of squares for:
   the columns (SS_C)
   the rows (SS_R)
   the interaction (SS_I)
   the within groups (SS_W)
2. Calculate their correlated degrees of freedom:
   $df_C = C - 1$
   $df_R = R - 1$
   $df_I = (R - 1)(C - 1)$
   $df_W = N - (R)(C)$
3. Divide the sums of squares by their appropriate degrees of freedom.
4. Calculate the F ratios.
5. Check the obtained F ratios with the critical Fs.
6. For each significant F, calculate the F_s to determine which groups were significantly different.

At this point it would be wise for the reader to compare these steps to those for a one-way ANOVAR design in Chapter Ten. Notice that the steps are identical; the only difference is that more Fs must be calculated. The way they are calculated does not change. Even the use and calculation of F_s is unchanged.

RANDOMIZED FACTORIAL DESIGNS

As previously mentioned, one of the main reasons for employing factorial designs is to save time and money by analyzing two IVs in the same experiment. Such was the case in the experiment designed to determine the importance of grading and exam frequency in college classrooms. A second reason for using the factorial design is that there might be an interaction between the two variables. That is, it was felt grading might be most effective when more exams were given. The rationale for such an assumption was the idea that the amount of feedback students would receive from many exams might provide enough motivation to stimulate academic achievement without grades. Table 11–7 shows the results of the investigation. The numbers in the cells represent the raw scores of the subjects on the final exam.[8] The design employed in this investigation was a 2 × 2 factorial design. Since the statistical calculations involved are

TABLE 11–7 *A 2 × 2 Factorial Design with Exam Frequency and Grading Conditions as IVs*

	IV 1 FREQUENCY OF EXAM	
	Weekly	*Monthly*
Graded	54	46
	47	43
	44	44
	48	41
	50	50
	45	47
	51	45
	49	45
	53	44
Not graded	31	35
	38	30
	40	40
	38	38
	37	35
	45	36
	36	35
	37	34
	40	32

IV 2 EFFECT OF EXAM

[8] Each group in the study actually had over thirty subjects. Nine were elected from each group in an effort to decrease the amount of statistical computation and make the example easier for the reader to follow. The results depict the actual results obtained in the investigation.

identical to the 2 × 2 (drug × temperature) presented in the preceding section of this chapter, the statistical computation is carried out here with little explanation. The reader may answer any questions that arise by comparing the two examples and noting the previous explanations. Table 11–8 (see pp. 296–297) shows the statistical calculations involved.

It is apparent from the statistical analysis that both grading and frequency of exam are significant variables in the academic achievement of students. Because the F for interaction was insignificant, it may be concluded that (1) grading is better than not grading irrespective of whether exams are given weekly or monthly, and (2) weekly testing is better than monthly, no matter whether the exams count toward the grade or not.

Randomized factorial designs are favored by many professional psychologists concerned with educational, social, and industrial field experiments because of their ability to convert secondary variables into measurable IVs. Field situations frequently include important secondary variables that cannot be eliminated. The factorial design allows the investigator to determine not only the influence of an IV brought into the situation but also the primary effect of some relevant secondary variable already present in the selected field situation.

As an example, the psychology department at a prominent university was interested in improving its introductory psychology course. It was decided to try three different teaching procedures and compare their effectiveness in terms of academic achievement and how well the students rated the procedure they experienced. The three procedures compared were three lectures a week procedure, go at your own pace discussion procedure, and no class, just a final exam procedure. This started out to be an investigation requiring a three-group one-way ANOVAR design. As the planning of the experiment progressed, several members of the department felt an important secondary variable already present in any classroom situation should be taken into strong consideration. That variable was student grade point average (GPA). It was felt by most of the faculty that students varying in GPA may differ in their responsiveness to the three procedures. For example, it was felt that the brighter student might function better in the nonclass situation, for he or she would not be held back by other students. It was also suggested that the less bright student might do better in the highly structured lecture situation.

After some discussion it was decided to get a measure of differences related to the brightness of the student by dividing the students involved in the experiment into groups according to their GPA. The students who enrolled in the introductory course were divided (without their knowledge) into three groups: group A, GPA 0.0–1.99; group B, GPA 2.00–2.99; group C, GPA 3.00–4.00. Table 11–9 shows the eventual design of the experiment. The result was a 3 × 3 factorial design. Notice that by

TABLE 11–8 *Statistical Calculations in a 2 × 2 Factorial Design*

GROUP I (WEEKLY EXAM, GRADED)		GROUP II (WEEKLY EXAM, NOT GRADED)	
X	X^2	X	X^2
54	2,916	31	961
47	2,209	38	1,444
44	1,936	40	1,600
48	2,304	38	1,444
50	2,500	37	1,369
45	2,025	45	2,025
51	2,601	36	1,296
49	2,401	37	1,369
53	2,809	40	1,600
$\Sigma X_I = 441$	$\Sigma X_I{}^2 = 21,701$	$\Sigma X_{II} = 342$	$\Sigma X_{II}^2 = 13,108$

GROUP III (MONTHLY EXAM, GRADED)		GROUP IV (MONTHLY EXAM, NOT GRADED)	
X	X^2	X	X^2
46	2,116	35	1,225
43	1,849	30	900
44	1,936	40	1,600
41	1,681	38	1,444
50	2,500	35	1,225
47	2,209	36	1,296
45	2,025	35	1,225
45	2,025	34	1,156
44	1,936	32	1,024
$\Sigma X_{III} = 405$	$\Sigma X_{III}^2 = 18,277$	$\Sigma X_{IV} = 315$	$\Sigma X_{IV}^2 = 11,095$

$$SS_C = \left[\Sigma \frac{(\Sigma X_C)^2}{n} \right] - \frac{(\Sigma X_G)^2}{N}$$

$$= \left[\frac{(441 + 342)^2}{18} + \frac{(405 + 315)^2}{18} \right] - \frac{(441 + 342 + 405 + 315)^2}{36}$$

$$= (34,060.5 + 28,800) - 62,750.25$$

$$= 110.25$$

$$SS_R = \left[\Sigma \frac{(\Sigma X_R)^2}{n} \right] - \frac{(\Sigma X_G)^2}{N}$$

$$= \left[\frac{(441 + 405)^2}{18} + \frac{(342 + 315)^2}{18} \right] - \frac{(441 + 342 + 405 + 315)^2}{36}$$

$$= (39,762 + 23,980.5) - 62,750.25$$

$$= 992.25$$

TABLE 11–8 *(Continued)*

	GROUP I (WEEKLY EXAM, GRADED)		GROUP II (WEEKLY EXAM, NOT GRADED)	
	X	X^2	X	X^2

$$SS_I = \left[\Sigma \frac{(\Sigma X_{RC})^2}{n} \right] + \left[\frac{(\Sigma X_G)^2}{N} \right] - \left[\Sigma \frac{(\Sigma X_C)^2}{n} \right] - \left[\Sigma \frac{(\Sigma X_R)^2}{n} \right]$$

$$= \left[\frac{(441)^2}{9} + \frac{(342)^2}{9} + \frac{(405)^2}{9} + \frac{(315)^2}{9} \right]$$

$$+ \left[\frac{(441 + 342 + 405 + 315)^2}{36} \right]$$

$$- \left[\frac{(441 + 342)^2}{18} + \frac{(405 + 315)^2}{18} \right]$$

$$- \left[\frac{(441 + 405)^2}{18} + \frac{(342 + 315)^2}{18} \right]$$

$$= [21{,}609 + 12{,}996 + 18{,}225 + 11{,}025]$$

$$+ [62{,}750.25] - [62{,}860.5] - [63{,}742.5]$$

$$= 2.25$$

$$SS_W = \Sigma X^2 - \Sigma \frac{(\Sigma X_{RC})^2}{n}$$

$$= 64{,}181 - 63{,}855$$

$$= 326$$

$$df_C = (C - 1) = 2 - 1 = 1$$

$$df_R = (R - 1) = 2 - 1 = 1$$

$$df_I = (R - 1)(C - 1) = (2 - 1)(2 - 1) = 1$$

$$df_W = (N - RC) = 36 - (2)(2) = 32$$

$$F_C = \frac{SS_C/df_C}{SS_W/df_W} = \frac{110.25/1}{326/32} = \frac{110.25}{10.19} = 10.82 \qquad \text{critical F} = 4.15$$

$$F_R = \frac{SS_R/df_R}{SS_W/df_W} = \frac{992.25/1}{326/32} = \frac{992.25}{10.19} = 97.37 \qquad \text{critical F} = 4.15$$

$$F_I = \frac{SS_I/df_I}{SS_W/df_W} = \frac{2.25/1}{326/32} = \frac{2.25}{10.19} = .22 \qquad \text{critical F} = 4.15$$

TABLE 11–9   *A 3 × 3 Factorial Design*

	IV 1 TEACHING PROCEDURE		
	Lecture	*Discussion*	*No class*
IV 2 GPA — 0.0–1.99			
IV 2 GPA — 2.00–2.99			
IV 2 GPA — 3.00–4.00			

blocking the subjects on their GPA and performing a statistical analysis of the differences in GPA levels, a one-way ANOVAR design can be converted into a factorial design.

The statistical analysis of this 3 × 3 factorial design is identical to a 2 × 2 design, except that the computation is a little more cumbersome due to the additional groups. An interesting aspect of the results was that the students who attended no class performed slightly better on the final exam than the students in the lecture group. Some students felt that this fact supported the idea that things learned while sleeping may inhibit active studying.

RANDOMIZED BLOCKED FACTORIAL DESIGNS

Blocking may be carried out in an experiment to remove differences between groups that may be due to a secondary variable rather than an IV. Returning to the drug-temperature example of a factorial design, suppose the rats used as subjects came from three different strains. It is known that different strains of rats differ in their sensitivity to various drugs. Rats from a certain strain could become anesthetized faster than rats from another strain, even though both strains are given the same drug with temperature and dosage held constant. The difference between the groups could then be due partially to strain differences in subjects from group to group. If different strains were involved in the situation, the wise investigator would equate the groups by blocking them on the variable (strain differences), as shown in Table 11–10. The dashed lines are included to show that each group is actually composed of three subgroups, but is treated as if the subgroups did not exist. By means of blocking, each major group has been equated on strain differences.

With blocking accomplished, the groups are equated on the variable of strain, and any differences between groups in the time it takes to become anesthetized cannot be attributed to strain. There is a good chance that randomization alone would automatically equate groups in an experiment on secondary variables such as this. However, one principle of randomization is that as a control technique it becomes more effective the larger the number of subjects in each group. That is, the probability that groups in an experiment are equated on all the secondary variables by randomization can be increased by increasing the number of subjects in the groups.

TABLE 11–10   *Blocked 2 × 2 Factorial Design*

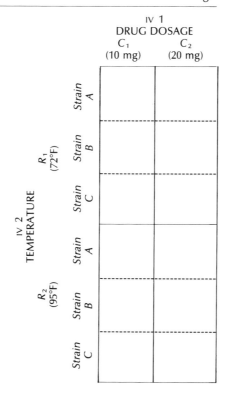

Generally speaking, as the number of groups in an experiment increases, the number of subjects per group decreases. This does not have to be so, but it is a common occurrence in social science investigations. Having fifteen subjects in each group of a two-group design is not uncommon. The total number of subjects in the study would equal thirty. It is generally not too difficult to find thirty subjects on which to carry out an investigation. Suppose however, you were carrying out a 3 × 2 factorial design. Now ninety subjects would be needed to have fifteen per group. It should not be hard for the reader to conclude from these statements that the number of subjects used per group in a factorial design is much smaller than in two-group designs. In fact, two or three subjects per group is not uncommon in factorial designs, whereas the same number of subjects per group is not acceptable in a two-group design.

One other point should be clear: as the number of groups in an experiment increases, the investigator must rely more heavily on alternative procedures for controlling secondary variables. For this reason, the investigator should give more consideration to blocking secondary variables in factorial designs than might be given in two-group designs.

Insight
Blocking, Stratifying, or Leveling

In the previous chapter it was mentioned that all psychologists do not mean the same thing when using the term blocking. In one sense, psychologists use the term blocking to mean the influence of some secondary variable in an investigation has been controlled by ensuring equivalent amounts of that secondary variable (e.g., sex, aptitude, littermate differences) are "blocked" in each group. Other psychologists employ the term blocking to mean the groups have not only been equated on the secondary variable, but the effects of that variable are determined by treating that variable as a second IV and running a statistical test on the blocked data.

While this point may make the reader somewhat uncomfortable, it points out an important aspect of science and technology. New terminology and designs are continually being coined and developed in psychology, like all other sciences. Those having adequate usefulness are kept, while the not-so-useful are dropped. In some cases the useful ones are initially used differently by various workers in the field until the most efficient use of the term is derived, like a piece in a jigsaw puzzle that is turned and rotated until its most proper relationship with the rest of the puzzle is determined so it may be laid to rest in its own niche. Any dynamic, constantly changing, and progressing field of science continually includes this terminological evolution.

While attempts to control secondary variables through design procedures such as those identified by the term blocking are not exactly new, the term blocking has not quite come to rest in a firm definitional niche. For example, Lee [1975, p. 48] states that the term blocking may be used to identify the procedure for equating any type of secondary variable, no matter whether the secondary variable is measured in terms of a nominal, ordinal, interval, or ratio scale. In other words, if the investigator equated groups in terms of sex (a nominal factor), socioeconomic class (an ordinal factor), or IQ (an interval factor), the term blocking should be used. On the other hand, Stanley [1973] limits the use of the term blocking to only those situations where the variable being controlled is nominal in nature. He uses the term *stratifying* to indicate the secondary variable being "blocked" throughout the groups if ordinal in nature, while *leveling* indicates the variable is measured in terms of an interval or ratio scale of measurement.

Throughout this text the term blocking has been used irrespective of whether the secondary variable being controlled was measured in terms of nominal, ordinal, interval, or ratio scales. And while the most common use of the term blocking in psychology includes the assumption that the blocked variable is treated like a second IV, thereby changing the statistical analysis, this text has used the term only to indicate the groups directly equated on the variable, while no statistical analysis of the secondary variable was included.

STATISTICAL CONTROL WITH FACTORIAL DESIGNS

Controlling a secondary variable with statistical methods is just as possible with factorial designs as it is with two-group and one-way ANOVAR designs. An analysis of the covariance statistical test is employed with factorial designs to statistically control for some secondary variable. The covariance statistical test for factorial designs is based on the same principle as the covariance statistical test illustrated in the previous chapter. The objective is to remove differences between DV scores due to some correlated fluctuating secondary variable. This is accomplished by *adjusting* the sum squares as shown in the last chapter.

It is important to keep in mind that more than one secondary variable may be statistically controlled in an experiment with analysis of covariance. The procedure for one covariate can be extended to experiments having two or more covariates. As you might expect, the statistical analysis becomes quite complicated. For examples of how analysis of covariance may be employed with factorial designs, the reader is referred to Keppel (1973) and Kirk (1969).

Statistical control, like blocking, is more important in factorial designs than in two-group designs for a couple of reasons. First, groups contain fewer subjects, making randomization less effective. Second, field situations in which factorial designs are used have more secondary variables to take into consideration than the more selective laboratory environment. Unexpected secondary variables frequently show themselves only after the investigation is underway. This problem is compounded in factorial designs, for the more IVs involved, the greater the possibility more secondary variables will interact with them.

Insight
Latin Square and Greco-Latin Square Designs

From the coverage of factorial designs in this chapter, it should be apparent to the reader that every time an investigator adds another IV to his or her study, the number of subjects required in the investigation is at least doubled (assuming the new IV had only two levels). A 3 × 4 factorial experiment with five subjects per group requires 60 subjects, while adding a third IV, and changing the design to a 3 × 4 × 2 factorial, would increase the number of subjects required to 120.

Psychologists have come up with a rather novel way of increasing the number of IVs in an investigation without increasing the number of subjects required. It entails systematically distributing the levels of the added IV throughout the groups (often called cells in a factorial experiment) in the investigation. To illustrate how this is done, let's start with a 3 × 3 factorial design as exemplified in Table 11–12. Suppose an investigator (Ann) wants to study the effects of two IVs (age and drug) on activity levels in rats. Realizing that strain differences may also be an important variable, Ann decides to add this IV by using three different strains of rats: Norwegian, Sprague Dawley, and Long Evans.

Holding to the number of nine groups originally decided upon with ten rats in each group, she simply systematically distributes strain differences throughout the design as shown in Table 11–13. The third IV is distributed in such a manner that the strain differences are equally distributed throughout the design. Table 11–14 shows how the effects of the different levels of the three IVs may be detected. By treating each of the three IVs one at a time (illustrated earlier on page 291), it is possible for Ann to isolate SS_{drug}, SS_{age}, and SS_{strain}. This is an example of what psychologists refer to as a *latin square design*. The name alludes to an important point to remember when one considers adding an IV to an investigation without increasing the number of groups involved. It is only possible to add an IV *if the design is a square*. That is, the number of levels for all the IVs must be the same. For example, 2 × 2, 3 × 3, 4 × 4, 5 × 5 factorial designs will allow you to add an IV without increasing the number of groups. However, 3 × 2, 2 × 4, 3 × 5, and 4 × 6 (nonsquare) designs do not.

It is also possible for an investigator to add two IVs rather than just one. These are called *greco-latin square designs*. Table 11–15 illustrates how two IVs may be systematically distributed throughout a *squared* design.

TABLE 11–11 *A 2 × 2 Factorial Design*

<table>
<tr><th colspan="5">IV 1
EXAM FREQUENCY</th></tr>
<tr><th></th><th colspan="2">Weekly</th><th colspan="2">Monthly</th></tr>
<tr><th></th><th>Y</th><th>X</th><th>Y</th><th>X</th></tr>
<tr><td rowspan="9">Graded</td><td>11</td><td>54</td><td>10</td><td>46</td></tr>
<tr><td>14</td><td>47</td><td>13</td><td>43</td></tr>
<tr><td>12</td><td>44</td><td>11</td><td>44</td></tr>
<tr><td>10</td><td>48</td><td>9</td><td>41</td></tr>
<tr><td>12</td><td>50</td><td>11</td><td>50</td></tr>
<tr><td>13</td><td>45</td><td>12</td><td>47</td></tr>
<tr><td>11</td><td>51</td><td>10</td><td>45</td></tr>
<tr><td>14</td><td>49</td><td>13</td><td>45</td></tr>
<tr><td>11</td><td>53</td><td>10</td><td>44</td></tr>
<tr><th></th><th>Y</th><th>X</th><th>Y</th><th>X</th></tr>
<tr><td rowspan="9">Not graded</td><td>5</td><td>31</td><td>4</td><td>35</td></tr>
<tr><td>7</td><td>38</td><td>6</td><td>30</td></tr>
<tr><td>6</td><td>40</td><td>5</td><td>40</td></tr>
<tr><td>5</td><td>38</td><td>4</td><td>38</td></tr>
<tr><td>6</td><td>37</td><td>5</td><td>35</td></tr>
<tr><td>7</td><td>45</td><td>6</td><td>36</td></tr>
<tr><td>5</td><td>36</td><td>4</td><td>35</td></tr>
<tr><td>7</td><td>37</td><td>6</td><td>34</td></tr>
<tr><td>6</td><td>40</td><td>5</td><td>32</td></tr>
</table>

(IV 2 — EFFECT OF EXAM)

TABLE 11–12 *Illustration of a 3 × 3 Factorial Design*

		IV 1 (DRUG)		
	Days	1	2	3
IV 2 (AGE)	30			
	60			
	90			

TABLE 11–13   *Illustration of How the IV of Strain Differences May Be Added to a 3 × 3 Factorial Design (N = Norwegian; SD = Sprague Dawley, LE = Long Evans)*

	Days old	IV 1 (DRUG LEVEL)		
		1 Gram	2 Grams	3 Grams
IV 2 (AGE)	30	N	SD	LE
	60	LE	N	SD
	90	SD	LE	N

TABLE 11–14   *Illustration Showing How the Effects of Different Levels of Three IVs Is Expected in a Latin Square Design*

	IV 1				IV 1				IV 3 (STRAIN)
	Days old	1 g	2 g	3 g	Days old	1 g	2 g	3 g	
IV 2 (AGE)	30	N	SD	LE	30	N	SD	LE	$\bar{X}_{30}$
	60	LE	N	SD	60	LE	N	SD	$\bar{X}_{60}$
	90	SD	LE	N	90	SD	LE	N	$\bar{X}_{90}$

N	SD	LE
30 day 1 g	30 day 2 g	30 day 3 g
60 day 3 g	60 day 1 g	60 day 2 g
90 day 2 g	90 day 3 g	90 day 1 g
$\bar{X}_N$	$\bar{X}_{SD}$	$\bar{X}_{LE}$

TABLE 11–15 *Illustration of a Greco-Latin Square Design Where the Three Levels of the Fourth IV are Labeled A, B, and C*

		IV 1 (DRUG)		
	Days old	1 g	2 g	3 g
IV 2 (AGE)	30	N C	SD B	LE A
	60	LE B	N A	SD C
	90	SD S	LE C	N B

ADVANTAGES AND DISADVANTAGES OF FACTORIAL DESIGNS

Factorial designs have several advantages over less sophisticated designs. First, factorial designs provide an additional control procedure—making a secondary variable a second IV. This is an important addition, because it is the only technique that not only controls the secondary variable, but also tells how much of an effect it has in a situation. Second, factorial designs are the only designs that allow the investigator to study interaction effects.

Factorial designs may be used in certain situations to conserve time and energy. It may not be feasible to carry out more than one experiment at a time because of inadequate physical facilities, not enough subjects, or lack of time. This type of problem can be alleviated by using a factorial design and administering more than one IV at a time to each subject.

Factorial designs may be more practical in many field situations because of the large number of secondary variables present and because of limited time to work. An industrial psychologist may be brought into a corporation to determine the cause of certain productivity problems. Results are required in a short time. To accomplish the task, several variables may be manipulated concurrently to save time. A clinical psychologist may employ a factorial design because of limited time to determine the effects of certain IVs on a group of mentally retarded children.

The disadvantages of factorial designs center mainly around the increased complexity over two-group and one-way ANOVAR designs. They include taking more time than one single two-group experiment, requiring more subjects, and a more complicated and cumbersome statistical analysis. There are also many situations in which factorial designs are impractical and unnecessary. A teacher may want to know whether students learn math better with a teaching machine than on their own. This question can be answered with a simpler two-group design. It should be remembered that an investigator should select the simplest design that will answer the particular question. Do not fit your interests to a design, let your design serve your interests.

SUMMARY

Experimental designs that involve more then one IV are called factorial designs. Factorial designs are classified according to how many IVs are involved (two factorial, three factorial, and so on). They are also defined in terms of how many levels of each variable are employed (e.g., 2 × 3 factorial design). The procedure for carrying out a factorial experiment is the same as for a one-way ANOVAR experiment, except that more groups are used. The F test and multiple-group comparison tests are used in analyzing factorial designs the same way they are used in ANOVAR designs. The statistical analysis for factorial designs is carried out by treating each IV as if it were the only one employed. The multiple-group comparison tests are also calculated in the same way as with one-way ANOVAR designs.

Factorial designs have three main advantages over other types of designs: (1) they allow more than one IV to be studied at one time; (2) they allow the interactive effects of two or more IVs to be determined; (3) they provide an additional control technique. The main disadvantage of factorial designs is the complex statistical calculations involved.

I. Origin of Small-*N* Designs
II. Logical Analysis of Small-*N* Designs
III. ABA Small-*N* Designs
IV. Other Types of Small-*N* Designs
   A. Staggered Baseline Designs
   B. Analytical ABAB Designs
   C. Concurrent Multiple Response Designs
V. Comparison of Small-*N* and Large-*N* Designs
   A. Types of Control Techniques
   B. Manipulation of the Dependent Variable
   C. Monitoring the Experimental Data
   D. Data Analysis
   E. Generality of Results
VI. Small-*N* Designs in the Applied Setting
VII. Advantages and Disadvantages of Small-*N* Designs
VIII. Summary

Small-*N*
Designs

Chapter Twelve shows how a scientifically sound experiment can be carried out using only one or two subjects. This concept may seem foreign to those who have a strong background in statistical analysis and have been taught that an investigation must include large numbers of subjects to be scientifically sound. This chapter presents an alternative approach to carrying out investigations that is not based on a statistical method of data analysis. Although it has been shown to be exceptionally effective in basic research, one of its strongest attractions is its effectiveness in applied settings. Small-N designs provide teachers, case workers, counselors, and other practicing psychologists the opportunity to demonstrate scientifically the effectiveness of their approaches in field settings where they deal with only one or two problem subjects. Notice that small-N designs involve the use of elimination and constancy as control techniques more than large-N designs do.

ORIGIN OF SMALL-*N* DESIGNS

The types of experimental designs covered up to now have been what are commonly termed large-*N* group designs. The procedural format for all these designs centered around choosing a large number of subjects, dividing them into groups, and statistically comparing the behavior of one group with the behavior of another. The group design approach, however, does not meet all the needs of psychology. In many instances the psychologist is faced with situations in which large numbers of subjects are not available. The clinical psychologist, for example, is generally faced with a problem involving only one or two persons and is expected to carry out an investigation to solve that problem.

In the past the psychologist was unable experimentally to demonstrate the effectiveness of a certain therapy, or scientifically to isolate certain principles of behavior because there were no strong means of controlling for secondary variables. A person would come in with a problem, the psychologist would apply a certain therapy over many sessions, the behavior would change, and the patient would leave. Feeling good about the results, the clinician would then present those results at a psychological convention, stating that the technique employed was responsible for the "cure." Often experimental psychologists would challenge the validity of these types of clinical investigations. Their criticisms would include, "You haven't controlled for proactive history," "You haven't controlled for retroactive history," "Where is your control group showing the person wouldn't have gotten better by himself," "How do you know it wasn't something else in the situation (your cute secretary, for example) that cured him rather than the therapy you used," "You don't have enough subjects to make a general statement that your therapy is effective." Realizing their points were well taken, the clinician would return to the office somewhat dejected by the fact that he or she was unable to apply most of the experimental control procedures considered necessary by the scientific community to demonstrate cause and effect reltaionships. The psychologist would return to performing correlational and case study investigations in an effort to isolate cause-effect relationships, for no control procedures had been identified so that a scientific manipulatory investigation could be carried out on only one or two subjects. As is true in most cases, however, where there is a will there is a way; so it was only a matter of time (and creative effort) until methods were devised that would allow controlled experimental investigations to be performed using only a small number of subjects. Before covering the procedures employed in small-N investigations, let us briefly review how large-N experimental designs became accepted for psychological investigations. This will help the reader understand why large-N designs are used and why a small-N design procedure was necessary.

Recall that at the turn of the century psychology (and other scientific disciplines, for that matter) was seeking to find better ways of determining cause and effect relationships. Prior to the early 1900s, the statistical tools so commonly used by psychologists today had not been perfected. Although experimental designs involving the comparison of one group to another had been employed since 1834 (in agricultural field research), psychology did not become strongly involved in group investigations until the early 1900s. Thorndike, McCall, and Chapman [1916], for example, carried out a four-group experiment on the effect of ventilation on mental work. Even at the time of this experiment, however, randomization as an effective control technique and the powerful statistical tests based on randomization (e.g., t-tests, F tests) has not been developed. It was not until the 1920s that randomization became generally accepted as a control technique in scientific circles. Prior to that time, elimination and constancy were the only techniques available for psychological investigation. With the acceptance of randomization as a control technique came statistical analytical procedures (e.g., the analysis of variance) based on random selection of subjects.

These statistical tests were a major step forward, for they were a much more powerful means of empirically determining whether the differences in DV measures between groups were significant. They provided a measure of variation (V_W) representing how much variation occurs between experimental subjects exclusive of the influence of the IV. The investigator could now make a comparative analysis (V_B/V_W) and determine the probability that such variation could occur by chance.

The statistical tests also became the springboard from which other control techniques were launched. Adequate development of statistical procedures was a prerequisite for the implementation of another control technique statistical control.[1] Because two of the five procedures for controlling secondary variables are related to statistical procedures, it should not be surprising that scientific investigators turned their efforts to an elaboration and refinement of statistical procedures. And much to the chagrin of most undergraduate psychology majors struggling through statistics courses, that is exactly what happened. For the next fifty years, mathematicians and researchers from all scientific disciplines began devoting a large portion of their time to investigating the application of statistical tools to research investigations. As with most scientific disciplines, statistics has become an integral part of the training program for psychology students.

One of the principles upon which these statistical tools are based is, "The more subjects an investigator employs in his project, the more effective are the statistical tests." An in-depth explanation of this point is left to books on statistical methods [Hays, 1973; Keppel, 1973], but an important point the reader should remember here is that the more subjects employed in an investigation when carrying out a large-N design, the greater the chance of obtaining a V_B/V_W that is significant.[2] Because of this principle, researchers were admonished to employ large numbers of subjects in their projects.

Although the development of more effective large-N designs and their related statistical procedures had advantageous effects on psychological research, it also had some drawbacks. Due to their great success in identifying cause and effect relationships, large-N statistical designs captivated most social scientists to such a degree that they began to equate good experimental research with large-N designs. This was more serious for psychology than for most other social sciences because psychology was the study of individuals more than of groups of people. Psychologists

---

[1] Statistical control requires statistical calculations involving the analysis of a variance in order for it to be used as a control technique.

[2] Actually, there is a limit, for one can have too many subjects. This does not happen very often, however, and the problem is usually in the opposite direction. There is no hard and fast rule as to exactly how many subjects there should be in a research project, but 15 to 30 is generally an acceptable number. Having over 100 subjects is not uncommon.

often deal with only a few people at a time. What they also needed was a scientifically sound experimental procedure that could be employed on one or two persons at a time. Unfortunately, however, the wave of enthusiasm for statistical procedures steered most researchers away from even attempting to develop sound experimental procedures involving only a few subjects.

Fortunately for psychology, not all psychologists turned their efforts toward statistical procedures. Among those who did not was B. F. Skinner. Skinner felt that an effective experimental analysis of behavior based on the behavioral study of only a few subjects was possible. Since the control techniques of randomization, making a secondary variable an IV, and statistical control were closely tied to statistical manipulations, Skinner's approach was based on elimination and constancy. Almost singlehandedly (at least in comparison to the hundreds of investigators working on statistical refinements), Skinner laid the foundation for a small-*N* experimental approach to analyzing behavior that most psychologists agree has been one of the two greatest achievements in research in the history of psychology. Although Skinner began his work on small-*N* designs only a few years after statistical methods entered the research scene, it was to be many years before the discipline of psychology accepted this approach as scientifically adequate. It did not receive the immediate recognition and acceptance given to large-*N* designs, due in part to the fact that Skinner's approach was based on two methods of control that had been employed for decades. With the popular appeal of the newly developed statistical tools, Skinner's emphasis seemed outmoded. Few psychologists realized that Skinner was developing an unusually sensitive analytical approach that involved the application of elimination and constancy in a unique way.

LOGICAL ANALYSIS OF SMALL-*N* DESIGNS

As previously mentioned, small-*N* designs are based on the control techniques of elimination, constancy, and making a secondary variable an IV. The way they are applied to control secondary variables when only a few subjects are involved is somewhat different than the way they are used in large-*N* designs. In large-*N* designs elimination and constancy are usually applied before the subjects begin responding in the experimental situation; they are not built into the design of the experiment. Prior to the actual carrying out of the experiment, some variables may be eliminated from the situation while others are held constant by ensuring that each group of subjects in the investigation has been equated on some important secondary variable. In small-*N* designs, constancy and elimination are employed not only before, but also while the investigation is in progress. This is accomplished by taking repeated measurements from each subject and continually monitoring the DV while the experiment is in progress. Thus, the investigator may "sense" irregularities in the DV due to secondary variables. They are then identified and eliminated or held constant.

Small-*N* designs are generally divided into three consecutive conditions, as shown in Figure 12–1. When setting up the experiment, the investigator takes special care in selecting his DV. First, some behavior is selected and recorded repeatedly by the investigator to obtain a stable measure of the DV prior to the administration of the IV. This is commonly referred to as the *baseline*. A DV used with small-*N* designs should have the following characteristics:

1. It should be objectively measurable.
2. It should be easily emitted by the subjects.
3. The subject should be able to emit the behavior at length without fatigue.
4. It should be sensitive to changes that may occur in the situation.

The characteristics listed here are the ones a researcher expects of a DV in basic research settings where the experimenter may choose the DV. In many situations (like clinical settings) the psychologist has no choice in the behavior to be dealt with (such as a patient's bedwetting problems); the DV is already determined. In such cases, the psychologist determines the *best* way to measure the behavior. Chapter Five lists the types of measures that may be chosen.

Frequently, in these experiments there is no set number of experimental sessions defined as the baseline. The decision as to when the IV condition is to start generally is made while the experiment is in progress. The criterion for deciding when to apply the IV is the stability of

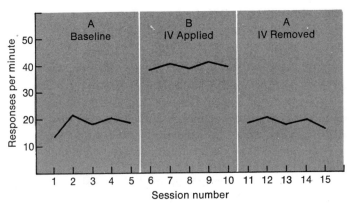

FIGURE 12–1 Basic format for small-*N* designs.

performance by the subject. How is stability defined? Stability may be defined in various ways, depending on the DV measure being used. If, for example, the subjects are in an experiment involving error responses and correct responses, stability may be defined as the subject making a certain percentage of responses as errors. If the experiment involves just getting a stable rate of responding, stability may be defined as 5 percent or less variability in responses per minute for four consecutive sessions. Stability, then, may be defined differently in various small-*N* experiments, depending on the type of response measure being used as the DV. By reviewing the literature of small-*N* designs employing the same type of DV, the investigator may find an appropriate way of defining stability in the experiment.[3] The criterion of stability should be set before the baseline is started.

After the criterion of stability is reached, the second condition of the investigation is implemented. The IV is administered with all other aspects of the experimental situation remaining exactly the same as during the sessions in which the baseline was being established. How long does the IV condition last? The B condition, like the baseline, continues until the DV again stabilizes, with stability again being defined in terms similar to the baseline (e.g., 5 percent variability from one session to the next). The criterion of stability for condition B is also generally set prior to the start of the experiment.

Once the DV in condition B has stabilized, the IV is removed so that the subject is again experiencing the same situation presented during the baseline. Why is the second A condition carried out? Recall from Chapter Three that the ability of the investigator to apply the IV whenever and to whomever he or she desires is considered one of the investigator's most important tasks, because that additional control of any situation greatly reduces the probability that some secondary variable was responsible for any concomitant change in a DV occurring when an IV enters the experimental situation. The ability of an investigator to demonstrate the DV changes when an IV is "removed" is just as powerful in indicating a cause-effect relationship as the demonstration that the administration of an IV influences the DV. The ability to apply and remove the IV, with the DV changing in some direction when the IV is given and returning to its original level when the IV is removed, is an even more powerful demonstration of a cause-effect relationship than simply applying or removing the IV and noting a change in the DV. The reverse condition (the second A condition) should be included when carrying out psychological research with a small-*N* design where possible.

---

[3] Good sources are *The Journal of the Experimental Analysis of Behavior*, the *Journal of Applied Behavioral Analysis*, Murray Sidman's *Tactics of Scientific Research*, and Honig and Staddon's *Operant Behavior*.

The ABA design is the major type of small-*N* design. It involves establishing a baseline, applying an IV, and removing that IV (returning to the pre-IV condition). It may be employed whenever the effects of the IV can be removed. Such IVs include drugs, visual cues, praise, deprivation, emotion-inducing stimuli, sounds, and almost any change in the environment.

Several years ago, two undergraduate students were conducting an experiment on pigeons for a class project. The purpose of the experiment was to determine the effects of a certain drug on behavior. They conditioned two pigeons to peck a small plastic key for food reinforcement. They were then going to inject the drug into the subjects during every other experimental session and compare the behavior of the pigeons when injected with the drug against their behavior when they were not influenced by the drug. After several days of running the experiment, the students complained that they were having trouble with the lights inside the pigeon test chamber. For some reason the chamber lights had been getting dimmer over the last four sessions and now were almost totally out. We located their electrical problem, but in looking over the data records, something caught my eye. Their records showed that the pigeons were pecking faster as the lights were getting dimmer. This was interesting, for generally pigeons roost when placed in a dark chamber.

After thinking the situation over for a while, I decided to carry out an investigation to see if light intensity did affect the behavior of pigeons. Eight pigeons were selected to serve as subjects in the experiment. Two of the pigeons were individually trained to peck a key on a fixed-ratio schedule of 100 key pecks (i.e., they were given grain every time they pecked the key 100 times), while two others were trained to peck the key on a variable interval schedule of reinforcement. The variable-interval schedule is a little difficult to conceptualize for someone who is unfamiliar with the idea of schedules of reinforcement. Basically, it involves two things: a certain amount of time must pass, and the pigeon must peck the key after that time is up before it will be rewarded. The length of time that must pass varies from one time to the next so that the pigeon generally responds at a somewhat low and constant rate when on this schedule of reinforcement. Two pigeons were trained on a variable-ratio (VR-100) schedule of reinforcement in which the birds were reinforced for pecking the key a certain number of times, but the exact number changed from one reinforcement to the next. This is the same schedule used by slot machines in Las Vegas. The customer must pull the lever a number of times to win, but the number of required pulls varies from one win to the next.[4] The last two pigeons were trained to respond on a fixed-interval

---

[4] A VR schedule generally gets the subject to respond more per unit of time than any of the other schedules, and is obviously why it is used in casinos.

schedule (FI). On an FI schedule, both a set amount of time must pass and the subject must respond after the time is up before being reinforced. Figures 12–2 and 12–3 show the number of responses per hour (the DV) emitted by the subjects during the whole experiment.[5]

The pigeons who were reinforced on a fixed-ratio schedule are labeled FR, those reinforced on a variable-interval schedule are labeled VI, those reinforced on a variable-ratio schedule are labeled VR, and those reinforced on a fixed interval schedule are labeled FI.

All the pigeons were run for 30 one-hour daily sessions during the first condition of the experiment. The last 10 of those sessions are shown in the figure and were used as the baseline in the experiment. At the start of condition B, the house and key light in the chamber were slowly reduced in intensity over the next few sessions until the pigeons were pecking the key in total darkness. The arrows indicate the first whole session each subject was run one whole session in total darkness, with no lights on in the chamber. Condition B lasted for a total of 20 sessions. The lights (house and key) were then turned on at full intensity at the beginning of session 51 and remained on for the last 10 sessions of the experiment. From the data shown in Figures 12–2 and 12–3, it is apparent not only that light intensity influences key-pecking behavior, but also that its effect on rate of behavior differs depending on which schedule of reinforcement the subject is on.

At this point, the reader may be somewhat skeptical and argue that the results simply show that the presence or absence of light did influence the behavior of the subjects, but that no real conclusions can be drawn because the direction the behavior changed and the amount it changed was different for each bird. The reader might argue that the difference obtained might simply be due to the individual differences of the few subjects employed and that to draw such conclusions properly many more pigeons need to be run.

The arguments would be incorrect for reasons that relate to two of the principles upon which small-N designs are based. First, the possibility of a small-N design being internally invalid is less than that of a large-N design because there is much better control of the experimental situation and a more accurate measure of the DV. The better control comes from the fact that the investigator monitors the experiment much more closely than is the case in large-N experiments. A continuous running measure of the DV during all phases of the experiment is obtained, rather than just a one-shot measure. Because each subject is used as its own control (commonly called *intrasubject* control), many sources of internal invalidity are automatically controlled for. Those secondary variables that did

---

[5] This example may be difficult to follow unless it is read over several times and the figure studied closely. This experiment was published in *The Journal of the Experimental Analysis of Behavior*, 1974, **24**, 14–21.

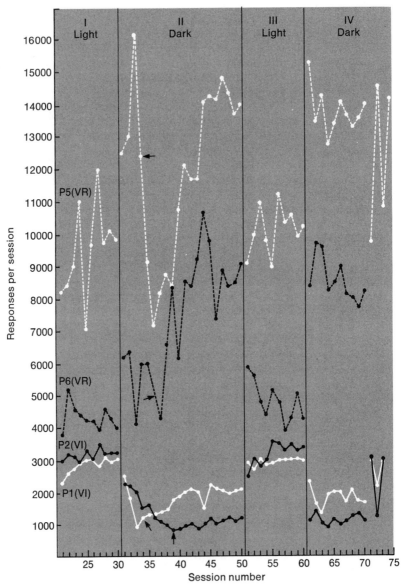

FIGURE 12–2   Total number of responses emitted per session for pigeons on a variable-interval (P1, P2) and a variable-ratio (P5, P6) schedule of reinforcement. (Adapted from Robinson and Shelley (1974), Figure 1. Reprinted by permission.)

happen to fluctuate during the experiment would show up as fluctuations in the DV. The investigator who is constantly monitoring the data during baseline would take note of the DV change, search for the cause, and remove it. Also the IV would not be applied until after the baseline behavior has been restabilized.

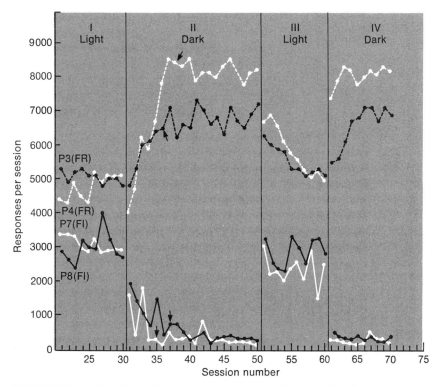

FIGURE 12–3   Total number of responses emitted per session for pigeons under the fixed-interval schedule of reinforcement (P7, P8) and under a fixed-ratio schedule (P3, P4).
(Adapted from Robinson and Shelley (1974), Figure 2. Reprinted by permission)

The second reason deals with the way of determining the generality of the findings. Although large-*N* experiments increase the generality of their findings by increasing the number of subjects employed in a particular investigation, small-*N* designs use a different means for determining whether the data are representative. This is called *interinvestigatory affirmation.* In small-*N* research the investigator is more dependent on previous research.[6] The small-*N* researcher checks the behavior against previous studies that have used the same DV. How did I know, for example, that the behavior emitted by the pigeons during the baseline was representative of the average pigeon's behavior on such a schedule of reinforcement? There have been literally thousands of sessions previously carried out on pigeons by researchers all over the country. Being familiar with the literature on pigeon behavior under the control of different schedules of reinforcement, I simply compared the behavior of the present subjects to

---

[6] Notice the phrase "more dependent" was used. Large-*N* investigations also employ inter-investigatory affirmation, but not as much.

that of those published in the literature. The fact that the behavior of these subjects was representative of pigeons was affirmed by comparing their behavior to that of pigeons in other similar investigations.

A knowledge of previous investigations comparing the behavior of pigeons on different schedules of reinforcement also helped explain the apparent contradiction in behavior of my subjects—some increased their response rate while others decreased it. Notice which of the subjects' behavior increased and which decreased. The pigeons whose ability to obtain reinforcement depended on their rate of responding (fixed and variable-ratio) increased their rates. This could indicate that the birds were attending more to their task because there were fewer distractions in the chamber when the lights were out, or it could indicate that pigeons are simply more active when the lights are out. A look at the behavior of the birds on interval schedules (both fixed and variable) helps in deciding which of the two conclusions could be correct. Now if the pigeons on interval schedules were to attend more closely to the schedule of reinforcement they were on, their response rates should not increase, but actually decrease. In this way they would be more efficient—get the same number of reinforcers for less work. Since that is exactly what happened, the conclusion drawn was that pigeons attended to the schedule of reinforcement they are on better in total darkness than in lighted chambers. The differences in the behavior of the pigeons in the experiment were then explained in terms of the differential effects of schedules of reinforcement and light intensity rather than capricious differences in the subjects.

It should be apparent that an investigator must be more familiar with the literature to employ a small-N rather than a large-N experimental design. This dependency of small designs on past literature is one reason small-N research has taken longer to gain acceptance as an appropriate technique. A backlog of data had to be accumulated to substantiate the validity of the procedure. Although the development of statistical tools and the development of small-N design procedures were begun about the same time, small-N designs have gained general acceptance by most psychologists only in the last twenty years, whereas statistical designs have been accepted for the last fifty years. The great success of large-N designs was probably responsible for inhibiting the acceptance of small-N designs, because so many researchers began to believe that the only means for determining whether the data of an experiment was generalizable to other subjects was by means of statistical analysis.

How well do small-N designs control for sources of internal invalidity? Proactive history is controlled for using each subject as its own control and by the constant monitoring of the DV during condition B and by the procedure of reversing the conditions. If the secondary variable varied during condition B at some time other than the exact point at which the IV was presented, the investigator would detect it as a fluctuation in the

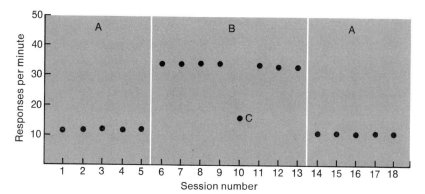

FIGURE 12–4 Illustration of a secondary variable fluctuation causing a notable change in the dependent variable, which is then fixed.

DV during that phase of the experiment. Figure 12–4 gives such a situation. In session 10 some secondary variable changed and it showed up in the DV.[7] If a secondary variable happens to change at exactly the same time the IV is introduced (a very unlikely situation in the first place), it will be detected when the IV is removed and the DV does not return to the level obtained during the baseline. Maturation may also be checked for by the removal of the IV. Retroactive history effects will show up as fluctuations in the DV during the experiment, and sometimes by the inability of the DV to reverse in the second A condition. Statistical regression is controlled for by using the subjects as their own control and also by the second A condition of the experiment. Experimental mortality is controlled for by the close monitoring of the investigation by the investigator.

Because few subjects are normally used, the investigator may more thoroughly check the circumstances under which that subject was lost and detect whether it was due to the IV or some secondary variable. Pretesting is controlled for by the use of each subject as its own control and the second A condition. If more than one IV is employed in the study, interaction may be checked for by adding additional B conditions, as shown in Figure 12–5. Any differences in the effects of the IVs alone or together would show up by comparing the DV measures in B_1, B_2, and B_3. The A conditions interspersed between the Bs allow the investigator to check for any carryover effects from the experiencing of more than one IV. Although an ABA design does not totally control for instrumentation

---

[7] The data given in Figure 12–4 are fictitious but do represent how the principle works. In a past class experiment using pigeons, the feeding mechanism jammed during the experiment and the response rate dropped. Noting the fluctuation in the DV, we searched for the cause of the change, found it, and corrected it. The DV then restabilized, and the experiment was continued.

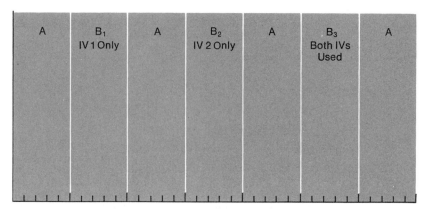

FIGURE 12–5   Illustration of a small-*N* investigation involving more than one independent variable.

and experimenter bias, it comes closer to controlling for them than large-*N* designs. Variation in DV due to instrumentation fluctuations, for example, will show up more easily because repeated measures are taken.

OTHER TYPES OF SMALL-*N* DESIGNS

The ABA experimental design is not the only type of small-*N* design an investigator may use. There are a number of different acceptable ways of setting up a small-*N* design, and although space does not permit an in-depth coverage here, a few types will be presented to give the reader a general idea of what is involved.[8]

Staggered Baseline Designs

In some situations the investigator may wonder whether the behavior of the subjects will revert to the original level obtained in the baseline. There are variables (e.g., learning experiences) that may change the subject's behavior in such a way that the behavior cannot reverse. Suppose, for example, a subject is trying to solve certain types of problems and is consistently making mistakes. You measure the number of mistakes made each day for several days and find that about 35 mistakes out of 100 attempts are made each day. This serves as the baseline. Now you teach the subject a new approach to deal with the problems (this is the IV). The number of mistakes now declines to 5 out of 100 for the next few days.

[8] See Sidman, *Tactics of Scientific Research.* He does an excellent job of presenting both the rationale and the procedures involved in small *N* research.

You want to reverse back to the original baseline condition now, but you realize you cannot remove the knowledge you gave the subject. Can small-N designs be used in such situations?

The answer is yes, and the procedure involves staggering when the IV condition is given to the different subjects. Figure 12–6 shows how this is done. The As represent a session in which the baseline is being established, while the Bs represent the application and presence of the IV. In the example given, the first B for each subject would represent the first session after which a subject had been taught a new approach. Staggering when the IV is applied decreases the probability that some secondary variable just happened to fluctuate at the same time the IV was administered and was actually responsible for the change in the DV. A second type of staggered baseline design involves only one subject. In this design, the investigator monitors three (the exact number may vary) behaviors of one subject rather than one behavior of three subjects. The IV is then applied to each of the behaviors at a different session. This approach is often used in behavior therapy.

Although the staggered baseline design is considered a good small-N design and includes the two characteristics essential for a small-N design (a large number of DV measures being taken, and a baseline phase), it is not generally considered to be as powerful as the ABA design. The ability to apply and remove an IV in an experimental situation with a concomitant change in the DV is more effective in inferring cause-effect relationships.

Analytic ABAB Design

Both small-N designs presented so far are what were previously termed exploratory experiments; that is, two conditions are compared, one with the IV and one without, to determine whether a certain IV had an effect. Analytical experiments are also possible with small-N designs. Suppose you want to determine the effect of different dosages of a particular drug that is a central nervous system depressant. Figure 12–7 shows how this

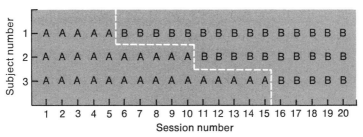

FIGURE 12–6   Diagrammatic representation of a staggered baseline design.

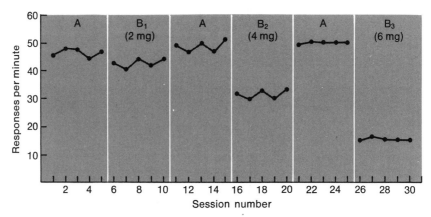

FIGURE 12–7   Diagrammatic representation of an analytical small-*N* design.

type of design could be set up with some fictitious data included. First a baseline rate of behavior is established during five daily one-hour sessions in which the subject emits about fifty responses per minute on some task. Then the subject is given 2 mg of the drug for each of the following five sessions. During the third set of five sessions, the subject is run without being given any drug. The last fifteen sessions of the experiment involved five sessions with 4 mg of drug given, five no-drug sessions, and finally five drug sessions with 6 mg of drug given. The relative effectiveness of different drug levels could then be determined by comparing the behavior of the subject under different levels of the drug.

This procedure can also be used to carry out investigations involving more than one IV that are called factorial experiments when large-*N* designs are employed. Rather than administer different levels of one particular IV, the investigator could substitute different IVs in the alternating B conditions.

Insight
Factorial Small-N Designs

In Chapter 10 factorial designs were defined as designed where more than one IV was involved. Small-*N* designs also have the ability to study more than one IV at a time. The study just mentioned concerning pigeons pecking in the dark exemplifies a small-*N* factorial design. The two IVs studied in this experiment were (1) lighting conditions (light versus dark) and (2) schedules of reinforcement (FR, FI, VI, and VR). In this study different levels of light were varied across *conditions*, while the different levels of schedules were varied across subjects.

It is also possible to have small-*N* factorial designs where *both* IVs are varied across conditions. It would be possible, for example, to carry out the previously mentioned study with just two pigeons using a design as shown.

The pigeons could be run through the following eight conditions:

Light FR	Dark FR	Light VI	Dark VI	Light VR	Dark VR	Light FI	Dark FI
1	2	3	4	5	6	7	8

CONDITION

The two birds could be shaped to an FR schedule in the first light condition and then put in the dark. Next they would be shaped to a VI schedule in light and then put in the dark. This approach could continue until each bird had experienced all eight conditions.

While the exact sequencing of the eight conditions would be varied more than shown here, the reader should get the basic idea that small-*N* factorial designs may allow IVs to be distributed in more than one way.

Concurrent Multiple Response Designs

Instead of investigating the effects of more than one variable using only one DV, a researcher may study the effects of two (or more) IVs on two different responses being emitted during the same experimental situation. In this situation two different responses are used to generate simultaneously two different baselines, each under the control of a separate set of maintaining contingencies. Suppose, for example, an investigator wants to determine whether extinction or punishment was a better means of eliminating behavior. Initially, a rat could be placed in a chamber containing two levers. The rat would then be taught to respond on both bars to get reinforced; pressing either bar would result in food. After the bar-pressing behavior had stabilized for both bars, the investigator could set it up so that the rat would be shocked every time it pressed the left bar (punishment), and simply not get food any longer (extinction) when it pressed the bar on the right side. Later, the original baseline conditions could be reinstated.[9]

Concurrent ABA designs can be employed to carry out both exploratory and analytical experiments. They also give the investigator an opportunity to study how the changing of conditions controlling one's behavior might influence other behaviors. Concurrent designs could be employed to deal with such practical questions as, "How does decreasing the working hours of a person affect work efficiency and leisure activity?"

[9] Concurrent ABA designs should be avoided by the novice investigator because there are several aspects of these designs that can lead to incorrect conclusions (e.g., the contingencies programmed for one behavior may exert control over the second also). Effective use of concurrent designs requires sound knowledge of concurrent design techniques.

A baseline for both work and leisure activity could be obtained for a couple of prison inmates, for example. The amount of work required could then be varied to determine how it affected their work output and the types of things they did in the exercise yard.

COMPARISON OF SMALL-*N* AND LARGE-*N* DESIGNS

At this point, it might be well to bring out some important distinctions between large and small-*N* designs.

In *Experimental Psychology: A Small-*N *Approach* by Robinson and Foster (1979), the differences between large-*N* and small-*N* analytical approaches on several methodological dimensions are discussed. These points are summarized in Table 12–1. Some of the points are elaborated on in more detail below.

Types of Control Techniques

Large-*N* designs may employ randomization and statistical control, whereas small-*N* designs typically do not. Small-*N* designs may use randomization as a means of subject selection, but not as a procedure for controlling secondary variables in the experiment. Although both large-*N* and small-*N* experiments employ elimination and constancy as control techniques, how they use them differs. In large-*N* designs secondary variables are eliminated or held constant at the beginning of the investigation. In small-*N* experiments, elimination and constancy are employed as the investigation is carried out, as well as at the beginning. If a secondary variable happened to vary during the baseline of a small-*N* experiment, the investigator would spot the effect on the DV, search for the responsible variable, remove it, and continue on with establishing the baseline. In such a case with a large-*N* design, the experiment would have to be scrapped or the investigator would need to obtain a covariate measure that would allow the effects of the fluctuating secondary variable to be removed. Notice that small-*N* designs allow the investigator to control for secondary variables after an experiment is in progress, even though statistical adjustment is not possible.

In small-*N* experiments the investigator not only tries to hold secondary variables constant but also increases the control of the experimental situation by getting a constant or continuous measure of the DV. This gives a truer measure of the DV with less chance that the DV measure dealt with is simply a measure of some chance fluctuation, which could be the case if only one measure of the DV per subject were taken. Large-*N*

TABLE 12–1   *Comparison of How Small-*N *and Large-*N *Analytical Approaches Handle Certain Aspects of an Investigation*

ATTRIBUTES OF AN INVESTIGATION	SMALL-*N* APPROACH	LARGE-*N* APPROACH
1. Typical number of subjects	2–5	30
2. DV measure	Repeated measures per subject	One measure per subject and repeated measures
3. Dependence on procedural technology	Strong	Medium
4. Monitoring data	Throughout experiment	Only after all data is collected
5. Control techniques employed	Elimination, constancy, making a secondary variable an IV	Randomization, constancy, elimination, statistical control, making a secondary variable an IV
6. Time sequence of comparison conditions	Consecutive comparisons (simultaneous comparisons possible)	Simultaneous comparisons (consecutive comparisons possible)
7. Adjustment of DV while experiment in progress	Yes	No
8. Adjustment of IV while experiment in progress	Yes	No
9. Means of determining significance of IV effects	Visual examination (intrasubject comparison, intersubject comparison)	Statistical tests (intergroup comparison, intragroup comparison)
10. Means of presenting data	Individual data presented in line graph, histogram, or cumulative records and tables	Group data presented in line graphs, histograms, and tables
11. Means of generality	Systematic replication, interinvestigatory affirmation	Random selection of subjects (minimal interinvestigation affirmation)
12. Types of investigations with which technique can be employed	Laboratory experiments, field experiments	Laboratory experiments, field experiments, EPF laboratory and field studies

325

investigations control for chance fluctuations by using an increased number of subjects; small-N designs control by using an increased number of responses per subject.

Manipulation of the Dependent Variable

In large-N experiments the investigator sets up an experimental design, controls for all the secondary variables possible, applies an IV, and most often takes a one-shot measure of the DV. Little is done about the DV except simply taking a measure of it. With small-N designs the investigator can actually manipulate the DV by varying secondary variables. This procedure is carried out in an effort to develop a more stable DV measure prior to the administration of the IV. Just as an auto mechanic may adjust variables such as the carburetor and the spark plugs to obtain a smooth-running engine before applying some chemical (an IV) to the gas to note its effect on engine performance, so may the psychologist change the value of certain secondary variables in an effort to smooth out and "tune up" measures of the DV before the IV is given. In this way the actual effects of the IV may become more apparent.

Monitoring the Experimental Data

In large-N experiments little analyzing of the data is done until the investigation is over. In small-N designs, however, the experimenter continually monitors the data. This is done to watch for changes in secondary variables that may occur during the experiment, and also because the shifting from one condition to the next is usually determined by the behavior of the subjects.

Data Analysis

Large-N experiments employ the use of statistical calculations to determine the significance of the data. A t-test, F test, or something similar is performed in the fifth step of carrying out a large-N experiment. Frequently, in small-N investigations no statistical test is used in evaluating the data. The data are simply presented in graphic form. Graphs such as Figure 12–1 which show an overall comparison of the subject's behavior from one session to another are often presented. Besides an overall graphical comparison, daily records such as those shown in Figure 12–8 are also included so that the reader can analyze more closely what the behavior (DV) of the subject was like from one moment to the next during a session. Figure 12–8, for example, consists of two daily session records,

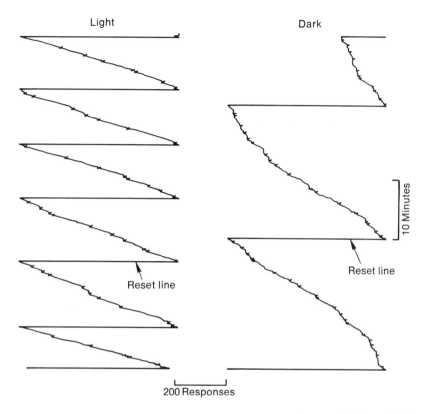

FIGURE 12–8   Cumulative records of a pigeon pecking in light and dark conditions on a variable interval schedule.
(Adapted from Robinson and Shelley (1974), Figure 3. Reprinted by permission.)

one recorded during the baseline when the house and key light were on (left record), and one taken when the pigeon was pecking in total darkness (right record).

To read these cumulative records correctly, one needs to understand how they are made. Figure 12–9 shows diagrammatically how a cumulative recorder operates. The paper is continuously being passed over roller A at a very slow speed (approximately 1 inch per 5 minutes). A pen rests on the paper and draws a vertical line on the record as long as no responses are made by the subject. When the subject does respond, the pen steps a fraction of an inch to the left. (It generally takes 500 steps for the pen to move all the way from the right to the left side of the paper.) When the pen reaches the left side, the recorder automatically resets the pen back to the right side so that it can continue to step each time a response is made. Two of the lines made by the recorder when the pen was reset are marked in Figure 12–8.

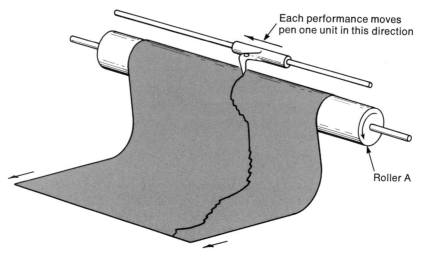

Each performance moves pen one unit in this direction

Roller A

FIGURE 12–9   A cumulative recorder.

By looking at records such as these, the trained researcher can tell quite a bit about how the subject was reacting during the experiment. One of the more obvious things Figure 12–8 tells the investigator is that the subject made over 3,000 responses during the light conditions (notice the recorder had to reset six times; 6×500 responses $= 3,000$), while the subject only responded about 1,200 times during the dark session.

The reader may wonder why so much attention has been given to explaining how to read records. The reason is that analyzing individual subjects' records is an important part of carrying out a small-N design. Just as a researcher who frequently uses statistical tests is able to use them to identify different interesting aspects of the data he or she is analyzing, so can the small-N researcher become proficient in analyzing cumulative records. By simply looking at cumulative records, well-trained investigators can tell such things as what schedule of reinforcement the subject was on, if some secondary variable changed during the session (in some cases the record can even identify the variable), if the subject was frustrated, if the subject was getting satiated, and if the equipment worked properly.

Generality of Results

A topic closely related to data analysis is the issue of generality of results. How well do the results obtained in the investigation represent what would be obtained with other subjects? There is an important distinction between the way large-N investigations control for generality of the results and the way small-N experiments accomplish the same task. In large-N experiments the investigator may increase the generality of the results by increasing the number of subjects in the investigation. It is a well-known principle of data collection that the larger the sample chosen from the population to be subjects in an experiment, the closer will the obtained mean and variance measures of the sample be to the true mean and variance measures of the population. This statistical principle is so well known, in fact, that many scientists have come to believe that generality of results can only be obtained by statistical methods. This assumption is not correct, however, for the concepts of generality and statistical methods are not exactly synonymous. To help bring out the fallaciousness of such reasoning, let us look at a situation in which increasing the number of subjects does not increase the generality of the experiment results.

Suppose, for example, you carried out an experiment on ten rats to see if shocking a rat intermittently while it was carrying out a particular task would influence its behavior. The results you obtained showed all ten rats stopped working and hovered in the corner when shock was applied. Is this reaction characteristic of all rats? The question deals with intraspecies generality. Is it true that the more rats you use in your experiment, the greater the possibility that the results you obtain are true. Can you generalize for all members of the species called rat? What about interspecies generality? Does increasing the number of rats used in the study increase the possibility that the results also hold true for dogs, cats, and humans? Suppose you found from an investigation that a certain teaching procedure was effective for teaching math to young grade-school children. Could you increase the possibility that it could also be effective for mentally retarded children by running additional normal children in your study? Obviously not. The procedure of generalizing from one species to another or from one type of situation to another is carried out through inductive reasoning. The investigator uses past experience and research to compare the similarities and differences of various species. From these similarities and differences, the investigator determines how generalizable the data are. Statistical methods can be employed to determine intraspecies generality because in such cases the investigator is comparing "quantitative" differences in varibles—not the case when comparing one species with another or one situation with another. Small-N designs, then, determine generality of results more by inductive reasoning and interinvestigatory affirmation than by random selection and inferential statistical methods, as is the case with large-N designs.[10]

---

[10] Sidman [1960] points out that many dimensions of intraspecies generality can be effectively handled in nonstatistical ways. In fact, he argues that increasing the number of subjects does not always increase the intraspecies generality of results. Robinson and Foster (1979) devote a whole chapter to the issue of generality and small-N experimentations.

SMALL-*N* DESIGNS IN THE APPLIED SETTING

It was mentioned in Chapter One and Chapter Two that present-day psychologists in the applied areas are required to be more familiar than practitioners of the past with ways of performing experimental research because advances in experimental techniques now make it possible for the applied psychologist to carry out a scientific experiment with only one or two subjects. The development of small-*N* designs is the major reason why applied psychologists now can and should perform such investigations. To illustrate how an ABA design may be applied to everyday problems, here is an experiment that was carried out several years ago.

Dave, a neighbor of mine, was the principal at a nearby school. At a social gathering one evening, he began expressing concern about a student, Mary, who for the past three years seemed to be withdrawing socially more and more from her classmates. He had referred her to the school psychologist three years ago because of her "poor socializing and reading ability," but she was not making progress. I suggested he might try some behavior modification therapy on her, but he said he did not think reinforcement therapy would be effective. In fact, he graciously stated he did not "believe such approaches were effective." He continued, "Although I don't believe it would work, I would certainly be willing to give it a try if I could find someone to do it." Humbly, I leaped into the breach. "I'll try it on one condition," I replied. "You must agree to let me carry out the investigation in such a manner that we may determine what it was that changed her behavior—assuming that it changes, of course." My purpose in making such an offer was simply to show him, if possible, that behavior modification therapy is an effective therapeutic approach, and one of the many alternatives available to the practicing psychologist. Not realizing that my condition meant reverting Mary to her original unsocial behavior once she was socializing, he accepted.

Mary was an attractive 15-year-old girl from a middle-class family enrolled in a class of educable retardates, homogeneous in terms of chronological age (14 to 16) and mental age (80 to 85). A portion of her teacher's report said, "Mary does not mix with any of her peers, just reads and does her work alone. . . . She has good art skills and shows a definite respect and friendliness to her art teacher. . . ." After reviewing the situation, I decided to work with Mary 30 minutes every school day during art period. First, a baseline was taken in which I sat in the back of the room and monitored Mary's behavior. Every 30 seconds I marked on a data sheet whether she was socializing (talking to other students, with other students, or even looking at other students) or not socializing (working alone at her desk or off somewhere by herself). These data were then converted into the percentage of the one-half hour session time she spent socializing and recorded on a chart, as shown in Figure 12–10.

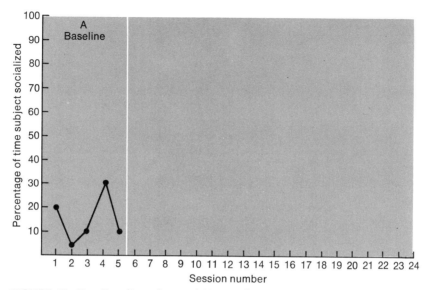

FIGURE 12–10   Baseline phase of Mary's therapy.

After a week of getting a baseline, condition B was begun. Since Mary enjoyed social interaction with her art teacher, the IV was designated as attention from him. Every time Mary socialized with her classmates, I cued her teacher to go over to Mary, smile, and verbally interact with her for 15 seconds, and then move away. Teacher attention was thus used to reinforce Mary's peer socializing. Reinforcement was carried out for the next two weeks, and the percentage of time Mary socialized was again recorded on the chart (Figure 12–11).

By the end of the second week of reinforcement, Mary was spending 95 percent of her time socializing with her classmates. As one might expect, the principal was overjoyed at the dramatic change in Mary's behavior.[11] At this time, I suggested that Mary's antisocial behavior was probably the result of increased attention by her teachers. Dave said he did not agree, but did not really care, for she was no longer antisocial with her peers, and that was what he was concerned with. I told him we were now ready to see if the attention was in fact the determining factor by removing the attention for socializing and seeing if she would return to her antisocial ways. Amazed that I should even suggest such a thing, he said he was pleased with the results and that the investigation could

[11] The change in Mary's behavior is actually not as astounding as it may seem. Prior to the start of the experiment, I checked with Mary's parents. They told me that she was not withdrawn at home. This information led me to conclude that Mary's abnormal sociability was not a deeply ingrained personality problem but a result of something specific at school. Since Mary was probably getting more than her share of attention from teachers when she acted antisocial, I hypothesized that the extra attention was actually causing her problem.

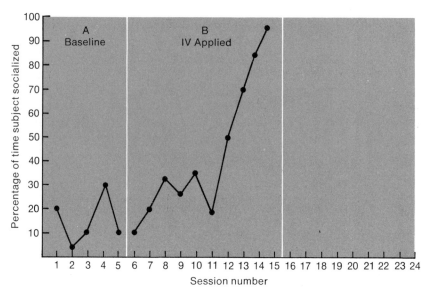

FIGURE 12–11   Mary's therapy through the baseline and independent variable administration phase.

terminate now. I then reminded him of his promise and told him not to worry. We would reimplement the attention later and bring her social behavior back up.

For the next three sessions Mary was no longer given teacher attention when she mingled with her classmates. In fact, she was given teacher attention for emitting antisocial behavior.[12] Notice in Figure 12–12 that the social behavior declines to the baseline level during the second A condition. The IV was reinstated in sessions 19 through 22, and the behavior again climbed to the final level obtained in the first B condition. At last report, one year following the investigation, Mary was doing fine and was no longer considered withdrawn.

Notice that only one subject was involved in this investigation, yet the conclusions drawn about teacher attention causing the withdrawal were substantiated in a scientifically acceptable way. The data obtained from this ABAB design leave little doubt that teacher attention was responsible for increasing Mary's social behavior. Prior to the development of an ABA small-*N* approach, the applied psychologist's investigations involved only the second stage of what has been done here. He or she would simply apply a technique and note the behavior that resulted. No attempt was made to establish a baseline or to reverse the conditions, both of which are

---

[12] This technique is commonly used in ABA designs. Not only is the reinforcer removed from the desired behavior, but it is applied to antagonistic behaviors. This procedure is more effective in determining cause-effect relationships than simply returning to baseline conditions.

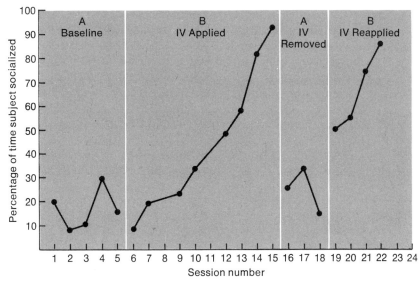

FIGURE 12–12   Mary's therapy through all conditions of the experiment.

extremely important in making this a scientifically acceptable investigation. The ABAB design is a welcome addition to the psychologist's arsenal of analytical procedures because it allows the research to be carried out in applied settings. In the normal, everyday routine, the practicing psychologist generally carries out only the AB portion of this design to help a patient. Whenever it is desired to substantiate cause-effect relationships, the psychologist needs to add at least the reversal condition to the investigation. When doing research, the applied psychologist will add the second B condition, whereas the basic researcher will not. The second B condition is necessary in the applied setting because the patient wants the problem cured, not simply a demonstration that it *could* be cured.

ADVANTAGES AND DISADVANTAGES OF SMALL-*N* DESIGNS

Obviously, the biggest advantage of a small-*N* design is the ability to carry out a scientifically sound investigation with only one or two subjects. This is more important to the psychologist than other social scientists because so much of her or his time is spent dealing with only one person. Small-*N* designs allow the investigator to control the experimental situation more effectively by establishing a continuous measure of the DV throughout the experimental situation. There is also less chance that some secondary variation may change during the investigation without being noticed because the investigator constantly monitors the data. The investigator may in fact "tune up" the DV, thereby making it more sensitive to the possible effects of an IV. No statistical tests need be performed, a point considered an advantage by many who dislike carrying out statistical computations. Both exploratory and analytical investigations may be carried out with small-N designs, as well as investigations involving two or more IVs. Small-N designs allow the investigator to eliminate and hold constant secondary variables that do not show up until after the investigation is under way. ABA designs are generally preferred over the staggered baseline design because the ability to reverse the conditions is a much more effective experimental procedure than varying the point at which an IV is applied. Small-N intrasubject comparison controls for secondary variables better than intersubject comparisons, which is the case for large-N designs.

In terms of disadvantages, small-N designs are not appropriate for certain types of psychological research such as surveys or ex post facto situations. One must have the ability to control and manipulate an IV to be able to use a small-N design. The investigator needs to be more versed in related research literature than is generally required to carry out a large-N experiment. This is true partly because the investigator must rely more on interinvestigatory affirmation rather than on statistical analysis of data. Two of the control techniques are not possible with small-N designs (this is not a very severe disadvantage because small-N designs use other means to accomplish the task). Small-N designs generally take months to complete, whereas many large-N designs can be carried out in one session.

SUMMARY

Small-N experimental designs allow scientifically sound investigations to be carried out on only a few subjects. The analytical assumptions underlying small-N and large-N designs are somewhat different.

Historically, the development of experimental procedures for employing large-N and small-N designs started about the same time. Yet, because of the initial success of large-N designs and the support they received from the scientific community, small-N designs have only recently been acknowledged as a scientifically sound approach to determining cause-effect relationships. The basic format of small-N designs involves using subjects as their own control in carrying out an experimental investigation. First, a baseline is established to determine the value of the DV prior to the administration of an IV. Next, the IV is administered for several experimental sessions with the DV continually being monitored.

The experimental conditions present during the baseline are then replicated by removing the IV for several sessions with the DV continually being monitored. The effect of the IV is determined by noting how the DV changed when the IV was applied and removed. Several different types of small-N designs were presented. These included the ABA design, the staggered baseline design, the analytical ABAB design, and the concurrent multiple response design.

Some of the more important distinctions between large-N and small-N designs were discussed. Although both large-N and small-N designs emphasize quantifiable data gathering and strong control of secondary variables in an investigation, the ways in which they accomplish these tasks differ. Large-N designs emphasize the use of randomization and statistical manipulations of data; small-N designs use elimination and constancy as control techniques and interinvestigatory affirmation as a means of determining the significance of the data. Advantages and disadvantages of small-N designs were also discussed.

I. Statistical Terms and Concepts
  A. *Normal Distribution*
  B. *Other Types of Distributions*
  C. *Sampling*
  D. *Developing a Hypothesis*
  E. *Testing a Hypothesis*
  F. *Significance Level*
  G. *Descriptive and Inferential Statistics*
  H. *Measurement Scales*
   I. *Parametric and Nonparametric Statistics*
   J. *Statistical Tests in Contrast*
II. Chi-Square Nominal Statistical Test
  A. *Two-Dimensional Chi-Square Tests*
  B. *Steps Involved in Calculating X^2*
  C. *Attributes of Chi Square*
III. Mann-Whitney *U* Test: An Ordinal Significance Test
IV. Summary

Data Analysis – Statistical Techniques

13

Few people would challenge the idea that the development of statistics did more for the advancement of psychology than any other development. The purpose of this chapter is to present the main statistical terms, concepts, and tests in such a way that the reader will have a stronger understanding of the way data are analyzed in psychological investigations. Generally, some students enrolled in experimental courses such as the one this text is designed for have had some statistics. It is hoped this explanation of statistics from a somewhat different vantage point than what was experienced before will strengthen their understanding of statistics. And hopefully, the information covered in this chapter is presented in such a way it may enlighten those readers relatively naive in statistical knowledge.

There is perhaps only one word whose mention can strike fear in the hearts of most college students majoring in psychology. That word is *statistics*. While statistical analysis is only one of six basic steps involved in carrying out an investigation (Chapter Three outlines the six steps), it is without question the most apprehensive step, for students and psychologists alike. This is true for several reasons. First, statistics deals with numbers, and numbers have very little personality in and of themselves. It would be hard to conceive of an undergraduate course that is "drier" and less palatable than statistics. It has been claimed that the main reason Freud's ideas were so quickly taken up by psychology in the early part of this century was because a course or two in statistics made his ideas even more appealing

Actually, statistics can be quite interesting. Take the sequence of numbers 36-24-35 for example. Working with statistics like those can be quite enjoyable. It should be apparent from this illustration that working with statistics is not all bad. And one way to make the study of statistics more interesting and valuable is to have a set of numbers represent something of value to you. This is done by letting them represent data you have collected to answer some psychological question. For example, can certain drugs improve intelligence? What causes people to be aggressive? How can one's memory be improved?

With collected data in hand, the psychological investigator turns to statistical tests in hopes of getting help in answering such psychological questions. Actually, running statistical tests are not half as difficult as the formulas themselves seem to imply. This is particularly true when the investigator is somewhat familiar with some of the more common statistical terminology and concepts. Terms such as inferential statistics, sampling, ordinal scales, nonparametrics, and hypothesis testing intimidate the student. Actually, such terms are easily understood once thay are tied into the overall fabric of an experimental investigation. Hopefully the terms, concepts, and tests presented in this chapter will enlighten and reassure the reader with the confidence necessary to employ statistical techniques in analyzing data.

STATISTICAL TERMS AND CONCEPTS

Normal Distribution

Suppose you came from a town of 5,000 inhabitants and wanted to know how intelligent the townspeople were. One way to get an indication would be to randomly select a person from the town and give that individual an intelligence test. Figure 13–1(a) illustrates such a situation. While the information on one person is informative, it gives you a relatively poor idea of what the town is like in terms of intelligence. A better idea would be to select a sample of 100 people, test them, and plot their IQs [Figure 13(b)]. A third choice you could make would be to measure every person's intelligence in the whole town and plot them as in Figure 13(c).

The type of distribution shown in Figure 13(c) is called a *normal distribution*. It is so called because almost any attribute, be it physical or mental, that a psychologist wants to study is distributed like this. This type of distribution is what we *normally* expect to find.

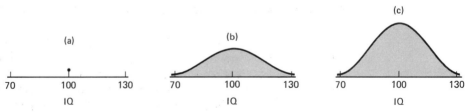

FIGURE 13–1   (a) Getting the IQ of one person; (b) getting the IQ of a group of 100 persons; (c) getting the IQ of everyone in town.

Other Types of Distributions

Some other types of distributions are shown in Figure 13–2. There are normal distributions [Figure 13–2(a)], bimodal distributions [Figure 13–2(b)], rectangular distributions [Figure 13–2(c)] and skewed distributions [Figure 13–2(d) and (e)]. While most physical and mental attributes are distributed normally, some attributes are distributed differently. For example, the genetic attribute of sex is found to be *bimodally distributed*. That is, while most humans are typically considered male or female, each of us varies in terms of degree of maleness and femaleness. The *skewed curve distribution* is often found when studying ages. The attribute of human skin color is distributed in a *skewed* manner over the earth's population.

Sampling

Getting back to the issue of intelligence in a town of 5,000, let's look at the best way to determine the town's intelligence. Notice that the normal distribution for 100 people has roughly the same shape and width as the normal distribution where all the townspeople were measured. One of the most interesting and valuable things that psychologists have found when studying distributions is that measuring some attribute in a *randomly selected sample* of people chosen from the total population of people you are interested in will give you a good indication as to how that attribute is distributed throughout the whole population. In other words, someone would only have to sample 100 people to know the limits (often called *range*) of intelligence in the town and the percentage of people at each level of intelligence. Measuring all the members of the town would not only be impractical, but also unnecessary.

Public opinion polls like the Gallup poll illustrate this point. By randomly sampling a minute portion of the whole population, they can fairly accurately determine such attributes as people's attitude on the holding of hostages in Iran, the distribution of socioeconomic status of black and white families or the height of Americans.

Sampling, then, is an important tool for experimentation in psychology. By administering an IV to only a small portion that has been randomly sampled from a population, the psychologist can learn how the *population* would react to some IV without having to test the whole population.

Developing a Hypothesis

Suppose a pharmaceutical company in that town was dumping waste water into a pond that supplied the town's water. And further suppose an astute

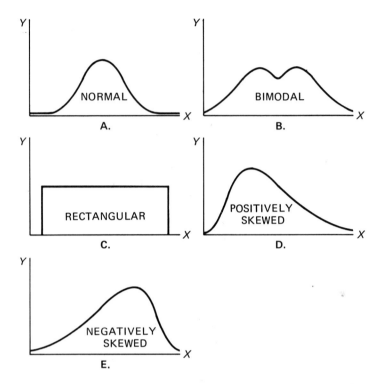

FIGURE 13–2   Five types of distributions: (a) normal distribution; (b) bimodal distribution; (c) rectangular distribution; (d) positively skewed distribution; and (e) negatively skewed distribution.
(Adapted from *Basic Statistics for the Behavioral Sciences*, Hopkins and Glass, Prentice-Hall, Inc., 1978, p. 36. Reprinted by permission.)

school teacher one day happened to plot the IQ scores for the third-grade students in her class. She then, out of curiosity, plotted the IQs from class files for all third-grade students in the school three years prior to the opening of the plant. Finding the IQ scores of the present third-grade class averaged 20 points higher than the former class, she might hypothesize that the chemical compound being released from the plant increased a person's IQ. Figure 13–3 shows two overlapping normal distributions for the third-grade classes obtained by the teacher. Curve (a) is the distribution of intelligence for the third-grade class three years prior to the opening of the plant while curve (b) shows what the distribution was after the pharmaceutical plant was in operation for two years.

   If someone had in fact measured the intelligence of the whole town before and after the plant was in operation, and if the two distributions shown in Figure 13–3 were the results obtained, one might easily conclude that the chemicals being dumped by the plant increase a person's intelligence.

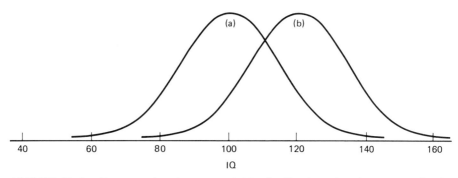

FIGURE 13–3 Two overlapping normal IQ distributions for the town's third-grade class: (a) represented the distribution of intelligence scores prior to opening of the pharmaceutical plant, and (b) represents the distribution after the chemicals affect the townspeople.

Figure 13–3 brings out an important point that many students fail to notice. The effect an IV has on some group or population shows up as a *shift* in the distribution. If the chemicals did in fact cause higher intelligence, they would result in the shift of the range of intelligence in the town. And the greater the effect of the chemicals, the greater the distance between the means of the two distributions.

The example made here exemplifies a prepost type of experiment in which the intelligence measures of the townspeople prior to the opening of the plant would serve as the *control measures*, or control condition as some call it, against which the intelligence measures obtained after the IV (the chemicals) was introduced. As mentioned in earlier chapters, however, a more common experimental paradigm entails concurrently comparing a *control group* of individuals against an *experimental group* of individuals.

Armed now with some basic information about distributions, samples, and effects of IVs on distributions, let's take a closer look at how one goes about testing a hypothesis.

Testing a Hypothesis

First, you select a hypothesis. Keeping in mind that the definition of hypothesis is a *testable statement of a potential relationship between two or more variables*, one looks at the two variables under consideration. In the present situation we are interested in determining whether certain chemical additives in the city water supply (the IV in our proposed experiment) influence intelligence (the DV in our proposed experiment). Having some information about the people in the town whose intelligence seems to be rising from drinking water contaminated by certain chemical compounds, we might hypothesize, "the chemical compounds can increase intelligence."

With this hypothesis we then begin selecting subjects. Knowing that testing a randomly selected sample of people from the population is just as good as testing the whole population, we randomly select sixty people.

Any findings made about these sixty people should hold true for the population. After randomly selecting sixty subjects from the population, they are randomly divided into two groups of thirty persons each.

After the two groups of people have been determined, the chemicals are administered to one of the two groups. If the chemical compounds do not affect intelligence, we would expect the normal distribution of intelligence scores for both groups to show up as perfectly overlapping normal distributions as in Figure 13–4. If the IV does increase intelligence, however, the normal distribution of scores for the experimental group will shift to the right, with the extent of the shift indicating the strength of the IV effect. We will let Figure 13–5 represent the intelligence scores obtained from the control and experimental groups.

Looking at the distribution of scores obtained from our experiment, we would likely want to conclude that the chemical compound does increase intelligence. There appears to be a rather large difference between the scores of the two groups. The question that should come to mind at this time is, "How different must the distributions of the two groups be before we can conclude that the IV had an effect?"

Significance Level

The next step in testing one's hypothesis is to run a statistical test on the data. Technically speaking, a statistical test compares the distribution of scores for the control sample to the distribution of scores for the experimental sample. Recall from Chapter 9 that the formula for the randomized t-test is

$$t = \frac{X_a - X_b}{\sqrt{\frac{SS_a + SS_b}{(n_a - 1) + (n_b - 1)}\left(\frac{1}{n_a} + \frac{1}{n_b}\right)}}$$

The distance the IV has shifted the distribution of scores for the experimental group from the distribution of the control group will show

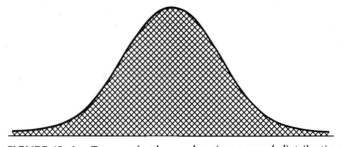

FIGURE 13–4   Two perfectly overlapping normal distributions.

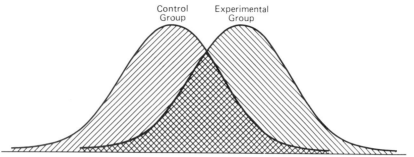

Control Group   Experimental Group

FIGURE 13–5   Plotted distributions of scores for the control and experimental groups in an experiment.

up as the difference between the two means, $\bar{X}_a$ and $\bar{X}_b$, in the numerator of the formula. Therefore, the greater the distance between the two means, the greater the effect of the IV.

This last statement has to be qualified to some extent. Actually, differences between the means can be caused not only by the IV but also by chance. We know that no person scores exactly the same on an intelligence test when tested two or more times, even if the repeated testing occurs within a few days. It is possible then that the distributions of scores for an experimental and control group will not overlap perfectly if the IV has no effect. It is even possible that the means of the two distributions could differ as much as is shown in Figure 13–3 simply as a function of chance. As one might expect, however, the greater the obtained distances between the means of the two distributions, the greater is the probability that the IV in fact caused the difference instead of chance. This fact is born out by *t* tables, which shows the probability that any *t* value is due to chance. (F tables do essentially the same thing.) In the tables you can see that the larger the *t* value, the smaller the probability that the difference between the scores in the experimental and control groups could have occurred by chance.

As mentioned in earlier chapters, psychologists have generally agreed on the 5 percent *significance level.* That is, whenever a statistical test is run, the obtained value (be it a *t* value, F value, or whatever) has to have less than a 5 percent probability of occurring by chance. Conversely, the 5 percent significance level indicates that there is a 95 percent probability that the difference between the groups was caused by the IV. Figure 13–5 shows how far apart the distributions of scores for the control and experimental groups could have been to exceed the 5 percent level of significance.

After the statistical test is run, and the 5 percent level of significance is reached, we would conclude two things. First, the IV did in fact have an effect on the experimental subjects tested in the experiment itself. Second, we would conclude that the chemical compound would improve the intelligence of the "population" from which the sample of sixty people was randomly selected.

Descriptive and Inferential Statistics

There are two types of statistics that experimenters often talk about, *descriptive statistics* and *inferential statistics*. One main reason experimentalists collect data is to get a better description of an event, a situation, or an individual. If someone tells you that a person is 6 feet tall and weighs 150 pounds, you have just heard some *descriptive statistics*. If you plot the distribution of scores from entering freshman on a college entrance exam, you have descriptive statistics. Descriptive statistics are data that have been collected, organized, and even summarized. Plotted distributions, calculated means, standard deviations, and percentiles are all examples of descriptive statistics. The scores collected from the subjects in the control and experimental groups of the previously discussed experiment on intelligence were descriptive statistics.

When the descriptive statistics of the control and experimental group were plugged into the t formula, they became inferential statistics. Statistical tests such as the t-tests and F tests were designed to take data collected from samples and make inferences. There are two main types of inferences (or conclusions) psychologists are interested in. First, should we conclude an IV did or did not affect the DV of the subjects tested? The statistical tests aid us in making the correct inference about what happened "within" the study. Second, should we conclude the IV would or would not affect the DV in the overall population? Statistical tests aid us in making the correct inference about what would happen beyond the study, throughout the population.

Measurement Scales

In Chapter Six it was pointed out that numerical data may be collected using any of the four different measurement scales. Due to the fact that the type of statistical test one may employ in an investigation depends to a large extent on the type of measurement scale used, it may be beneficial in this chapter to repeat what was said about measurement scales in Chapter Six.

There are four basic measurement scales that may be used to assign numbers to objects and events: the *nominal, ordinal, interval,* and *ratio* measurement scales. The nominal scale is the simplest measurement scale and entails nothing more than the mere assignment of an identifying number to each stimulus. The number on marathon runners' uniforms exemplify nominal scaling. Nominal numbers may categorize stimuli but

TABLE 13–1   *Illustration of the Four Types of Measurement Scales*

RUNNER	NOMINAL (NUMBER ON JERSEY)	ORDINAL (ORDER AT FINISH LINE)	INTERVAL (TIME ON WRISTWATCH AT FINISH LINE)	RATIO (TIME TO RUN TWO MILES)
A	8	1	3:46-27″	6′-27″
B	2	2	3:46-58″	6′-58″
C	14	3	3:51-07″	11′-07″
D	7	4	3:52-03″	12′-03″

say nothing about how they are ordered (first, second, etc.), how different they are from each other, or how big the differences are between the stimuli. Interval scaling is the assignment of numbers to stimuli using a number scale where the units intervals being used are equal. Grades on a multiple-choice test exemplify this scale. A score of 83 on an exam is 3 units less than a score of 86. The scores of 53 and 56 differ in the same 3-unit amount. Numbers on a yardstick exemplify a ratio scale, but also have an absolute zero point. While the difference between an interval and ratio scale of having an absolute zero point may seem unimportant to the reader, it makes a big difference in terms of what statistical operations may be performed.

Table 13–1 illustrates the use of each of the four measurement scales. Four long distance runners ran a practice race prior to a sanctioned meet. Runner A has the number 8 on his jersey, player B is number 2, player C is 14, and player D is 7.

A second illustration the reader may more easily relate to is shown in Table 13–2. Six students took an exam in an experimental psychology class. As each turned in his or her exam, the exam paper was assigned an identification number (column 1). The second column indicates how the students ranked, with number 1 being the highest scoring paper. Column

TABLE 13–2   *Illustration of the Nominal, Ordinal, and Interval Scales on Student Exam Papers*

STUDENT NUMBER	RANK ON THE EXAM	INTERVAL SCORE ON THE EXAM
4	1	97
1	2	91
6	3	86
3	4	80
2	5	63
5	6	42

3 indicates the actual scores obtained in terms of an interval scale. Notice that the interval scale scores provide more exacting information than the ranking does. Students typically want to know more than just where they ranked in class. They want to know how well they did in terms of answering the questions.

Parametric and Nonparametric Statistics

Inferential tests available to investigators may be divided into two types: *parametric statistical tests* and *nonparametric statistical tests*. *Parametric statistical* tests are inferential statistical tests run on data that are interval or ratio in nature. Chapters Nine through Eleven illustrated two-group designs, multilevel one-IV designs, and factorial designs. In each example presented in those three chapters, the inferential tests run were *t*-tests or F tests. This was done because most of the experiments in psychology entail using interval or ratio data.

It is important to keep in mind, however, that two-group, multilevel one-IV, and factorial experiments may be conducted with data being collected using nominal or ordinal measurements. When nominal and ordinal data are collected, the type of inferential statistical test one needs to employ is a *nonparametric statistical test*. While *t*-tests and F tests are parametric tests, the most common nonparametric tests include the chi square, the sign test, the Mann-Whitney U, the Wilcoxon, and the Kruskal-Wallis test.

Statistical Tests in Contrast

Psychologists tend to divide statistical analyses employed in research investigations into three major categories: (1) parametric statistical tests, (2) nonparametric statistical tests, and (3) correlational techniques. Figures 13–6 and 13–7 employ flow charts to show how these three statistical techniques are related.

The first question an investigator asks is whether the investigation is out to determine whether two variables have some degree of relationship, or whether one variable is causing a second variable to change. If the investigation is studying the degree of relationship between variables, a correlational study is what you have. By looking at what measurement scale is being employed, you may then select which correlational technique to employ. Table 7–3 (page 190) points out the more common correlational techniques employed with the different measurement scales.

If a person is interested in studying situations where one variable "affects" some behavior, then parametric or nonparametric statistical tests are appropriate. By looking at the measurement scale used, one either

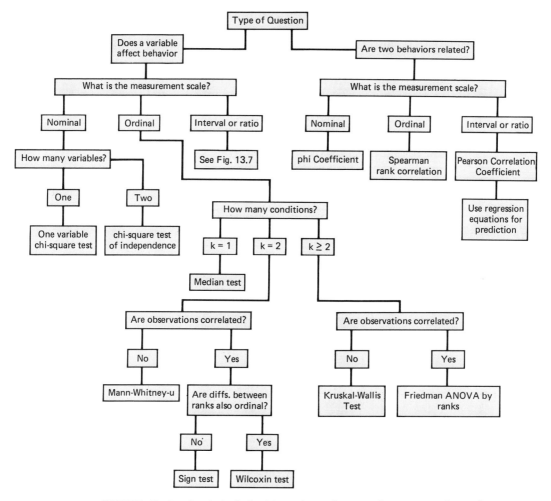

FIGURE 13–6   Statistical decision chart showing how one selects the proper nonparametric statistical test or the proper correlational technique.

selects a parametric test (for interval and ratio scales) or a nonparametric test (for nominal or ordinal measurement scales). Figure 13–6 shows which nonparametric tests are appropriate for the different measurement scales and conditions (e.g., nominal scale with only one variable).

Figure 13–7 shows which conditions require the different parametric tests. By following the flow charts in these two figures, it should be fairly easy to select the appropriate statistical test for the needs of almost any investigation.

Due to the fact that almost every parametric statistical test is previously illustrated in Chapters Nine through Eleven, the remainder of this chapter focuses on two of the more commonly used nonparametric statistical tests.

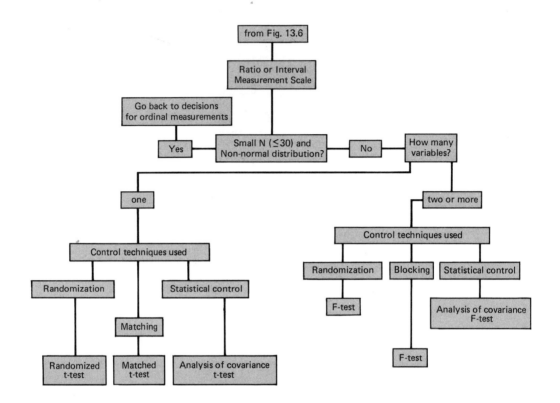

FIGURE 13–7   Statistical decision chart for showing how one selects the proper parametric statistical test.

A more in-depth coverage of nonparametric tests may be found in a variety of statistical texts, including Noether's *Statistics: A Nonparametric Approach*, 1978, Keppel's *Design and Statistical Analysis*, 1978, and Siegel's *Nonparametric Statistics*, 1956.

CHI-SQUARE NOMINAL STATISTICAL TEST

In the southern Utah area surrounding the town of St. George, people are claiming that radioactive fallout from atmospheric atomic tests conducted at nearby federal testing grounds years ago has caused sickness and death. To determine whether their claim is justified, the state of Utah

TABLE 13–3	Number of Deaths due to Leukemia in Three Utah Towns, Price, Logan and St. George (hypothetical data)

PRICE	LOGAN	ST. GEORGE
20	17	38

is conducting an investigation that involves comparing two similarly populated areas to the St. George area. The DV being studied is deaths resulting from leukemia, a blood problem that can be induced by exposure to radioactivity. The populations surrounding three towns (Price, Logan, and St. George) are studied with the number of deaths due to leukemia being the data collected.[1] Table 13–3 shows the number of leukemia deaths recorded over the past 20 years in all three areas. With such data available, how does one go about conducting a statistical test to determine whether there is a significant difference in deaths between the three towns?

Realizing there are three groups of data, the enthusiastic reader may feel he can run an F test similar to those discussed in Chapter Ten, where statistical tests for investigations involving three or more groups (and only one IV) were presented. There is, however, an important difference between the data collected on leukemia deaths in this chapter and the data discussed in Chapter Ten when F tests were illustrated. *The data collected here on leukemia deaths do not include within group variability.* The numbers listed for Price, Logan, and St. George are simply count totals. Each death is represented by the number 1, and those numbers are added together to get one total value for each town area. Recall from Chapter Four that two main data ingredients are necessary for running an F test: (1) a measure of differences between groups, and (2) a measure of variation between scores *within* each group. The first required ingredient has been referred to in this text as V_B; the second has been labeled V_W. In the F formula ($F = V_B/V_W$), both V_B and V_W measures are essential.

The reason no V_W is possible with the leukemia death data is because they are *nominal scale data.* Nominal scale data are nothing more than frequency counts by categories. In this case there are three categories: Price, Logan, and St. George. The most common statistical test employed by psychologists for analyzing nominal data is the *chi-square test.*

Chi square, like the *t*-test and F test is a test of significance. While the *t*-tests and F tests are applied to interval and ratio data, chi square is

---

[1] While it is true that southern Utah residents are making such a claim, the data presented here are contrived specifically to illustrate how a chi square may be run and are not the true data being studied by the state of Utah and the federal government.

TABLE 13–4   *Expected and Observed Leukemia Death Frequencies For Three Utah Towns*

TOWN	PRICE	LOGAN	ST. GEORGE
Observed frequency (O)	20	17	38
Expected frequency (E)	25	25	25

designed for nominal data. All three tests of significance just mentioned require some comparison to be made. With F tests and t-tests, the comparison is essentially the difference *within* the groups to the differences *between* the groups. The chi-square test, having no within differences, compares *obtained frequencies* to *expected frequencies*. The expected frequencies play the same role in chi-square tests that within variance plays in F and t-tests; it is a measure of what would be without the effects of some IV being present.

Expected frequencies in this case are determined simply by adding up the total number of deaths, 75, and dividing by the total number of categories, 3. All three categories should have the same number of deaths if there is no variable differentially affecting any of the categories.

Table 13–4 shows the observed cell frequencies (O) and the expected cell frequencies (E) for the leukemia death situation. Essentially, a chi-square test entails calculating the difference between the observed and expected frequencies and then determining if that difference could occur by chance less than five times out of 100.[2] In this particular case concerning leukemia deaths, the calculations for chi square (χ^2) would go as follows:

$$\chi^2 = \sum \frac{(O - E)^2}{E}$$

$$= \frac{(20 - 25)^2}{25} + \frac{(17 - 25)^2}{25} + \frac{(38 - 25)^2}{25}$$

$$= 1 + 2.56 + 7.04 = 10.60$$

Once the chi-square value, 10.60 in this case, is determined, the investigator turns to a chi-square table, which looks quite similar to a t table.[3] A chi square table may be found in the Appendix, page 401. Both t and chi-square tables require the investigator to calculate degrees of freedom. Typically, degrees of freedom for chi square is calculated the same way one calculates the degrees of freedom for *between variance*. In this case it is the number of cells, or categories, minus 1. The critical chi-square value listed in the table ($df = 2$; 0.05 significance level) is 5.991. The obtained

---

[2] Obviously, this assumes we selected the 0.05 level of significance. Like F tests and t-tests, the investigator may choose any level.

[3] Notice that the expected frequencies have to be recalculated.

chi-square value (10.60) is larger than 5.991, so it is concluded that the towns' death rates from leukemia do differ significantly from the other towns. Once the overall chi square is found to be significant, the investigator compares each cell to every other to find out where the differences lie—between which towns. Instead of running a special multiple-group comparison test, as would be the case with an F test, the investigator would simply run three more chi squares comparing (1) Price to Logan, (2) Price to St. George, and (3) Logan to St. George, as follows:[4]

$$Price\text{-}Logan: \quad \chi^2 = \frac{(20 - 18.5)^2}{18.5} + \frac{(17 - 18.5)^2}{18.5}$$

$$= 0.24$$

$$Price\text{-}St.\ George: \quad \chi^2 = \frac{(20 - 29)^2}{29} + \frac{(38 - 29)^2}{29}$$

$$= 2.79 + 2.79$$

$$= 5.58$$

$$Logan\text{-}St.\ George: \quad \chi^2 = \frac{(17 - 27.5)^2}{27.5} + \frac{(38 - 27.5)^2}{27.5}$$

$$= 3.28 + 3.28$$

$$= 6.56$$

It is apparent that the death rate from leukemia is significantly higher in St. George than in the other two Utah towns.

Two-Dimensional Chi-Square Tests

The chi-square example concerning leukemia deaths illustrates what may be referred to as a *single-dimension* chi-square test. There are also *two-dimensional* chi-square tests. The distinction between one- and two-dimensional chi-square tests may be made clearer by drawing a somewhat imprecise analogy of single versus multiple IV experimental designs. Two-group and one-way ANOVAR designs previously discussed in Chapters Nine and Ten are single-dimension designs while factorial designs involve two or more dimensions.

Suppose an investigator wanted to determine whether handedness is related to the sex of an individual. He or she could go out, sample 100 men and 90 women and obtain the data presented in Table 13–5. The first step after the "observed" data were collected would be to determine the expected frequencies. In the leukemia example, the expected fre-

---

[4] Notice that the expected frequencies have to be recalculated.

TABLE 13–5 *Hypothetical Data Concerning Sex and Handedness of Individuals*

	HANDEDNESS			
	Right	Left	Ambidextrous	Total
Male	52	38	10	100
Female	48	32	10	90
Total	100	70	20	190

quency for each cell was determined simply by taking the total number of deaths (75) and dividing by 3, the number of groups. It was naturally assumed that all three groups would have exactly the same number of deaths related to leukemia if no IV was causing differences. In many chi-square situations the expected frequencies cannot be so logically determined. In the present case, for example, most people know handedness (right, left, ambidextrous) is not equally distributed in people. In such cases the expected frequency can be readily obtained using a well-known multiplication theorem of probability. Briefly, the multiplication theorem states that given a two-dimensional table, the expected frequency of any cell in that table is equal to the sum of frequencies in the row *times* the sum of frequencies in the column *divided* by the *total* number of frequency counts made in the whole investigation. Symbolically, the formula is

$$f_{E(RC)} = \frac{f_R f_C}{N}$$

where $f_{E(RC)}$ is the expected frequency for a cell in row R and column C and $f_R f_C/N$ is the frequency of the column (f_C) times the frequency of the row (f_R) divided by total number of subjects in the investigation.

Table 13–6 illustrates what has been said by showing how the expected frequencies are calculated for the sex-handedness investigation.

TABLE 13–6 *Means for Obtaining Expected Frequencies for Sex-Handedness Investigation*

(a)				(b)				(c)		
$\dfrac{f_{C1}f_{R1}}{N}$	$\dfrac{f_{C2}f_{R1}}{N}$	$\dfrac{f_{C3}f_{R1}}{N}$	R_1	$\dfrac{(100)(100)}{190}$	$\dfrac{(70)(100)}{190}$	$\dfrac{(20)(100)}{190}$	100	52.6	36.8	10.5
$\dfrac{f_{C1}f_{R2}}{N}$	$\dfrac{f_{C2}f_{R2}}{N}$	$\dfrac{f_{C3}f_{R2}}{N}$	R_2	$\dfrac{(100)(90)}{190}$	$\dfrac{(70)(90)}{190}$	$\dfrac{(20)(90)}{190}$	90	47.4	33	9.5
C_1	C_2	C_3	N	100	70	20	190			

Figure 13–4(a) indicates the formulas by which the expected frequencies for each cell are calculated. For example, the expected frequency for right-handed males would be the total frequency count for column 1 (C) times the total frequency count for row 1 (R), divided by the total frequency count for all cells together (N).

Table 13–4(b) substitutes the proper numbers, and Table 13–4(c) indicates the actual expected frequencies. The chi-square calculation for this two-dimensional situation is then carried out as follows:

$$\chi^2 = \sum_{}^{R} \sum_{}^{C} \frac{(O - E)^2}{E}$$

$$= \frac{(52 - 52.6)^2}{52.6} + \frac{(38 - 36.8)^2}{36.8} + \frac{(10 - 10.5)^2}{11}$$

$$+ \frac{(48 - 47.4)^2}{47.5} + \frac{(32 - 33)^2}{33} + \frac{(10 - 9.5)^2}{9.5}$$

$$= 0.007 + 0.04 + 0.02 + 0.008 + 0.03 + 0.03$$

$$= 0.135$$

Next, the degrees of freedom are calculated using the formula $df = (C - 1)(R - 1)$.[5] With $df = 2$ and 0.05 as the chosen level of significance, the critical value listed in the χ^2 table is 5.991. It would then be concluded that sex and handedness are not related; one does not influence the appearance of the other.

Steps Involved in Calculating χ^2

Due to the fact that chi square is a test of significance, the steps involved in calculating it are essentially the same as for running a *t*-test or an F test:

1. Collect and arrange the data in its proper groups.
2. Assume the null hypothesis and set out to disprove it.
3. Perform the appropriate statistical calculations for χ^2.
4. Determine the appropriate degrees of freedom for χ^2.
5. Select an appropriate level of significance (i.e., 0.05 or 0.01).
6. With chosen degrees of freedom value and level of significance value, look up the critical χ^2 value from the appropriate table.
7. Compare your calculated χ^2 value to the critical χ^2 value.

The main difference between the chi-square test and the F test is in step 3, where chi square compares *obtained frequencies* to *expected frequencies* rather than *within-group variance* (V_W) to *between-group variance* (V_B) as is the case with F tests.

---

[5] Notice that this formula is identical for df_1 in factorial designs.

Attributes of Chi Square

As previously mentioned, chi-square is designed to be used when *nominal data* are collected. It can also be used on any data that are reduced to proportions and percentages. Most statistics books illustrate how chi square may be calculated using proportions [e.g., Ferguson, 1976, p. 199–201]. It may also be used on ordinal, interval, and ratio data because such data can obviously be reduced to nominal scale. However, power of analysis is lost (see page 158) when converting higher-level data to nominal data, so such conversions are not generally done. As a statistical test, chi square is relatively easy to compute and does not require the population to be normally distributed as do the *t*-test and F test.

In cases where the expected frequency is less than 5 for any of the cells, the chi-square calculations need to be adjusted or corrected. A correction known as *Yates' correction for continuity* may be applied in such situations [see Ferguson, 1976, p. 201–202]. With two or more degrees of freedom, the error in chi square introduced by small expected frequencies is of less consequence than with only one degree of freedom. Also, when expected cell frequencies are small, it is not uncommon for cells to be combined.

The application of chi square with a 2×2 group arrangement is so common that a formula has been devised for such occasions that does not require expected frequencies to be calculated [see Ferguson, 1976, p. 198–199].

MANN-WHITNEY *U* TEST: AN ORDINAL SIGNIFICANCE TEST

The Mann-Whitney *U* test is designed to determine the significance of experimental data when the dependent variable is recorded in terms of ranked measurements, and when two groups are to be compared.[6] Suppose the music department asks an experimental psychologist to devise an investigation to determine whether two teaching methods differentially influence a child's musical achievement. One class of twenty students is randomly divided into two groups of ten students each. Students in group A are taught using the zilthy method while students in group B are taught using a more typical rehearsal approach. At the end of one year of training, a recital is given where all twenty students are ranked by a panel of judges according to their skill. Table 13–7 shows the final rankings of the twenty students.

---

[6] Actually the Mann-Whitney *U* test may be employed where there are more than two groups. In such cases you simply compare two groups at a time in the fashion of a multigroup comparison test such as the Scheffé.

TABLE 13–7	*Ranking of the Students in Groups A and B According to Musicial Skill*
GROUP A	GROUP B
1	3
2	5
4	6
8	7
10	9
11	14
12	15
13	16
18	17
20	19

The statistic U is then calculated with the formula

$$U_{obs} = N_A N_B + \frac{N_A(N_A + 1)}{2} - T_A$$

N_A and N_B represent the number of cases in groups A and B, respectively, and T_A stands for the total (T) of the ranks for one group ($T_A = 1 + 2 + 4 + 8 + 10 + 11 + 12 + 13 + 18 + 20$), the Mann-Whitney U in this example would be calculated as follows:

$$U_{obs} = (10)(10) + \frac{10(10 + 1)}{2} - 99$$

$$= 100 + \frac{90}{2} - 99$$

$$= 100 - 54$$

$$= 46$$

With the calculated U value in hand, one now turns to Table D in the appendix to see if the two rankings differ significantly. Using N_A and N_B in much the same way as df_B and df_W are used in multilevel one IV designs, the experimenter looks for the critical U value in Table D. A Mann-Whitney U table differs from t and F tables in that *two* values of U are given, one smaller than the other. These two values are such that if the observed U falls *between* these two values it is concluded that there is *no* significant difference between the groups. With N_A and N_B each equaling 10, the critical values in the table are 16 and 84. Our observed U value of 46 lies between 16 and 84. Therefore, we conclude that the zilthy method was not better than a standard rehearsal method for training music students. If our U value were larger than 84 or smaller than 16, we would have concluded that the two methods produce different results.

The formula for Mann-Whitney U just given is employed in situations where neither group contains more than twenty subjects. If there are more than twenty subjects in a group, the following formula should be used:

$$z = \frac{U_{\text{obs}} - (N_A N_B / 2)}{\sqrt{\dfrac{(N_A)(N_B)(N_A + N_B + 1)}{12}}}$$

Once the z score is calculated, the investigator turns to a z table (found in most statistic texts). The number listed in the table tells you what level of significance a particular z score reaches. For example, if a z of 1.50 reaches the 0.0668 level of significance, this is higher than the 0.05 level that is commonly accepted as the point at which we conclude the groups did differ.

The Mann-Whitney U is a statistical test of significance designed to be used when (1) data are collected as an ordinal measurement, and (2) when only two groups are involved. If more than two groups are involved in a situation where ordinal data are collected, the Kruskal-Wallis test is most commonly employed. Illustrations of how one runs a Kruskal-Wallis test may be found in McCall [1975, p. 313–316], and Ferguson [1976, p. 392–394].

SUMMARY

The chapter presents the main statistical terms, concepts, and nonparametric tests used in conjunction with data analysis. Normal curves play a major role in the testing of hypotheses. Statistical tests are run to determine whether the data of experimental and control groups are significantly different. Descriptive statistics summarize data while inferential statistics are tests employed to determine the significance of data. There are four measurement scales—nominal, ordinal, interval, and ratio. Parametric statistics involve interval and ratio scales while nonparametric statistics involve nominal and ordinal scales. Psychologists tend to divide statistical analyses into three major categories—parametric statistics, nonparametric statistics, and correlational techniques. The statistical analyses one should employ depends on several variables: measurement scale used, number of groups involved, and the number of IVs. Figures 13–6 and 13–7 show which statistical test is appropriate for the different types of psychological investigations. Illustrated use of the Chi-square test and the Mann-Whitney U test complete the chapter.

I. Role of the Report
II. Objectives of the Report
III. Organization of the Report
    A. Title and Title Page
    B. Abstract
    C. Introduction
    D. Method
    E. Results
    F. Discussion
    G. Conclusions and/or Summary
IV. Dry Facts and Some Requirements of Style
    A. Accuracy
    B. Length
    C. Typing
    D. Tense and Person
    E. Headings
    F. Footnotes
    G. Abbreviations and Symbols
    H. References
V. Peer Communication
    A. The Journal
    B. Locating Journal Articles
    C. Conventions
VI. Summary

Communication in Psychology

14

Almost every undergraduate psychology program in the country requires its students to learn how to write reports according to the rules of the American Psychological Association. The purpose of this chapter is to present the guidelines set down by the APA along with sample published reports. Also included is a section devoted to showing students how to look up journal articles in the Psychological Abstracts.

Conducting psychological investigations is not the only responsibility of a psychologist; the objective of research is not simply gratification for the investigator. It is the responsibility of any psychologist to communicate information that would be useful for the advancement of the discipline. The most common means of communication in scientific communities is the written report. After the investigator has designed an investigation, carried out the procedural steps, and analyzed the data, there is still one thing to do—write a report summarizing the investigation. This is generally considered an arduous task. The actual carrying out of the experimental routine is usually fascinating and the statistical analysis merely a necessary step; even the drawing of conclusions and inferences is a challenge. But to most, the drudgery of having to write up the findings is looked upon as an unrewarding, laborious task to be put off as long as possible. Most research psychologists have a drawer full of data from past projects that they cannot seem to find the time to report.

ROLE OF THE REPORT

The obvious question raised by beginning research students is why are journal reports so dreadfully dull. As one student put it, "I barely got to sleep when I realized I was still on the introduction and I had only 10 more minutes before class," or "Why don't they ever say this in English?" Though scientific journal reports have yet to win Pulitzer prizes, their role in communication is important.

Why do reports in general seem to be so uninteresting to the student or uninformed general reader? Reports are exactly that—reports. They are reports of observations and collections of data culminating in conclusions and inferences drawn by the experimenter. All observations, relevant manipulation techniques, and apparatus require description in a particular scientific vocabulary so that the experimenter can communicate precisely what is meant. Precision in definition is the crux of the question. Although a specific action or process can be defined by many different slang expressions and colloquialisms in everyday life, the scientist must seek exactness in universally accepted definitions understood by all in the same or similar situations. Therefore, the scientist must seek detail and exact meanings in order to transmit intentions or method.

Take, for instance, the simple observation of a subject's behavior. In an everyday life situation, a common observation could be this: "Upon giving the medicine to the subject, he seemed to be worried and anxious until the negative thing was taken away." The statement is vague on several points. A researcher reading such a communication would wonder what was actually involved. What were the exact living conditions of the subject? Who was the subject? What was the dosage and the mode of application of the IV? and so on. If the statement was in a journal report, the reader would expect all important terms to be operationally defined.[1] What did the observer mean when the subject was described as being "worried" and "anxious"? If the subject was nonhuman, a rat, did it run about the confinement or chew its toenails? Just what behaviors led the observer to think it was "anxious"?

The scientist would also inquire about the operational definition of the "negative thing" mentioned by the observer. The definition of a "negative thing" may be a punishment to the observer, whereas the researcher reading the report may define it personally as merely a noxious but not necessarily punishing stimulus. Because individuals have their own personal definitions of words, some kind of universal standard of definition is necessary. Since scientific writing is precise, using exactly defined words and phrases, it is not unusual for it to be termed "dull" and "uninteresting." Reports are written in a pure, unambiguous way, so no question about how the experiment was conducted or the definitions entailed is left unanswered.

---

[1] An *operational definition* is one in which a term is defined by the operations used to measure them. For example, someone trying to operationally define a chocolate cake would describe the operations used to measure its properties: its color, texture, composition, and so on. Try to operationally define hunger. It could be operationally defined as so many hours of food deprivation.

OBJECTIVES OF THE REPORT

Let us take a look at what makes writing the report a "chore." Need it cause anxiety and ulcers for both student and researcher?

We agree that communication is the most oft-used source of learning; it is the key to the transfer of knowledge from one individual to another. It is also the intrinsic component of report writing. The report is the transmission of one's efforts, observations, conclusions, and inferences to another, with the assurance that the same or similar results will be derived by others if the directions are followed as outlined by the original experimenter. Can you imagine the frustration if a second researcher decided to duplicate a particular study and found that the results indicated a large degree of insignificance when the original study resounded with significance and purported to be a valuable discovery? This frequently occurs because the initial report was vague and unclear on important points that need to be replicated exactly in order to obtain the reported results. One principle for the student to remember is that every relevant aspect, each important observation or manipulation of variables, should be noted and included in the report.

In effective communication, organization is clearly an important asset for the writer as well as the reader. The writer can rely on an effective organization of material to help ensure that his or her thoughts and data are communicated correctly. It acts as a guide to enable the writer to progress in a logical manner. Organization also helps the writer to be concise and stick to a planned pattern and avoid the temptation to ramble or slip off on a tangent. Most of all, the writer's own thinking is enhanced by efficient organization, and he or she is assured a point will be thoroughly discussed. To the reader, tight organization of the material is an advantage. The burden of "plowing through" is lessened considerably, and it is easier to understand the point the author is making.

Deeply entwined with organization are the following: clarity, accuracy, and conciseness. These four points distinguish the good writeup from the mediocre. Readers assume the accuracy of the printed material they quote as "authority," and journals, being sources of authority, demand it. Of deeper consequence is the original purpose of scientific writing—the relaying of observations and data accrued in the study situation. When accuracy is sacrificed, the study (and the reason to do the study) is worth very little to the reader and in turn much less to the scientific world.

Accuracy, clarity, and conciseness are important attributes in any report. Accuracy is dulled by an inconsistent and unreadable text. The novice investigator usually finds it difficult to incorporate these attributes into a report. The novice is not alone, however; seldom is a report submitted to a journal for publication not returned to the author for editing.

How does one go about writing a well-organized, concise, accurate, clear report? There are few places a researcher can go to get help in making a report accurate, clear, and concise. These attributes generally depend on the literary abilities of the writer and improve with practice. There is, however, quite a bit of help available to aid the writer in organizing a report because psychologists have selected a particular format for acceptable reports. Actually, several different types of formats could have been used, but the American Psychological Association realized that it would ease the problems of both reading and writing reports if a standardized form was adopted. A large portion of this chapter is devoted to presenting the standardized aspects of report writing found in a well-written psychology report.

Insight
Changes in Organization of Journal Articles

The reader might find it interesting to peruse through psychology journals starting with *Psychological Review*, which was first published in 1884. By thumbing through every tenth-year volume of *Psychology Review* and the *Journal of Experimental Psychology* (begun in 1916), one can see changes in the organization of reports. Near the turn of the century few guidelines were adhered to when submitting an article for publication. The report was similar to the log in a diary or a typed talk. Few subsections were labeled, and information concerning subjects used, results obtained, and apparatus employed could be found anywhere throughout the report. For example, if one wanted to find out what type and how subjects were employed in the investigation, one would have to search throughout the report. Today there is a special *subjects* subsection, which is labeled and easily identified. Currently, line graphs are most commonly employed to present data results, whereas data in early journal articles were predominantly reported in tabular form. The trend to line graphs occurred because line graphs provide more information at a glance to the reader.

From the 1940s to 1960s, it was common for the abbreviations *E* and *S* to be used for experimenter and subject, respectively, with little mention, other than the subject section, as to exactly what type of subject (i.e., child, rat, pigeon) was employed. Now such abbreviations are discouraged in many journals, and the writer is encouraged to state exactly what the subjects were throughout the writeup [i.e., the children (not *Ss*) were seated in front of the test console and . . .].

The changes that have been made over the years have occurred for one main reason—to make journal articles easier to read and more informative. In 1974 the American Psychological Association published a revised *Publication Manual* containing all current requirements concerning organization and writing style criteria acceptable by psychological journals.

While most psychological journals subscribe to the writing requirements listed in the *Publication Manual*, a journal may deviate somewhat from the manual. Different headings may be required, references may be cited differently, or special forms of data presentation may be required. Generally, the specialized style requirements for a journal are listed in the first yearly issue (i.e., the January issue) on the inside of the front cover of that journal.

ORGANIZATION OF THE REPORT

One aid to both reader and researcher is a formal written outline of intentions and conclusions. In scientific writing, certain organizational procedures and conventions have become fairly standardized. The finest and most accessible source is the *Publication Manual* of the American Psychological Association, commonly known as the "Webster's" of psychological report writing. It is a useful addition to the library of every psychology student or researcher.

The standard experimental writeup includes the following primary sections and subsections: title and title page, abstract, introduction, method (including subjects, apparatus, and procedure), results, discussion, and conclusions. To help the reader visualize what a published journal article looks like, an article written by Frank Logan and Douglas Spanier published in the *Journal of Comparative and Physiological Psychology* has been reproduced here in its entirety (Figure 14-1). While somewhat shorter than the average published journal article, it illustrates the organization and style of writing outlined in the *Publication Manual.*

Although Figure 14-1 shows a complete published article, it does not exemplify what the typed write-up looks like that is submitted to the journal. Due to the fact that most undergraduate experimental psychology courses require such a write-up, Figure 14-2 shows the correct form for writing up a psychological investigation. Notice that while the journal publishes the title of the article and authors, the abstract, and the introduction of the article on the same page, the write-up includes a separate title page and a separate page for the abstract. The printing of journals is expensive; therefore, editors must conserve space as much as possible. The main divisions of a write-up are explained below.

Title and Title Page

The title should be short but clearly indicative of the exact topic covered. It is generally known that the report is "a study of . . ." or "an investigation of . . ." so that type of introductory phrase should be avoided. The IV and the DV employed in the investigation should be stated in the title.

The title page information, commonly centered on a separate page, should include the following: the title of the experiment, the researcher or those involved, and the affiliation of the authors. Although optional

Journal of Comparative and Physiological Psychology
1970, Vol. 72, No. 1, 102-104

RELATIVE EFFECT OF DELAY OF FOOD AND WATER REWARD[1]

FRANK A. LOGAN[2] AND DOUGLAS SPANIER[3]

University of New Mexico

Hungry or thirsty rats were given the appropriate reward after 1- or 30-sec. time of delay in a between-groups 2 × 2 design. In one experiment, delay was imposed in the goal box; in another experiment, delay was imposed in the straight alley just before the goal box. In both experiments, the thirsty rat ran somewhat slower at the short delay and somewhat faster at the long delay, producing significant interactions. Hence, delay of water reward was found to be relatively less detrimental than delay of food reward. This finding may be related to the degree to which incompatible responses are elicited by the different drive stimuli during the time of delay.

Among the most clearly established principles of learning is that the effectiveness of reward is reduced the longer the time it is delayed after a response. The detrimental effects of delay may be attenuated by minimizing incompatible responses during the time of delay (Harker, 1956) or by bridging the time of delay with chained behavior (Ferster, 1953). Nevertheless, organisms certainly prefer shorter to longer delays of reward (Logan, 1965).

In spite of the quite substantial body of literature concerning delayed reward, it appears that this research has been done exclusively using hungry organisms responding for food reward. While the principle is undoubtedly of wider generality than that, it is at least possible that the parameters of the gradient of delay of reinforcement depend importantly upon the nature of the motivating conditions. Perhaps there is no a priori basis for anticipating this possibility, but preliminary research in the related context of decision-making by rats strongly suggested that delay of water reward was not as detrimental as delay of food reward.

The present study was designed to test this possibility in a conventional instrumental-learning context. Specifically, hungry or thirsty rats were trained to run for food or water under conditions of immediate or delayed reward. Given reasonably comparable conditions of drive and incentive, the resulting performance should reveal whether delay of reward interacts with the nature of the motivating conditions.

METHOD

Subjects

The subjects were 76 male hooded rats bred in the colony maintained by the Department of Psychology at the University of New Mexico. They were about 100 days old at the beginning of the experiment and were housed in individual cages with water freely available for the hungry rats and food freely available for the thirsty rats. Twelve grams of laboratory chow daily were given the hungry rats, and 15-cc water were given the thirsty rats immediately after each experimental session.

Apparatus

The apparatus was an 8-ft. straight runway with a solid black floor, black plastic sides, and clear plastic top. Its inside dimensions were 4 × 4 in. A 3 × 6 in. aluminum start box provided access to the runway when a spring-loaded aluminum door was released. At the goal end of the alley was a brass block containing two cups 1 in. in diameter and 1 in. deep. A goal door 2 ft. from the reward cups was operated manually. Reward of three 45-mg. Noyes pellets or .1-cc distilled water was delivered into the appropriate cup. Timing started when the rat broke a photobeam located 1 in. into the runway and terminated when the rat broke a photobeam inside the reward cup (Experiment 1) or a photobeam located 6 in. before the closed goal door (Experiment 2). The entire apparatus

[1] This research was supported by a grant to the first author by the National Science Foundation. The authors are indebted to William Candelaria and William Wither for assistance in running the subjects.

[2] Requests for reprints should be sent to Frank A. Logan. Department of Psychology. University of New Mexico. Albuquerque, New Mexico 87106.

[3] Now at Stanislaus State College.

102

FIGURE 14–1 Reproduction of a complete journal article.

(Copyright 1970 by the American Psychological Association. Reprinted by permission.)

was housed in a sheet-metal enclosure with a blue plastic top providing ventilation and indirect lighting from below.

Procedure

The rats were run six trials/day, rotated in squads of four to provide an intertrial interval of about 3 min. In Experiment 1, the goal door was open when the rat was released from the start box and was closed after it broke the photobeam inside the reward cup. Reward was then delivered automatically after the appropriate delay timed by a Hunter timer. In Experiment 2, the goal door was closed when the rat was released from the start box, and a second door located 2 ft. further back from the goal was closed to detain the rat in that section for the appropriate delay interval. The rat was then released to run to the goal where reward was delivered immediately upon breaking the photobeam in the reward cup. Training continued for a total of 312 trials (52 days) in both experiments.

Design

Each experiment comprised a 2 × 2 factorial, animals being either hungry or thirsty and receiving the appropriate reward after either 1- or 30-sec. delay. The only difference was that this delay was imposed in the goal region with access to the empty reward cups in Experiment 1 and in a comparable 2-ft. section of the runway away from the reward cups in Experiment 2. Ten rats were randomly assigned to each of the four groups in Experiment 1 and 9 rats to each group in Experiment 2.

RESULTS

Terminal running speeds averaged over the last 10 days of the experiments are shown in the two panels of Figure 1. Both experiments showed a significant overall effect of delay (Experiment 1: $F = 25.3$, $df = 1/36$, $p < .01$; Experiment 2: $F = 542.5$, $df = 1/32$, $p < .01$). More importantly, however, both experiments also showed a significant interaction between delay and the nature of the motivating conditions (Experiment 1: $F = 7.2$, $df = 1/36$, $p < .02$; Experiment 2: $F = 9.6$, $df = 1/32$, $p < .01$). This interaction can not be attributed to unequal units of measurement or to gross differences in motivation, since the conditions employed were such that the thirsty rats ran somewhat slower under the 1-sec. delay and somewhat faster under the 30-sec. delay.

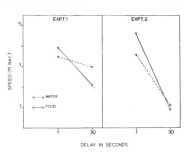

Fig. 1. Asymptotic running speeds produced by 1- or 30-sec. delay of food or water reward.

DISCUSSION

The principle of the gradient of delay of reinforcement applies when a thirsty animal is running for water much as it does when a hungry animal is running for food. But the parameters of those gradients are not the same. Specifically, delay of water reward is relatively less detrimental to performance than delay of food reward. This obtains whether the delay is imposed in the goal box or in the maze before the goal box.

A possible basis for this difference might be found in the nature of the fractional anticipatory goal responses appropriate to the two rewards. It is at least conceivable that food-anticipatory responses such as salivating are more frustrating than water-anticipatory responses such as lip-licking. However, the fact that organisms can survive longer without food than without water would provide little evolutionary justification for such a speculation.

A more probable account relates to the delay-engendered competing responses. While no objective records are available, it is reasonable that thirsty animals would maintain greater orientation toward the goal during a delay than hungry animals. This clearly appeared to be the case in the first experiment where the thirsty rats tended to lick longer at the dry water cup than the hungry rats licked at the empty food cup, and a similar though less conspicuous effect could have occurred in the

FIGURE 14–1   (Continued)

maze. This would suggest that there are different unlearned responses to the drive stimuli provided by hunger and thirst, an interpretation distantly related to the difference in these two drives with respect to alternation behavior (Petrinovich & Bolles, 1954). Insofar as competing responses occur during a delay and become anticipatory to interfere with the instrumental response, an inherent difference in the tendency to make such responses as between hunger and thirst would account for the differential effects of delay under these two sources of motivation.

REFERENCES

FERSTER, C. B. Sustained behavior under delayed reinforcement. *Journal of Experimental Psychology*, 1953, **45**, 218–224.

HARKER, G. S. Delay of reward and performance of an instrumental response. *Journal of Experimental Psychology*, 1956, **51**, 303–310.

LOGAN, F. A. Decision-making by rats: Delay versus amount of reward. *Journal of Comparative and Physiological Psychology*, 1965, **59**, 1–12.

PETRINOVICH, L., & BOLLES, R. Deprivation states and behavioral attributes. *Journal of Comparative and Physiological Psychology*. 1954, **47**, 450–453.

(Received August 30, 1969)

FIGURE 14–1   (Continued)

for some journals, the title page is considered a handy source for identification and for that reason is required by many editors.

Abstract

Most psychological journals require the submission of an abstract with the manuscript. Often located at the beginning of the work, the abstract sometimes takes the place of the summary traditionally put at the end of the article. The abstract should be no more than 12 to 15 lines in length (approximately 100 to 120 words), and it should be written in complete sentences. A main heading is used to identify the abstract section in the typed manuscript, although it does not show up in the actual publication. The abstract is centered on a page by itself.

An abstract generally has four parts:

1. The objective of the investigation.
2. A brief description of the experimental procedures.
3. A statement of the results.
4. The conclusions or implications of the findings.

Only pertinent data are included, and they should be stated in condensed form. Be sure to mention the number and kind of subjects used as well as the design and the significance level of the results. The results should be mentioned or at least the trend of the results should be included. The suggested length may follow this pattern: objective, one or two sentences; procedure, five or six sentences; results, one or two sentences; and conclusion, one sentence. The results and conclusion are sometimes combined into one sentence.

Relative Effect of Delay of Food
and Water Reward

Frank A. Logan
and Douglas Spanier

University of New Mexico

Running Head: Delay of Food

Relative Effect of Delay of Food and
Water Reward

Abstract

Hungry or thirsty rats were given the appropriate reward after 1-
or 30- sec. time of delay in a between-groups 2 x 2 design. In one experiment, delay was imposed in the goal box; in another experiment, delay was
imposed in the straight alley just before the goal box. In both experiments, the thirsty rat ran somewhat slower at the short delay and somewhat faster at the long delay, producing significant interactions. Hence,
delay of water reward was found to be relatively less detrimental than
delay of food reward. This finding may be related to the degree to which
incompatible responses are elicited by the different drive stimuli during
the time of delay.

Among the most clearly established principles of learning is that the
effectiveness of reward is reduced the longer the time it is delayed after
a response. The detrimental effects of delay may be attenuated by minimizing
incompatible responses during the time of delay (Harker, 1956) or by bridging
the time of delay with chained behavior (Ferster, 1953). Nevertheless,
organisms certainly prefer shorter to longer delays of reward (Logan, 1956).

In spite of the quite substantial body of literature concerning delayed
reward, it appears that this research has been done exclusively using hungry
organisms responding for food reward. While the principle is undoubtedly
of wider generality than that, it is at least possible that the parameters
of the gradient of delay of reinforcement depend importantly upon the nature
of the motivating conditions. Perhaps there is no a priori basis for anticipating this possibility, but preliminary research in the related context of decision making by rats strongly suggested that delay of water reward
was not as detrimental as delay of food reward.

The present study was designed to test this possibility in a conventional
instrumental-learning context. Specifically, hungry or thirsty rats were
trained to run for food or water under conditions of immediate or delayed
reward. Given reasonably comparable conditions of drive and incentive, the
resulting performance should reveal whether delay of reward interacts with
the nature of the motivating conditions.

FIGURE 14–2   Reproduction of a complete write-up.

366

Method

Subjects

The subjects were 76 male hooded rats bred in the colony maintained by the Department of Psychology at the University of New Mexico. They were about 100 days old at the beginning of the experiment and were housed in individual cages with water freely available for the hungry rats and food freely available for the thirsty rats. Twelve grams of laboratory chow daily were given the hungry rats, and 15-cc water were given the thirsty rats immediately after each experimental session.

Apparatus

The apparatus was an 8-ft. straight runway with a solid black floor, black plastic sides, and clear plastic top. Its inside dimensions were 4 x 4 in. A 3 x 6 in. aluminum start box provided access to the runway when a spring-loaded aluminum door was released. At the goal end of the alley was a brass block containing two cups 1 in. in diameter and 1 in. deep. A goal door 2 ft. from the reward cups was operated manually. Reward of three 45-mg. Noyes pellets of .1 cc distilled water was delivered into the appropriate cup. Timing started when the rat broke a photobeam located 1 in. into the runway and terminated when the rat broke a photobeam inside the reward cup (Experiment 1) or a photobeam located 6 in. before the closed goal door (Experiment 2). The entire apparatus was housed in a sheet-metal enclosure with a blue plastic top providing ventilation and indirect lighting from below.

Procedure

The rats were run six trials/day, rotated in squads of four to provide

---

an intertrial interval of about 3 min. In Experiment 1, the goal door was open when the rat was released from the start box and was closed after it broke the photobeam inside the reward cup. Reward was then delivered automatically after the appropriate delay timed by a Hunter timer. In Experiment 2, the goal door was closed when the rat was released from the start box, and a second door located 2 ft. further back from the goal was closed to detain the rat in that section for the appropriate delay interval. The rat was then released to run to the goal where reward was delivered immediately upon breaking the photobeam in the reward cup. Training continued for a total of 312 trials (52 days) in both experiments.

Design

Each experiment comprised a 2 X 2 factorial, animals being either hungry or thirsty and receiving the appropriate reward after either 1-or 30-sec. delay. The only difference was that this delay was imposed in the goal region with access to the empty reward cups in Experiment 1 and in a comparable 2-ft. section of the runway away from the reward cups in Experiment 2. Ten rats were randomly assigned to each of the four groups in Experiment 1 and 9 rats to each group in Experiment 2.

Results

Terminal running speeds averaged over the last 10 days of the experiments are shown in the two panels of Figure 1. Both experiments showed a significant overall effect of delay (Experiment 1: $F = 25.3$, $df = 1/36$, $p < .01$; Experiment 2: $F = 542.5$, $df = 1/32$, $p < .01$). This interaction can not be attributed to unequal units of measurement or to gross differences in motivation, since the conditions employed were such that the thirsty rats

---

```
------------------------------
    Insert Fig. 1 about here
------------------------------
```

ran somewhat slower under the 1-sec. delay and somewhat faster under the 30-sec. delay.

Discussion

The principle of the gradient of delay of reinforcement applies when a thirsty animal is running for water much as it does when a hungry animal is running for food. But the parameters of those gradients are not the same. Specifically, delay of water reward is relatively less detrimental to performance than delay of food reward. This obtains whether the delay is imposed in the goal box or in the maze before the goal box.

A possible basis for this difference might be found in the nature of the fractional anticipatory goal responses appropriate to the two rewards. It is at least conceivable that food-anticipatory responses such as salivating are more frustrating than water-anticipatory responses such as lip-licking. However, the fact that organisms can survive longer without food than without water would provide little evolutionary justification for such a speculation.

A more probable account relates to the delay-engendered competing responses. While no objective records are available, it is reasonable that thirsty animals would maintain greater orientation toward the goal during a delay than hungry animals. This clearly appeared to be the case in the first experiment where the thirsty rats tended to lick longer at the dry water cup than the hungry rats licked at the empty food cup, and a similar though less conspicuous effect could have occurred in the maze. This would suggest that

---

FIGURE 14–2 (Continued)

there are different unlearned responses to the drive stimuli provided by hunger and thirst, an interpretation distantly related to the difference in these two drives with respect to alternation behavior (Petrinovich & Bolles, 1954). Insofar as competing responses occur during a delay and become anticipatory to interfere with the instrumental response, an inherent difference in the tendency to make such responses as between hunger and thirst would account for the differential effects of delay under these two sources of motivation.

References

Ferster, C. B. Sustained behavior under delayed reinforcement. Journal of Experimental Psychology, 1953, 45, 218-224.

Harker, G. S. Delay of reward and performance of an instrumental response. Journal of Experimental Psychology, 1956, 51, 303-310.

Logan, F. A. Decision-making by rats: Delay versus amount of reward. Journal of Comparative and Physiological Psychology, 1965, 59, 1-12.

Petrinovich, L., & Bolles, R. Deprivation states and behavioral attributes. Journal of Comparative and Physiological Psychology. 1954, 47, 450-453.

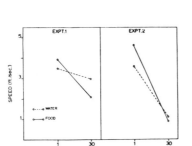

Fig. 1. Asymptotic running speeds produced by 1- or 30-sec. delay of food or water reward.

FIGURE 14–2 (Continued)

Introduction

The purpose of the introduction is to state the question asked of the experiment and the rationale behind the study. In other words, the theoretical propositions from which your hypothesis are drawn are stated in the introduction. The logic used, summarized relevant arguments, and supporting data are also included.

Two points need to be emphasized: (1) a statement of and background to the problem, and (2) a statement of the objective of the study. The statement of the objective is the formally stated hypothesis and should be written in terms of the IV and the DV. If needed, additional sentences are added to more exactly define the IV and DV.

A brief review of the literature is often advantageous, for it gives the reader a foundation for a more complete understanding of the issue. It also gives the writer a foundation on which to start the report. The heading "Introduction" is neither needed nor recommended for this section. The introduction section starts on a separate page following the abstract and is preceded by the title of the article.

Method

The method section is the body of the report. In this section the reader should be given the precise manner in which the experiment was conducted. Enough detail should be included to allow the replication of the experiment by the reader; remember, however, that too much detail obscures the facts.[2] Remember, too, that the functional value of each fact determines whether it should be mentioned in the write-up. Quality exceeds quantity in the final evaluation of any report. The test for any material should be the answer to these questions: "Was it used during the experiment?" and "Is this necessary for the reader to replicate the experiment?" Include in this section the following:

1. Subjects involved.
2. Sampling procedures used.
3. Control devices used.
4. Design of the study.
5. Techniques of measurement and observation.
6. Logic of the data.

To help clarify what is involved, the method section is frequently divided into three subsections, and in some cases four. The three subsections are subjects, apparatus, and procedure. In instances where the design

---

[2] The problem most report writers have is usually the opposite: they fail to be thorough in their procedural explanation.

of the experiment is rather complicated, a subsection called design is included.

Subjects.   The first step of any recipe is to define and describe what is going to be used in the work. First define and describe the population and how it was sampled in detail. It is important to notice if any subjects were unused or taken out of "active service" (students who did not show up for appointments, rats that died), since a change in the population may lead to unrepresentative and inconsistent results due to the loss of randomness.

Apparatus.   As the heading tells us, all relevant aspects of the devices and machinery, quizzes or questionnaires used should be included in the report. Remember, the reader may wish to repeat the study and to do so accurately she or he requires conditions similar to those originally experienced by the subjects of the experiment. When complicated machinery is used, a diagram is useful, though in some journals it is not required. Where standard types of apparatus are used, often you may see only the name of the apparatus. Note that any material or device used with which the subject came in contact is considered apparatus.

Procedure.   Detail, precision, and readability are the keys in discussing the collection of data. This is the "how" subsection: how the IV was manipulated, how the DV was recorded, and so on. Three basic criteria should be considered: design, steps for conducting the experiment, and how the measurement of the subjects' behavior was accomplished. Summarize instructions if you, the experimenter, gave them to the subjects; or, if the subjects were not human, describe the schedules of reinforcement used. Refer to the planning form described in Chapter One.

Design.   Type of design, the method of experimental versus control group comparison, is the essential part of this subsection. Specification of subjects or groups and the identification labels assist the reader in understanding further references to them later in the write-up (e.g., group X = experimental group; group Y = control group). Here, also, the variables mentioned in the hypothesis need to be operationally defined. Mention should be made of the IVs and the DVs as well as of the experimental control devices and techniques used.[3] This subsection, though helpful in some instances, can be absorbed by the preceding subsection and need not be separate.

Does a method section have to be divided into subsections? Not all the time. Remember, the purpose of subsections is to help clarify potentially complex material. Do not use subsections unnecessarily. For example, if the only materials used in the investigation were paper and pencils, a separate apparatus subsection would be unnecessary.

---

[3] Such detail as the experimental control, definition of variables, and so on can be placed in the procedure subsection instead.

Results

All data aiding the formation and justification of your conclusions are found in the results section. A summary statement of the results obtained (e.g., "Errorless learning was obtained with the experimental group") generally comes near the beginning of the results section. This is followed by an elaboration of the results. Data may be expressed not only verbally, but also in graphs, figures, and tables. Be sure to include means, deviations, percentages, and the like in the body of the results section. Expound in detail on the data you collected, pointing out similarities and differences where they exist. One should be careful not to include conclusions or discussion issues in this section. Stick to stating what data were gathered. Raw data are merely summarized and explained in detail. Clear and concise observation is needed.

Notice also the advantage of using graphs and tables. These condense much valid and important material into a small space and give the reader an opportunity to see a whole procedure or its results at a glance. Let us examine in more detail the acceptable form for figures and graphs.

Figures and Tables. Within the results section, you may want to include a graph of the data gathered. The *raw* data are often not included, however; neither are the calculations.[4] Figures, tables, or both serve as a *summary* of the data: a condensation of the major finding of the study in numerical and tabular form. These data are used as support for the conclusions and must be presented as systematically and accurately as possible. Main points of the data pertinent to the conclusion should be readily apparent in the table. Taken from another study, the table in Figure 14-3 is an example of a well-organized tabular presentation of data.

A figure is commonly a graph, a chart, or a photograph. Certain kinds of data are best shown by a figure. Again, the criteria for a figure are much like that for a table: be accurate, readable, and systematic. In experimental research, figures are most often similar to the illustrations in Figure 14-4. A general rule of thumb when drawing a table or a graph is to make it three units high for every four units wide.

Labeling and captioning a figure is important both for identification and for understanding. The captions for tables go *above* the tables, while the captions for figures go *below* the figures. What the figure shows should also be reviewed in the body of the results section. Thus, in referring to the bottom graph in Figure 14-4, the results of the data could be written as follows:

> As Figure 14-4 (*bottom*) reveals, there were differences in extinction perform-
> ance among the five groups. . . .

[4] For student reports, the professor may often ask that an appendix be added in which raw data are placed and can be easily evaluated.

TABLE 2

BRAIN NOREPINEPHRINE LEVELS
IN EXPERIMENT 2

Triplet	Brain norepinephrine level (ng/g)		
	Avoidance-escape	Yoked	Nonshock[a]
1	475	372	395
2	496	359	410
3	360	329	345
4	393	357	358
5	466	451	477
6	309	226	300
7	400	333	372

$p < .01$ $p < .02$

$p < .05$

[a] Lower NE values in this experiment than in Experiment 1 were due to use of a catecholamine-specific method (see text).

FIGURE 14–3   Example of a well-organized table.
(From Weiss, Stone, and Harrell (1970), p. 158. Copyright 1970 by the American Psychological Association. Reprinted by permission.)

When reviewing the journals, the reader may note that there is a trend toward using line graphs instead of tables. Over the years psychologists have become aware of the fact that line graphs show data more quickly at a glance than tables, which require the reader to study them more carefully. Relationships between groups stand out better with line graphs. This trend illustrates an important point about journal publications: their objective is to make articles clearer and easier to read. If one type of presentation does this better than another, it is adopted into report formats.

The results section of an unpublished report does not actually include the figures or tables. The author indicates in the manuscript where the figure or graph should be inserted in the published article, but actually places the figures on separate pages at the end of the report.

Discussion

Now that the facts are stated and the statistics gathered and presented, interpretation of those facts and data becomes necessary. Of what value are bare facts without some discussion or explanation of them and of their relation to other studies? It is here, in the discussion section, that the explanation of the presented data is expected. In no other section of the report should any attempt be made at interpretation or discussion of data.

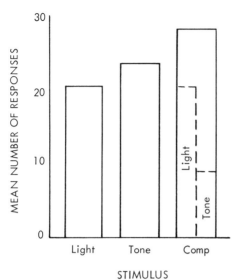

Fig. 2. Mean number of responses emitted during presentations of the single and compound S^Ds by Subjects 13 to 18 for the two test days combined. Each S^D was correlated with its own lever and both levers were always extended. That portion of compound responses emitted on the light- and tone-correlated levers is indicated by the dotted lines within the bar graph denoting compound responding.

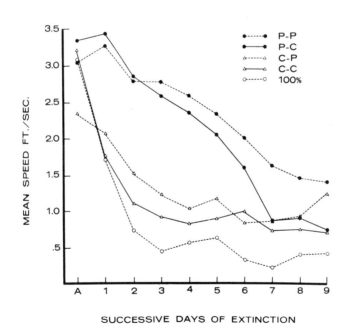

Fig. 4. Mean running speed for the various groups as a function of successive days of extinction testing.

FIGURE 14–4   Two examples of typical graphs in research articles.

(*Top*: Miller (1961), Figure 2. Reprinted with permission from the author and the *Journal of the Experimental Analysis of Behavior*. *Bottom*: Rudy, Homzie, Cox, Graeber, and Carter (1970), Figure 4. Copyright 1970 by the American Psychological Association. Reprinted by permission.)

Other literature relating to the study may be brought into the write-up at this point. The present results may be related to previously stated ones; concurrent research or related studies may provide new insights into your study. Other studies may confirm your hypothesis; or if other findings run counter to yours, alternate explanations can be pointed out or a slightly altered hypothesis may be advanced for possible future investigation. If some unexpected incongruence appears in your results, an unforeseen bump in a graph or line, do not hesitate to question, examine, and maybe offer a hypothesis on that fluctuation.

Every experiment has limitations, so it is not in any way degrading to the work done to point these out. Usually, such limitations are valid and provide the reader with valuable information. It is wise for the researcher to determine the extent to which conclusions and hypotheses may be generalized. Can you safely generalize your study using rats as subjects to a human population or human behavior? Note and state to what extent the uncontrolled variables hinder generalization of that particular study. This is the place to discuss every crucial uncontrolled variable. It is in this section also where you may state possible modification of design and/or procedure. Also, review additional problems uncovered by the study that were obscure before and that now need to be changed in future study.

Consider for a moment the possibility of obtaining a negative relationship and inferences. Some experimenters mistakenly find this to be humiliating and embarrassing. As was mentioned previously, this is *not* a "bad" possibility; in fact, it is not uncommon to find negatively corresponding results. They can even be valuable for possible future studies. In such cases, a long dissertation on the possible reasons why such results were obtained is *not* recommended. Instead, a brief discussion with some speculation as to why the results were obtained and possible changes for future investigations is appropriate.

Conclusions and/or Summary

Although the abstract has usurped the place of the summary, often the abstract is limited in scope. Some journals still require the author to end the report with a brief formal statement of the problem, the results, and the conclusions.

Final compilation of the write-up is next. This general format or order may prove to be helpful:

1. Title page
2. Abstract (also title, author, affiliation of the author)
3. Text
4. References (start on a new page)
5. Footnotes (start on a new page)
6. Tables (each on a separate page)
7. Figures (each on a separate page)

Study examples in journals and texts to determine similarities and differences in good and poor examples of figures and tables. You will find the best are those that are easy to discern and read.

DRY FACTS AND SOME REQUIREMENTS OF STYLE

Style is the culmination of many techniques, but the best and easiest is adherence to elementary rules of good grammar and sentence structure. The following portion of the chapter is subdivided for quick reference to some of the more common helpful hints and rules for effective report writing.

Accuracy

Of major importance is the completeness and accuracy of references and citations. Careful checking of the original publication should be routine.

Length

Because of the number of articles being submitted to journals daily, conciseness is mandatory. Length varies with each study and the amount of comment needed. In general, however, rewrite and condense that which is necessary. The upper limit over which special permission from the journal editorial staff is needed for publication is approximately 16,000 words. Many times the journal for which you are writing will specify the precise length of the report.

Typing

Typing the manuscript is considered a common and expected procedure. Double spacing with margins of one inch or more on top, sides, and bottom of the page is the rule. Avoid block-style typing by using paragraphs and headings accurately. The only copy to be typed in all capital letters is the title, centered, at the top of the first page of the manuscript, with a deep margin above it.

Tense and Person

Since the research has already been done, the description of procedure as well as statements concerning the review of literature should be stated in the past tense. Of course, this generalization is not rule of law; however, it should be used in context with clarity and understanding as the criteria. The present tense may be used to discuss the results (e.g., "Rats do work harder for more food"), whereas a description of the results may be in the past tense (e.g., "Twelve rats ran the maze with fewer than six errors").

In scientific writing, the third person is more effective than "I", "me," or "we" to establish an objective tone. Generally, use of the third person is preferred, although the first person may be used by the author to state what was done (e.g., "To control that secondary variable, I employed a matched group design").

Sample
  Poor: I found that whenever my difference obtained was significant, the mean score of the total student population fell between the mean scores of the experimental groups.
  Better: Whenever a significant difference appeared, the mean score of the total student population fell between the mean scores of the experimental groups.

Headings

The headings should indicate clearly the organization of the paper. In the APA requirements, three types of headings are usually employed. Main headings, used for identifying the method, results, discussion, and summary sections, are centered and typed with first letter of each word capitalized. Do not use all capitals or any end punctuation. Main headings are underlined. Side headings are typed flush to the left margin and are italicized (underlined). To continue the text, double space, then indent for continuation. Paragraph headings are indented, and only the initial letter of the first word is capitalized. They should be italicized and followed by a period. Continue the text directly with no special spacing. Use side and paragraph headings when making subsections. Side headings are generally used for identifying subsections such as subjects, apparatus, procedure, and design, although paragraph headings can be used for these if no subdivisions are required within them. For further helpful hints, refer to the APA *Publication Manual* and other journal articles.

Sample

Main Heading

Side Heading
    Paragraph heading

Footnotes

Footnotes may sometimes prove more of a hindrance than a help to clear, concise writing. They should be used primarily for citations to supporting evidence. Footnotes may also acknowledge help in the preparation of the manuscript or give the author's address. In general, try to avoid putting tangential material or parenthetical discussions in footnotes.

Sample
[1] The literature on the nature and bodily mechanism of emotion is extensive. The following works contain discussions and references: Ruckmick [1936], Lund [1939], Young [1943], Woodworth and Schlosberg [1954].

Abbreviations and Symbols

Abbreviations are used sparingly in psychological journals. Longer technical terms or names of specific techniques may be initially spelled out, then followed by the abbreviation in parentheses. The abbreviations are then used alone throughout the report. The use of abbreviations such as S (subject), E (experimenter), and I (investigator) is discouraged. In APA journals and most psychology writings, researchers have established a general vocabulary that includes certain abbreviations (e.g., t, N, df), which are acceptable in reports.

References

References to other studies or authors commonly appear both in the text and in a list at the end of the manuscript. In the text, references should be cited by enclosing in brackets the author's surname and the year of the publication. For example, if we were referring to a certain study, we would say "Jones [1953] said. . . ." If a reference has more than two authors, include the surnames of all authors the first time, and thereafter use only the surname of the senior author and the abbreviation et al.

Sample
A recent study [Salvador, Fuentes, Smith, and Black, 1968] shows. . . . The study previously cited [Salvador et al., 1968] shows. . . .

If the author has completed many works relevant to the data you wish to support, place the dates in sequence by year of publication.

Sample
Recent studies [Jones, 1973, 1974, 1976] have shown. . . .

PEER COMMUNICATION

As you recall from Chapter One, the psychologist requires five basic skills. The first, analytical prowess, describes the ability of the psychologist to analyze a situation accurately. The second skill is knowledge of psychological principles. The third and fourth skills deal with the ability to communicate. Last is the skill of evaluation and of interpretation.

Let us go back to the second skill, knowledge of principles, and look at it more closely. As an authority in his or her field, the psychologist's familiarity with the major works as well as with the newest discoveries should be both deep and broad. Like a medical doctor, the psychologist is looked upon as one having solutions to many problems because of his or her wide range of knowledge. If the psychologist does not know the answer from his or her background, the psychologist does know where to go to find the answer in a book, journal, or from colleagues having close connections with that particular problem. To examine that last statement further, let us look at an example.

Remember the last time you felt queasy inside, experienced dizzy spells, and your hands were cold, wet, and shaky? After making the decision to go to the doctor, you made your way to his office. When the nurse took you to the back room and ordered you to undress, you complied slowly. Remember waiting for the doctor, twiddling your thumbs (only too aware of your appearance)? The doctor arrives and inquires in a very businesslike way about your health. After finishing the examination, the doctor tells you to dress, and leaves the room. Did you ever wonder what the doctor was doing while you dressed? Your guess is probably right. He most likely was off to his library to look up possible answers to your particular symptoms. By the time you are through dressing, he has a diagnosis (a solution to the problem) and three prescriptions with the appropriate medicine, dosage, and price. The doctor demonstrated knowledge of his field both with the accuracy of his analysis and with his knowledge of where and how to look up the answer quickly. A thorough and up-to-date knowledge of the field is required of an authority, in this example, a doctor, as it is of a psychologist.

Psychology is not a "stand-still" science. New principles are being discovered and old principles are being built upon everyday. With information arriving at such a rapid pace, effective communication is a problem. How can this information be transmitted to those who need it? Consider for a moment the problem faced by researchers in the field. New areas being opened have had research started but are by no means considered to have solutions yet. If this initial information is given to another authority working on the same or similar information, the addition of this new input could mean an earlier solution. Each small advance of a particular subject may also be a clue to later studies. One small step found by a colleague somewhere else in the world may prove to be the missing key to the solution to another's problem. The distribution of this material must be continuous and rapid, and a book requires years in writing, compilation, printing, and distributing. By the time it is finished, the information it contains may be obsolete. This problem is currently being solved by the use of journals and conventions.

The Journal

As a source of quick reference and up-to-date discoveries, the journal is an invaluable aid to both the medical doctor and the psychologist. The journal solves many dilemmas.

Journals provide a record of recent significant advances in the field so that at any time the psychologist can easily refer back to that study to enhance her or his newest research. Another hurdle partly overcome by the journal is sheer reading load. To keep abreast of current research, the psychologist must read a great amount of current material. In view of the fact that thousands of articles are published in over a hundred journals in psychology alone, reading everything is physically impossible. The authority in whatever field usually reads only that material pertaining to his or her area of expertise or specific problem. Knowing where to look as well as how to look up a particular study is a great advantage. We will look at how to approach the guides to journals later in the chapter.

Journals assist the professional since they must be selective of the information sent to them. Often journals are known for their particular content coverage. This helps the professional narrow reading to those topics that deal most closely with a specific field. For instance, a clinical psychologist would most likely refer often to journals dealing mainly with human subjects, whereas the experimental psychologist would want to read mainly journals carrying experimental articles with more emphasis on nonhuman subjects. Table 14-1 lists the major psychology journals along with the types of investigations (e.g., EPF, large or small-N experiments, and so on) they specialize in reporting, the types of subjects used in the investigations they report, the content areas they emphasize, and whether or not they publish review and/or theoretical articles.

Psychologists are not the only professionals plagued with the problem of how to keep up with the field. Most areas of research have an information pool much like psychology, where some journals are devoted just to reviews of the latest findings and publications. The professional can quickly scan what is available and can more easily choose those articles and journals most applicable to a particular field of study.

Another advantage of the journal is the assistance it gives the professional in problem areas lying *outside* a field of expertise. Remember the example in Chapter One in which the psychiatrist's behavioral principles did not work with the girl using obscene language. It was obvious that the psychiatrist was not an expert on behavior modification. The area was out of his field of expertise. Perhaps, if he had been more widely read

TABLE 14–1 *Major Psychology Journals and the Types of Investigations, Subjects, and Content Areas They Emphasize*

Journal	Ex post facto studies	Experiments—large N	Experiments—small N	Animal subjects	Human subjects	Theory and systems	Research technology and statistics	Perception and sensation	Motivation and emotion	Learning and thinking	Physiological psychology	Pharmacology	Genetics	Developmental and child psychology	Educational psychology	Social psychology	Personality	Mental retardation	Clinical psychology	Review articles	Theoretical articles
American Behavioral Scientist	×	×	×		×	×		×	×	×				×	×	×	×		×	×	×
American Journal of Mental Deficiency	×	×	×		×			×	×	×	×	×	×	×	×	×	×	×	×	×	×
American Journal of Psychiatry	×				×						×	×	×	×	×	×	×	×	×		×
American Journal of Psychology	×	×		×	×			×	×	×	×	×	×	×							
American Psychologist	×		×	×	×	×	×	×	×	×	×	×	×	×	×	×	×	×	×	×	×
American Scientist	×	×		×	×		×	×	×	×	×	×		×	×	×	×	×	×	×	
American Statistical Association Journal	×	×		×	×		×													×	×
American Statistician	×	×			×	×										×					
Animal Behavior	×	×		×		×		×	×	×	×	×		×							
Annual Review of Psychology	×	×	×	×	×	×	×	×	×	×	×	×	×	×	×	×	×	×	×	×	
Archives of General Psychiatry	×		×	×	×		×		×		×	×	×	×		×	×	×	×	×	×
Behavior		×		×				×	×	×	×	×	×								×
Behavior Research and Therapy		×	×	×	×			×	×	×	×				×			×	×		
Behavioral Science	×	×		×	×	×			×	×						×	×	×			×
Biometrics	×	×					×														
British Journal of Educational Psychology	×	×	×		×		×		×	×					×	×	×			×	×
British Journal of Medical Psychology	×	×	×		×			×	×	×	×			×	×	×	×	×		×	×
British Journal of Psychology	×	×		×	×		×	×		×	×			×					×	×	×
Canadian Journal of Psychology	×	×	×	×	×	×		×	×	×	×	×		×	×	×	×				×

TABLE 14–1 (Continued)

Journal	Ex post facto studies	Experiments—large N	Experiments—small N	Animal subjects	Human subjects	Theory and systems	Research technology and statistics	Perception and sensation	Motivation and emotion	Learning and thinking	Physiological psychology	Pharmacology	Genetics	Developmental and child psychology	Educational psychology	Social psychology	Personality	Mental retardation	Clinical psychology	Review articles	Theoretical articles
Canadian Psychologist	×		×			×	×	×	×	×	×	×		×	×	×	×	×	×	×	×
Child Development	×	×	×			×								×							
Cognitive Psychology		×				×	×		×	×				×	×					×	×
Counseling Psychologist		×				×													×	×	×
Developmental Psychology	×	×		×	×	×			×	×	×			×	×	×	×	×	×	×	
Dissertation Abstracts	×	×	×	×	×	×	×	×	×	×	×	×	×	×	×	×	×	×	×	×	×
Educational and Psychological Measurement	×	×					×							×	×			×			
Genetic Psychology Monographs		×				×								×	×			×	×	×	×
Journal of Abnormal Psychology		×			×	×			×	×				×		×	×	×	×	×	×
Journal of Applied Behavioral Analysis	×	×	×		×	×	×	×	×	×	×	×		×	×	×		×	×	×	
Journal of Applied Psychology	×	×			×		×	×		×				×	×	×	×	×	×	×	
Journal of Biological Psychology	×	×		×		×			×	×	×	×	×								
Journal of Child Psychology and Psychiatry	×	×	×	×	×								×	×	×	×	×	×	×	×	×
Journal of Clinical Psychology	×	×			×													×		×	
Journal of Comparative and Physiological Psychology	×	×		×	×			×	×	×	×	×	×								
Journal of Consulting and Clinical Psychology	×	×			×									×	×			×	×	×	
Journal of Educational Measurement	×	×	×		×		×								×						
Journal of Educational Psychology	×	×			×	×		×	×	×				×	×		×		×		

TABLE 14–1   (Continued)

Journal	Ex post facto studies	Experiments—large N	Experiments—small N	Animal subjects	Human subjects	Theory and systems	Research technology and statistics	Perception and sensation	Motivation and emotion	Learning and thinking	Physiological psychology	Pharmacology	Genetics	Developmental and child psychology	Educational psychology	Social psychology	Personality	Mental retardation	Clinical psychology	Review articles	Theoretical articles
Journal of Experimental Child Psychology	×	×			×			×		×				×		×		×			
Journal of Experimental Psychology	×	×		×	×			×	×	×				×						×	×
Journal of Experimental Research in Personality	×	×		×	×												×				
Journal of Experimental Social Psychology	×	×			×									×		×					
Journal of General Psychology	×	×		×	×	×	×		×	×											
Journal of Genetic Psychology	×	×			×						×	×						×	×	×	×
Journal of Mathematical Psychology							×													×	×
Journal of Mental Deficiency Research	×	×		×	×					×	×	×	×					×			
Journal of Personality	×	×	×		×	×								×		×	×		×		×
Journal of Personality and Social Psychology	×	×		×	×				×					×		×	×				
Journal of Social Psychology	×	×			×											×	×				
Journal of the Experimental Analysis of Behavior	×		×	×	×	×	×	×	×	×	×	×	×	×		×	×			×	×
Journal of Verbal Learning and Verbal Behavior		×			×					×					×						
Perception and Psychophysics		×		×	×		×	×	×											×	×
Perceptual and Motor Skills	×	×		×	×	×	×	×			×	×								×	×
Physiology and Behavior		×		×	×			×	×	×	×	×	×							×	×
Psychological Abstracts	×	×		×	×	×	×	×	×	×	×	×	×	×	×	×	×	×	×		×

TABLE 14–1 *(Continued)*

Journal	Ex post facto studies	Experiments—large N	Experiments—small N	Animal subjects	Human subjects	Theory and systems	Research technology and statistics	Perception and sensation	Motivation and emotion	Learning and thinking	Physiological psychology	Pharmacology	Genetics	Developmental and child psychology	Educational psychology	Social psychology	Personality	Mental retardation	Clinical psychology	Review articles	Theoretical articles
Psychological Bulletin	×	×		×	×	×	×	×	×	×	×	×	×	×	×	×	×	×	×		×
Psychological Record	×	×	×	×	×	×	×	×	×	×	×	×	×	×	×	×	×	×	×	×	×
Psychological Reports	×	×	×	×	×	×	×	×	×	×	×	×	×	×	×	×	×	×	×	×	×
Psychological Review	×	×		×	×	×		×	×	×	×	×	×	×	×	×	×	×	×		
Psychology Today	×	×	×	×	×	×		×	×	×	×	×	×	×	×	×	×	×	×		×
Psychometrika		×		×	×	×	×														
Psychonomic Science	×	×	×	×	×	×	×	×	×	×	×	×	×	×	×	×	×	×	×	×	×
Psychopharmacologica	×	×		×	×			×	×	×	×	×									
Psychophysiology		×		×	×		×			×	×	×		×							
Quarterly Journal of Experimental Psychology		×		×	×		×	×	×	×				×							
Review of Educational Research	×	×			×	×	×			×					×	×	×		×	×	×
Science	×	×	×	×	×	×		×	×	×	×	×	×	×		×	×	×			
Scientific American	×	×	×	×	×	×		×	×	×	×	×	×	×				×	×		

Note: The information in this table was obtained from questionnaires sent to each journal by the author.

on the subject and been more familiar with the details, he could have discovered that certain rewards are not effective because of a principle called individual reward hierarchy. He could also have found out how to remedy the problem and find a more effective reward rather than giving up. Psychologists, like other professionals, often rely on colleagues who may themselves be authorities in similar fields. If no peer is available for consultation, journals may also fill this need for an information source.

Locating Journal Articles

One of the most frustrating tasks for the undergraduate is looking up published material from which to make a report. The student is often faced with rows and rows of volumes of journals, all in chronological order instead of by title, author, or subject. The confused student sees no possible route to finding the one article needed in those thousands of books. The student is not alone; even professionals are often confused about how to search for that one tiny but vital article in the mass of published material.

The best guide to the journals is *Psychological Abstracts*, a tool to help find that hidden article the psychologist or student needs. *Psychological Abstracts* contains summaries of technical reports, journal articles, and books. Some have likened it to a small catalog of directions. Compiled into two volumes each year, *Psychological Abstracts* has a cumulative index for each. Each index lists the national and international journals regularly reviewed in the *Abstracts*.

In using *Psychological Abstracts*, you will notice that it provides summaries of journal articles. It also refers the searcher to books and specific chapters in books. A code is used for easier searching. Near the front of

---

SUBJECT INDEX

Hodgkin's disease, psychosomatics of, 4439
Holism, psychologists' attitudes toward, 7212
Holland (*See* Cultures)
Holland Vocational Preference Inventory, as personality inventory, 9955
Hollingsworth, H. L., obituary, 179
Home (*See* Family)
    running away from (*See* Runaways)
Home Environment Diagnosis Test, & Effort Quotient, 2165
Homemaker service, for family stability, 8306
Homeostasis (*See also* Equilibrium)
    activity level &, rat, 9470
    concept analysis, 2425
    consolation &, 7187
    normality concept &, 10269
    in puberty, 5832
    in schizophrenia, 8767
Homer, Odyssey, Penelope, psychoanalysis, 864
Homing, bats, 542
    in fish, California rocky shore, 567
    magnetic theory, pigeons, 2988
    in nonmigratory bats, 5483
    rodents, 5493
Homogeneity, factor analysis vs. analysis of variance in, 9287
    test of, item selection methods, 5070
        by item-test regression, 3833
        for normal distribution, 7265
Homosexuality (*See also* Lesbianism)
    avoidance learning of rat &, 523
    in college students, 10457
    diagnosis & treatment of, 10610
    in drug addiction, 3921
    effeminate passive obligatory, 10596
    etiological theories of, male, 8695
    fetishism, case study, 1699
    group, behavior, male, 4211
        therapy, 6366
    impotence & frigidity, 1824
    inversion vs. term distinction, 8692

Howard Ink Blot Test, 6289
"How I Feel About Things" Test, validity of, childhood, 7947
How Supervise?, Supervisory Practices Test vs., 11124
H-Technique scales (*See* Stauffer's H-Technique)
Hull, C., motor performance theory of, 7683
Human (*See* Man)
Human engineering (*See* Engineering psychology)
Human figure drawing (*See* Drawing)
Human relations, 4872
    attitude change in, 8407
    cases, 4866
    changing technology, 2336
    classification & typology, 5055(a)
    concepts of, 4762
    faith as basis of, 4887
    in growing company, 2326
    inservice program, 7152
    international, 8172
    inventory of problems in, 4860
    on-the-job, 2346
    & management principles, 2328
    manipulating vs. understanding approach to, 10105
    in officers, test for, 2304, 2305, 8407
    science of, 7039
    supervision &, 9105, 9136
    supervisor selection &, 4871
    test construction, user's role, 2305
    training evaluation method, 11142
Human Relations Inventory, vs. MMPI, social conformity, 3491
Humanism, & scientific training, 5054
Humidity (*See also* Air; Climate; Temperature)
    peripheral vision in, 9559
    suicide notes &, 10605
Humm-Wadsworth Temperament Scale, critique of, 9102

FIGURE 14–5 Section of a page from the subject index in *Psychological Abstracts*. (*Psychological Abstracts*, 1953, vol. 33, no. 6, p. 1179.)

BRIEF SUBJECT INDEX

Physiological Correlates (see also Stress/Physiological) 13718, 13961, 14144, 14151, 14157, 14246, 14395, 14399, 14946, 14974, 14980, 14982, 14998, 15449
Physiological Psychology 13709, 13736, 13851, 13857, 13951, 14157, 15369
Physiology (see also Electrophysiology) 13644, 13645, 13843, 13847, 13852, 13855, 13867, 14565, 15089
Physiology/Sensory (see also Vision/Physiology of) 13855, 13952, 13976, 13983
Physique (SEE Body)
Piaget/J. 14318, 14324, 14325, 14329, 14332, 15504
Picture 13672, 14157, 14346, 15179, 15308, 15485
Picture-Frustration (SEE Projective Technique)
Pigeon 13910, 13931, 14081, 14184, 14185, 14201, 14210, 14219, 14220, 14231, 14247, 14249, 14252
Pilot (SEE Aviation, Personnel/Military)
Pitch (SEE Sound, Audition)
Pituitary (SEE Gland, Hormone)
PK (SEE Parapsychology)
Placebo (SEE Drug Effects)
Play (SEE Game, Recreation)
Play Therapy (SEE Therapy)
Pleasure (SEE Emotion)
Poisson Distribution (SEE Mathematics)
Police (SEE Crime & Criminals, Law)
Political Behavior

Problem Solving (see also Choice Behavior, Decision Making, Childhood/Concept Formation & Problem Solving in) 13656, 13832, 13833, 13905, 14162, 14332, 14427, 14505, 14597, 14613, 14672, 14901, 15066, 15135, 15228, 15509
Profile (SEE Score & Scoring)
Programed Instruction (see also Teaching Aids) 13782, 15158, 15346, 15484, 15501, 15502, 15503, 15504, 15505, 15506, 15507, 15508, 15509, 15510, 15511
Programing (SEE Computer)
Projection (SEE Defense Mechanism, Cerebral Cortex, Visual Cortex)
Projective Technique (see also Rorschach Test) 13841, 14366, 14374, 14389, 14393, 14425, 14564, 14578, 14640, 14646, 14654, 14666, 14883, 14894, 15084, 15282, 15283
Propaganda (SEE Communication, Communication/Mass, Persuasion)
Proprioception (SEE Kinesthesis, Somesthesia)
Prostitution (SEE Occupation, Sexual Behavior)
Protestantism (SEE Religion)
Psychedelic Experience (SEE Drug Effects—Human)
Psychiatric Diagnosis (SEE Psychodiagnosis)
Psychiatric Hospital (SEE Mental Hospitalization)
Psychiatric Patient (see also Patient) 14591, 14637, 14654, 14659, 14666, 14668, 14673, 14689, 14705, 14745, 14754, 14757, 14760, 14835, 14836, 14840, 14845, 14850, 14869, 14870, 14871, 14873, 14875, 14885, 14896, 14920, 14921, 14932, 15035, 15037,

Psychology 13581, 13582, 13593, 13596, 13597, 13598, 13599, 13600, 13601, 14437, 14889, 14895, 15069, 15199
Psychology Abroad 13590, 13594, 13640, 13843, 13855, 14401, 14606, 14626, 14639, 15254
Psychology/History of 13563, 13564, 13565, 13648, 13720, 13855, 14401, 14671, 14843, 14938, 15065, 15068, 15232
Psychometrics (SEE Test & Testing, Psychophysics, Statistics)
Psychomotor Performance (SEE Motor Performance)
Psychoneurosis (SEE Neurosis)
Psychopathology 13562, 13593, 14154, 14464, 14575, 14624, 14660, 14664, 14674, 14692, 14710, 14722, 14798, 14836, 14878, 14896, 14962, 15003, 15042, 15089
Psychopathy (SEE Mental Disorder)
Psychopharmacology (SEE Drug Effects, Drug Therapy, Biochemistry)
Psychophysics 13655, 13658, 13711
Psychophysiology (SEE Physiological Psychology)
Psychosis & Psychotics (see also Mental Disorder, specific psychoses) 14740, 14773, 14795, 14798, 14807, 14810, 14820, 14874, 14880, 14931, 14932, 14939, 15003, 15017, 15020, 15023, 15024, 15027, 15214, 15215
Psychosis/Children (SEE Childhood/Psychosis in)
Psychosomatic

FIGURE 14–6 Section of a page from the brief subject index in *Psychological Abstracts*. (*Psychological Abstracts*, 1970, vol. 44, no. 9, p. xi.)

each issue is a table of general area content. However, a subject index is also provided (Figure 14-5). For recent unbound issues, similar information can be found using the brief subject index found usually at the end of each monthly issue (Figure 14-6).

The *Abstracts* contain a summary or a statement representing each of the areas of a research report: introduction, method, results, and conclusion. The first sentence of the summaries also tells whether it is a research article, a review article, or a theoretical discussion (Figure 14-7). *Psychological Abstracts* is a time-saving device. By using it, you can decide whether or not to take the time and trouble to go to the original source. An author index for the names of the authors whose articles you have previously found helpful is also available.

Let us go through a simulated search. Suppose you noted a significant effect on the behavior of your rat when you delayed the reinforcement it received. You first would go to the cumulative index and look for a reference. Maybe "reinforcement, delay" or "reinforcement schedules" will lead you to the right reference article. You decide to look under "reinforcement, delay" and you find it has the number 14224 after it. You search then for the number 14224 in the volume describing that year, 1970, and the approximate month, July–December, and soon find the material shown in Figure 14-8. The running head at the top corner of the page includes the number 44: 14217–14225. The title, author, journal, volume, number, and page are all listed there. You then can choose to discard it after reading the abstract or go to the stacks and look up the article itself.

SOCIAL PSYCHOLOGY

5886. **Abramson, E., Cutter, H. A., Kautz, R. W., & Mendelson, M.** (Pennsylvania State U.) **Social power and commitment: A theoretical statement.** *Amer. sociol. Rev.,* 1958, **23**, 15–22.—A statement and analysis of a general theory of the relationship of social power and social interaction.—*G. H. Frank.*

5887. **Adler, H. G. Ideas toward a sociology of the concentration camp.** *Amer. J. Sociol.,* 1958, **63**, 513–522,—Indicates possible methods for studying the concentration camp sociologically. The concentration camp reached its most extreme and cruel stage of development in the totalitarian state. One of the primary dangers of contemporary life is the concentration camp.—*R. M. Frumkin.*

FIGURE 14–7   Two summaries from *Psychological Abstracts.*

by either shock-level group. Under the present conditions, fear conditioning to visual cues in a 1-trial passive-avoidance situation could not be demonstrated. —*Journal abstract.*

14217. **Nagy, Z. Michael, Misanin, James R., & Newman, Judith A.** (Susquehanna U.) **Anatomy of escape behavior in neonatal mice.** *Journal of Comparative & Physiological Psychology,* 1970, **72**(1), 116–124.—6 groups of Swiss-Webster albino mice (N = 96), 5–15 days of age, were given 25 trials in a straight-alley shock-escape task to examine the possibility of instrumental learning at these ages. Several different measures reflected improved escape behavior by the end of the training session for Ss as young as 5 days of age. By comparing performance measures, it was possible to rule out maturation, fatigue, and habituation as factors leading to the improved escape behavior. The data are interpreted as providing evidence that 5-day-old Ss are capable of learning instrumental escape responses. (20 ref.)—*Journal abstract.*

Reinforcement

14218. **Birkimer, John C. & Aylworth, Charles E.** (U. Louisville) **Rapid extinction of conditioned reinforcement effects in the signaled absence of primary reinforcement.** *Psychonomic Science,* 1970, **18**(1), 31–32.—Trained 6 male albino Sprague-Dawley rats on a multiple schedule involving intermittent white noise and sucrose solution for bar-pressing in the presence of 1 stimulus and extinction in the presence of the 2nd. When responding in the 2nd stimulus context reached a low level, the noise was made available for each response in that context. The noise functioned as a conditioned reinforcer, temporarily raising response rates in the 2nd stimulus context above their earlier level. The reinforcing effects of the noise quickly extinguished, suggesting procedural or species-specific differences between the current study and recent research by J. R. Thomas with pigeons.—*Journal abstract.*

14219. **Brownstein, Aaron J. & Hughes, Ronald G.** (U. North Carolina, Greensboro) **The role of response suppression in behavioral contrast: Signaled reinforcement.** *Psychonomic Science,* 1970, **18**(1), 50–52. —After responding was maintained on multiple variable-interval schedules of reinforcement, a signaling procedure was added to 1 component. 4 adult white Carneaux pigeons served as Ss. The signaling procedure consisted of illuminating the key, the only source of illumination in the chamber, only when responding would be reinforced. Rate of responding in the unaltered component increased. When the signaling procedure was removed, rate of responding decreased in the component in which reinforcement had never been signaled. Obtained rates of reinforcement in both components were equal throughout the experiment.—*Journal abstract.*

14220. **Brownstein, Aaron J. & Newsom, Crighton.** (U. North Carolina, Greensboro) **Behavioral contrast in multiple schedules with equal reinforcement rates.** *Psychonomic Science,* 1970, **18**(1), 25–26.—After responding was maintained on multiple fixed-interval schedules of reinforcement, with 4 Silver King pigeons, a cuing procedure was added to 1 component. Cuing was accomplished by illuminating a lamp just prior to reinforcement availability. This procedure produced positive behavioral contrast. The rate of responding in the cued component decreased, and the rate in the

uncued component increased. When the cue was removed, negative behavioral contrast occurred. Rate of responding in the component from which the cue had been removed increased, and in the other component decreased. Throughout the experiment, rates of reinforcement in both components were held constant. —*Journal abstract.*

14221. **Capaldi, E. J., Ziff, D. R., & Godbout, R. C.** (Purdue U.) **Extinction and the necessity or non-necessity of anticipating reward on nonrewarded trials.** *Psychonomic Science,* 1970, **18**(1), 61–63.—Male Holtzman rats receiving nonrewarded trials but not previous rewarded trials showed a PRE. These data are similar to those produced in initial nonreward effect studies, except that fewer nonrewards were employed here. Results are not consistent with the hypothesis that at least 1 rewarded trial must precede nonrewarded trials in order to obtain a PRE, nor do they support the idea that reward must be expected on nonrewarded trials in order to obtain a PRE. Reinforcing this view were the results of studies that did not attempt to eliminate expectancy, as here, but rather manipulated its strength prior to extinction. (17 ref.)—*Journal abstract.*

14222. **Farrell, Walter M.** (U. Miami) **Some motivating and reinforcing functions of an auditory stimulus.** *Dissertation Abstracts International,* 1969, **30**(5-B), 2435.

14223. **Logan, Frank A. & Spanier, Douglas.** (U. New Mexico) **Chaining and nonchaining delay of reinforcement.** *Journal of Comparative & Physiological Psychology,* 1970, **72**(1), 98–101.—Exp. I pitted a differential in amount of reward against a comparable differential in nonchaining delay of reward, at 2 different lengths of chaining delay accomplished by different runway lengths. 28 male albino rats served as Ss. Ss tended to choose the smaller more immediate reward in short runways and the larger delayed reward in long runways. Exp. II pitted a short chaining delay combined with a nonchaining delay against a long chaining delay. Ss tended to choose the short chaining delay even when the added nonchaining delay resulted in a longer total time of delay of reward. Results indicate that Ss combine both sources of delay in choosing between alternatives, with chaining delay more deleterious than nonchaining delay. This latter finding is interpreted in terms of immediacy of secondary reinforcement.—*Journal abstract.*

14224. **Logan, Frank A. & Spanier, Douglas.** (U. New Mexico) **Relative effect of delay of food and water reward.** *Journal of Comparative & Physiological Psychology,* 1970, **72**(1), 102–104.—Gave 76 hungry or thirsty male hooded rats the appropriate reward after 1- or 30-sec time of delay in a between-groups 2 × 2 design. In 1 experiment, delay was imposed in the goal box; in another experiment, delay was imposed in the straight alley just before the goal box. In both experiments, the thirsty S ran somewhat slower at the short delay and somewhat faster at the long delay, producing significant interactions. Hence, delay of water reward was found to be relatively less detrimental than delay of food reward. This finding may be related to the degree to which incompatible responses are elicited by the different drive stimuli during the time of delay.—*Journal abstract.*

14225. **McHewitt, Earl R. & McHose, James H.** (Southern Illinois U.) **Role of nonreward in differential conditioning.** *Journal of Experimental Psychology,* 1970,

FIGURE 14–8 Page from *Psychological Abstracts* containing the summary for the Logan and Spanier article shown in Figure 14–1.
(*Psychological Abstracts,* 1970, vol. 44, no. 9, p. 1455.)

Conventions

A second way of disseminating newly discovered information is through conventions. The United States is divided into geographical regions. Within these regions, psychological conventions are held, usually annually. A large national convention is also held. At these conventions, speakers present papers, and smaller discussion groups present the most recent developments within their topic area.

Two basic objectives are accomplished by conventions. This convening of professionals from often great distances allows each authority to tell the others of the most recent studies. This is a great help, since even with the journal an author has to deal with what is called publication lag, the time it takes to publish and review the material.[5] Conventions also allow professionals to get together for personal discussion of their research. Since some may be working on the same or similar fields, this personal interaction is a valuable information source.

SUMMARY

The report is the final effort to communicate all facets of the experiment undertaken: the reasons for the experiment, the method used in carrying it out, the precise measurements taken, and the conclusions drawn from the results. In writing, the researcher seeks to communicate to both the professional and the layman. In doing so, precise definitions and wording are used so that everyone will interpret the words similarly. Often the researcher uses operational definitions to make the meaning clear. This scientific writing, though "boring" to many unfamiliar with the style, is precise and aimed at exact understanding. The objective of the report is to transmit the exact information so that another researcher doing the same experiment can replicate the previously derived results. Organization, accuracy, clarity, and readability are the vital elements in a good report.

The universally accepted form of the report is as follows:

Title
Abstract

---

[5] Traditionally, for a journal the publication lag ranges from twelve to eighteen months. Though some journals take only three to four months, they are usually review journals specifically for the purpose of giving an introduction to a certain study in hopes that it will be elaborated on in a future article. The latter situation described may be found in *Bulletin of the Psychonomic Society* and *Science*, two journals specifically having brief (two-page) research reports. Articles in those journals are characterized by a short time period from submission to publication.

Text
  Introduction
  Method
    Subjects
    Apparatus
    Procedure
    Design
  Results
  Discussion
References
Footnotes
Tables and Figures

The psychologist, considered to be an authority in his or her field, faces the ever-present problem of keeping up with the masses of new material being published every day. One solution to the problem is the journal. Journals are subdivided and categorized according to subjects, content areas, and the types of investigations they publish. A psychologist can refer to that journal most applicable to a particular current problem or field of expertise. Thus the journal assists the professional by narrowing the reading spectrum. Another advantage is the assistance journals give as sources of information to the professional in problem areas lying outside his or her field of expertise. In the absence of authorities, the journal plays another important role as an information source.

Finding journal articles poses yet another hurdle. *Psychological Abstracts*, containing summaries of journal articles, is a time-saving device and an invaluable tool for finding material.

Besides the journal, another solution to the problem of distribution of new information is the convention. Conventions aid professionals by sidestepping the publication lag to the newest information and by allowing personal discussion of problems so that data can be compared and other authorities can be consulted on particular research problems.

Appendix

TABLE A *Table of t*

df	P 0.9	0.8	0.7	0.6	0.5	0.4	0.3	0.2	0.1	0.05	0.02	0.01
1	0.158	0.325	0.510	0.727	1.000	1.376	1.963	3.078	6.314	12.706	31.821	63.657
2	0.142	0.289	0.445	0.617	0.816	1.061	1.386	1.886	2.920	4.303	6.965	9.925
3	0.137	0.277	0.424	0.584	0.765	0.978	1.250	1.638	2.353	3.182	4.541	5.841
4	0.134	0.271	0.414	0.589	0.741	0.941	1.190	1.533	2.132	2.776	3.747	4.604
5	0.132	0.267	0.408	0.559	0.727	0.920	1.156	1.476	2.015	2.571	3.365	4.032
6	0.131	0.265	0.404	0.553	0.718	0.906	1.134	1.440	1.943	2.447	3.143	3.707
7	0.130	0.263	0.402	0.549	0.711	0.896	1.119	1.415	1.895	2.365	2.998	3.499
8	0.130	0.262	0.399	0.546	0.706	0.889	1.108	1.397	1.860	2.306	2.896	3.355
9	0.129	0.261	0.398	0.543	0.703	0.883	1.100	1.383	1.833	2.262	2.821	3.250
10	0.129	0.260	0.397	0.542	0.700	0.879	1.093	1.372	1.812	2.228	2.764	3.169
11	0.129	0.260	0.396	0.540	0.697	0.876	1.088	1.363	1.796	2.201	2.718	3.106
12	0.128	0.259	0.395	0.539	0.695	0.873	1.083	1.356	1.782	2.179	2.681	3.055
13	0.128	0.259	0.394	0.538	0.694	0.870	1.079	1.350	1.771	2.160	2.650	3.012
14	0.128	0.258	0.393	0.537	0.692	0.868	1.076	1.345	1.761	2.145	2.624	2.977
15	0.128	0.258	0.393	0.536	0.691	0.866	1.074	1.341	1.753	2.131	2.602	2.947

16	0.128	0.258	0.392	0.535	0.690	0.865	1.071	1.337	1.746	2.120	2.583	2.921
17	0.128	0.257	0.392	0.534	0.689	0.863	1.069	1.333	1.740	2.110	2.567	2.898
18	0.127	0.257	0.392	0.534	0.688	0.862	1.067	1.330	1.734	2.101	2.552	2.878
19	0.127	0.257	0.391	0.533	0.688	0.861	1.066	1.328	1.729	2.093	2.539	2.861
20	0.127	0.257	0.391	0.533	0.687	0.860	1.064	1.325	1.725	2.086	2.528	2.845
21	0.127	0.257	0.391	0.532	0.686	0.859	1.063	1.323	1.721	2.080	2.518	2.831
22	0.127	0.256	0.390	0.532	0.686	0.858	1.061	1.321	1.717	2.074	2.508	2.819
23	0.127	0.256	0.390	0.532	0.685	0.858	1.060	1.319	1.714	2.069	2.500	2.807
24	0.127	0.256	0.390	0.531	0.685	0.857	1.059	1.318	1.711	2.064	2.492	2.797
25	0.127	0.256	0.390	0.531	0.684	0.856	1.058	1.316	1.708	2.060	2.485	2.787
26	0.127	0.256	0.390	0.531	0.684	0.856	1.058	1.315	1.706	2.056	2.479	2.779
27	0.127	0.256	0.389	0.531	0.684	0.855	1.057	1.314	1.703	2.052	2.473	2.771
28	0.127	0.256	0.389	0.530	0.683	0.855	1.056	1.313	1.701	2.048	2.467	2.763
29	0.127	0.256	0.389	0.530	0.683	0.854	1.055	1.311	1.699	2.045	2.462	2.756
30	0.127	0.256	0.389	0.530	0.683	0.854	1.055	1.310	1.697	2.042	2.457	2.750
∞	0.12566	0.25335	0.38532	0.52440	0.67449	0.84162	1.03643	1.28155	1.64485	1.95996	2.32634	2.57582

Source for Appendix Tables A and B: Reprinted from Table 4 of R. A. Fisher, *Statistical methods for research workers*, 14th ed. Copyright © 1972 by Hafner Press, a division of Macmillan Publishing Co., Inc.

TABLE B *Table of F*

df Associated with Denominator	P	\multicolumn{10}{c}{df Associated with Numerator}

df Associated with Denominator	P	1	2	3	4	5	6	8	12	24	∞
1	0.01	4052	4999	5403	5625	5764	5859	5981	6106	6234	6366
	0.05	161.45	199.50	215.71	224.58	230.16	233.99	238.88	243.91	249.05	254.32
	0.10	39.86	49.50	53.59	55.83	57.24	58.20	59.44	60.70	62.00	63.33
	0.20	9.47	12.00	13.06	13.73	14.01	14.26	14.59	14.90	15.24	15.58
2	0.01	98.49	99.00	99.17	99.25	99.30	99.33	99.36	99.42	99.46	99.50
	0.05	18.51	19.00	19.16	19.25	19.30	19.33	19.37	19.41	19.45	19.50
	0.10	8.53	9.00	9.16	9.24	9.29	9.33	9.37	9.41	9.45	9.49
	0.20	3.56	4.00	4.16	4.24	4.28	4.32	4.36	4.40	4.44	4.48
3	0.01	34.12	30.81	29.46	28.71	28.24	27.91	27.49	27.05	26.60	26.12
	0.05	10.13	9.55	9.28	9.12	9.01	8.94	8.84	8.74	8.64	8.53
	0.10	5.54	5.46	5.39	5.34	5.31	5.28	5.25	5.22	5.18	5.13
	0.20	2.68	2.89	2.94	2.96	2.97	2.97	2.98	2.98	2.98	2.98
4	0.01	21.20	18.00	16.69	15.98	15.52	15.21	14.80	14.37	13.93	13.46
	0.05	7.71	6.94	6.59	6.39	6.26	6.16	6.04	5.91	5.77	5.63
	0.10	4.54	4.32	4.19	4.11	4.05	4.01	3.95	3.90	3.83	3.76
	0.20	2.35	2.47	2.48	2.48	2.48	2.47	2.47	2.46	2.44	2.43
5	0.01	16.26	13.27	12.06	11.39	10.97	10.67	10.29	9.89	9.47	9.02
	0.05	6.61	5.79	5.41	5.19	5.05	4.95	4.82	4.68	4.53	4.36
	0.10	4.06	3.78	3.62	3.52	3.45	3.40	3.34	3.27	3.19	3.10
	0.20	2.18	2.26	2.25	2.24	2.23	2.22	2.20	2.18	2.16	2.13

df	α										
6	0.01	13.74	10.92	9.78	9.15	8.75	8.47	8.10	7.72	7.31	6.88
	0.05	5.99	5.14	4.76	4.53	4.39	4.28	4.15	4.00	3.84	3.67
	0.10	3.78	3.46	3.29	3.18	3.11	3.05	2.98	2.90	2.82	2.72
	0.20	2.07	2.13	2.11	2.09	2.08	2.06	2.04	2.02	1.99	1.95
7	0.01	12.25	9.55	8.45	7.85	7.46	7.19	6.84	6.47	6.07	5.65
	0.05	5.59	4.74	4.35	4.12	3.97	3.87	3.73	3.57	3.41	3.23
	0.10	3.59	3.26	3.07	2.96	2.88	2.83	2.75	2.67	2.58	2.47
	0.20	2.00	2.04	2.02	1.99	1.97	1.96	1.93	1.91	1.87	1.83
8	0.01	11.26	8.65	7.59	7.01	6.63	6.37	6.03	5.67	5.28	4.86
	0.05	5.32	4.46	4.07	3.84	3.69	3.58	3.44	3.28	3.12	2.93
	0.10	3.46	3.11	2.92	2.81	2.73	2.67	2.59	2.50	2.40	2.29
	0.20	1.95	1.98	1.95	1.92	1.90	1.88	1.86	1.83	1.79	1.74
9	0.01	10.56	8.02	6.99	6.42	6.06	5.80	5.47	5.11	4.73	4.31
	0.05	5.12	4.26	3.86	3.63	3.48	3.37	3.23	3.07	2.90	2.71
	0.10	3.36	3.01	2.81	2.69	2.61	2.55	2.47	2.38	2.28	2.16
	0.20	1.91	1.94	1.90	1.87	1.85	1.83	1.80	1.76	1.72	1.67
10	0.01	10.04	7.56	6.55	5.99	5.64	5.39	5.06	4.71	4.33	3.91
	0.05	4.96	4.10	3.71	3.48	3.33	3.22	3.07	2.91	2.74	2.54
	0.10	3.28	2.92	2.73	2.61	2.52	2.46	2.38	2.28	2.18	2.06
	0.20	1.88	1.90	1.86	1.83	1.80	1.78	1.75	1.72	1.67	1.62
11	0.01	9.65	7.20	6.22	5.67	5.32	5.07	4.74	4.40	4.02	3.60
	0.05	4.84	3.98	3.59	3.36	3.20	3.09	2.95	2.79	2.61	2.40
	0.10	3.23	2.86	2.66	2.54	2.45	2.39	2.30	2.21	2.10	1.97
	0.20	1.86	1.87	1.83	1.80	1.77	1.75	1.72	1.68	1.63	1.57
12	0.01	9.33	6.93	5.95	5.41	5.06	4.82	4.50	4.16	3.78	3.36
	0.05	4.75	3.88	3.49	3.26	3.11	3.00	2.85	2.69	2.50	2.30
	0.10	3.18	2.81	2.61	2.48	2.39	2.33	2.24	2.15	2.04	1.90
	0.20	1.84	1.85	1.80	1.77	1.74	1.72	1.69	1.65	1.60	1.54

TABLE B (Continued)

		df Associated with Numerator									
df Associated with Denominator	P	1	2	3	4	5	6	8	12	24	∞
13	0.01	9.07	6.70	5.74	5.20	4.86	4.62	4.30	3.96	3.59	3.16
	0.05	4.67	3.80	3.41	3.18	3.02	2.92	2.77	2.60	2.42	2.21
	0.10	3.14	2.76	2.56	2.43	2.35	2.28	2.20	2.10	1.98	1.85
	0.20	1.82	1.88	1.78	1.75	1.72	1.69	1.66	1.62	1.57	1.51
14	0.01	8.86	6.51	5.56	5.08	4.69	4.46	4.14	3.80	3.43	3.00
	0.05	4.60	3.74	3.34	3.11	2.96	2.85	2.70	2.53	2.35	2.13
	0.10	3.10	2.73	2.52	2.39	2.31	2.24	2.15	2.05	1.94	1.80
	0.20	1.81	1.81	1.76	1.78	1.70	1.67	1.64	1.60	1.55	1.48
15	0.01	8.68	6.36	5.42	4.89	4.56	4.32	4.00	3.67	3.29	2.87
	0.05	4.54	3.68	3.29	3.06	2.90	2.79	2.64	2.48	2.29	2.07
	0.10	3.07	2.70	2.49	2.36	2.27	2.21	2.12	2.02	1.90	1.76
	0.20	1.80	1.79	1.75	1.71	1.68	1.66	1.62	1.58	1.53	1.46
16	0.01	8.53	6.23	5.29	4.77	4.44	4.20	3.89	3.55	3.18	2.75
	0.05	4.49	3.63	3.24	3.01	2.85	2.74	2.59	2.42	2.24	2.01
	0.10	3.05	2.67	2.46	2.33	2.24	2.18	2.09	1.99	1.87	1.72
	0.20	1.79	1.78	1.74	1.70	1.67	1.64	1.61	1.56	1.51	1.43
17	0.01	8.40	6.11	5.18	4.67	4.34	4.10	3.79	3.45	3.08	2.65
	0.05	4.45	3.59	3.20	2.96	2.81	2.70	2.55	2.38	2.19	1.96
	0.10	3.03	2.64	2.44	2.31	2.22	2.15	2.06	1.96	1.84	1.69
	0.20	1.78	1.77	1.72	1.68	1.65	1.63	1.59	1.55	1.49	1.42

18	0.01	8.28	6.01	5.09	4.58	4.25	4.01	3.71	3.37	3.00	2.57
	0.05	4.41	3.55	3.16	2.93	2.77	2.66	2.51	2.34	2.15	1.92
	0.10	3.01	3.62	2.42	2.29	2.20	2.13	2.04	1.93	1.81	1.66
	0.20	1.77	1.76	1.71	1.67	1.64	1.62	1.58	1.53	1.48	1.40
19	0.01	8.18	5.93	5.01	4.50	4.17	3.94	3.63	3.30	2.92	2.49
	0.05	4.38	3.52	3.13	2.90	2.74	2.63	2.48	2.31	2.11	1.88
	0.10	2.99	2.61	2.40	2.27	2.18	2.11	2.02	1.91	1.79	1.63
	0.20	1.76	1.75	1.70	1.66	1.63	1.61	1.57	1.52	1.46	1.39
20	0.01	8.10	5.85	4.94	4.43	4.10	3.87	3.56	3.23	2.86	2.42
	0.05	4.35	3.49	3.10	2.87	2.71	2.60	2.45	2.28	2.08	1.84
	0.10	2.97	2.59	2.38	2.25	2.16	2.09	2.00	1.89	1.77	1.61
	0.20	1.76	1.75	1.70	1.65	1.62	1.60	1.56	1.51	1.45	1.37
21	0.01	8.02	5.78	4.87	4.37	4.04	3.81	3.51	3.17	2.80	2.36
	0.05	4.32	3.47	3.07	2.84	2.68	2.57	2.42	2.25	2.05	1.81
	0.10	2.96	2.57	2.36	2.23	2.14	2.08	1.98	1.88	1.75	1.59
	0.20	1.75	1.74	1.69	1.65	1.61	1.59	1.55	1.50	1.44	1.36
22	0.01	7.94	5.72	4.82	4.31	3.99	3.76	3.45	3.12	2.75	2.31
	0.05	4.30	3.44	3.05	2.82	2.66	2.55	2.40	2.23	2.03	1.78
	0.10	2.95	2.56	2.35	2.22	2.13	2.06	1.97	1.86	1.73	1.57
	0.20	1.75	1.73	1.68	1.64	1.61	1.58	1.54	1.49	1.43	1.35
23	0.01	7.88	5.66	4.76	4.26	3.94	3.71	3.41	3.07	2.70	2.26
	0.05	4.28	3.42	3.03	2.80	2.64	2.53	2.38	2.20	2.00	1.76
	0.10	2.94	2.55	2.34	2.21	2.11	2.05	1.95	1.84	1.72	1.55
	0.20	1.74	1.73	1.68	1.63	1.60	1.57	1.53	1.49	1.42	1.34
24	0.01	7.82	5.61	4.72	4.22	3.90	3.67	3.36	3.03	2.66	2.21
	0.05	4.26	3.40	3.01	2.78	2.62	2.51	2.36	2.18	1.98	1.73
	0.10	2.93	2.54	2.33	2.19	2.10	2.04	1.94	1.83	1.70	1.53
	0.20	1.74	1.72	1.67	1.63	1.59	1.57	1.53	1.48	1.42	1.33

TABLE B *(Continued)*

df Associated with Denominator	P	\multicolumn{10}{c}{df Associated with Numerator}

df Associated with Denominator	P	1	2	3	4	5	6	8	12	24	∞
25	0.01	7.77	5.57	4.68	4.18	3.86	3.63	3.32	2.99	2.62	2.17
	0.05	4.24	3.38	2.99	2.76	2.60	2.49	2.34	2.16	1.96	1.71
	0.10	2.92	2.53	2.32	2.18	2.09	2.02	1.93	1.82	1.69	1.52
	0.20	1.73	1.72	1.66	1.62	1.59	1.56	1.52	1.47	1.41	1.32
26	0.01	7.72	5.53	4.64	4.14	3.82	3.59	3.29	2.96	2.58	2.13
	0.05	4.22	3.37	2.98	2.74	2.59	2.47	2.32	2.15	1.95	1.69
	0.10	2.91	2.52	2.31	2.17	2.08	2.01	1.92	1.81	1.68	1.50
	0.20	1.73	1.71	1.66	1.62	1.58	1.56	1.52	1.47	1.40	1.31
27	0.01	7.68	5.49	4.60	4.11	3.78	3.56	3.26	2.93	2.55	2.10
	0.05	4.21	3.35	2.96	2.73	2.57	2.46	2.30	2.13	1.93	1.67
	0.10	2.90	2.51	2.30	2.17	2.07	2.00	1.91	1.80	1.67	1.49
	0.20	1.73	1.71	1.66	1.61	1.58	1.55	1.51	1.46	1.40	1.30
28	0.01	7.64	5.45	4.57	4.07	3.75	3.53	3.23	2.90	2.52	2.06
	0.05	4.20	3.34	2.95	2.71	2.56	2.44	2.29	2.12	1.91	1.65
	0.10	2.89	2.50	2.29	2.16	2.06	2.00	1.90	1.79	1.66	1.48
	0.20	1.72	1.71	1.65	1.61	1.57	1.55	1.51	1.46	1.39	1.30
29	0.01	7.60	5.42	4.54	4.04	3.73	3.50	3.20	2.87	2.49	2.03
	0.05	4.18	3.33	2.93	2.70	2.54	2.43	2.28	2.10	1.90	1.64
	0.10	2.89	2.50	2.28	2.15	2.06	1.99	1.89	1.78	1.65	1.47
	0.20	1.72	1.70	1.65	1.60	1.57	1.54	1.50	1.45	1.39	1.29

30	0.01	7.56	5.39	4.51	4.02	3.70	3.47	3.17	2.84	2.47	2.01
	0.05	4.17	3.32	2.92	2.69	2.53	2.42	2.27	2.09	1.89	1.62
	0.10	2.88	2.49	2.28	2.14	2.05	1.98	1.88	1.77	1.64	1.46
	0.20	1.72	1.70	1.64	1.60	1.57	1.54	1.50	1.45	1.38	1.28
40	0.01	7.31	5.18	4.31	3.83	3.51	3.29	2.99	2.66	2.29	1.80
	0.05	4.08	3.23	2.84	2.61	2.45	2.34	2.18	2.00	1.79	1.51
	0.10	2.84	2.44	2.23	2.09	2.00	1.93	1.83	1.71	1.57	1.38
	0.20	1.70	1.68	1.62	1.57	1.54	1.51	1.47	1.41	1.34	1.24
60	0.01	7.08	4.98	4.13	3.65	3.34	3.12	2.82	2.50	2.12	1.60
	0.05	4.00	3.15	2.76	2.52	2.37	2.25	2.10	1.92	1.70	1.39
	0.10	2.79	2.39	2.18	2.04	1.95	1.87	1.77	1.66	1.51	1.29
	0.20	1.68	1.65	1.59	1.55	1.51	1.48	1.44	1.38	1.31	1.18
120	0.01	6.85	4.79	3.95	3.48	3.17	2.96	2.66	2.34	1.95	1.38
	0.05	3.92	3.07	2.68	2.45	2.29	2.17	2.02	1.83	1.61	1.25
	0.10	2.75	2.35	2.13	1.99	1.90	1.82	1.72	1.60	1.45	1.19
	0.20	1.66	1.63	1.57	1.52	1.48	1.45	1.41	1.35	1.27	1.12
∞	0.01	6.64	4.60	3.78	3.32	3.02	2.80	2.51	2.18	1.79	1.00
	0.05	3.84	2.99	2.60	2.37	2.21	2.09	1.94	1.75	1.52	1.00
	0.10	2.71	2.30	2.08	1.94	1.85	1.77	1.67	1.55	1.38	1.00
	0.20	1.64	1.61	1.55	1.50	1.46	1.43	1.38	1.32	1.23	1.00

TABLE C *Critical Values of the U Statistic of the Mann-Whitney Test*

To use these tables, first decide what level of significance you want with either a one- or two-tailed test. For example, if you want p = .05, two-tailed, use (c). Then locate the number of cases or measures (n) in both groups in the particular subtable you have chosen. The U value you have calculated must be *less* than that at the appropriate place in the table. For example, if you had 18 subjects in each group of an experiment, and calculated U = 90, then you could conclude that the null hypothesis can be rejected because the critical U value with groups of these sizes is 99 (see subtable c).

(a) Critical Values of *U* for a One-Tailed Test at .001 or for a Two-Tailed Test at .002

n_1 \ n_2	9	10	11	12	13	14	15	16	17	18	19	20
1												
2												
3									0	0	0	0
4		0	0	0	1	1	1	2	2	3	3	3
5	1	1	2	2	3	3	4	5	5	6	7	7
6	2	3	4	4	5	6	7	8	9	10	11	12
7	3	5	6	7	8	9	10	11	13	14	15	16
8	5	6	8	9	11	12	14	15	17	18	20	21
9	7	8	10	12	14	15	17	19	21	23	25	26
10	8	10	12	14	17	19	21	23	25	27	29	32
11	10	12	15	17	20	22	24	27	29	32	34	37
12	12	14	17	20	23	25	28	31	34	37	40	42
13	14	17	20	23	26	29	32	35	38	42	45	48
14	15	19	22	25	29	32	36	39	43	46	50	54
15	17	21	24	28	32	36	40	43	47	51	55	59
16	19	23	27	31	35	39	43	48	52	56	60	65
17	21	25	29	34	38	43	47	52	57	61	66	70
18	23	27	32	37	42	46	51	56	61	66	71	76
19	25	29	34	40	45	50	55	60	66	71	77	82
20	26	32	37	42	48	54	59	65	70	76	82	88

SOURCE: Adapted from Tables 1, 3, 5, and 7 of D. Aube, "Extended Tables for the Mann-Whitney Statistic," *Bulletin of the Institute of Educational Research at Indiana University*, 1953, 1, No. 2. From S. Siegel, *Nonparametric Statistics for the Behavior Sciences*. New York: McGraw-Hill Book Company, 1956. Reprinted by permission of the Institute of Educational Research and McGraw-Hill Book Company.

TABLE D *Critical Values of Chi-Square*

PERCENTILE:	50	75	90	95	97.5	99	99.9
df	*α:* .50	.25	.10	.05	.025	.01	.001
1	.45	1.32	2.71	3.84	5.02	6.63	10.8
2	1.39	2.77	4.61	5.99	7.38	9.21	13.8
3	2.37	3.11	6.25	7.81	9.35	11.3	16.3
4	3.36	5.39	7.78	9.49	11.1	13.3	18.5
5	4.35	6.63	9.24	11.1	12.8	15.1	20.5
6	5.35	7.84	10.6	12.6	14.4	16.8	22.5
7	6.35	9.04	12.0	14.1	16.0	18.5	24.3
8	7.34	10.2	13.4	15.5	17.5	20.1	26.1
9	8.34	11.4	14.7	16.9	19.0	21.7	27.9
10	9.34	12.5	16.0	18.3	20.5	23.2	29.6
11	10.3	13.7	17.3	19.7	21.9	24.7	31.3
12	11.3	14.8	18.5	21.0	23.3	26.2	32.9
13	12.3	16.0	19.8	22.4	24.7	27.7	34.5
14	13.3	17.1	21.1	23.7	26.1	29.1	36.1
15	14.3	18.2	22.3	25.0	27.5	30.6	37.7
16	15.3	19.4	23.5	26.3	28.8	32.0	39.3
17	16.3	20.5	24.8	27.6	30.2	33.4	40.8
18	17.3	21.6	26.0	28.9	31.5	34.8	42.3
19	18.3	22.7	27.2	30.1	32.9	36.2	43.8
20	19.3	23.8	28.4	31.4	34.2	37.6	45.3
21	20.3	24.9	29.6	32.7	35.5	38.9	46.8
22	21.3	26.0	30.8	33.9	36.8	40.3	48.3
23	22.3	27.1	32.0	35.2	38.1	41.6	49.7
24	23.3	28.2	33.2	36.4	39.4	43.0	51.2
25	24.3	29.3	34.4	37.7	40.6	44.3	52.6
26	25.3	30.4	35.6	38.9	41.9	45.6	54.1
27	26.3	31.5	36.7	40.1	43.2	47.0	55.5
28	27.3	32.6	37.9	41.3	44.5	48.3	56.9
29	28.3	33.7	39.1	42.6	45.7	49.6	58.3
30	29.3	34.8	40.3	43.8	47.0	50.9	59.7
40	39.3	45.6	51.8	55.8	59.3	63.7	73.4
50	49.3	56.3	63.2	67.5	71.4	76.2	86.7
60	59.3	67.0	74.4	79.1	83.3	88.4	99.6
100	99.3	109.1	118.5	124.3	129.6	135.8	149.5

Source: Adapted from table 8 in E. S. Pearson and H. O. Hartley (Eds.), *Biometrika Tables for Statisticians*, 3rd ed. (1966), by permission of the *Biometrika* Trustees.

Notes: 1. The α-values pertain to nondirectional hypotheses.

2. For *df* > 30, the central *chi*-square distribution is approximately normally distributed with a standard deviation of 1. Appendix Table B can be used for *df* > 30 using

$$z = \sqrt{2\chi^2} - \sqrt{2df - 1}$$

References

AMERICAN PSYCHOLOGICAL ASSOCIATION, Ad Hoc Committee on Ethical Standards in Psychological Research. *Ethical principles in the conduct of research with human participants*. Washington, D.C.: American Psychological Association, 1973.

BARRY, H. Prolonged measurements of discrimination between alcohol and non-drug states. *Journal of Comparative Physiological Psychology*, 1968, **65**, 349–352.

BELLVILLE, R. E. Control of behavior by drug-produced internal stimuli. *Psychopharmicologia* (Berl.), 1964, **5**, 95–105.

BERGIN, A. E. & GARFIELD, S. L. (Eds.) *Handbook of psychotherapy and behavior change: an empirical analysis*. New York: Wiley, 1971.

BORING, E. G. *A history of experimental psychology*. Englewood Cliffs, N.J.: Prentice-Hall (Appleton-Century-Crofts), 1950.

BRADY, J. V. Ulcers in "executive" monkeys. *Scientific American*, 1958, **199**, 95–100.

BRELAND, K., & BRELAND M. *Animal behavior*. New York: Macmillan, 1966.

BURKE, R. L., & BENNIS, W. G. Changes in perception of self and others during human relations training. *Human Relations*, 1961, **14**, 165–182.

BUTLER, J. M., & HAIGH, C. V. Changes in the relation between self-concepts and ideal concepts consequent upon client-centered counseling. In C. R. Rogers and F. R. Dymond (Eds.), *Psychotherapy and personality change*. Chicago: Univ. of Chicago Press, 1954.

CAMPBELL, D. T., & STANLEY, J. C. *Experimental and quasi-experimental designs for research*. Skokie: Rand McNally, 1966.

CHADDOC, R. E. *Principles and Methods of Statistics*. Boston: Houghton Mifflin, 1925.

COHEN, E., MOTTO, J. A., & SEIDEN, R. H. An instrument for evaluating suicide potential: a preliminary study. *American Journal of Psychiatry*, 1966, **22**, (8), 886–891.

COLLMANN, R. D., & STROLLER, A. A survey of mongoloid births in Victoria, Australia, 1942–1957. *American Journal of Public Health*, 1962, **52**, 813–829.

_____. Virus aetiology for Down's syndrome. *Nature*, 1965, **208**, 903–904.

CONRAD, H. S. Clearance of questionnaires with respect to "invasion of privacy," public sensitivities, ethical standards, etc. *American Psychologist*, 1967, **22** (5), 356–359.

403

CRONBACH, L. J., & GLESER, G. C. *Psychological tests and personnel decisions.* Urbana: Univ. of Illinois Press, 1957.

DEMBER, W. N. *The psychology of perception.* New York: Holt, Rinehart and Winston, 1963.

DODWELL, P. C., & BESSENT, D. E. Learning without swimming in a water maze. *Journal of Comparative Physiological Psychology*, 1960, **54**, 422–425.

FECHNER, G. T. *Elemente der Psychophysik.* Leipzig: Breitkopf und Hartel, 1860.

FERGUSON, G. A. *Statistical analysis in psychology and education.* New York: McGraw-Hill, 1966.

_____. *Statistical analysis in psychology and education.* New York: McGraw-Hill, 1976.

FERSTER, C. B., & SKINNER, B. F. *Schedules of reinforcement.* New York: Appleton-Century-Crofts, 1957.

FISHER, R. A. *Statistical methods for research workers.* Edinburgh: Oliver & Boyd, 1925.

GEE, W. *Social science research methods.* Englewood Cliffs, N.J.: Prentice-Hall, Inc. (Appleton-Century-Crofts), 1950.

GIRDEN, E., & CULLER, E. A. Conditioned responses in curarized striate muscle in dogs. *Journal of Comparative Psychology*, 1937, **23**, 261–274.

GOLDSCHMIDT, W. The brideprice of the Sebei. *Scientific American*, 1973, **229** (1), 74–85.

GOODWIN, D. W., POWELL, B., BREMER, D., HOINE, H., & STERN, J. Alcohol and recall: state dependent effects in man. *Science*, 1969, **163**, 1358–1360.

GOSSETT, W. S. Standard error of the mean. *Biometrika*, 1908, **6**, 1–25.

GUILFORD, J. P. *Psychometric methods.* (2nd ed.) New York: McGraw-Hill, 1954.

GUTTMAN, N., & KALISH, H. I. Discriminability and stimulus generalization. *Journal of Experimental Psychology*, 1956, **51**, 79–88.

HALACY, D. S. *Man and memory.* New York: Harper & Row, 1970.

HAYS, W. L. *Statistics for psychologists.* New York: Holt, Rinehart and Winston, 1973.

HOLMGREN, B. *Drug dependent conditioned reflexes.* Paper read at the international symposium on cortical-subcortical relationships in sensory regulation. Havana, Cuba, 1965.

JEFFRY, R. The psychologist as an expert witness on the issue of insanity. *American Psychologist*, 1969, **19**, 838–843.

JOHNSON, R. C., & MEDINNUS, G. R. *Child psychology.* New York: Wiley, 1969.

KELMAN, H. C. Humane use of human subjects: the problem of deception in social psychological experiments. *Psychological Bulletin*, 1967, **67** (1), 1–11.

KEPPEL, G. *Design and analysis: a researcher's handbook.* Englewood Cliffs N.J.: Prentice-Hall, Inc., 1973.

KERLINGER, F. N. *Foundations of behavioral research.* New York: Holt, Rinehart and Winston, 1973.

KIRK, R. E. *Experimental design: procedures for the behavioral sciences.* Monterey: Brooks-Cole, 1968.

KLING, J. W., & RIGGS, L. A. *Experimental psychology.* New York: Holt, Rinehart and Winston, 1971.

KORNHAUSER, A., & SHEATSLEY, P. Questionnaire construction and interview procedure. In C. Selltiz et al. (Eds.), *Research methods in social relations.* New York: Holt, Rinehart and Winston, 1959.

LEE, W. *Experimental design and analysis.* San Francisco: W. H. Freeman & Co., 1975.

LOGAN, F. A., & SPANIER, D. Relative effect of delay of food and water reward. *Journal of Comparative and Physiological Psychology*, 1970, **72** (1), 102–104.

LOVELL, V. R. The human use of personality tests: a dissenting view. *American Psychologist*, 1967, **22** (5), 383–393.

McCALL, R. B. *Fundamental statistics for psychology.* New York: Harcourt, Brace, & Jovanovich, 1975.

MARTIN, D. W. *Doing psychology experiments.* Monterey: Brooks-Cole, 1977.

MATHESON, D. W., BRUCE, R. L., & BEAUCHAMP, K. L. *Introduction to experimental psychology.* New York: Holt, Rinehart and Winston, 1970.

MAXWELL, A. E. *Basic statistics in behavioural research.* Baltimore: Penguin, 1970.

MILLER, N. E. Some recent studies of conflict behavior and drugs. *American Psychologist*, 1961, **16,** 12–24.

MOORE, R. & GOLDIAMOND, I. Errorless establishment of visual discrimination using fading procedures. *Journal of Experimental Analysis of Behavior*, 1964, **7,** 269–272.

MURCH, G. M. *Visual and auditory perception.* New York: Bobbs-Merrill, 1973.

MURDOCK, B. B., Jr. The serial position effect of free recall. *Journal of Experimental Psychology*, 1962, **62,** 482–488.

NOETHER, GOTTFRIED E. *Introduction to statistics.* Boston: Houghton Mifflin Company, 1978.

OVERTON, D. A. State-dependent or "dissociated" learning produced with pento-barbital. *Journal of Comparative Physiological Psychology*, 1964, **57,** 3–12.

PARTEN, M. *Surveys, polls, and samples.* New York: Harper & Row, 1950.

PETTIGREW, T. Regional differences in anti-Negro prejudice. *Journal of Abnormal Psychology*, 1959, **59,** 28–36.

PUBLICATION MANUAL. Washington, D.C.: American Psychological Association.

REESE, E. P. *Experiments in operant behavior.* New York: Appleton-Century-Crofts, 1964.

ROBINSON, H. B., & ROBINSON, N. M. Mental retardation. In P. H. Mussen (Ed.), *Manual of child psychology.* New York: Wiley, 1970.

ROBINSON, P. W., & FOSTER, D. F. *Experimental psychology: A small-N approach.* New York: Harper & Row Publishers, 1979.

ROBINSON, P. W. & SHELLEY, M. F. The effects of total darkness on schedule control. *Journal of the Experimental Analysis of Behavior, 1974*, **22,** 391–400.

ROSENBERG, M. *The logic of survey analysis.* New York: Basic Books, Inc. 1968.

ROSENTHAL, R. *Experimenter effects in behavioral research.* New York: Appleton-Century-Crofts, 1966.

ROSS, S., & LOCKMAN, R. F. *A career in psychology.* Washington, D.C.: American Psychological Association, 1963.

RUEBHAUSEN, O. M., & BRIM, O. G. J. Privacy and behavioral research. *American Psychologist*, 1966, **21** (5), 423–437.

RYAN, T. A. Multiple comparisons in psychological research. *Psychological Bulletin*, 1959, **56,** 26–47.

SAINSBURY, P., & BARRACLOUGH, B. Differences between suicidal rates. *Nature*, 1968, 220–1252.

SASSON, R., & NELSON, T. M. The human experimental subject in context. *Canadian Psychologist*, 1969, **10** (4), 409–437.

SEEMAN, J. Deception in psychological research. *American Psychologist*, 1969, **24** (11), 1025–1028.

SEIGEL, S. *Nonparametric Statistics*. New York: McGraw-Hill, 1956.

SIDMAN, M. *Tactics of scientific research*. New York: Basic Books, Inc., 1960.

SIDMAN, M., & STODDARD, L. T. The effectiveness of fading in programming simultaneous form discrimination for retarded children. *Journal of Experimental Analysis of Behavior*, 1967, **10**, 3–15.

SISSON, R. F. Aha! It really works! *National Geographic*, 1974, **145** (1), 142–147.

SKINNER, B. F. A case history in scientific method. *American Psychologist*, 1956, **2**, 221, 233.

SULZBACHER, S. I., & HOUSER, J. E. A tactic to eliminate disruptive behaviors in the classroom: group contingent consequences. *American Journal of Mental Deficiency*, 1966, **1**, 182–187.

TERRACE, H. S. Discrimination learning with and without errors. *Journal of Experimental Analysis of Behavior*, 1963, **6**, 1–27.

THOMAS, D. S. Statistics in social research. *The American Journal of Sociology*, 1929, **35**, 1–9.

THORNDIKE, E. L., McCALL, W. A., & CHAPMAN, J. C. Ventilation in relation to mental work. *Teachers College Contributions in Education*, 1916, 78.

WALK, R. D., & GIBSON, E. J. A comparative and analytical study of visual depth perception. *Psychological Monographs*, 1961, **75**, Whole No. 519.

WARWICK, D. P., & OSHERSON, S. *Comparative research methods*. Englewood Cliffs, N.J.: Prentice-Hall, Inc., 1973.

WHALEY, D. L., & MALOTT, R. W. *Elementary principles of behavior*. New York: Appleton-Century-Crofts, 1971.

WHALEY, D. L., & SURRATT, S. L. *Attitudes of science*. Kalamazoo: Behaviordelia, 1968.

WINCH, W. H. The transfer of improvement of memory in school-children. *British Journal of Psychology*, 1908, **2**, 284–293.

WINER, B. J. *Statistical principles in experimental design*. (2nd ed.) New York: McGraw-Hill, 1971.

WIXEN, B. N. *Children of the rich*. New York: Crown, 1973.

WOLF, M. M., RISLEY, T., & MEES, H. Application of operant conditioning procedures to the behavior problems of an autistic child. *Behavior Research and Therapy*, 1964, **1**, 305–312.

WOODWORTH, R. S. *Experimental psychology*. New York: Holt, Rinehart and Winston, 1938.

Index

A

ABA design, 314
Absolute threshold, 147–148
Abstracts:
  psychological, 18, 19, 24,
    138, 384, 386
  section in experiment
    write-up, 365
Achievement tests:
  standardized, 168
  unstandardized, 168
American Humane
    Association, 132
American Psychological
    Association, 52
Amplitude, response,
    136–137
Analysis of covariance:
  factorial designs, 301–304
  one-way ANOVAR
    designs, 277
  two-group designs,
    242–249
Analysis of variance:
  factorial designs, 289–293
  illustrative explanation,
    256–263
  one-way ANOVAR
    designs, 265–268

two-group designs, 260-
    263
Analytical, courses in
    psychology, 8
Analytical ABAB design,
    321–322
Analytical experiments, 210,
    322
  definition, 210
Analytical prowess, 11, 377
Animism, 37
ANOVAR designs (see One-
    way ANOVAR
    designs)
ANOVAR experiments (see
    One-way ANOVAR
    designs)
Apomorphine, 18, 19, 20,
    22, 27
Apparatus:
  section in write-up, 370
  use (see
    Instrumentation)
Aptitude tests, 168–169
Assumptions, in statistical
    testing, 241
Astrology, 37
Auld, 182
Averages, 89
Average variation, 90–92

B

Background variables, 46
Balancing, 210
Barnett, S. A., 122
Barraclough, B., 194
Barry, 56
Baseline, 312
Beauchamp, K. L., 187
Behavior, measurements of,
    133
Behavioral phenomenon,
    demonstration of, 75
Behaviorism, 42, 44
Beil, C., 40
Bellville, 56
Bender-Gestalt, 172
Bessent, D. E., 69
Between-groups variance
    (see Variance,
    between-groups)
Bias:
  experimenter, 133,
    141–142
  selection, 114–115
Bimodal distribution, 339
Binet, A., 171–172
Biometrika, 51
Blocked designs, 272
Blocking, 207–208, 210,

235, 236, 300–301
Blough, D., 152
Boring, 50
Brady, J., 4
Brain dynamics, 299
Breland, K., 124
Brim, O. G., 123
Broca, P., 40
Bruce, R. L., 187
Burt, 194
Buskist, W., 161

C

California Achievement
    Test, 168
Campbell, D. T., 219
Cancer, 82
Carry-over affects, 280
Case study designs, 197–201
    deviant case analysis, 197
    isolated clinical case
        analysis, 197–201
    systematic observation,
        199–201
Catch trials, 154
Cause-effect relationships,
    182, 188, 321, 333
Cells, factorial designs, 285
Census information on
    questionnaires, 166
Chaddock, 51
Chapman, J. C., 309
Chicks, as subjects, 123
Chi square, 348–354
Choice selection, response
    measure, 137
Chronical age, psychological
    testing, 172
Clinical method, 42, 43
Coefficient of concordance,
    164
Coefficient of consistence K,
    163
Collmann, R. D., 188
Comparative investigations,
    226

Conclusions, drawing of, 26
Concomitant variation, 193
Concurrent multiple
    response design, 323
Conrad, H. S., 123
Constancy, as a control
    technique:
    definition, 101–102
    experimental design use,
        46, 207
    nondesign experimental
        technique, 141
    quasi-experimental design
        use, 181
    small-N design use,
        309–311, 324
Constant error, 154
Content courses, in
    psychology, 8
Contrast designs, ex post
    facto approach,
    195–197
Control conditions, 48
Control data, measures for
    comparison, 226
Control group:
    reasons for, 249
    role in two-group designs,
        225
Controlled laboratory
    experiments:
    advantages and
        disadvantages of,
        75–76
    definition, 22, 67
    example, 67
    ex post facto comparison,
        83–84
    reasons for, 75
    steps involved in, 69–75
Controlling background
    variables, 46
Control subjects, 48
Control techniques:
    constancy, 101–102,
        207–208
    elimination, 100–101,
        207–208

experimental vs. statistical,
    105, 207
make a second IV,
    102–104, 207
randomization, 104–105,
    207
statistical control,
    105–107, 207
Conventions, 388
Correlation:
    calculation of, 243, 247
    coefficient, 185
    formula, 247
    type of design, 189–195
Correlation psychology, 73
Counterbalance designs, 115
Covariance (see Analysis of
    covariance)
Covariate:
    definition, 216
    in factorial designs,
        301–304
    in one-way ANOVAR
        designs, 275–277
    in two-group designs, 229
Critical F:
    definition, 267
    in factorial designs,
    in one-way ANOVAR
        designs, 267
Cronbach, L. J., 73
Culler, 55, 56
Cumulative recorder, 327

D

Darwin, C., 40
Data collection techniques:
    application of, 176
    interviews, 165–167
    psychological tests,
        experimental uses of,
        167–176
    scaling techniques,
        156–165

threshold measurement, 147–156
Degrees of Freedom (df):
between groups (df_B), 267
definitions of, 231, 264
matched two-group design, 233
one-way analysis of covariance ANOVAR design, 277
randomized factorial designs, 293
randomized one-way ANOVAR design, 264
randomized pretest-posttest control group design, 227
randomized two-group design, 231
within-groups (df_W), 267
Dependent variable (DV):
analysis of fluctuation, 74
definition, 15, 18, 22
how to select, 138
recording of, 76
types, 133
ways of measuring, 133–137
Descartes, R., 40
Descriptive research, 176–177
Descriptive statistics, 344
Design, definition of, 23
Design, in experimental write-up, 18, 20, 369, 389
Determinism, 61, 67
definition, 33
violation of, 35
Deviant case analysis, 197
Dewey, J., 40
Difference threshold, 147–148
Direct relationship, in correlation, 201–202
Distributions, types of, 339
Dodwell, P. C., 69–72
Double-blind, control

procedure, 133
Down's syndrome, 187–188
D score, 233

E

Ebbinghaus, H., 54
Elements der Psychophysik, 156
Elimination, as a control technique:
definition, 46, 100–101
in experimental designs, 207
nondesign experimental technique, 140–141
small-N designs, 309–311, 324
Empirical investigations, 39
Empiricism:
definition, 33, 61, 67
route to knowledge, 38
violation illustration, 35
Errorless learning, 121
Error variance:
definition, 25, 85, 143
means of reducing, 206
Escape conditioning, 136
Ethics:
Animals, 131
Humans, 130
in research, 126
Evaluation, 378
Experiential control, 46, 48
Experiment:
plan for, 101
(see Controlled laboratory experiment)
Experimental control procedures, 105
Experimental designs:
comparison, 207–208
criterion for categorizing, 206–209
definition, 205–206
major function of, 206

relationship to control procedures, 207
symbol definitions, 212
types of, 212–217
Experimental investigation, 17–27, 66
Experimental method, 42, 50
Experimental mortality, 108, 111, 319
Experimental psychology, 50, 51, 73
Experimental research, 15 (see also Experimental designs)
Experimentation, reasons for, 45, 53, 75
Experimenter bias, 320
Experiments:
controlled laboratory
advantages and disadvantages, 75–76
definition, 67
example, 68–69
reasons for, 75
steps involved, 69–75
field
advantages and disadvantages, 79–80
definition, 76–77
example, 77–78
reasons for, 78–79
steps involved, 78
Exploratory experiments, 210, 250, 322, 323
Ex post facto:
field studies
advantages and disadvantages, 83
comparison to experiments, 82
definition, 80
example, 80–81
reasons for, 83
investigations, 80–86
comparison to experiments, 66
types of, 67

laboratory studies
  advantages and
    disadvantages, 85–86
  definition, 83
  example, 84
  reasons for, 84–85
  steps involved, 84
  research, 15
External validity:
  causes of, 113–115
  definition, 113
  in field experiments, 79
Eysenck, H. J., 194

F

Factorial designs, 207, 209,
    211, 272
  advantages and
    disadvantages, 305
  control techniques
    possible, 288
  definition, 284
  distinction from one-way
    ANOVAR designs,
    288
  logical analysis of,
    288–293
  reasons for use, 286
  small-n designs, 322
  steps involved, 288
  steps in statistical
    calculations, 293
  symbolic representation,
    284
  types
    analysis of covariance,
      301–304
    randomized, 294–298
    randomized blocked,
      298–301
Factorial experiments, 305
Fechner, G. T., 156
Ferguson, G. A., 164–165,
    354, 356
Ferster, C. B., 122

Field experiment, 22 (see
    also Experiments,
    field)
Field studies (see Ex post
    facto, field studies)
Fisher, R. A., 47, 48, 51,
    217
Forced choice response, 152
Foster, D. F., 50
F prime (F'),
  definition, 269
  formula, 269
F ratios:
  calculation of
    factorial designs, 293
  one-way ANOVAR
    designs, 267
Frequency, as a DV
    measure, 133–134,
    143
Freud, S., 42, 198
Fritsch, G., 40
F table, 51
F test (see F ratios)
Functionalism, 43, 61
Functionality, 39

G

Gain score, 238, 241
Galton, F., 40, 51
Galvanic skin response, 137
Gee, 45, 51
General Aptitude Test
    Battery, 169
Generality:
  interspecies, 317, 328, 329
  rule rather than
    exception, 124
Gestalt, school of
    psychology, 42, 44, 61
Girdon, 55, 56
Goldiamond, I., 121
Goldschmidt, W., 196–197
Gosset, 48, 51
Grand Mean ($\bar{X}_G$), 258–260

Greco-latin square design,
    302–303
Guinea pigs, 123
Guiras, 160
Guttman, N., 152

H

Halacy, D. S., 201
Hall, M., 40
Hans the Wonder Horse,
    140
Hartley, D., 40
Hawthorne effect, 114
Hays, W. L., 74
Headings, in a report:
  main, 376
  paragraph, 376
  second order, 376
Hedonic scaling, 161
Heistad, 56
Higbee, K. L., 128
Hitzig, E., 40
Hobbes, T., 40
Holmgren, 56
Houser, J. E., 134
House-Tree-Person Test,
    172
Hypothesis
  development of, 339–341
  formulation of, 69–70
  testing of, 341–342
  types of, 70

I

Identification information,
    for interviews, 166
Independent variable (IV),
    15, 18
  definition, 21
  example, 20
  how to select, 139–140
  making a secondary
    variable an IV,
    102–104, 310, 324

manipulation of, 71–74
Individual instruction
    program, 85
Individual psychology, 50,
    51
Inductive reasoning, 329
Inferential statistics, 344
Instrumentation, 112, 143,
    320
Interaction, 115
    concept of, 286–287
    diagram, 287
Internal invalidity, 108, 143
    definition, 108
    sources of
        experimental mortality,
            111, 112
        experimenter bias, 113
        instrumentation,
            112–113
        interaction effects, 112
        maturation, 110
        proactive history, 109
        retroactive history, 109
        statistical regression,
            111
        testing, 110
Internal validity:
    definition, 108
    in field experiments, 79
    small-N designs, 317, 318
    two-group designs, 250
Interpretation, 378
Interviews, 165–167
    selection of questions,
        166–167
    structured vs.
        unstructured,
        165–166
Intrasubject control, 315
Introspection, 41, 61
Inverse relationship, in
    correlation, 201–202
Investigations, types of, 17,
    66–67
Investigatory affirmation,
    317

Isolated clinical case analysis,
    197–281

J

James, W., 40
Jarvik, O. O., 302
Jeffry, R., 172
Johnson, R. C., 196
Journal, purpose of, 379
Journal articles, locating,
    383–386
Journal of Applied
    Behavioral Analysis,
    52
Journal of Experimental
    Psychology, 361
Journal of the Experimental
    Analysis of Behavior,
    52
Journals in psychology, list
    of, 380–383
Just noticeable difference
    (JND), 148

K

K, 277
Kalish, H. I., 152
Kelman, H. C., 123, 128
Keppel, G., 74, 348
Kerlinger, F. N., 167
Keysor, R., 70
Knowledge, means of
    obtaining:
    empiricism, 38
    metamorphism, 38
    rationalism, 38
Kofka, K., 42
Kohler, W., 42
Kornhouser, A., 167
Kruskal-Wallis test, 346, 356

L

Laboratory studies (see Ex
    post facto, laboratory
    studies)
Large-N experimental
    designs:
    contrast with small-N
        designs, 309
    data analysis, 326, 327
    generality, 328–329
    manipulation of the DV,
        326
    monitoring data, 326
    types of control
        techniques used, 324
Latency, 135, 143
Latin-square design,
    302–303
Leahy, A. M., 290
Learning psychology, 318
Lee, 249, 272, 300
Leveling, 300–301
Levels, in factorial designs,
    285
Locke, J., 40
Logan, F. A., 362
Logical empiricism, 39
Loveli, V. R., 123

M

McCall, W. A., 309, 356
Mackenzie, W. A., 51
Magendie, F., 40
Magnitude estimation, 160
Magnitude production, 160
Malott, R. W., 221
Manipulation of variables,
    73–74
Manipulatory investigations
    (see Experimental
    investigation,
    experimental designs)
Mann Whitney U test, 346,
    354–356

Martin, D., 59
Masking, 141
Matched design, 240
Matching, 207, 208, 210, 235
Matheson, D. W., 187
Maturation, 110
Maxwell, A. E., 73
Maze, water, 68–69
Mean, 89–90
Measurement scales, 344–346
Medinnus, G. R., 196
Mees, 55
Mendel, G., 75, 114
Mental age, 172
Metamorphism, 38
Metaphysical explanations, 38
Method of average error, 150, 153, 156
Method of constant stimuli, 150–153, 156
Method of limits, 15–151, 156
Method of signal detection, 150, 154–156
Michael, J., 122
Mill, J., 40, 193
Miller, H. L., 56, 161
Minnesota Multiplhasi Personality Inventory (MMPI), 169
Mongolism, 187, 188
Monkeys, as subjects, 122
Moore, R., 121
Morton, W., 211
Muller, J., 40
Multiple group comparison tests:
  definition, 269
  example, 269–270
  factorial designs, 293
Multiple group designs (see One-way ANOVAR designs)
Multiple personality, 34, 35

Multiple treatment interaction effect, 115
Murdock, B. B., 134
Mythology, 37

N

Naturalistic studies, 199
Nelson, T. M., 123
Noether, 348
Nominal scale data, 349
Nonexperimental designs:
  advantages and disadvantages, 201–203
  case study designs, 181, 197–201, 203
  contrast designs, 181, 195–197, 203
  correlational designs, 181, 183–189, 203
  quasi-experimental designs, 181–183, 203
Nonhuman species:
  advantages of, 122–123
  generality issue, 124–126
  use of, 122–123
Nonmanipulatory investigations (see Ex post facto investigations)
Nonparametric statistics, 346, 347
Normal distribution, 338, 339

O

Objective Analytical Test Battery, 169
One-group designs, 209, 213, 217–222
  posttest only design, 217–220

pretest-posttest design, 220–221
  times series design, 221–222
One-way ANOVAR designs, 207, 209, 211
  analysis of covariance, 272–278
  definition, 254
  logical analysis, 255–263
  procedures involved, 254
  randomized, 264–270
  randomized blocked, 270–271
Operational definition, 139, 359
Organization of journal articles, 361
Osherson, S., 197
Overton, 56

P

Paired comparison scaling, 162–164
Paradigm, internally verifiable, 47–48
Paradigm, scientific, 45
Parametric investigation, 210
Parametric statistics, 346, 347, 348
Parsimony:
  assumption of scientific method, 32–34, 67
  definition, 32–34
  violation of, 36
Parten, M., 166
Pavlov, I. P., 124
Pearson, K., 51
Pearson product correlation:
  formula, 185
  illustration, 185–186
  rationale behind it, 184
Penfield, W., 199
Personality tests, 169
Pettigrew, T., 81

Phenomenology, 42, 61
Phi-gamma hypothesis, 156
Pigeons, as subjects, 122
Pilot study, 142
Placebo, 14
Plan of an experiment:
  analyzing the results,
    24–26
  basic steps involved, 17
  classifying variables,
    . 21–22
  drawing conclusions,
    26–27
  planning the method,
    23–24
  selecting a design, 22-23
  selecting a topic, 17–19
Point of subjective equality,
  154
Porter, R. W., 84
Prediction, 177
Pre-experimental designs,
  217, 218
Prejudice, 80–81
Pretesting:
  one-group designs, 220,
    221
  small-N designs (baseline),
    312, 313, 320, 321
  source of invalidity, 114
  two-group designs, 237,
    242
Pretest-posttest designs, 241
Proactive history, 109, 318
Pseudoexperimental designs,
  . 216–218
Psychoanalysis, 42, 61
Psychological abstracts, 18,
  19, 24, 138, 384–386
Psychological review, 361
Psychological scaling, 157
Psychological tests:
  development of, 170–172
  experimental uses of,
    169–170
  misuse of, 172–176
  types, 168–169

Psychology:
  roots of
    philosophical, 39, 50
    physiological, 40–41
  schools of
    Behaviorism, 42, 44, 61
    Functionalism, 42, 43,
      61
    Gestalt, 42, 44–45, 61
    Psychoanalysis, 42, 43,
      61
    Structuralism, 41–42, 61
  subfields in, 4
  work activities in, 5–6
Psychophysical Methods, 156
Publication manual, of the
  APA, 362

Q

Quasi-experimental designs,
  181–183

R

Rabbits, 123
Randomization:
  as a control technique,
    104–105
  in experimentation, 48,
    76, 217
  in factorial designs, 300
  in small-N designs, 309,
    324
Range, 339
Rank order scaling, 164–165
Rationalism, 38
Rats, as subjects, 122
Rectangular distributions,
  339
Reese, E. P., 122
Regression analysis, 243
Related measure designs,
  240–248

Reliability, 195
Repeated measure design,
  241
Repeated measurements,
  277
Reports, 359
Report writing:
  objectives of, 360
  organization, main
    sections
    abstract, 365
    conclusions and
      summary, 374
    discussion, 372–374
    introduction, 369
    method, 369–370
    results, 371–372
    title page, 362, 365
  role of, 358–359
  style
    abbreviations and
      symbols, 377
    accuracy, 375
    figures and tables, 371
    footnotes, 376–377
    form, 387
    headings, 376
    length, 375
    references, 377
    tense and person,
      375–376
    typing, 375
  subsections
    apparatus, 370
    design, 370
    procedure, 370
    subjects, 370
Research design:
  definition, 18
  types of:
    experimental, 212–217
    nonexperimental,
      180–203
Research problems, things to
  consider, 59
Research topic, selection of,
  18, 19

Response criterion factor, in signal detection, 155
Response duration, as a DV, 136
Response latency, 135
Response measures:
  amplitude, 136–137
  choice selection, 137
  duration, 136
  frequency, 133–136
  latency, 135
Retroactive history, 109, 319
Review of literature, need for, 24
Risley, 55
Robinson, H. B., 188
Robinson, N. M., 188
Robinson, P. W., 50, 79, 128
Rorschach Test, 169, 172
Rosenberg, 194
Rosenthal, R., 113, 194
Rosnow, 194
Ruebhausen, D. M., 123

S

Sainsbury, P., 194
Sampling, 339
Sasson, R., 123
Scaling techniques:
  methods, 189
  paired comparison, 156–157, 162
Scheffe F (F_s):
  definition, 269
  factorial designs, 293
  formula, 269
Scholastic Aptitude Test (SAT), 221
Scientific approach, history in psychology, 37–41
Scientific method, assumptions of, 32–36, 61
Secondary variables, 14, 15, 20, 318

Secondary variance:
  control effectiveness, 105
  means of controlling, 100–107, 206
Secondary variation:
  means of control, 14, 75–76
  sources of, 108–115
Seeman, J., 123
Selection bias, 114–115
Sensitivity factor, in signal detection, 155
Sensitize, effect of pretesting, 110
Sequential Tests of Educational Progress (STEP), 168
Sheatsley, P., 167
Shelley, M., 79
Shock, 84
Sidman, M., 53, 121, 320, 329
Siegel, 348
Sigma (Σ), 230
Signal detection theory, 156
Significance level, 255, 342, 343
Sisson, R. F., 199
Skewed distributions, 339
Skills, required of a psychologist, 9–13
Skinner, B. F., 48, 55, 125, 311
Small-N designs, 16, 202, 308
  advantages and disadvantages, 333
  comparison with large-N designs, 324–329
  data analysis, 326
  generality of, 328
  manipulation of DV, 326
  monitoring of data, 326
  types of control techniques used, 324
Smoking, 82
Solomon four-group design, 111, 207, 214

Somerfield, E., 51
Spanier, D., 362
Specific nerve energies, 40
Stability, definition of, 313
Staggered baseline design, 320
Stanley, J. C., 219
Statistical control:
  experimental uses of, 207
  factorial designs, 301–304
  one-way ANOVAR designs, 272–278
  situations for use, 105–107
  small-N designs, 310, 324
  two-group designs, 242–249
Statistical regression, 111, 319
Statistical testing, 48
Stevens, 160
Stimulus presentation methods:
  method of constant stimuli, 150–153
  method of limits, 150–151
Stoddard, L. T., 121
Strain differences, 298
Stratifying, 300–301
Stroller, A. A., 188
Structuralism, 41–43, 47, 61
Subjects:
  humans
    advantages and disadvantages of, 123–124
    ethical responsibility, 126–131
    number used, 126
    selection of, 119–122, 177
    types of, 122–124
Suicide, 194
Sulzbacker, S. I., 134
Sums of Squares (SS):
  algebraic explanation of, 259
  calculations involved factorial designs,

290–292
one-way ANOVAR
  designs, 265–266
two-group designs,
  230–231
divisions in factorial
  designs, 289
Swets, 155–156
Systematic observation, 226
Systematic variance, 206
Systematic variation, 15,
  94–95
Szondi Test, 172

T

Tanner, 155–156
Ten containments, 127
Terrace, H. S., 120
Testability:
  definition, 34, 61, 67
  violation of, 36
Testing, 110
t-formulas:
  matched group design,
    233
  randomized two-group
    design, 229
  static group design, 242
Thematic Apperception
  Test, 169, 172
Theory, evaluation of, 75
Theory of signal
  detectability, 156
Thomas, D., 46
Thorndike, E. L., 309
Threshold measurement:
  calculations of, 149–150
  stimulus of, 150–156
  types of, 147–148
  use of, 147
Thresholds:
  absolute, 147–148
  difference (jnd), 148
  sensory, 40
Titchner, E., 41, 42
Torres, 56

Total sums of squares (ss$_T$),
  260–261
  computational formula,
    263
  raw score formula, 262
Totem, 37
Treatment, in factorial
  designs, 285
True experimental designs,
  217
t-test, assumptions behind:
  homogeneity of variance,
    242
  normalization, 241
Two-group designs, 207,
  209, 211
  advantages and
    disadvantages,
    249–251
  analysis of covariance, 242
  logical analysis, 225–228
  matched, 232–236
  nonrandomized pretest-
    posttest, 242
  pretest-posttest control
    group, 236–240
  randomized posttest only,
    228–232
  static group, 241–242

U

Ulcers, 84

V

Validity,
  differences in designs
    used, 13–14
  external, 113–115
  field experiment, 78–79
Variables, relationship
  between, 74–75
Variance:
  between groups (V$_B$)
    definition, 90–93

divisions of, 93–94
formula, 264, 265
one-way ANOVAR 256,
  262–263, 265–267
two-groups designs, 227
within-groups (V$_W$)
  divisions of, 95–96
  means of calculations,
    265, 266, 296
Variation:
  average variation, 90
  controlling for, 71–73
  statistical analysis, 96–99
  systematic, 94–95
  types of, 15
  within
    error, 95
    secondary, 95

W

Warwick, D. P., 195, 197
Watson, J., 64–65, 119
Weber, E., 40
Wechsler Memory Scale, 172
Weldon, W. F. R., 51
Wertheimer, M., 42, 44
Whaley, D. L., 221
Wilcoxon test, 346
Winch, W. H., 48, 51
Winer, B. J., 74
Within-group variance,
  formula, 265 (see also
  Variance)
Within variation (see
  Variance)
Wixin, B. N., 198
Wolf, M. M., 55, 221
Woodworth, 45
Work activities, of
  psychologists, 5–7
Write-ups (see Report
  writing)
Wundt, W., 41, 42

X

X$_{ig}$, 259